HERMANN BECKH (18. later Sanskrit, becoming P. at the University of Berlin ... and modern languages, he wro... ...ensively on religious and philosophical subjects, including Buddhism, Indology, Christianity, Alchemy and Music. In 1911, he heard a lecture by Rudolf Steiner and was inspired to join the Anthroposophical Society, where he soon became a valued co-worker. In 1922, he helped found The Christian Community, a movement for religious renewal. His many books are in the process of being translated from the original German and published in English.

HERMANN BECKH
A CELEBRATION

Items from Professor Beckh's Literary Estate

With Essays and Appreciations

Translated and Edited by Neil Franklin, Katrin Binder,
Maren Stott and Alan Stott

TEMPLE LODGE

Temple Lodge Publishing Ltd.
Hillside House, The Square
Forest Row, RH18 5ES

www.templelodge.com

First published by Temple Lodge 2025

A CIP catalogue record for this book is available from the British Library

ISBN 978 1 915776 32 7

Cover by Morgan Creative
Typeset by Symbiosys Technologies, Visakhapatnam, India
Printed and bound by 4Edge Ltd., Essex

Contents

Introduction

Celebration is the last projected volume in the series 'The Collected Works of Rev. Prof. Hermann Beckh (1875-1937)' in English, not counting the forthcoming re-issue of The Language of Tonality. This volume introducing the man and his work at the same time celebrates his life by offering glimpses of his influence today. In assessing the significance of 'the Professor'—who believed the future of civilization depended upon a complete change of thinking—future perspectives may certainly emerge.

What is the leading characteristic of this universal scholar? Concerning The Hymn to the Earth, the translator in his Introduction claims, 'Quite possibly we could call … the oldest modern poetical work, or the most modern piece of ancient poetry.' Typical of Beckh, an innocent sentence reveals his habitual comprehensive viewpoint. He invariably points beyond 'either-or' to 'not only but also', for example, in music 'to view … the facts and connections in a new light' and, in language, to research 'the union of sound and sense'. The Hymn begins by mentioning the theme of universal, cosmic rhythms that Beckh endeavoured to explain in ever new ways. 'Cosmic religion,' he notes,[1] 'is the revelation of the spirit in the earthly realm.' We are clearly meant to develop; the human constitution itself, however, is a constant.

Soon after the new millennium arrived, a small group of independent scholars and artists volunteered to translate and publish everything of Beckh's that could be found—initially without the early academic legal and linguistic work. The general aim was to meet, if not anticipate, the centenaries of the original publication dates. The present volume includes the most useful articles from Festschrift: Essays in Honour of Hermann Beckh (2016); the same goes for Hermann Beckh and the Spirit-Word (2015), both now out of print. However, the important essays by Beckh himself are now all available elsewhere. Here we include seven items from the master's literary estate plus some surviving correspondence, along with some appreciations and essays by scholars and artists who draw on Beckh's insights in spirituality, language and music. The Professor's main concern was to share his insights, which indeed is why the English translation of the 'Collected Works' was undertaken. A reassessment of this universal scholar is long overdue.

The man

What did his colleagues stress about this independent, universal scholar and the first founder-priest of The Christian Community to cross the threshold of death (1937)? 'He seemed like a messenger from a different world order.' 'I learnt to love about him his real spiritual over-abundance.' 'He repeatedly undertook, even at an advanced age, to climb mountains alone. His nearness to heaven of the high peaks drew him aloft.' 'He was a child of the heights.' 'He carried in his soul love for the word, love for the stars, and love for music.' 'He was like one of the ancient Rishis of India suddenly transported into a completely uncongenial civilization.'

These are just a few of the cameos capturing the essence of Beckh's being, written by those remarkable founder-priests and colleagues.[2] Gottfried Husemann,[3] a colleague and a successor at the Priests' Seminary in Stuttgart, sums up:

> To Hermann Beckh, Wagner and Bruckner enthusiast, who as a 'leisure activity' learned a new language in addition to the many he knew already, we are indebted for the translation of the most important things from the Sanskrit, amongst other works the well-known *Hymn to the Earth*. He generously shared his gifts. Beckh carried the East in himself in a spiritually appropriate manner. He was an important personality. One also felt this when he lectured. His writings witness to his deep research. Because he also carried the characteristics of an absent-minded professor, he was the centre of much merriment, but in this Beckh joined in, laughing at his own expense. We all loved him.

In 1922 Beckh insisted on joining the founders of the non-sectarian 'Movement for Religious Renewal', The Christian Community. He experienced it as *the* fulfilment of his life. Those 'out front' were deeply astonished. But according to Rudolf Meyer,[4] 'Without him, our beginnings are inconceivable'. Beckh, it is clear, was a spiritually guiding star. During his fifteen years of service teaching in the Seminary, Beckh inspired a generation of priests. Dr Alfred Heidenreich and Adam Bittleston both learnt from his example; they devoted their careers to working in the UK. A year before he died, Emil Bock, who after Dr Rittelmeyer steered The Christian Community 1938-1959, in an appreciation (1959) finally admitted, 'An abundance of books came into existence whose significance perhaps will only be properly appreciated in the future.' That future could be our present.

Today, one hundred years on, perspectives have widened to embrace world concerns. In the twenty-first century Beckh's pioneer example can now come into its own, for he also wrote for posterity.

Research

One story concerning Beckh's attitude to research is worth knowing. While attending Rudolf Steiner's lecture-course, *Christ and the Spiritual World, the Search for the Holy Grail*, Leipzig 1913 (GA 149), which calls for a new star-wisdom, Beckh asked what astrological literature he should read. 'Nothing,' came the answer, 'only anthroposophy.' *Beckh kept to this advice; it makes his work uniquely valuable.* When the astrologers at that time failed to take the hint, Hermann Beckh did take it up. Moreover, the Professor, as he claimed several times, had found direct access to the creative archetypes from his musical studies. He took pains to emphasize the *inner movement* of his suggested tone-zodiac. Moreover, what seems clear now is that had *The Language of the Stars* appeared earlier,[5] we would have a different astrosophy from what we have today.

The clues Steiner left regarding cultivating 'a good style'—perhaps his best-kept secret—are explored in an article here. As Beckh points out, we all live in several rhythms at the same time, of the day, the week, the months and years, in which the stars play their roles, and which also reflect in what we can summarize with the word 'creation'. Did Steiner keep to his own advice concerning 'good style', illustrating what Beckh summarizes in the word *ṛta*, 'rhythmical order'? If the kingdom of God will come on Earth as it is in Heaven, 'we shall know as we have been known' (cf. 1 Cor. 13:12)—in down-to-earth terms, learn to collaborate by mastering the rhythms in which we live. This also explains Beckh's habitual use of the word 'Mystery' as a technical term, recognizing its religious derivation, and hence, too, the capital letter in English. The 'traditionalist' René Guénon, another holistic thinker of the twentieth century, speaks of the 'primordial human being' and the 'primordial revelation'. Beckh, too, recognizes the original human unity—he is fond of quoting Gen. 2:7—and, researching the story further, traces in detail 'The One who says "I" in me ...', as his translation of Psalm 23 begins.

An English theologian of Beckh's generation with a strong interest in German theology, Sir Edwyn Hoskyns (1884-1937), who translated Karl Barth's influential *The Epistle to the Romans* (1919/22; Eng. tr.

1933), like Beckh possessed a musical nature and a great sensitivity to language. Hoskyns commentary on the Fourth Gospel, left unfinished at his death, was edited and completed by Noel Davey.[6] Hoskyns believed one could learn not only from history and culture but also of faith. He began one of his sermons[7] by asking,

> Can we rescue a word, and discover a universe? Can we study a language, and awake to the Truth? Can we bury ourselves in a lexicon, and rise in the presence of God? … [I]t may happen that a historian regains his balance only as he turns to decipher the meanings of words, and the theologian escapes from the sand only as he follows a phrase to its source.

The casual reader may suspect rhetoric; the serious student recognizes clear echoes. Faith has genuine epistemological status. Precisely here our dilemmas are depicted; here Beckh fruitfully concentrates his prodigious energies. Readers of Beckh may experience moments of affinity with Hoskyns. People of prayer, creative artists, farmers and parents all know the practical links between technical details and results—call it 'performance', 'produce', a 'home'—it boils down to sustained and patient *application*. 'One word of truth shall outweigh the whole world', says the Russian proverb,[8] made famous by Aleksandr Solzhenitsyn. Our essential humanity is the focus. Professor Beckh himself, however, leads the celebration with his translation and edition of the *Hymn to the Earth* (1934). It stands as a reminder that a balanced vision of the *future* cannot fail to take note of our *origins*. Indeed, to counteract dire threats such an exercise appears to be essential—which is why Rudolf Steiner wrote *Occult / Esoteric Science* (1910), describing the inner story of earthly Creation itself, which begins with enthusiasm.

Beckh's faithfulness to his revered teacher is also apparent in his surviving letters, where we also glimpse at work the devoted researcher of specific fairytales and alchemical themes. In his writings, too, Beckh takes the stories of Elijah and Jezebel, Parsifal and Klingsor, Christ and Herodias, and so on, as actual and ongoing. He supported the initiative in Dornach to create a working-centre for spiritual renewal. Building the Goetheanum attracted people from seventeen different countries who collaborated despite the struggles of the time. For Beckh the *struggle for cultural renewal out of the spirit* provided the only lasting solution to the threatened loss of everything. Neither Beckh nor Rittelmeyer lived to experience the complete prohibition during the *Dritte Reich* of The Christian Community, the Anthroposophical Society and the educational and artistic institutions they nourished, including the pulping of books. The struggles of the time reach beyond narrow national concerns—as Beckh's almost exact contemporary, the composer Ralph Vaughan Williams (1872-1958) points out, blaming the politicians fairly and squarely for the pejorative meaning of the word 'national'. V-W, a tolerant, self-confessed 'agnostic', felt called to edit the music *The English Hymnal* (1906 and 1933) and to help with *The Oxford Book of Carols* (1928/1964) as *cultural* contributions. It is worth mentioning that, when speaking of the creative future for society (Torquay, 22 August 1924. GA 243), Rudolf Steiner gave some seminal indications to do with musical research, that is, inspiration from *audition*, not only vision. What he points to is proactive inner listening: 'It all depends on people.'

Selected letters of Professor Beckh to Rudolf Steiner here supplement Gundhild Kačer-Bock's biography; the extra material supplements an appreciation of Beckh's richly productive life. For readers' information one or two details: the Professor's 'fairytale' with delightful illustrations by Tatiana Schellhase is included in the English translation *Hermann Beckh: Life and Work* (TL 2021). The search for copies of Beckh's lost service music has so far largely drawn a blank. That apart, with some precious discoveries in the literary estate, supplementing *Collected Articles 1922-1938*, all the available products of Beckh's pen from 1916-1938 are now available in English.

Our contributions

In his contributions, Neil Franklin, General Editor of the 16-volumes of 'Collected Works' in English, takes the unprecedented step to reveal Beckh's inner pilgrimage through his life and entire *oeuvre*—it forms the centrepiece of *Celebration*. Rev. Christoph Rau (1928-2018), a remarkable theologian who knew how to use his musical training, wrote: 'What you have done for Beckh will be acknowledged in due time.' (Hopefully acknowledgement of Christoph Rau's considerable contributions will in its turn save his original discoveries from unjustified neglect.) Other contributors share how Beckh's example bears fruit in linguistic and musical pursuits. As the twenty-first century unfolds, others may be fruitfully inspired by this universal scholar. No end is in sight. The present volume not only rounds off the 'Collected Works'—it also introduces a remarkable personality, a largely unrecognized spiritual leader whose outstanding work for cultural and religious renewal is all of a piece and as contemporary as ever.

My sincere thanks to everyone who has made possible this *Celebration* and the translation project itself as an entirety. As with the earlier *Festschrift* (now a collector's item) special thanks to all contributors of new material, who join Susana Ulrich-Alvarez Ulloa (Sanskrit scholar and eurythmist), Oliver Heinl (linguist), Katrin Binder (Indologist, translator and eurythmist) and Maren Stott (eurythmist and co-translator); both Dr Binder and Dr Franklin (Blake and Böhme scholar) burnt midnight oil as 'more than editors'. We thank most warmly the librarians and archivists Wolfgang Gaedeke and Thomas Prange and the team at the *Zentralarchiv der Christengemeinschaft* (Berlin), Georg Ewertowski (Stuttgart), and the team at the *Nachlass* (Dornach). Although engaged in other projects, Neil Franklin gave precedence to the Beckh-project, unstintingly sharing his many insights; a steady, warm south-westerly breeze filled the sails of this barque. The late Rev. Christoph Rau leads those priests who expressed their moral support—Christward Kröner, Georg Dreissig, Michael Debus, Erhard Keller and Rüdiger Lunkeit and others—and whose appreciation of Hermann Beckh has been most encouraging. Michael Jones, Christopher Cooper, Dr Kenneth Gibson and Rev. Douglas Thackray were kind enough to write reviews. The late Tim Clement of Anastasi Ltd gave his considerable practical support during the initial years. Last but not least, our courteous publisher Sevak Gulbekian of Temple Lodge (TL) took over the project and with his team once again has given many hours to prepare yet another handsome volume. Remaining blemishes I acknowledge mine.

Alan Stott
Epiphany 2024

FROM THE LITERARY ESTATE

Some hitherto unpublished articles and lecture notes by Prof. Hermann Beckh. Unless otherwise stated, held in the *Zentralarchiv der Christenge-meinschaft*, Berlin. Our thanks for every assistance to Thomas Prange, archiv@christengemeinschaft.org

Ātman and Brahman

(An unpublished article, undated; from the handwritten MS in Sütterlin script, transcribed by Gundhild Kačer-Bock, translated by Marin & Alan Stott.)

Familiar to all who have studied Indian philosophy before is the teaching of the unity of *ātman*, the highest human 'I' or Self, with the *brahman*, the world-soul or the world-'I', expressed in the Upanishads. The actual development of the meanings of *ātman* and *brahman*, through which they have finally become the centre of Indian thought, is not so well known. Only knowledge of this development process of the meaning of the words gives us a hint of the depth of the doctrine of the unity of *ātman* and *brahman* which is expressed and repeated by so many people. We have to learn to grasp that change in imagination, in soul-experience, of which the change in the meaning of the words is only the external expression.

Brahman

It is well known that in the earlier Vedic language, *brahman* does not yet have the meaning 'world-soul' it has acquired in the later Vedas. In the earlier texts, something more subjective is described, namely 'devotion to the gods', the power of prayer and the holy word, prayer and the sacred word itself, or as it similarly has been attempted in the dictionaries to describe this term of the Vedic *brahman*. It has become common to point out that this Vedic *brahman* is something different from the *brahman* concept of later metaphysics, yet this change of meanings has not been treated as a problem in itself. Precisely this problem will be focused on here.

   The word *brahman* goes back to a root √*bṛh*, which, if we are allowed to follow Wackernagel (*Indische Grammatik*), also underlies the German word '*Berg*' ['mountain'], and which means 'to be big, to be wide, to expand widely' and the like. With the word '*brahman*', the early Vedic Indian describes an experience of soul-and-spirit. It is difficult for us today to find a word in our language to cover this, because the experience itself of the earlier Indian, in its intensity and immediacy, has become foreign today. How can we penetrate the essence of such questions, especially the essence of Indian philosophy and mysticism, if we imagine that people's soul-life was always the same? Rather, like everything else in the world, it is subject to change and development.

Brahman names much more than our words 'devotion' or 'prayer' today. To the mystical disposition of the ancient Indian it was the foremost mystical experience, an expansion and stretching of the soul beyond the limits of the physical, a striving toward and a being led to the cosmic-divine, to the divine that in ancient India was initially viewed as a multitude of divine beings and forces in the universe. *Unity* first creates thinking (the beginnings of which can certainly be traced back to the Rigveda, as shown in the Cantos in Book 10, e.g. 10, 129). For *visual* experience of world-phenomena and forces—and in ancient times, in the childhood of the race, human beings everywhere beheld the living and divine element behind the external appearances and forces—there is initially a multiplicity. But the more this experience permeates the visual impressions of the outer senses, the 'external illusion of the sensory world', the more it penetrates from multiplicity to unity.

The 'word' also meant more for that earlier experience of *brahman* than it means to us today. In the word the living force was felt that linked the soul not only to the outer conceptual envelope of visible things, but especially to the invisible living divine presence hidden behind the sensory appearances. *Brahman* was the *holy* word, the 'Word', in so far as the strength lived in it that united the soul with the divine in all things and beings. The power striving towards the divine from this human contemplation and from the holy word pronounced in prayer was felt to be nourishment and strength for the gods. All nuances of imagining and soul-experience, which later theology associates with the term 'the sacred', also lay in the Vedic *brahman*, only that *brahman* was perceived as something much more real. Thus, we can understand how in the later Indian thinking it became the reality of all realities, the one and only reality, compared to which everything else in the world is only *māyā*.

From this subjective experience of 'the sacred', *brahman* has become the great holy and divine [element] itself, beheld objectively in the universe; *brahman*, originally the experience that lifts the soul beyond the physical, carries it to the divine being, and allows it to expand into the cosmic divine nature, then becomes this cosmic-divine itself, which is viewed in thought as the great unity, the world-soul, the world 'I', the sacred word pronounced in prayer in the mantra becomes the 'cosmic word'.

Ātman

Conversely, the word *ātman*, which in the philosophy of the Upanishads means the core of our being, the highest human self, shows a change in the meaning from the objective to the subjective. Originally, this word *ātman*, which ultimately simply acquired the meaning of a reflexive pronoun, 'self' [myself, yourself, him/her/itself, etc.], really expresses something like our German word *'Atmen'*, 'breathing'. *Ātman* is the divine breath in the universe, the breath of the gods, and we are reminded of the imagination of the Germanic Odin when in the Rigveda, Book 10, the storm wind is revered as a divine entity, called *ātmā devānām*, 'breath of the gods'. From the cosmic widths, from the cosmic-divine world, this divine breath is then breathed into the human body as it moves through the body into the human inner life.

> And the Lord God formed man of the dust of the ground, and breathed into his nostrils the breath of life; and man became a living soul [Genesis 2:7].

It is in the breath that the Indian sees the forces of life that build up and form the outer body. This relates to the fact that, for example, in Buddhism the breath (*prāṇa*) is referred to as *kāya-saṃskāra*, as the 'formative force of the physical body'. Also, in the Indian context, *ātman* means not only the transcendental subject, the metaphysical highest 'I' of the human being, but it also and in particular means the visible self, the physical body itself. Only in philosophy this concept of the self, perceptible to our senses, is raised to the higher self, to the supersensible human essence. *Ātman* is thus the divine breath in the human being that builds up the bodily shell as the physical respiratory forces, and from there has moved into the innermost soul, deeply hidden beneath the surface of ordinary consciousness, and there acts as our innermost essence, our highest self. A whole series of mental coverings and layers of consciousness is mentioned in the later Vedānta-philosophy and Sāṃkhya-philosophy, as already in the Upanishads and in Manu. When all of these layers are penetrated, we finally find in the most inner realm that divine *ātman*, the 'divine breath', the divine self in the human being.

And now the great doctrine, the great recognition of the early Indian mystics, is this. That divine being, to which the soul comes when, penetrating the boundaries of the senses and the physical, connecting with the cosmic reality is none other than that divine being which it also meets when, penetrating and piercing all of its soul shells, it penetrates to its innermost soul-core, to what is most deeply hidden beneath the surface of outer consciousness. The invisible divine found outside in the universe is of the same nature, when the appearance of the senses is pierced; it is what emerges as our innermost soul-kernel, our innermost spiritual being in the deepest consciousness, when all the envelope or sheaths of the soul are sequentially penetrated. It is ultimately one and the same cosmic being that is found on the way out and on the way in. *Ātman* is *brahman*.

The Twelve Deeds / Acts of the Buddha[9]

A study on the relationship of the 12-fold Buddhist series, the causal-connections, to the zodiac[10]

x   x

x

♈ [Aries] 1st member of the series: *avidyā* 'the not-knowing', 'the error' also termed in Indian 'primal matter' (*mūlaprākṛti*), in the sense of spiritual science used to characterize the principle of the physical element, the substance of the Thrones. [♈] here again the sign of entering into the evolution of time and space.

Here too the meaning comes about, by proceeding 5 signs further in the zodiac. That is, the next sign:

♍ [Virgin] 2. *saṃskāra*, the primordial principle of the etheric element. In outer science the meaning of *Saṃskāra* is very contested ('the given, tendencies, dispositions, latent impressions', or rather: unconscious formative forces), the literal translation is 'working over'. Cf. on this *O.S.*[11] p. 144. [Trans. Monges p. 133] 'Thus the whole of Saturn evolution appears like a fashioning, a working over of what has streamed out of the Spirits of Will, by the Spirits of Wisdom, of Motion, Form, and so forth.' *Saṃskāra* is then certainly occult [= hidden]: the substance of the Spirits of Wisdom, as the primordial principle of the etheric element.

♒ [Waterman] 3. *vijñāna* 'consciousness', occult, the substance of the Spirits of Motion as the primordial principle of the etheric element (which also agrees with the sign ♒).

♋ [Crab] 4. *nāma-rūpa* 'Name and Form', the double concept corresponds nicely to the pincers of the Crab, occult: the *substance of the Spirits of Form*, that is, the primordial principle of the Sentient Soul (cf. *O.S.* p. 201 [Monges p. 180] on the evolution of the Earth). The actual 'I' is missing in Buddhism, consequently it is characteristic in what follows that the actual 'I'-beings, the Αρχαι are passed over, and the next member of the Buddhist causal series points directly towards.

♐ [Archer] 5. *ṣaḍāyatana* (the 6 realms, i.e. the *senses*, in the sense of *O.S.* (p. 106) that is the substance of the Archangels, the ker-

nel of the senses are worked on by the Archangels, at the same time the primordial principle of the Mind-Soul (*Occ. Sci.* pp. 202f. [Monges p. 181]). (And the Mind-Soul says to itself, 'These are the Archangels'.)

♉ [Bull] 6. *sparśa* 'touch' would have to be brought into connection with the sign of the Bull and to the hierarchy of the Angels [scan 1, left], as well as to the primordial principle of the Consciousness-Soul (to which the ♉ corresponds). Cf. *Occ. Sci.* p. 204 [Monges, p. 183; Creeger, p. 204].

♎ [Scales]. *vedanā* 'the feelings' would occultly have to signify what in *O.S.* p. 134 [Monges, p. 129] is described as the 'most simple, dullest form of consciousness' of the human seed at this stage beginning to stir its own forces. To the hierarchy of the angels (♉) there would be connected under the sign ♎ 'the human being', beautifully expressing the point of balance reached by the development working from above downwards.

These 7 first members of the Buddhist causal series would consequently express that Mystery expressed in the creative activity of the
[heavenly] hierarchies on the Thrones right down to the human beings
that had begun to develop on [Ancient] Saturn and was repeated on
[Ancient] Sun, [Ancient] Moon and the Earth.

II

The still remaining five members of the causal series would then signify that which belongs only to the *evolution of the Earth*. The entangle-
ment in the luciferic and ahrimanic element by the human seed that
was worked on by the gods, I would like to characterize as the Mystery
'with the point turned downwards'. Here too the Mystery begins with
the sign of the Fishes:

♓ [the Fishes] 8. *tṛṣṇā* 'the sensual desire', sensual love (which can
certainly in fact be described as the Mystery). In Buddha's development ♓ in the ascending Mystery signifies the opposite, the overcoming of sensual desire before entry into the Bodhi-circle.

♌ [Lion] 9. *upādāna* 'the laying hold', i.e. the satisfaction of sensual
desire, the succumbing to temptation, the biting of the apple. (In Buddha's development the same sign stands for the overcoming of the
Tempter).

♑ [Goat] 10. *bhāva* 'becoming', [i.e. conception.] The connection
with the sign of the Goat I do not yet quite understand. Here too probably are parallels to Buddha's development: in the course of Buddha's
life ♑ signifies the *becoming* of the Buddha, of the higher human being,
here in the descending causal series it signifies the 'conception' of the
earthly human being.

♊ [Twins] 11. *jāti* 'birth'. The sign of the Twins also signifies here
Lucifer-Ahriman.

occult: Ahriman [this insertion probably comments on the next
step—see table]

♏ [Scorpion] 12. *jarāmaraṇa* 'old age and death' (as also in the course
of Buddha's life), understandable without more ado.

4.

1.

2.

3.

6.

7.

8.

5.

Complete overview of the signs in connection to Buddha's development and its causal chain

Symbol	Buddha's development	causal chain
♈	descent from the gods	*avidyā*, primordial principle of the physical element (Thrones)
♍	entry into the womb	*saṃskāra*, primordial principle of the etheric element (Spirits of Wisdom)
♒	birth	*vijñāna*, primordial principle of the astral element (Spirits of Motion)
♋	youth, meeting the outer world, meditation under the rose-apple tree (impulse of the sentient soul)	*nāmarūpa*, primordial principle of the sentient soul (Spirits of Form)
♐	shooting the arrow, betrothal	*ṣaḍāyatana* (the senses), primordial principle of the mind-soul (Archangels)
♉	the great farewell, beginning of the life's course of the Buddha, impulse of the consciousness-soul	*sparśa* 'touch', primordial principle of the consciousness-soul (Angels)
♎	asceticism, meditation preparation, cleansing of the astral body for Spirit-Self	*vedanā* 'the feelings', one's own feeling of the human seed ('the human being')
	[pentagram pointing up]	[pentagram pointing down]
♓	entry into the Bodhi-circle, (entry into the Mystery)	*ṭṛṣṇā* 'sensual love' as the entry into the descending Mystery
♌	victory over the Tempter (Lucifer)	*upādāna* the laying hold of the sensory world, succumbing to temptation

♑	the coming into being, the *becoming* of the higher Spirit-Man	*bh[ā]va* the *becoming* in conception, the *becoming* of the lower human being
♊	Sermon of Benares on the 2 paths (rejection of the path of Lucifer and of Ahriman)	*jāti* 'birth' (from Lucifer to Ahriman?)
♏	death, the great *parinirvana*	*jarāmaraṇa* 'old age and death' (Ahriman)

The Zodiac and the Human Supersensory Members

[in answer to an enquiry[12]]

The thing about the circle of fifths and the zodiac is not new. I once talked about this with Dr Steiner, in relationship to my Buddha-book that had appeared in the Göschen series [1916], that is, the 12 main deeds in the life of the Buddha:

1. descent from the gods,
2. entering his mother's womb,
3. birth,
4. experience as a youth under the rose-apple tree,
5. arrow shot in the battle for the bride,
6. the great parting from the palace,
7. the time of asceticism and meditation,
8. entering into the circle of enlightenment,
9. fight with Mara,
10. enlightenment under the fig tree,
11. first proclamation of the teaching,
12. Nirvana.

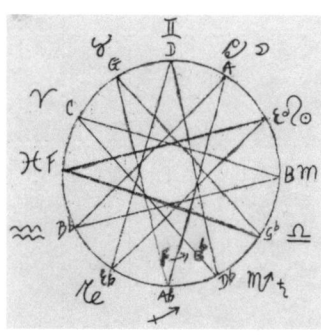

The sequence is ordered according to the zodiac, yet not in the normal sequence Ram-Fishes, but according to the sequence of the circle of fifths: Ram, Virgin, Waterman, Crab, Archer, Bull, Scales, Fishes, Lion, Goat, Twins and Scorpion, in which the death-sign of Scorpio expressively comes last. ('Circle of fifths' here means that in the zodiac circle one proceeds from the 1st to the 6th sign, to the 11th, the 4th, 9th, 2nd, 7th, 12th, 5th, 10th, 3rd, and the 8th sign.) It is really beautiful to see how with the birth the two streams of water of Waterman correspond, how the bowshot takes place in the sign of the Archer, the death in the Scorpion, and so on. Of course, I could not write these things, which already I carried inwardly, right into the book first published by Göschen [Berlin & Leipzig 1916, 1928[3], latest ed. Freies Geistesleben, Stuttgart 1998]. Till today, they are not publicly known. Also, the twelve members of the Buddhist series (see *Buddha's Life and Teaching*, TL 2019, 34-81) can be ordered in the same sequence of the zodiacal circle of fifths. The main viewpoint of this sequence of the circle of fifths (I have spoken of this with an older anthroposophist, and Dr Steiner agreed with it), however, is that in the sequence the individual signs correspond to the human supersensory members.

I never published this, because one always hears the objection, how can you prove this? These things cannot be 'proved' in a normal way, but if one meditates them through then the evidence opens up. One also doesn't want anyone to accept this like a dogma, but that one only accepts what has become clear by whatever way. To this the other side also belongs: that one does not over-quickly object to these things as merely 'thought out', but truly pays the necessary devotion and soul-attention it deserves.

Now, on the one hand, the problem has been pointed out. On the other hand, many things are contained in my recent contributions on the gospels, through which this matter too can be supported. I would like to risk here with the following, to present the matter with the human supersensory members and the zodiacal circle of fifths.

♈ The Ram, which also in the gospel always means the laying-hold of the earthly element, as placing oneself on the firm earth (after the Storm on the Lake, the experiences in the astral and etheric realm), the human *physical body* would come here as the lowest human member.

♍ The Virgin, a nocturnal sign in the circle of fifths, in the gospel lies at the basis of the revelations of the etheric Christ (the Feedings, the Last Supper, etc.) would be the *etheric body*.

♒ The Waterman would be the *astral body*. Think of the 'flowing, waving of the astral element' as it plays a role in the gospel with the Storm on the Lake. Also, think that when on Ancient Moon the human being received the addition of the astral body. The human being was a 'water man'.

♋ The Crab as *sentient soul* can be understood if one thinks that in the constitution of the sentient soul (turned towards the world of the senses) lies a certain revulsion against the spiritual element, a plunge into the sensory world. Cf. the sign of the Crab, ♋, how it also relates to the creation of Eve, out of Adam's rib (Gen. 2:22). ♋ is the 'rib'. This process, too, coincides with the arrival of the sentient soul in the human being. In the gospel, too, ♋ (besides the 'turning point of time') also means all the enclosing aspects of homely things and the lower, humble existence.

♐ The Archer, the next sign in the circle of fifths, as the sign of the *mind-soul*, of the deadly earthly [intellectual] thinking, is very clear.

♉ Taurus, *consciousness-soul*; one recalls the connection of consciousness-soul with the word.

♎ The Scales, the sign of inner balance, of meditation, of 'watch and pray' in the gospel, is arranged very meaningfully to manas, *Spirit-self*, the astral element transformed by the 'I' and brought into balance.

♓ The Christ-sign of the Fishes, also most meaningfully arranged to buddhi, *Life-spirit*, the etheric element transformed through the 'I' of Christ.

The signs of the Virgin ♍ and the Fishes ♓, ether-body and Life-spirit, stand here beautifully and expressively mutually opposite as zodiac coordinates. ♓ is also related to the [Greek] X of Xristos. The further connection arising through this, of the connection of Life-spirit and feet (Washing of the Feet) has deep esoteric backgrounds.

In the circle of fifths Leo ♌ follows, as *Spirit-man*, atma. Concerning the connection of this sign and Spirit-man, the physical body laid hold of and transformed by the 'I', the transformed and transubstantiated blood, I have already extensively described in my contributions on the gospel, to which I refer the reader.

Then, on the circle of fifths, the Goat ♑, the Twins ♊ and the Scorpion ♏, as three higher supersensory members, reaching still deeper into the Holy Trinity, as they initially are to be recognized in Christ Jesus Himself. The ♑, the overcome Lucifer, can be related to the 'Holy Spirit'; the overcome Ahriman (the ♍) to the 'Father'; the ♊ in the narrow sense, to the 'Son', to Christ, as to the One standing in the midst, holding the balance between the Twins, Lucifer and Ahriman. In this sense one can also bring the ♑ to relate to the 'first temptation' of Christ (through Lucifer), ♊ with the 'second temptation' on the pinnacle of the temple (through Lucifer and Ahriman), ♍ with the 'third temptation' (through Ahriman, stones into bread).

That this tone-zodiac circle of fifths—according to the scheme applied in my essay on the musical keys—results in the descending chromatic scale can be easily noticed and was already pointed out by me (♈, C-major; ♍, B-major, ♒, B♭-major, etc.). One always comes across the fact that behind all the keys lies more (in particular, cosmic matters), then those tending today to ignore the keys [atonality] can take notice. Even the wind which likes so much to howl in that descending sequence would consequently (as an important 'cosmic wind') relate to our cosmic, zodiacal circle of fifths.

With all this, the various relationships of the zodiacal signs are very far from being completely mentioned. Something more interesting

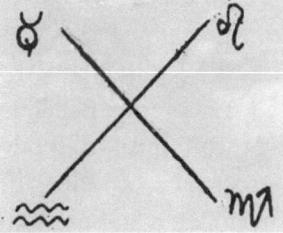

is their relationship to the *human temperaments*. We could start from the third of the three crosses, presented in my work on the gospel, the cross of the 'Holy Spirit'. This at the same time is the cross of the four beasts and of the four evangelists, that is (see fig.).

Here at the same time we have the four temperaments, that is, ♉ (Bull—Luke, sanguine); ♌ (Lion—Mark, choleric); ♏ (Scorpion = Eagle, John, melancholic); ♒ (Waterman—Matthew, phlegmatic). To each temperament there belong two further signs, forming each time a triangle, which one can easily find if one continues in steps of a *fourth* on the circle, consequently connecting the 1st sign with the 5th & the 9th; the 2nd with the 6th & the 10th; the 3rd with the 7th & 11th. This can easily be drawn as a diagram, putting in the triangles with different colours. The zodiac, consequently, divides into three crosses as shown with the gospel; it also divides into four triangles. Each of the four corners of one and the same cross belongs to another triangle, and each of the three corners of a triangle belongs to another of the three crosses.

> To the sanguine temperament belong: Bull, Virgin and Goat,♉, ♍, ♑;
> to the choleric belong: Lion, Archer and Ram, ♌; ♐, ♑;
> to the melancholic belong: Scorpion, Fishes and Crab, ♏, ♓, ♋;
> to the phlegmatic belong: Waterman, Twins, Scales, ♒, ♊, ♎.

One can feel through the cross and everything lying in the Christian cross, the four temperaments are again connected to form; a higher unity, brought into a higher harmony. Cf. on this Friedrich Doldinger, 'Viergetier', in *Gegenwartsrätsel im Offenbarungslicht*, Band 16 'Christus aller Erde', Stuttgart 1925, p. 101f.

The Apocalypse and The Act of Consecration of Man[13]

Still more directly than in the gospels, we find in the Apocalypse, the Revelation of John, this book [written] above all others for priests, in this Christian, future initiation text, and the most meaningful of all biblical initiation texts, the form of The Act of Consecration of Man. The pictures of the Apocalypse unfold before our eyes like a tremendous cosmic service at the altar, a service in which earthly events and cosmic events take place directly; an invisible, spiritual, cosmic altar-service connected to the outer earthly altar-service.

The Apocalypse itself clearly places the altar in our view. In particular Chapter 8, where in that cosmic-service the offering of incense, the tremendous cosmic Offertory begins. In Chapter 6:9, too, and in Chapter 11:1. Of course, it is not an outer altar; the events at the altar are not outer events. It is a cosmic altar-service and as such it cannot be a sensory experience, but only an experience of spiritual consecration, a meditation-experience. Experiences of this kind can only be sought and found in a quiet solitude of soul. Here the Apocalyptist also seeks them and here, too, the revelation comes to him. In the picture of the lonely island of Patmos—which we can also imagine geographically as the place where these experiences took place—he places before us this loneliness of the soul, which opens to these spiritual revelations. Here he is no longer in space and time of the sensory world, but in the spirit (Chap. 1:10, cf. 4:2, 21:10). He stands before us as the one initiated into the Mysteries of the spirit, the one raised by Christ Himself, the only disciple who experienced the tremendous consecrating event of Golgotha right to the end. He who stood with the mother under the cross (John 19:27) was amongst the first to experience the Risen One (Jn. 20:2-8). Where the consecrating experience of the gospels ends, the Apocalypse begins—the Risen One Himself stands spiritually before John, in the midst of the seven lampstands, also present with the cosmic altar-service (1:12, 13), 'holding the seven stars' (the spirits of the seven planets) in His right hand. The seven lights on the altar point towards the sevenfold revelation of the divine creative power.

The earthly altar-service begins with the 'Epistle' (read on the right side of the altar); the cosmic Act of Consecration of the Apocalypse begins with the Letters to the Communities (Chaps. 2 & 3). The seven major Mystery-communities of that time are the next to receive the tremendous impulse flowing through the revelations to the apocalyptist. In the word 'Amen', which here becomes the name of the Representative of Humanity Himself (3:14), the Mystery of the development of humanity is contained as the beginning and end of time connecting tremendous consecrating events.[14]

The 'open door' in heaven (4:1) pictures a still deeper view into the spiritual worlds, a new stage in the experience of consecration. We read in verse 2, 'At once I was in the spirit', that is, a still higher stage in the spirit. The picture of the cosmic-altar is completed for the spiritual gaze. He now sees not only Christ (as the living Risen One; He is also alive and invisible, yet pictorially present in the earthly altar-service) and the seven candles on the altar (once again, indicated in the seven 'torches of fire', v. 5), but, in the picture of the 'four living creatures', the spiritual human form, which receives its ultimate consecration in the tremendous and initial cosmic altar-event, and the 24 elders, who are the spiritual leaders of the individual epochs of humanity. Above all, the great picture of the altar is now completed (5:1) with the enthroned Christ, through the book in His hand, the gospel book of world-history, of all that happens in the world inscribed in the spiritual ether, sealed with seven seals for the one not initiated into its Mysteries. This scroll, or book, which has to be there if the great cosmic altar-service is to proceed to the Reading of the Gospel (just as in the earthly service the Gospel-reading follows the Epistle). As in The Act of Consecration the priest has to pray for Christ's blessing, to purify his heart and his lips, to be worthy to proclaim the divine gospel—in the earlier Mass we find here the reference to Isaiah 6, when the divine angel purifies with glowing charcoal the prophet's lips—so with the cosmic Reading of the Gospel the first thing to arise here is the question of worthiness: 'Who is worthy to open the scroll and break its seals?' (5:2). And no one in heaven or on earth or under the earth is found to be worthy—even into his meditation-experience, carried by the calmness of the spirit, the beholding apocalyptist is shaken by this knowledge (5:4, 'and I wept much that no one was found worthy to open the book or to look into it.'). The only one worthy is the Lamb that was slain, Christ Himself, not in His eternal form as the King here on the throne, but in the form in which He passed through space and time, standing as the great Martyr of the human race, as the slain Lamb. At the earthly altar, the human priest who has passed through the sickness of sin reads the gospel and who first has to ask for worthiness; the cosmic Gospel of the great revelation is read by the One who 'did go forth without sickness from the Father-God', Who is the divine Priest, according to the order of Melchizedek [Ps. 110:4, Heb. 5: 6, 10, etc.]. The tremendous song of praise at the end of Chapter 5 corresponds to the 'Gloria in excelsis' before the Gospel-Reading of the earlier Mass. Mysteries of human development in the past and future—Mysteries that remain incomprehensible unless we understand that development as one of consciousness—are revealed by the unsealing of the book, the cosmic Gospel Reading itself (Chap. 6). The worship of the angels, the elders and the four beasts (7:11f) stands like a great cosmic Credo in the same place where the earthly action at the altar has its Credo.

The content and goal of the entire earthly events, the great cosmic Deed at the altar, is nothing other than the great transformation and purification process of the Earth. Through Christ, Who united Himself with the Earth in the Mystery of Golgotha—who, as Novalis beautifully puts it, 'laid himself in the Earth as the foundation stone of a city of God'—is the decisive seed of this change implanted into all earthly and human events. This germ has been sunk into the spirituality of the Earth and into the souls of the people on Earth. The great process of change on Earth that began with Golgotha continues until the end of earthly time. Just as the transformed Earth then became the resurrection body of Christ, so everything in the Earth and humanity that has proven itself capable of this transformation and resurrection will then pass over to the new earthly embodiment. In anthroposophy it is called the Jupiter-existence, in the Apocalypse The New Jerusalem. Ultimately, it is this change in the Earth's being and in human beings that represents the change (transubstantiation) in the Deed at the altar.

As in the cosmos itself, the Transformation at the altar is not something passive, but something eminently active; it takes place when the soul that carries the Christ-seed within itself, the 'Christened' soul, sacrifices itself to the divine worlds in prayer, in meditation. That is why the change (Transubstantiation) is preceded by the sacrifice, the Offertory (Chapter 8). The rising incense is the ritual image of prayer, meditation, rising to the spiritual worlds. 'Out of the Christened soul may the smoke ascend, and upon us descend Your grace.' In this sense, in the cosmic act of the Apocalypse, the actual change is preceded by the Offertory, the Sacrifice, into which the opening of the seventh seal leads (Chapter 8:1ff). The silence in heaven brings to consciousness the transition into a new event. From the 'Christened' souls of the saints—the previous chapter presents them as the chosen ones in the white robe of the priest, bearing the seal of God—prayer, meditation rises up to God as a holy offering of incense.

> And another angel came and stood at the altar with a golden censer; and he was given much incense to mingle with the prayers of all the saints upon the golden altar before the throne; and the smoke of the incense rose with the prayers of the saints from the hand of the angel before God [8:3f].

The earlier Mass already names the angel standing to the right of the altar of incense and playing a role in the incense offering, Michael ('*Per intercessionem beati Michaeli Archangeli, stantio a dextris altaris incensi et omnium electorum suorum, incensum istud dignetur Dominus benedicere, et in odorem savitatis accipere.*'

'Through the intercession of blessed Michael the Archangel, standing at the right of the altar of incense, and all his elect, may the Lord deign to bless this incense and, in the odour of sweetness, to accept it.').[15] It is no doubt the same hierarchical being who is already encountered in the Apocalypse (7:2) as the angel who bears the seal of the living God, and in Chapter 10 stands there as the Sun-countenance of Christ, the same angel (or archangel), who is then mentioned by name in Chapter 12 as Michael.

> Then the angel took the censer and filled it with fire from the altar and threw it on the earth, and there were peals of thunder, loud noises, flashes of lightning, and an earthquake [8:5].

Even in the earlier pre-Christian sacrificial system, it was already evident that all devotion and meditation calls on adversaries who want to disrupt and break through the communion of devotion. The Christian ritual sacrifice is also always threatened by these demonic adversaries. As the prayers of the saints rise up to God in incense, all those sub-human beings that want to oppose the consecration of human beings, the great Act of Consecration of Man, also emerge from the abyss. In shockingly powerful images, behind which we have to learn ever more to find spiritual realities (most of them already in the present time), the Apocalypse lets these forces of the abyss hostile to the 'I' pass by us with the trumpet blasts of the seven angels. Their climax is the 'apocalyptic riders' (9:13-21).[16]

Just as the powers of the abyss arise during the great cosmic sacrifice with the incense of devotion and the prayers of the saints—our present time is in the midst of such events of the abyss—so too the last decisive change of the Earth, the fate of the future, cannot be carried out without everything falling away during that change that ultimately opposes divine love and does not want to, and cannot, take part in the change. This final decision and division takes place in the great universal Act of Consecration in the pouring out of the bowls of wrath (Chapter 16). In this outpouring during that cosmic action, the event of change, as it were, takes place at the altar. If this outpouring contains more of the negative side of the change, its positive side lies in all the images that are presented to the apocalyptist before and accompanying the change. In particular, in Chapter 10, the transformed human being of the future himself with the Sun-countenance of love reconnects 'sea' and 'land' in a deep occult meaning—as 'power' and 'wisdom'. It is those resurrected human beings who have realized the Christ-impulse within themselves. This picture is followed in the next, the 11th, chapter by the 'Measurement of the Temple'.

*

The Text of The Act of Consecration of Man in relation to the Text of the Old Latin Mass

[Transcript 2023, from the handwritten Sütterlin MS, undated, probably penned for the colleagues soon after the founding in 1922 and the 1928-article 'Michael in The Act of Consecration of Man' (CA No. 41). Probably unpublished since not traceable in the *Rundbrief*. Original held in the *Zentralarchiv der Christengemeinschaft*, Berlin. ACM = Act of Consecration of Man, MWH = *Menschenweihehandlung*. Subtitles added. A word or two ending the FN could not be deciphered. Novalis *Fragment* added.

NB Dr Frieling enters into more detail in his *Messe-Studien*, Eng. tr. 'Studies on the Mass' in Rudolf Frieling, *Experiencing Renewal*, TL 2024.

Text of the Old Latin Mass is available online, e.g. https://extraordinaryform.org/ExtraordinaryFormTextLandscape.pdf *or* http://www.latinliturgy.com/OrdinaryFormD20.pdf—accessed Jan. 2024. A.S.]

The text of the ACM given to us is far from being a 'translation' in the ordinary sense of the word. It is something creatively new, but in a certain sense it has absorbed the substance of something ancient, a Mystery that is even older than Christianity. For this last reason alone, any [Roman] Catholic accusation that the Old Latin Mass text of their Church has been translated here in an inadmissible and inadequate way—from a Catholic point of view—could not justifiably be made. The [Roman] Catholic Church did not create the sacrificial acts either, but rather adopted them from older Mystery traditions. But it then allowed what was taken over to solidify ever more into a certain form. It should be kept alive by taking the form that corresponds to the respective human consciousness in the spirit of living development. Only from such a living idea of development can a viable ritual of the future arise.

Just as the Latin text of the Mass corresponds to the [Roman] Catholic Church's view of the past, which is only concerned with preserving an old tradition as firmly as possible and protecting it from all temporal fluctuations, a ritual supported by the spirit of living development demands living language. This living language is particularly necessary where the rite no longer addresses subconscious emotional forces, but rather the consciousness, the fully conscious forces of the human 'I', or ego. In such a new community, the ritual act, The Act of Consecration of Man, can only become what it should be if every single one of its words can be absorbed and processed by every participant in the Act in fully conscious meditation. Just as Latin, as a fixed ecclesiastical language, belongs to the ritual of the past, so the living language belongs to the ritual of the future.

But this means that what was now to be given as a future-effective wording of an Act of Consecration of Man could not be an ordinary, mere literal translation. Such a translation, as can be found in Missals of the Catholic Church—to this extent the Catholic Church with its preference for Latin is correct—could not match the original Latin text. The words become pale in such an ordinary translation, the content of eternity that we can feel in the Latin wording no longer flows through them, and the language pales [compared to] that mantric power and effect which the Latin Mass text has, especially uniquely in its older, original parts. In the text of the Mass, not enough attention can be paid to this aspect of the mantra, i.e. the word that has an effect through the entire arrangement of the sounds, through the phonetic and rhythmic coordination of the whole. The Catholic Church has everywhere consciously cultivated this mantric spirit. But the German text of the MWH given to us is a mantra of the most powerful kind, precisely as a linguistic document, we will always be able to justify this text anew and draw new depths from it.

The standard of an ordinary 'translation', consequently, cannot be applied to this text of The Act of Consecration of Man. Rather, if it can be called a translation at all, or to the extent that it *can* be called a translation at all—Rudolf Steiner himself once called it that with reservations—it is a translation in a higher degree,[17] a free, creative translation that, by breaking away from the external word-for-word transliteration, seeks to capture the eternal content of the original words by giving its content the form and imprint that can be absorbed in a living way by today's human consciousness.

But the text of the Latin Mass has actually been transformed into something completely new. In the Catholic Church it is attuned to a certain biblical and denominational tone, whereas the text of the ACM appears to be entirely attuned to what is universal and human. It puts the cosmic in relation to the human perspective, the human in relation to the cosmic perspective. Anyone who feels the living Christ can take part in this wording, regardless of their affiliation with this or that denomination.

It will not be a question here of comparing the Mass text word for word, but rather of showing the spirit of the new 'translation' in individual characteristic places.

Gospel Reading

The *Munda cor meum ac labia mea omnipotens Deus*, which is effective in Latin, loses much of its mantric effect in the usual translation 'Cleanse my heart and my lips, O Almighty God'. A completely different power of words and meaning, something much purer and more majestic lies in our 'May my heart be filled with your pure life, O Christ. From my lips let flow the word purified by You'. The entire relationship between God and Christ, between the Ground of the World and the divine Son, has become different in the text of the ACM, in accordance with the deep understanding of the essence of the Trinity. The sacrifice is offered to the divine Ground of the World, which does not exist at all in the personal sense, but rather subsists on all being. But what is creative in human beings and in all becoming is the Christ, the creative cosmic Word, to which human beings relate their own word and from Whom they ask for the purification of this word. The biblical allusion to Isaiah 6 is missing in the ACM. [In the earlier Mass we find here the reference to Isaiah 6, when the seraph purifies the prophet's lips with glowing charcoal.][18]

The text of the ACM also seems to be carried by a higher degree of vividness: *ut digne et competenter annuntiem Evangel tuum*, 'so that I may proclaim your Gospel worthily and well', in the ACM 'So live Your word worthily upon my lips and borne by Your Spirit reach into those to whom it shall be proclaimed. Then from a worthy source and in a right stream, Your gospel is proclaimed.'

In the spirit of what was said above, the place of *Dominus vobiscum* now reads 'Christ in you', *Gloria tibi, Domine*, 'May it be revealed through You, O Christ'.

Per Evangelica dicta deleantur nostra delicta 'Through the words of the Gospel may our sins be wiped away', in the text of the ACM more expressive and more related to the word: 'The word of the Gospel wipes out that which lives impure in our word.'

The Creed

The text of the Creed, which was inserted into the Mass at this point, requires independent, in-depth attention and should consequently not be included in the considerations here for the time being.[19]

The Offertory

The opening of the Offertory also addresses the Father in the Latin Mass: *Suscipe, sancte Pater, omnipotens, aeterne Deus, hanc immaculatam hostiam,* 'Accept, holy Father, almighty and eternal God, this immaculate victim'. The ACM says here, in accordance with the deepening of the concept of the Trinity and the Father, the 'Divine Ground of the World'. What should be underlined is the strange emphasis that is always placed on the predicate *aeternus* in the ACM. It is not simply translated as 'eternal', but rather the eternal is translated according to its cosmic aspect or presented more concretely according to its human side; *sancte Pater omnipotens, aeterne Deus* becomes 'divine Ground of the World, weaving in widths of space and in depths of time', *ut mihi et illis proficiat ad salutem in vitam aeternam,* 'so that it [the offering] may effectively gain for me and for them salvation and eternal life' gains in this literal translation a personal touch, which the ACM uses exclusively through the wording: 'so that they bury not their eternal being for the sake of their temporal'. Here, in keeping with the true meaning of the original text, the idea itself has received a pure twist. It is similar with the *pro innumerabilibus peccatis et offensionibus et negligentiis meis,* which in literal translation does not fully exploit the meaning 'for my uncountable sins, offences, and omissions'. A greater dignity of expression combines with a deeper logic of thought (here too in harmony with the true meaning of the original text) our 'I bring it because to You have also flowed my strayings from You, my denials of Your being, my weaknesses'. There is also more to be gained from the *sed et pro omnibus fidelibus christianis vivis atque defunctis* than the mere literal translation 'but also for all faithful Christians living and dead'. In place of only 'faithful' Christians come the *true* Christians 'may there bring it all true Christians who are born', and the idea of the participation of the dead in the Act (which is so infinitely important for the deeper meaning of the Mass) is more independent and actively worked out: 'may there bring it all who have died'.

When invoking the Ground of the World in the ceremony of mixing water and wine, the idea of the connection between the human soul's members and the essential members of the Godhead has the effect of something completely new: the will, which is addressed to the Father, the Ground of the World itself, the feelings that unite with Christ, the eternal Son, Who lives in the life of the Father, and the thinking that lives in the life of the Holy Spirit. And yet this logically follows from the opening 'Divine Ground of the world, Who has fashioned out of the members of His being, the being of mankind' (*mirabiliter*, 'won-drously', receives the precise interpretation 'in the supersensible'),[20] and this lies as the germinal sense in the Latin *Deus, qui humanae substantiae dignitatem mirabiliter condidisti*, 'who wondrously created the dignity of our human nature'. Then comes the request to participate through the Mystery of water and wine in the divinity of Jesus Christ 'Who lives and reigns with You in unity with the Holy Spirit, God for ever and ever' (*qui tecum vivit et regnat per omnia saecula saeculorum*) to the clearer expression that emphasizes the interrelationship of the human soul's members with the members of the divine being: 'Divine Ground of the World ... to You I turn my willing; may this willing spring from feeling that unites with Christ, Who lives in your life, and may my thinking live in the life of the Holy Spirit through all cycles of the Earth to come.'

The following *Offerimus tibi domine calicem salutis* (or, grammatically incomprehensible *calicem salutaris*) 'We offer to you, O Lord, this chalice of salvation' speaks, not quite clearly in meaningful terms, of the chalice rising up with the smoke invoking divine grace. Here the text of the ACM says with full clarity what ascends to the heavens (namely something spiritual in connection with the external fragrance). The invocation of divine clemency becomes a more objective wish: 'May it enliven the good, that that also can raise itself to the heavens which has fallen to the Earth. May the fragrance ascend, as this God-willed being is descended. Yes, so be it.'

The following has also been completely redesigned in the 'translation'. First of all, the contrite, emotional quality of the initial request has been toned down. *In spiritu humilitatis et in animo contrita suscipiamur a te, Domine* ('with humble spirit and contrite heart may we be accepted by You, O Lord') has become the simple 'We all draw near to You in soul, O Christ.' The general invocation of God has again been replaced by the invocation of Christ. Accordingly, the following mention of the sacrifice had to be given a different twist: it no longer simply says, 'may our sacrifice in your sight this day be pleasing to you, Lord God' (*et sic fiat sacrificium nostrum in conspectu tuo hodie*) but 'that you offer us with You'. The creator of the wording of The Act of Consecration of Man took a deep inspiration from the words *in conspectu tuo* and *hodie*, which then finds expression in the words 'and Your light shine upon our day'. The idea returns later: 'Christ's light in our day-light', after the preceding 'Christ in the lifting of our hands'. The Latin text of the Mass has *elevatio manuum mearum sacrificium vespertinum*

[Ps. 140 (141):2], 'the raising of my hands like an evening sacrifice'. The *desire for consciousness*, which is hardly (only weakly) hinted at in the Latin text of the Mass, is brought very intensively to the fore in the new version; it is emphasized how the spiritual light of Christ connects with the daylight that shines on the external consciousness. With the following 'almighty, eternal God' the term *aeternus* appears again concretely dissolved into 'spirit of the widths of space and of the depths of time'.

Michael and the Censing

To bless the rising incense, the Latin text of the Mass brings an invocation 'through the intercession of blessed Michael the Archangel, standing at the right of the altar of incense, and to all his elect' (*per intercessionem beati Michaelis Archangeli stantis a dexteris altaris incensi, et omnium electorum suorum*) through the blessing power of spiritual beings the smoke and that which lives spiritually in the smoke is carried upwards. This idea is given the general form it deserves in the ACM: 'May our grounding in the Spirit fill the smoke with blessing's / blessed Spirit'; it is not the mere intercession of Christians that brings this about, but it is now said 'through Christ's living in our praying'. We ourselves arise through Christ in the Spirit that carries the incense upward in blessing. Here the smoke is no longer just taken externally, but it appears connected with what rises to the Spirit from the soul united with Christ Himself. This 'Christened soul' replaces the mere blessing of incense by a divine being. So, despite all the similarity of the thought and wording, the progress in consciousness cannot be overlooked, as it lies in the translation, 'Christ in us—out of the Christened soul may the smoke ascend, and upon us descend Your grace'. (Latin, *Insensum istud ad te benedictum ascendat ad te, domine, et descendat super nos misericordia tua.* 'May this incense, blessed by You, rise up to you, O Lord, and let your mercy come down upon us.')

Love

The entire creative depth of the wording of the ACM can be seen in the saying that concludes the actual Offertory and reads in Latin: *Accendat in nobis dominus ignem sui amoris, et flammam aeternae caritatis.* ('May the Lord enkindle in us the fire of his love and the flame of eternal charity.') The usual literal translation fails particularly at this point; above all, it does not find adequate words for *amor* and *caritas* in German. For *amor* it simply takes 'love', and for *caritas* it finds nothing other than a mere change in expression '*Minne*' ('*es entzünde in uns der Herr das Feuer seiner Liebe und die Flamme ewiger Minne*'). But '*Minne*' should be more *amor* than *caritas*. A more spiritual translation must be linked here to the very concrete idea of *amor* as the (initially in the physical) creative essence of love, and yet again in such a way that it is felt how the thoughts here relate to a spiritual creating, referring to the creative production of the higher human being. So here *amor* expressively becomes 'true, creative love' (compare 'Love's blessing warms soul beside soul, to bring all worlds to happiness' [Benedictus, Sc. 7, in Rudolf Steiner's Mystery Play] in *The Portal of Initiation*). In *flammam aeternae caritatis*, the concept of *timeless being*, which is created by the flame, is taken from the *aeternus*, from which the specifically spiritual concept of *caritas* finds its expression in the addition 'that the good endure'. *Caritas* appears as the perpetuating of good in the world, a devotion of the inner self, love in the highest spiritual sense. So one can find all the elements of the Latin saying in its version in the ACM, but you feel this new German version as something completely new, something received through independent inspiration from the spiritual world, through the direct power of words and meaning mantrically moving the soul: 'In the offering be born the fire of love, creative of being, and the flame beget timeless existence, that the good endure.'

The Transubstantiation

This is then followed in preparation for the third part of the Mass, the Transformation (Transubstantiation), by what is called the Canon, or the silent Mass. The translation in the ACM, if such a translation can still be spoken of here, appears to be particularly free and independent. All denominational allusions to the [Roman] Catholic Church and its saints and the catholic and apostolic faith are eliminated as such. They are replaced by the universal human reference to the community of Christ ('communities whose members feel the Christ within themselves, may feel united in a Church to which belong those who are aware of the healing-bringing power of the Christ'; 'feel', as the renewed Creed says). So, when the Latin Mass says of the sacrifices offered, *quae tibi offerimus pro ecclesia tua sancta catholica; quam pacificare, custodire, adunare, et regere digneris toto orbe terrarum*, 'which we offer you firstly for your holy catholic Church. Be pleased to grant her peace, to guard, unite and govern her throughout the whole world (together with your servant, our N. our Pope and N. our Bishop, and all those who, holding to the truth, hand on the catholic and apostolic faith)'. In the ACM the very general, human, pure thought emerges: 'We unite in the offering so that we may be the community of Christ', and what lies in the very original sense of the word 'catholic' ['universal'] is included in the request, 'May He may be in us, He who makes hearts to be at peace, who strengthens wills and unites mankind. So grant He unity to His believers. May He grant it to all who look towards Him and would follow Him.'

Of the commemoration of all the apostles and saints with the long list of names included in the section *Communicantes, et memoriam venerantes, in primis gloriosae semper Vírginis Mariae,* 'In communion with those whose memory we venerate, especially the glorious ever-Virgin Mary', no version can be found in the ACM. From all of these invocations the decisive idea is taken and expressed in the short phrase: 'May our prayer unite with all those who, bringing Christ to life within themselves, went before us; may their sheltering power ray forth to us.' The ancient Indian Mystery-system already knows this acceptance into this meditation of the saints of ancient times, of all those who have progressed in meditation. There is something new and independent in the request that concludes the Canon: 'This offering is sent to You by the Christian Communion, which knows Christ in freedom as its helping guide.'

At the beginning of the Transformation there is the request 'be pleased … to make this offering ... reasonable and acceptable, *so that it may be for us the Body and Blood* of Your most beloved Son, our Lord Jesus Christ' (*Quam oblationem tu, ... rationabilem, acceptabilemque facere digneris: ut nobis Corpus, et Sanguis fiat dilectissimi Filii tui Domini nostri Jesu Christi*). Instead, the simple 'Let live, O Father God, in this Christ-offering, the body and blood of your Son Who has His being in love' expressing the Christian attitude towards the spiritual fact of transformation, is decidedly freer than the Catholic one.

When it comes to the words of institution of the Lord's Supper, the ACM essentially follows the old text, but the expression has become simpler, and consequently even greater (e.g. in *sanctas ac venerabiles manus suas,* 'in His holy and venerable hands', has been omitted), for *benedixit* ('said the blessing') is expressly said 'and uniting His soul therewith', and 'bread' is given the significant addition 'for the revealing of salvation'. For 'Take and eat all of it, for this is my body' (*Accipite et manducate ex hoc omnes. Hic est enim Corpus meum*) the shorter and more mantrically expressive 'Take with the bread my body' has been substituted.

The phrase concerning the cup, *praeclarum calicem* 'this precious cup' is clarified as 'for the attainment of true salvation', in accordance with the supplementary phrase with the 'bread', 'for the revelation of salvation', for the passage is initially worded analogously to the previous passage. In a deeply meaningful way, too, *'calix sanguis mei'* ('chalice of my blood') unfolds in a novel manner; the meaning of the words *novi et aeterni testament: mysterium fidei: qui pro nobis et pro multis effundetur in remissionem peccatorum* ('the blood of the new and eternal covenant, the Mystery of Faith') is brought to a new development, which makes us feel that the 'Mystery of Faith' meaningfully reinterpreted already in the Latin text, is here explained in its depths: 'And he went on. "With this word is Godhead given to man [this paraphrases *novi aeterni testamenti*, 'new and eternal testament'] for the body will bear the new confession and from the cross will flow in the blood the new faith"' (this is the true content of the *Mysterium Fidei*, 'the Mystery of Faith'). The admonition contained in the words *mysterium fidei* to consider the particularly meaningful words also corresponds in the ACM to the added admonition 'Take this into your thinking'.

The following passage also brings new and meaningful inspiration to the ACM. In the Latin Mass it only says, 'Therefore, O Lord, as we celebrate the memorial of the blessed Passion' and so on (*Unde et memores, Domine, nos servi tui, sed et plebs tua sancta, ejusdem Christi Filii tui Domini nostri tam beatæ passionis*, etc); in the ACM it has become: 'So *live* in our thoughts the new confession, the new faith,' and then the meaningful 'so *thinks* in us Christ's Passion and death, His resurrection, His revelation through all ages of the Earth to come'.

The reference to the sacrifice of Abel, Abraham, Melchizedek in the Latin text of the Mass is again replaced by placing in the foreground the simple, basic idea of the relationship of the Christian to the pre-Christian sacrifice: 'You, O Father God, did once receive the offerings of those who had not yet Christ. So may You receive the offering of those who bring it in the name, the being, the power of Christ.'

The following *Supplices te rogamus, omnipotens Deus: jube haec perferri per manus sancti Angeli tui in sublime altare tuum, in conspectu divinae majestatis tuae* etc. ('In humble prayer we ask you, almighty God: command that these gifts be borne by the hands of your holy Angel to your altar on high in the sight of your divine majesty') replaced in the ACM with the short and expressive: 'Your Spirit's power of grace works earthward, as this offering strives heavenwards.'

In the Latin Mass there is still a longer invocation to the apostles and saints, *intra quorum nos consortium, non aestimator meriti, sed veniae, quaesumus, largitor admitte* ('admit us, we beseech you, into in their company, not weighing our merits, but granting us your pardon'). In the ACM this is summarized as 'Before You, we can do no works; before you we would overcome sin through Christ—through Whom You ...' in Lat. *Per quem haec omnia, Domine, semper bona creas, sanctificas, vivificas, benedicis, et praestas* ('Through whom you continue to make all these good things, O Lord, you sanctify them, fill them with life, bless them, and bestow them'), in the ACM, 'Create, heal and ensoul'. Compared to the Old Mass, the idea that the Son-God is the Creator in the broadest sense—not just *bona creas* ('good things')—appears new. From the concept of *gloria*, that of revelation is brought out again, from the eternity of *saecula saeculorum*, once again the relationship to space and time: *Per ipsum, et cum ipso, et in ipso, est tibi Deo Patri omnipotenti, in unitate Spiritus Sancti, omnis honor, et gloria, per omnia saecula saculorum* ('Through him, and with him, and in him, O God, almighty Father, in the unity of the Holy Spirit, all glory and honour is yours, for ever and ever'), for this in the ACM 'through Christ through whom You, together with the Healing Spirit, fulfil the revelation, the ordering of space, the course of time'.

The Lord's Prayer

The Latin Mass also inserts the Lord's Prayer at this point, before the Communion. The continuation of the last petition (*Libera nos, quaesumus, Domine, ab omnibus malis, praeteritis, praesentibus, et futuris*: etc) ('Deliver us, Lord, we pray, from every evil, past, present, and future ...') has no parallel in the ACM.

Communion

At the beginning of Communion, in addition to the new and expressive rendition of the *Pacem relinquo vobis, pacem meam do vobis: ne respicias peccata mea* ('peace I leave you, my peace I give you, look not on my sins'), it also turned into the active: 'Therefore make strong, O Christ, that in me which wrests itself free from the load of sin' and, instead of the reference to 'the faith of your church', mention is made of what 'in thinking and willing joins with You, that it stand at peace with the world and unite with the world's evolving' (in the Catholic Mass text also with reference to the Church: 'deign to grant her peace and to unify her according to Thy will'). *Qui vivis et regnas Deus per omnia sae-*

cula saeculorum ('Who lives and reigns God, forever and ever'), in the ACM related to 'becoming' [= 'nascent being']: 'which can come to pass through You in all cycles of time to come'.

One of the freshest new creations of the entire text is the following section: 'O Christ, who came forth without sickness from the Father God' (*Domine Jesus Christe, Fili Dei vivi*). For *Spiritus Sanctus* the Holy Spirit, 'the Healing Spirit' becomes meaningfully in the ACM: and 'Who did with the Healing Spirit give continued life to the spirits of human beings' (in the Latin text of the Mass appears *qui ex voluntate Patris, cooperante Spiritu Sancto, per mortem tuam mundum vivificasti* more one-sidedly turning to the past). The following request for salvation takes on a much more active meaning in the ACM; it no longer simply means: 'free me by this, your most holy Body and Blood, from all my sins and from every evil; keep me always faithful to your commandments, and never let me be parted from you'.

The following request for redemption takes on an essentially more active meaning in the ACM; it no longer simply says 'Deliver me through this Your most holy body and Your most holy blood from all my sins and from all evils, and make sure that I always receive Your commandments, and do not allow me to ever be separated from You,' but rather 'quell through Your health-bearing body the might of the sickness of sin and strengthen me in my wrestling soul with Your health-bestowing blood, that I live evermore with You ...' *Qui cum eodem Deo Patre, et Spiritu Sancto vivis et regnas Deus in saecula saeculorum* ('Who with the same God the Father and the Holy Spirit, lives and reigns, God, forever and ever'). Here too, the concept *'Healing Spirit'* is used for 'Holy Spirit': 'You who bear and order the life of the world, as You receive it from the Father and make it whole through the Spirit in all cycles of time to come.' In the following, too, compared to the concept of unworthiness in the Catholic Mass text, the ACM text emphasizes the *sickness* more. ... *quod ego indignus* ('which I unworthy') ... ACM 'be unto me who is sick ...'. Compared to the *tutamentum mentis et corporis* ('a safeguard both of mind and body') of the Latin text, the ACM emphasizes the etheric body: 'but for the life of the soul and the *forces that form* me the healing medicine'. The same emphasis on *illness* can be found in the following: Latin Mass *Domine, non sum dignus* 'Lord, I am not *worthy'*, ACM: 'O Christ, *sick* is the dwelling into which you enter ...'.

Corpus Domini nostri Jesu Christi custodiat animam tuam in vitam æternam ['May the Body of our Lord Jesus Christ preserve your soul unto everlasting life']: the term *aeternus* 'everlasting, eternal' is, as everywhere reproduced in a special way; the general expression 'eternal life' has been replaced by the request for continued life: 'the body of Lord heal my soul, that it *continue to live*,' also in what follows: 'The blood of the Lord keep strong my soul, that in the time to come it die not.' This request for life goes back to the oldest Mysteries; we also find it in a strange way in the Lamaistic Eucharist as communicated in the book by [Laurence Austine] Waddell, *The Buddhism of Tibet, or Lamaism* [1895].[21]

The question *Quid retribuam Domine per omnibus quae retribuit mihi?* ('What return shall I render unto the Lord for all He has given me?') takes a positive turn in the ACM, 'Take me, for as much as you have given Yourself to me'. The free translation of the following brings out the true thought. 'I will take the cup of the Lord and call on the name of the Lord, and I will be safe from my enemies' (*Calicem salutaris accipiam, et nomen Domini invocabo. Laudans invocabo Dominum, et ab inimicis meis salvus ero*) does not concern external enemies, but applies to the soul's adversaries (cf. Matt. 20:28), which is why the ACM, using an expressive paraphrase of the term *nomen* ['name'] has more correctly developed the original meaning of the entire passage: 'I take the cup and do this in the name of the Lord, calling, O Christ, I confess what has been revealed through You, and the might of man's adversary You take away from me.' The *pura mente capiamus* in what follows ('What we have eaten with our mouths, O Lord, let us receive with a pure heart') becomes, in a logical deepening of the thought in the ACM, 'What my mouth has received, *become spirit* in my soul.'

Instead of the 'blemish of sin' (*scelerum macula*), the 'sickness of sin' is spoken of again in the following. Accordingly, *quem pura et sancta refecerunt sacramenta* ('whom these pure and holy mysteries have refreshed') is rendered as 'through the healing medicine, the sacrament', and thus the idea of illness and healing [comes out] even more than would be the case if the text of the Mass were simply translated literally.

Richard Wagner's 'Lohengrin': A Pentecostal Mystery[22]

The more one concerns oneself with the life's work of Richard Wagner [1813-1883], the more colourful the characters [of his music dramas] appear. The characters, which out of old sagas and legends he re-enlivened for the present age, gradually appear to us as embodying life's riddles. They repeatedly appeal to us. We are to interpret their meaning. One discovers how the individuals are inwardly connected. As in nature, after the root come stem, leaf and blossom [together] forming a total organism, it is similarly shown that the total work of a genial master like Wagner is an organism, built not according to natural law but according to human spiritual laws. The individual characters are stages, degrees on a path of development. (Here it is beside the point that the works are conceived at different times.) In this we can compare Siegfried, Parsifal and Lohengrin.

Siegfried

Siegfried passes through the sea of flames after struggling through many escapades, reaches the mountain and marries the divine maiden Brünhilde. He finds his eternal self. We perceive the final hour of farewell where Siegfried descends into the valleys for new experiences. There his tragedy is fulfilled. Through the enchantment of the draught of oblivion, he succumbs to Gudrun, the darkening of the soul, indeed death through Hagen's spear. In him we behold the human tragedy of descent to earth.

Christmas

When we seek in our own lives for inklings of such paths of experience, we are guided to the cycle of the year. A more sensitive soul-observation can find in winter the earth becomes rigidified into a rock. Starry light shines more clearly and unobscured. In snowflakes the starry life floats down to earth. We feel we are close to the power of the starry world. In ourselves a soul slumbers, which in virginal purity is akin to heaven. Like Siegfried we would like to awaken the divine maiden. Then we celebrate Christmas when we feel heavenly life in earthly existence.

Good Friday

The sprouting splendour of colours in spring entices us in our devotion to the earth. The chaste juices of life in the plants become in our blood the draught of forgetting, which darkens the memory of the starry clarity of Christmas. Forgetfulness, indeed, the death of the soul of a heavenly existence, comes about. The soul celebrates Good Friday. The path from Christmas to Good Friday in nature contains the destiny of Siegfried.

Parsifal

Parsifal approaches the realm of the Grail as Siegfried achieves the height of the mountain. He has to leave it again because he fails to understand. When he faces Kundry in the voluptuous garden of Klingsor, Parsifal has also himself to undergo Siegfried's experience. But at that moment, when he is threatened to succumb to the danger of sensual love, there arises mightily in him another love not bound to the senses, which Siegfried, the pre-Christian hero, could not yet experience—*compassion* with the suffering Amfortas. 'Amfortas! The wound! It burns in my heart!' He feels the effect of Golgotha, the Holy Grail. For Christ suffered on Golgotha in order to save the forces of love, to wrest them from the earth.

Easter

Resurrection from the threatening death of soul is thus experienced by Parsifal. Siegfried arrives twice at the cave in the rock. The second occasion he has forgotten Brunhilde.

Parsifal comes twice to the Grail, the second time as victor over the death of soul. Easter in him has become a fact. From Good Friday to Easter is as Siegfried to Parsifal.

If we remained with Easter, we would experience the forces of resurrection only in our inner being. We would remain blissful in the realm of the Grail. But out there unredeemed humanity is suffering. The further degree of becoming human is to sacrifice one's own blissfulness and return to the unredeemed situation, not as unredeemed but as messengers of the Holy Grail. Then one becomes a Grail knight, a Knight of the Swan. One progresses from Parsifal to Lohengrin (Parsifal is the father of Lohengrin), from Easter to Pentecost.

Pentecost (Whitsun)

What is Pentecost? What is not Pentecost?

F. Miller [points to] Lenin and Ghandi. Both want to save humanity. Both want to speak the redeeming word. Both know that suffering encompasses all humanity. Suffering is international.

- Lenin [maintains to fight] the war against the class system and Western civilization right into the most extreme mechanization of all aspects of life.

- Ghandi [advocates] brotherly love and the simple culture of the forefathers.
- Lenin [maintains] Western technology redeems. He ravaged Eastern spirituality.
- Ghandi [maintains] Eastern spirituality redeems. He does not see the reason to become free from nature.

These [thinkers] assist the further separation of humanity. What is the Word redeeming humanity that reaches from West to East, in which the freedom of the West and the truth of the East are united? Longing for Pentecost is living in the present time. A tremendous longing for the festival of Pentecost should today arise in souls. For what was the festival of Pentecost?

The Festival of Pentecost

The Twelve [the Eleven and, according to tradition, Mary] are gathered in one accord. Behind them lies the terrible event which they did not understand. Tormenting days. The Thirteenth is missing. He has gone through death and resurrection. Dulled by their pain they experienced it yet did not understand its meaning. Then their moment came. The suffered pains tore open heaven for them. They heard the 'rushing' wind. The echo, the sounding musical creation of spiritual powers, and they found Christ, the Living One, humanity's presiding genius 'until the end of days'. Now they understood that a new life of the spirit should begin, renewing humanity. In beholding Christ, they found their eternal task. To be teachers. Each was filled with the fiery tongues of the Spirit. Twelve teachers for the world stand before us at Pentecost. They know now:

This experience of the spiritual world, of Christ, can come to all human beings, to the Roman in the West, to the Asian in the East, to the Greek and Jew in the middle. The redeeming Word is the annunciation of the knowledge of the spiritual world. Everyone is yearning for this. Out of the knowledge of spiritual beholding there arises the Word of Pentecost, experienced by each individual as a personal strength of freedom. A truth that makes you free [cf. Jn. 8:32]; this is the Spirit of Pentecost.

Grail Streams

In Christianity there always existed below the surface a secret longing to find that mysterious light-filled world where the Thirteenth lives, the Sun-Spirit of Humanity, to find that realm of the Grail, where wisdom, the understanding of the Mystery of Golgotha is to be found. This was sought by all the souls dissatisfied with blind authoritative belief.

From the legends of the Arthurian Cycle of the Knights of the Grail—
to the Mysteries of Goethe, Mörike's (1804-1875), 'Gesang Weylas'.

Du bist Orplid, mein Land!
Das ferne leuchtet;
Vom Meere dampfet dein besonnter Strand
Den Nebel, so der Götter Wange feuchtet.

Uralte Wasser steigen
Verjüngt um deine Hüften, Kind!
Vor deiner Gottheit beugen
Sich Könige, die deine Wärter sind.

You are Orplid, my land!
That shines afar;
Your sunlit shore sends up sea—
Mists, that moisten the cheeks of the gods.

Ancient waters climb,
Rejuvenated, child, about your waist!
Kings, who attend you,
Bow down before your divinity.
[Translation © Richard Stokes, author of *The Book of Lieder* (Faber, 2005)]

People sought the mysterious spirit-kings who attend the god.

Parsifal describes the path to this mysterious realm.

Lohengrin shows us the destiny of such a Grail-initiate, who with Pentecostal strength appears as the leader in humanity.

In 1841, Wagner writes, 'Here a whole new world opened for me. At first, I did not find the figure with which I could supersede *Lohengrin*. This picture continued to live indelibly in me.'

Lohengrin

Opening situation

In the country, the old king has died. Through this a new age arises. His daughter Elsa shall rule the country. Elsa from Brabant, as it were, represents the progressive time. The soul of the new time. Under what sign will the future come? Who will become her husband? Originally, Friedrich von Telramund was to become her husband. With him she was to create a new future. But he had succumbed to the strong magic forces of a woman who through signs made clear to him that from her race the rulers of the country were still to arise; she came from ancient, heathen Frisian descent. She venerates the old gods; she wants to evoke the long gone times. She is the enemy of Elsa. Progressive human souls and those who have become reactionary and demonic face each other. Through Telramund she seeks to destroy Elsa. She is accused of fratricide.

In humanity meaningful turning points always come where the old powers are finished, when a time arises where the progressive souls in humanity face many dangers. The old order no longer works. The worrying question is, what spirituality will the leadership support? From heathendom to Christianity, from the Roman Empire to the Middle Ages and from there to modern times such turning points occurred. But here the eternal powers of the past arise who resist progress, who call up ancient spirituality and with this become demonic counterforces of the new.

When Elsa, already accused, stands trial, the hero appears whom she has seen in her dream. The radiant knight comes with the Swan gliding over the water in silver armour with a golden horn and a sharp sword.

Second situation

In the centre of the battle stands Elsa von Brabant, the heir of the orphaned country, the soul of progressive humanity. As an enemy: Friedrich von Telramund, distinguished through many praiseworthy deeds. The earthly consciousness of his time. But, as is often the case, because the ordinary earthly consciousness does not see through to the deeper forces, he is under the spell of the old, doom-brooding Ortrud (luciferic world of the gods).

As helper: Lohengrin: brightly shining Sun-figure, behind him the wonderful Mystery of the world of the Grail. The Golden Horn to herald, 'Change your thinking'. Silver armour: robe of wisdom. Sword of his word: the proclamation of his insights. Thus he fights with Friedrich von Telramund, the consciousness of the age, for the soul of humanity, Elsa von Brabant.

The Condition

Wagner's wonderful insight that at the turning point of the ages the great leaders will come from 'yonder', who, consecrated to humanity's sacred future goals, will fight for it on the path of freedom and truth. Yet:

Nie sollst du mich befragen,
noch Wissens Sorge tragen,

woher ich kam der Fahrt,
noch wie mein Nam' und Art!

One thing you must solemnly promise me:
you must never ask me
or be at pains to discover
from whence I journeyed here,
nor what is my name and lineage!

The people suspect that he comes from a higher world. They greet him with, 'You God-sent hero'.

There is an important key in this condition. Lohengrin is saying: I appeal to no authority, to no position (type), to no personal abilities (name). The initiate wants to work freely through the trust that is freely placed in him. He should be recognized by his deeds, his fights with his opponents. He does not say: I am sent by God, Christ gave the command. 'Where I came from' is not authoritative. That belongs to charlatans. He does not says: *My* abilities are such and such. He wants to say, do not look at the outside; my name is one you do not know.

He reveals himself as a spirit of freedom; he wants to work in freedom. And people should look to him with free trust.

Christ before Pilate answers the question, 'Are you a spiritual king? You have to answer.' The personal life of the initiate should remain shrouded in secret. 'He will not speak on his own authority, but whatever he hears he will speak' [Jn. 16:13]. In freedom, proclaimer of the truth. Elsa accepts the condition. The battle is fought. The initiate carries his spiritual knowledge into the consciousness of the times.

Third situation

Suspicion; the purity of his person is being attacked. Technically, no one is a match for him. It remains in Elsa's soul. The Grail customs are defenceless against personal insults. At the hour when the most intimate marriage is to take place—the bridal chamber—what is human and all–too–human strikes the initiate. The night passes in intrusive questions and benevolent defence. The secret shall be unchastely torn from him and the deepest Mysteries used for personal defence.

Elsa: Whence have you come?
Lohengrin: Alas!
Elsa: What is your lineage?
Lohengrin: Alas! What have you done?

The hour of farewell is here. As a most wonderful gift he gives the [auto]biography of the one who was heaven sent.

> In a far-off land, inaccessible to your steps,
> there is a castle by the name of Montsalvat
> a light-filled temple stands within it,
> more beautiful than anything on earth;
> therein is a vessel of wondrous blessing
> that is watched over as a sacred relic:
> that the purest of men might guard it,
> it was brought down by a host of angels;
> every year a dove descends from Heaven
> to fortify its wondrous power:
> it is called the Grail, and the purest, most blessed faith
> is imparted through it to the Brotherhood of Knights.
> Whosoever is chosen to serve the Grail
> is armed by it with heavenly power,
> the darts of evil prove powerless against him,
> once he has seen it, the shadow of death flees him.
> Even he who is sent by it to a distant land
> appointed as a champion of virtue,
> will not be robbed of its holy power,
> provided that he, as its knight, remains unrecognized there.
> For so wondrous is the blessing of the Grail
> that when it is revealed it shuns the eye of the uninitiated;
> thus no man should doubt the knight,
> for if he is recognized he must leave you.
> Hear how I reward the forbidden question!
> I will send to you by the Grail:
> my father Parsifal wears its crown,
> I its knight—am called Lohengrin.

The marriage had not taken place. Earth-soul and Grail-soul cannot yet become one. Consequently, new Grail messengers must always come at every turning point.

But his work was not in vain. Elsa's brother is redeemed. The Swan becomes a human soul-force that leads in purity to the spiritual world. A new soul-force is thus incorporated into the existence of the initiate.

Conclusion

Lohengrin takes us deep into the riddles of humanity. In the fight for progress, Christ promised to send the Spirit of truth. He comes ever and again in the great teachers. Ever and again a Pentecost messenger comes from the region of the Grail who wants to lead humanity to freedom (tongues of flames) and to experience the spiritual world (rushing mighty wind). Everyone has to become a messenger of the Holy Grail.

We are living at a most serious turning point in the world. New Pentecost proclamation! Do we not perhaps have among us the messenger of Pentecost, the herald of spiritual knowledge, and do we not need a Christianity today as an answer to the needs of the present day, which combines the sure experience of the living Christ with the spirit of true freedom?

The Peoples of Europe in Schiller's Plays: A Pentecostal Mystery[23]

One of the ideas that emerged after the catastrophe of the Great War [1914-18] and is increasingly represented today is the idea of Pan-Europe, the United States of Europe. What is very important, however, is the way in which the idea of Pan-Europe is spread: as an economic organization (removal of customs barriers, etc.) and as a political institution to prevent wars. Europe should feel like a large unit.

Without criticizing this idea, one must say: it is only an echo, and a materialistic one, that is, without the essence of that European feeling that was there in Central Europe 100, 150 years ago [written 1927].

I recall a scene in Erfurt, in 1808. Napoleon and Goethe met—both men of Europe. Napoleon sought the unity of Europe through politics. He submitted to it: 'Politics is fate', he says to Goethe. He fails because of England, the power that actually says that the economy is fate. But confronted with Goethe, he said, '*Voilà, un Homme!*' 'Spirit is fate.'

All the peoples of Europe looked at the red-glowing Martian star Napoleon, but in common fear and rejection. People looked at the bright star of Jupiter [Goethe] in awe and admiration. This is where the human element expresses itself. Goethe's *Faust* is a European book. He has the language of contemporary people. Goethe is a good European.

In the time of Goethe [1749-1832] and Schiller [1759-1805] and their contemporaries there was a European feeling that could have become the basis for a free spiritual life between the peoples. But instead, the materialism that wages war in the world arose.

But today, after the catastrophe, we have to go back to the spiritual foundation and build on it to prepare for cultural progress.

Schiller's Christianity

But can we bring that time together with Christianity? We called this lecture 'a reflection on Pentecost'. Goethe's dislike and Schiller's statement are both well known: 'What religion do I profess? None of the ones you name me. And why none? [I've learnt this] from religion!' (Goethe & Schiller, *Musen-Almanak für das Jahr 1797*).

Pentecost: The group of Twelve [Apostles] experienced a spiritual centre, an invisible Thirteenth. In Him they experienced the divine human Archetype.

In Goethe's poem *'Geheimnisse'* [which concerns a Rosicrucian fraternity. Their leader] Humanus is the representative of humanity. If you read Schiller's ethnic dramas (leaving out *Don Carlos* and *William Tell*), then you think you are walking through such a group, around an invisible spiritual centre, the divine human Archetype. He [Schiller] goes from people to people, listens to his [the Archetype's] soul, and all together creates the full 'music of humanity'.

With Schiller's Christianity you have to consider the what, but more the *how*. In the 'how' of his work, the Pentecostal spirit lives, the language of the understanding of nations based on the ideal of a pure, divine human being. He created this ideal in his *Aesthetic Letters* [1794]. Through his friendship with Goethe, his spirit expanded and became saturated with reality.

Out of this he wrote the series of great national dramas. This would have become a true Pan-Europe if such impulses had continued to be cultivated. Embedded in Schiller's dramas is a recognition of the peculiarities and tasks of the individual European folk-souls. The fact that through the artistic element one can also see the truth behind it is already contained in Schiller's sentence [from the poem *'Die Künstler'*]:[24]

Nur durch das Morgentor des Schönen	Only through beauty's morning-gate
Drangst du in der Erkenntnis Land.	do you penetrate the land of knowledge.

Rudolf Steiner penetrated this 'land of knowledge' and fully developed Schiller's inklings. We would like to follow Schiller's method. He pre-heard musical motifs according to his feelings, which he then clothed in subject matter and character.[25] With the soul, we want to hear the primal sound of the individual dramas. We do not take the chronological order of the poetic dramas. We start with one of his last dramas.

The Bride of Messina [1803]

The high level of artistry is reflected in the fact that he no longer included his personal judgements. This play is not a German drama; it is an Italian drama. Hence the cool reception. Italy's soul itself lives within him. We are directed to Sicily, where everything is full of elementary forces, to the homeland of Empedocles, who still saw love and hate in nature. The drama speaks of the elementary powers of the soul. The ruling family has two sons. Since childhood, they have hated each other in endless arguments. A dream shows the father that the coming daughter will be the bane of the house. The mother's dream allows her to be saved. [She] grows up in loneliness. Both brothers get to know and love her. Through their mother's mediation, the two reconcile. Then he finds his brother in his lover's house. He kills him and then commits suicide under the most shocking circumstances. Let us listen to the primal sound of the drama. It is the song of love and hate. Equally powerful forces of nature influence the feelings here. People are just the arena in which they express themselves. Without the reins of reason, passions run wild.

> *Chorus*:
> We did not reflect on the warrior's anger
> and did not advise ourselves
> because we were beguiled by the rushing blood.

The sensations change at the moment when new impressions arise. Alternation of hatred, reconciliation for eternity, glow of love, murder of brother. People live in their sensations, with the impressions of the eye and the senses. 'Whoever pleases the eyes is king here.'

Nothing about inner problems; the rich sensual life [itself] supplies all sorts of problems. The subsoil of dreams on which everything is built—the whole glowing world of passion [is built] on the surging sea of dreams. Devoted to the senses, especially the eye. Cf. Catholicism; veneration of the Pope. Dante gives colourful descriptions of the spiritual world. The Italian's love of his homeland. He is the 'stranger' in other countries.

Conclusion:

'Life is not the most valuable thing.' 'But the greatest evil is guilt.' Sensation becomes compassion in pity.

The Maid of Orleans [1801]

A completely different world of soul. No longer the dull rage of passion. The bright light of beauty shines in the enthusiasm with which the drama is filled.

Plot: in the war between England and France, when the court is powerless, the lion-hearted maiden sent by the Lord appears and drives the English out of the country. Listen to the primal musical sound: the unconscious enters not as a dream and in a passion, but in the form of beauty.

At the court: the beautiful Agnes Sorel. People adore form. In the souls, the worship of form becomes the concept of honour (Knights and Troubadours).

> *King*: 'Yes, now I recognize my deep fall. For trust is given to my *honour*.'

The Maid appears to save the honour of the nation.

> 'Shall this empire fall? This land of glory?
> The most beautiful thing that the eternal Sun sees in its course.'

> 'The nation is worthless if it does not put all its joy into its honour.'

The third form is the Glorification of the Maid. The spiritual [shines] directly in the heroism of the Maid.

Schiller immerses this entire French world in the Greek perception of beauty. The intelligent mind-soul grasps the spiritual element in its revelation as beauty. Molière, Racine, Corneille—are 'barbarians'.

Mary Stuart [1800]

Schiller wrote to Goethe:

> The English history I have been reading since then has influenced me to keep English premises and essence always vividly before my imagination.

Here we enter a completely sober region. From the unconscious forces of drunkenness and enthusiasm we emerge into a sober world.

> Two formidable rivals, queens, are struggling for control. *Mary Stuart* is a drama concerning power. The queens are each other's competitor.

> *Mary*:
> For 'tis not justice, but mere violence,
> which is the question 'tween myself and England.

> What are the duties that I owe to England?
> I should but exercise a sacred right,
> Derived from sad necessity, if I
> Warred with these bonds, encountered might with might,
> Roused and incited every state in Europe
> For my protection to unite in arms.

Everyone wants to assert themselves here. Competition. Power without, dignity within (meeting of the queens). Wise consideration, prudence, beyond conscience.

Shakespeare, Darwin: the struggle for existence.

> Italy—sensations, feelings
> France—grace, form
> England—dignity

Wallenstein [1798-1799]

Germany brings conscience to the world. The German descends into the depths of his inner being. With *Wallenstein*, the conflicts are no longer external. For Germans, like the Slavs, it all takes place within.

Stuart is destroyed by her rival.
The Maid—because the nation leaves her.
The Bride—because the circumstances of life are tragic.
Wallenstein—perishes having himself to blame.

Max Piccolomini says of him:

> His spirit cannot be grasped like another's,
> how it ties its fate to the stars.
> Thus he resembles them in a strange,
> secret, eternally incomprehensible way.

His misfortune is that he cannot be one-sided. He stands above the parties. He is the brooding, thinking person. Such a person always has to look at the matter from two sides. 'The equivocal demeanor of my life bears witness on my prosecutor's party.' [*Wallenstein's Death*. I, 4.] He feels responsible for the whole situation.

> *Max*: Because he cares more about the best of Europe than a few feet
> Which Austria has more or less—[*Wallenstein* I:4]

Because he is like that, he comes close to the sphere of betrayal. But he only considered it in his thoughts; he had to, because as a *thinker* he has to look at things from different sides:

> ... it was not
> My serious meaning, it was ne'er resolved.
> I but amused myself with thinking of it.
> The free-will tempted me, the power to do
> Or not to do it. Was it criminal
> To make the fancy minister to hope,
> To fill the air with pretty toys of air,
> And clutch fantastic sceptres moving toward me? [*Wallenstein's Death* I, 4.]

He does this to ensure the best for himself. Not as an employee of the emperor.

> *Max*: He should ask the oracle within himself, the living source—
> not dead books, old orders, not mouldy papers.

Wallenstein is *a freedom seeker*. Since he became a thinker, he has felt the harmony of his inner being with the starry order: the order of wisdom in space and my fate are one. Within, an objective world of spiritual wisdom emerges. *A German person seeks the spirit in the 'I'* (Cf. *Faust*).

But Wallenstein has bad friends: Illo and Tertzky. That which is spiritual wealth for Wallenstein, feeling independent of the emperor and adopting a different point of view, becomes treason for them. They force him for the sake of freedom to perform externally the deed that he only entertained in thought. '... I must realize it now in earnest, because I toyed too freely with the thought!' [I, 3.] They cause the crash.

The German spirit always has its Illos and Tertzkys that persuade it to convert its spiritual possibilities into actions: to do business like the English, to turn diplomatic like the French, to feel like the Italian, to feel like the Roman in religion. Wars arise from such things. Outer things will be destroyed. 'In the night only Friedland stars can beam.' [III:10.] Germany has always given the greatest gift to humanity when it was in political and economic ruin. This is how the German man striving for freedom and an objective spirit stands before us in Wallenstein. He represents German greatness and at the same time its tragedy.

Demetrius [1804-1805]
The drama of the Slavs—left unfinished. Plot: Demetrius is to be executed although innocent of murder. One can see the mark of the Czar's son on him. He himself grew up in this consciousness and wants to take the throne of his forefathers with the help of Poland. He does become Czar, but his mother Marfa does not recognize him. Before that, the Czarevitch's murderer discovers that he is actually a false Czar. Nevertheless, Demetrius asks her to become his mother in order to prevent new misfortune. Romanov. The drama would have become sacrifice and devotion to the spirit. Solov'ev: new brotherhood in Christ. The Slavic spirit will only mature in its significance for humanity in the future.

Conclusion: this is how the folk-souls of the people speak in Schiller's dramas. He finds a language of the folk. This language is the Spirit of Pentecost, the Healing Spirit. Beyond all conventional barriers, the Christian spirit bubbles up from the great creators. Christianity is a mystical fact. At the end of his life, Goethe said: 'May spiritual culture continue to progress, may the natural sciences grow ever broader and deeper, and may the human spirit expand as it pleases! It will not supersede the sovereignty and moral culture of Christianity, as this shimmers in the gospels.'

Even though it may still be uncomfortable for many representatives today, real Pentecost will only come about when all free spirits feel comfortable in a renewed form of Christianity, when they can feel their deepest vision and striving understood. Then a Christian Community will be there as a gathering place for truly free spirits who, from their own free experience, seek the figure of Christ as the Representative of the human spirit. And the representatives of all nations and peoples and languages, standing in a circle with Humanus as the hidden Thirteenth, as the leader in the middle. Christ, the divine Archetype of what is fully human. This Church of free spirits will be the Church of Pentecost.

Surviving Letters to Rudolf Steiner

Held in the Rudolf Steiner *Nachlass*, Dornach. Transcribed and translated by M. & A. Stott.

From a visit, July 2017, I am grateful to the *Nachlass* for permission to see the file containing the existing letters Prof. Beckh wrote to Dr Steiner. No replies are known to exist. I was allowed to copy by hand whatever would assist my research. The following translations of a selection were made with Maren Stott. According to the Index in the file, omissions are apparent, raising the question whether more letters, also from the 'gap' year, were once extant. Some bibliographical details are added in [ ], also brief comments from Beckh's biographer, Gundhild Kačer-Bock. (Extracts from some letters and those to other recipients are included in her 1997 biography, *Hermann Beckh: Life and Work*, TL 2021)—A.S.

Check list:

29 Oct. 1912 and card 1 Nov 1912	8 Dec. 1916 (missing)
9 February 1913	8 Feb. 1917
11 February 1913	18 Feb. 1917
2 March 1913	Kiel, 4 March 1917
15 March 1913	Kiel, 17 March 1917
27 Oct. 1913	27 March 1917 (missing)
24 March 1914	Kiel, 1 July 1917
23 Feb. 1915	Kiel, 10 June, 1917
10 June 1915	Kiel, 23 July 1917
12 Dec. 1915	Kiel, 31 August 1917
24 January 1916	29 June 1918, 10 Aug. 1919 (missing)
23 Feb. 1916	Stuttgart, 13 January 1924
12 May 1916	Stuttgart, 13 March 1924
11 June 1916	Stuttgart, 6 June 1924
20 July 1916	
30 July 1916	Buddha's 12 deeds (see above,
Im Felde 26 Nov. 1916	pp. 13-19)
18 Feb. 1917	

*

Steglitz, 29 October 1912
Most esteemed Herr Doktor!

The request I make to you with these lines is in the first instance that you might grant the opportunity to meet you in person for a conversation. I am a private tutor[26] at the University of Berlin; my subject is Indian and Tibetan philology. When someone belonging to that 'hostile' materialist science turns towards a man of your way of thinking with the plea as is expressed here, he has to be prepared for some concerns that he can meet from the theosophical side. With the relationship as it still unfortunately exists between official studies and spiritual research in a higher sense (but perhaps also based on a passing necessity in the plan of world-development), those concerns appear most obvious and understandable. When the writer of this letter nevertheless dares to persist in his request, the serious importance he will not hide, then it is the love for the truth of occult spiritual research that gives him the courage for this.

Amongst the prevailing lower intellectualism and the intellectualism of official science, nobody suffers more than the one who thinks differently when he is placed in the midst of that environment. It would be for me the highest longing and the noblest content of my existence to be able to place insights still to be gained from spiritual realms into the service of life and development and to collaborate in the great tasks of our time to overcome that materialism ('to redeem science as one values it today with early sacred mysticism'). In his striving to fight against the materialistic stream of our time the individual has to overcome a tremendous resistance. On the one hand steadfast patience and certainty belongs to this, and on the other hand careful mindfulness, tact and no doubt also a certain degree of higher knowledge and concentration in order to fulfil the task adequately. When these characteristics are to be developed in the right manner, in order to become the truly effective weapon in the battle of life, they have to flow from a hidden source which your spiritual leadership might reveal to me, as far as in your judgement the conditions for this are right.

If with this I ask you in all earnestness to become my spiritual leader and guru, then I am aware of the significant difficulties that have to be overcome in the outer conditions as well as in one's own nature (or at least as far as is so far possible for my possibly limited self-knowledge). I do not want to force anything that in the given circumstance cannot be achieved but also do not want to leave anything untried, for which in the potentially existing possibilities could be developed, an opportunity might be given (according to the principle: 'not to do anything lying outside one's strength, but also not to omit what lies within those strengths').[27] Fear of danger does not hold me back, at least regarding my outer fortune in life, official career, and so on. Once before in my life I have possibly hastily sacrificed a profession from the standpoint of higher wisdom, but out of a strong inner impulse. I was a lawyer (in Munich), successfully completing all exams (state exam and doctorate) and found myself just prior to entering the Civil Service. Experiencing strange difficulties, I began new studies with the result that up to now I have been a private tutor here for some years. I could completely understand it if a spiritual researcher disagreed with the step I took then. Yet at the moment of writing, I do not entertain the wish to undo what has happened. For the occupation with early India—however sober and dry it appears within the limits of academic philosophy—has nevertheless given a richness of valuable stimuli for my spiritual strivings for which I can be grateful to my destiny. With this there is nothing further removed from me, by the way, than the limited neo-Buddhist or similar standpoint; I am rather—after thorough and mature deliberations—especially concerning these Indian things in the strictest sense of the word of *one* opinion with you. What you say in your writings and lectures about the position and significance of India in human development has especially spoken to me, indeed I confess with joy in this regard that through you I have received new and surprising stimuli and that my love with which I meet the study of Indian sacred texts—for example, Buddha's addresses, which are particularly delightful in the original text—has increased and intensified since acquaintance with your writings and lectures. The same applies especially to my relationship to the New Testament, more than anywhere else you have become the spiritual leader for me.

The Grail Mystery appeared to me as the highest symbol of the truth in Christianity and behind Christianity, higher than any Indian symbols known to me. Already in early childhood I dimly divined hidden Mysteries in this, a feeling that also in later life was kept awake through consecrated impressions from Bayreuth and other things.

Within the treasure of German fairytales, the fairytale of Sleeping Beauty / Snow White appeared to me—and still appears to me—to possess an especially deep, profound (occult) meaning (interpreted in the direction of the sleeping seed of our transcendental consciousness).

Besides your writings—although I have only become acquainted with them quite recently—I have nearly read them all; concerning serious literature I have known for some time the works of H.P. Blavatsky (*Isis Unveiled* and *Secret Doctrine*, as far as it is possible here to find a way through the thicket of a confused style to follow the high ideas of the writer). Also, the books of Annie Besant, Sinnett and Mabel Collins and some others—especially Bulwer[-Lytton] I do not want to leave unmentioned here. The new revelations from Adyar touch me less, yet I would still like to withhold judgement about it. I would like to connect with the Theosophical Society here. I also heard about an Anthroposophical Society. Before undertaking a step in the one or other direction, I would like to request a conversation with you—with regards to the special situation. In the case of my joining the Theosophical Society here I could name as referees those among the members of the Theosophical Society who belong to my study-group (e.g. Frl. Else Krause, who took a diligent part in my studies and exercises).

In any case, I will attempt on 31 October, at the end of the first lecture-evening at the Architects' House to approach you. But because many strive for the same thing, it might be possible that my intention will remain unsuccessful on that evening. Consequently, I would be most grateful—although, of course, I do reckon that you will have many reasons to forego any kind of written reply—if I could receive the enclosed postcard with a few added words.

With warm respect and esteem,
your devoted,
Dr Hermann Beckh
Private tutor[28]

[After the public lecture in the Architects' House on 31 October on the theme 'How does one justify spiritual science?' it seems only an initial meeting was possible and an agreement for Hermann Beckh to write to Rudolf Steiner a short letter the next day with the times: due to his commitments, he would not be able to visit Rudolf Steiner—G. K-B., from the biography.]

Steglitz 1 November 1912
Schloßstraße 41
Most esteemed Herr Doktor!

Regarding our conversation yesterday I may allow myself briefly to communicate to you the times when outer professional duties (partly at the University, and partly at the Königlichen Bibliothek) keep me occupied. These are: Tuesday, Wednesday, Friday and Saturday in the mornings 11–3, and Monday and Wednesday in the afternoon (4–6). Any other time I am absolutely at your service. I would be most happy if I may visit you.

With deep and utmost gratitude
for your kindness,
Dr Hermann Beckh

Steglitz
15 Jan. 1913

Highly esteemed Herr Doktor!

Since the matter is definitely important and I am not quite clear about a few points, I would like briefly to tell you about my first meditation.

At first I was surprised at how easy I managed to keep intruding thoughts at bay, indeed I even felt such thoughts did not want to come. On other occasions I always had to struggle with this. But this time it was as if something, which until then had not been experienced, supported me in this meditation. I am very grateful that you immediately gave me a sublime meditation. I felt I was lifted away from the earth, a sensation which I might have had in the high mountains, but very rarely in the big city. I kept my eyes closed (was that right?), as from the twilight darkness of the depths of the world, the rose cross appeared to me (which for some days has appeared clearer to my inner eye than ever before). When imagining the background of the colour scale I had at the first meditation attempt—but only very briefly and temporarily—experienced colour visions of wonderful beauty (whether imagination or illusion I do not yet know), especially green, blue, violet; these visions did not return until now during the repeat of the meditation. I am still not entirely clear how the background of the colours relates to the circle of the roses. The roses are all light pinks, but the colour scale goes from red down to purple. Do the roses then rise above the field of the other colours (not red ones), or do these colours begin only at those parts of the cross where the roses end?

If I understand correctly, I, A, O sounds from the three upper roses; the echo sounds come from the lower roses, as if they again emanate from three roses each; one rose would be left over, because (and certainly for deep reasons) there are but seven roses. By the way, according to your drawing, the echo tones would fall between the fourth and fifth, the fifth [and] sixth, the sixth and seventh rose, i.e. not emanate from the centre of the roses, is that correct? (Excuse my probably childish questions!)

Is it possible for this part of the meditation, in addition to the vowels, to specify certain musical tonal relationships (tones, intervals, chords) in which the vowels sound? In previous attempts, the desire to coordinate the tones musically came naturally to me, but I don't know whether I made the right choice. With my psychological constitution, music, especially harmony, is important as a gateway to esoteric [matters]. In this regard, it was one of the strongest influences on my inner being that I have met in my life.

The light in my meditation actually came about by itself after a while; this morning it seemed to be connected to a strong vision of light. The 'peace of mind' also came by itself; I didn't feel any effort to keep intruding thoughts at bay, but rather the feeling of a real soothing and deep resting, not disturbed in any way. I was also able to open my eyes again during this part of the meditation. I feel as if my body is permeated with strong and cool (very intense and pleasantly cool, almost cold) etheric currents. After finishing the meditation, I always had a feeling of increased vitality and faster blood circulation, also, as sometimes before, a feeling of lightness and hovering, and today, all day long, that of a strong but calm bliss. The physical inhibitions that I suffered from yesterday (I mean on the days I was with you) were resolved through the exercises, and not in one go.

This evening in order to bring balance in my ether-body I introduced the meditation with some gentle music-making (piano). The *Parsifal* Prelude seemed to me especially suitable—with its calm arpeggios and with a view to forming the subject of meditation. And here—perhaps introduced through *Parsifal*—a picture that seemed to me to be useful as a preparation for what you gave me (if an error, something wrong here, you will certainly draw my attention to it?). This picture creates the red of the roses through a mystical transformation. Around the black cross (the crossing point of the two beams) seven roses are ordered, as in the rosy cross, but initially white, the white roses of mystical death, the life of eternity. From the heights, carried by the hosts of the hierarchies, the Holy Grail descends, filled with the blood of Christ. A dazzling beam of light proceeds from the Grail; met by this light beam, the roses suddenly begin to glow in delicate glowing red, as if penetrated by the sacred blood of the Redeemer. The lighting up of the red colour is accompanied by a corresponding modulation of the musical harmony sounding from the roses of the cross.—As I said, all of this should only facilitate the structure of the given meditation and does not claim an independent meaning.

---

16 January 1913

Today, too, the meditation succeeded without any intrusion of estranged thoughts. Only the picture itself is probably not yet lively enough, still too shadowy. The fact that I have at least partially done the right thing I would like to conclude from the strong (especially physical) effects the meditation has on me: I feel something decisive in the blood. All professional work is now even easier than before. One question still, regarding breathing exercises. Some deep breathing always comes by itself when attempting to meditate. For the time being, however, I will omit actual breathing exercises because they seem rather to be a danger for me; at least in previous years I had adverse effect with such exercises from Indian books. At times the effects seemed good, at other times the opposite. On this or the other point mentioned in this letter I will take the opportunity to ask you in the Architects' House, if the circumstances are favourable for this.

With the feeling of thanks,
I remain
your devoted,
Dr Hermann Beckh

Steglitz
29 January 1913
Schloßstr. 41

Highly esteemed Doktor!

So far I was fortunate with meditation. However, because I am currently at a point where there is a risk of deception and attacks of different kinds, I would like to allow myself to impose on your kindness again through some questions.

I initially felt the colour impressions already mentioned in my last letter that soon after the meditations began, I felt initially to be illusion.

But I am very clear in myself, the clearer I am the more beautiful and precise the appearances occur; on unfavourable days the colours also fade without completely disappearing. They are most beautiful at the time of twilight (for example, wonderful again this evening). So much is certain that they are something different from colours in the outer world, but also something completely different from just colours presented in the imagination; they really are colours 'freely hovering in the room', like little flames but always one and the same colour tone, a delicate blue (possibly approaching violet), more beautiful than all outer colours. Sometimes the phenomena fill my entire room, so that the (very delicate) impression is similar to the cloud background of a picture by Raphael.

Perhaps all of this is a reflex of the meditation image, a kind of counter colour or something? The right thing will certainly be not to make too many assumptions at first, but to take up the impressions as calmly as possible. Perhaps with this communication I have already crossed my limits, the compliance with which the pupil is advised on p. 182 of your book *Knowledge of Higher Worlds: How is it Achieved?* You will certainly be so kind as to point out this failing. But it has nevertheless not to fall prey to false imagination. I never believed earlier on to be open to perceive impressions of the grain of seed described on p. 76 of your book; all my earlier attempts in this direction remained negative. Then I noticed a few days ago after the meditation of the rosy cross that my gaze as if by chance fell on a seed grain lying before me at a distance (a sunflower seed, as I use them to feed the bluetits) and I truly perceived this covered there in a clear, although not sharply defined, blue (or blue-violet) appearance of light; also since then I have always had the appearance, sometimes significantly weaker. The closest explanation is probably that I have happened to see the colour blue of the colour I would otherwise have seen freely floating now by change seen on a sunflower seed (of course, I don't see them on any object, only on my mountain crystals, I have perceived them similarly even if significantly weaker and smaller). But the danger that I imagine, as you describe it, of seeing the appearance of the etheric body of the plant, or something like that, is of course one of the big dangers, although I dismiss this imagination in my consciousness, it can still exist in my subconscious, and such imaginations are often the most dangerous. (Stronger than such a tendency is with me, as I believe, the striving for simple knowledge of the truth.)

An even greater danger, than the one just described, threatened me last evening during the lodge lecture. I saw the blue light phenomenon around the lecturer, this time especially strong (perhaps in this case I saw only a reflex of the blue panelling of the room, but the tonal colour of the appearance was deeper, more towards violet). For a long time I saw the appearance and didn't think further, when suddenly the thought of the aura struck me, because truly the colour phenomenon showed itself in a special strength on the head and on the hands. It could probably only be what are called the third aura (if I follow your *Theosophy*), the other two are definitely out of the question, and also in relation to the 'third aura' a lot is wrong with the descriptions given in books, especially that it was only blue (and blue-violet) awakens my suspicion.

I immediately tested whether I would be able to see the same appearance in the others present in the hall; with some I saw it, although weaker, but in most I saw nothing.—I am not aware of any predisposition from earlier on of seeing human auras. However, I always felt it most strongly, since the earliest times of my life that I can recall.—The impression of the appearance yesterday was that I was at first somewhat shocked.

The climax of the various appearances as well the meditation was on January 20. For I had the impression of a great clarity that has not been reached since then, indeed an almost unearthly bliss, a walking on 'flowery colours'. Also in the previous five days I was also without any hope, as in a higher condition. The last few days have brought various challenges and the feeling (not yet overcome) of a physical resistance (which at least for the moment I was almost able to overcome through meditation). During meditation itself, I succeed in what I want to call its 'negative side' (I mean holding off obtruding thoughts) in a better way than the 'positive side' (wherein I understand the most living Imagination of the picture for meditation), yet already regarding the latter there seems to be some progress. At the beginning it was difficult for me to imagine everything at the same time (colour and roses or tones and echo tones), and the idea of blue—indigo—violet at first succeeded much better than imagining the upper colours [of the colour circle]. I found a relief in imagining the rainbow colours on dispersing water (all in bright sunshine); are such helps allowed? I do not clearly recall what moral ideas with the three upper [colours] are to be connected to the four lower roses. With the upper one, I thought more of strong, courageous ones, with the lower part of devotional, humble love. Also the meditation taken from your lecture-cycle on John's Gospel about the four members of the physical body, ether-body, astral body and 'I' as body, life, light and love [*Leib, Leben, Licht, Liebe*], I believe I can draw strength (even the four L's with the change of the vowels seem to me significant, as well as from my favourite saying Rev. 12:10 (recent lecture-cycle); is it possible with this saying to think of the rosy cross?

With warmest respect
Your devoted,
Hermann Beckh

———————————

Steglitz, 9 February 1913

Highly esteemed Herr Doktor!

... Diving into such a theosophical sharing of life which I had never known before was somewhat overwhelming. In your third lecture of the cycle (Mysteries of Isis) in the midst of feelings of happiness an incredible longing came over me towards all that mourning, towards all that pain, towards all that forsakenness, towards all the shadows of death. This longing was still stronger after the last lecture of the cycle (for which I am eternally grateful to you) for here with the Parsifal and Grail motif you have touched my innermost being, the thought with which I have been living since early childhood, without which I would never have found the way to you (this is a completely assured fact). The longing to be led by you now more deeply into this Mystery will never and can never evade me. But the feeling of the heavy load has disappeared again, replaced by a deep calm and lightness.

At one time in 1899 I experienced something tremendous, of which since yesterday I now know that I can call it an esoteric experience; a similar but weaker one I experienced some years previously, and again still much earlier, I believe at the age of five; all these three experiences in the loneliness of the mountains. The most recent of these three experiences was preceded by much suffering. The consequence of these experiences was a strong urge to give my inner life an esoteric direction. The strongest suffering and attacks were the consequence of this (especially after giving up the legal profession), especially strong and sometimes almost suffocating, the suffering under one's own personality (Amfortas), then at times there repeatedly existed an upward striving (Parsifal). When I turned to you with the plea for occult instructions, I believed I should be prepared for a terrible increase of those sufferings and attacks, nevertheless, with this step I had the clear feeling that it meant an unavoidable necessity for my life; to omit this was unimaginable. And what I now at first have experienced as a consequence of all this, was the most blissful of all surprises, and when I look back especially on the last two days, then I stand indeed before experiences which in power and greatness over-top everything I have ever dared to dream. The reactions (which were not absent) were at least much weaker than what I experienced earlier on in this regard. I believe one of the most important tasks of an aspiring anthroposophist is that he aspires as much as is possible (for it is often difficult) also to extend his activities beyond himself into the world and to carry in any way a life that in our group has so splendidly blossomed, so that from the esoteric life a glorifying lustre falls on to exoteric life. Thus after all those magnificent impressions of the past week, it was difficult for me yesterday to decide to take part in the Centenary celebration (Prussian Festival) at the University, yet I overcame the arrogant stance and did not regret it. I recognized how I experience such things now quite differently from earlier on, there were impressions that lead over into the esoteric realm. For example, the ending of Schiller's 'Reiterlied':[29]

> Und setzet Ihr nicht das Leben ein
> Nie wird Euch das Leben gewonnen sein
> 'And deep be the stake, as the prize is high—
> Who life would win, he must dare to die!'

sounded like an occult admonition. It is as if a transformation is taking hold of everything …

In warm gratitude and
yours most faithfully,
Hermann Beckh

_____

11 February 1913

Highly esteemed Doktor!

Since yesterday, very clear pentagrams (✿) also double triangles (✿) with small figures in the middle (✿ with 'r') are recorded and other more complicated figures that my memory cannot yet grasp, furthermore, crosses, flowers with stars of all kinds and of often changing colours.

The most beautiful big pentagrams and crosses still remaining in a delicate and shining blue. All of this makes it impossible for me to stop at the mere joy of such appearances, I feel I have to love what is revealed so beautifully and kindly, and a strong longing lays hold of me to recognize what I love with my being and to enter into a conscious relationship with it.

Hoping for your friendly advice and support
in faithful loyalty
yours,
Hermann Beckh

---

2 March 1913

Highly esteemed Doktor!

The lecture took place successfully last Tuesday. It was a great pleasure for me to be able to speak before the Berlin theosophical friends about the rosy cross. I felt penetrated by a quite special power that hitherto I have never experienced in such strength, as if it had come from outside without my doing anything. I think I have never spoken with such concentration; it was like a state of higher consciousness. The unsatisfactory feeling of not entering in the right way into a magnetic exchange with the listeners that otherwise occurs during lectures, especially when it comes to lectures at the University, was this time not present. The fact that the topic was not taken from my specialist Indian studies was certainly useful, because some might have thought that I wanted to speak here as a scholar and philologist and not as a theosophist (although this of course is not my intention). The lecture was intentionally kept purely theosophical.

There are other things about which such an occult point of view could be discussed. Above all, there is Byron, in whom I was once interested a great deal (in a time of my life already lying far back). However, and this is a concern, the luciferic element is very strong in Byron, indeed, you can almost see him like an embodiment of the luciferic principle, and yet there is so much high and noble in him that points to the overcoming of the luciferic element, and some of his works, especially 'Manfred' and 'Cain', are rich in truly occult depths. In Byron's 'Cain', for example, various things are included that directly remind one of the way Lucifer's seductions as described in your last

Kristiania cycle 1912, lecture 8, p. 5ff. In the works of this poet, mostly in 'Manfred', a mighty, occult fire glows, which also in our age, when we know in the right way how to change and purity it through the fire of the Christ-impulse, is able to ignite living forces. In Byron himself, the urge was strong after such purification, as shown at the end of his life. In early Atlantean times, and later still in the original Persian and Chaldean times, he must have been a mighty personality, a magician and occultist.

So that would also be a topic for another time, but first I wanted to talk to you about it. There is no shortage of material for lectures. So once many years ago when I was a practicing lawyer, I collected everything from Shakespeare that has a relationship with occultism. This really rich material I have since then never been able to use in any way.

I am also ready to talk about Indian things (as I have already done in Nuremberg). Especially from the viewpoint of theosophy taught in our circles certainly allows the right understanding of these things, while those who prefer to consider everything Indian as their private domain actually do not understand very much of India, and above all pay too little attention to the occult historical viewpoints, according to which the Indian development is placed in the entire development of the Earth.

The Buddhist gospel of death (Mahaparinibbanasutta) and the Buddha legend (especially Lalitavistara) offers a lot of material for theosophical lectures. Pentagrams and similar figures have no longer shown themselves, that was only then when I wrote the last letter to you and then only for a few days. But it was so strange. What in the following period I experienced as appearances can best be described as flowers, colourful flowers in all kinds in bright colours, of course, unlike the flowers here in the physical world, a similarity with very specific flower types, for example with asters, but is still available, and as far as the colour is concerned, the flowers of mountain meadows with their intense bright colours come closest to these appearances. Perhaps the joy that we have in flowers (and particularly in the flora of the high mountains) will partly find explanation in the similarity with certain phenomena of the 'higher worlds', the picture of which the soul unconsciously carries in itself. Often it is shown to me in the chalice of such a supernatural flower as a shining point, which then detaches itself out of the flower and then stands there as a dazzling light. For some time (especially since I was working intensively with my lodge lecture), the phenomena have subsided, and now they have almost completely disappeared; only the blue cross I still see from time to time. Perhaps the phenomena will return again. But even if this is not the case, it will always be a beautiful memory for me to have had them in my life. Perhaps there is the opportunity to talk to you at the end of the next lodge evening?

In warmest grateful devotion,
Hermann Beckh

---

15 March 1913

Highly esteemed Doktor!

The flower appearances were weaker for a while, but from today they have increased in splendour. I believe I now know what the 'heavenly flowers' (*divyaphuspa*) are that are so often mentioned in Indian books. They are also mentioned a lot by Buddha. The appearances are now becoming clearer and certain types can be distinguished, for example [sketch of a lotus flower] (always yellow in the core, blue on the outside towards violet), similar to the mountain aster, others show other colours and forms, for example milkweeds, anemones, gentians and other flowers that I know precisely but I don't know the names. The calm, friendly nature of these supernatural phenomena stands in striking contrast to the disharmonies and sufferings of the outer physical suffering. Also, despite all the friendliness of their own nature, these things seem to be completely indifferent to the suffering of the external world. So (unlike humans) they probably don't derive from the soul that feels compassion for all beings and cannot be happy when others are unhappy but derives from another spiritual principle that is even more inwardly closed than the soul that shows indifference towards physical sufferings and feels only attracted to the supersensible world. Both principles can (and probably should) coexist.

I would like to find out more about the relationship between these supernatural flowers and the Moon. I'm surprised that the Moon, which plays a large role in my horoscope (unfortunately!) and has had a strong influence on me in the past, so that I actually see it as my occult opponent, that this Moon now conjures up such lovely things for me. Perhaps the relationship will improve with time as we both (I mean the Moon and I) accept each other.

In addition to the flowers, there are particularly phenomena of light (sometimes coming from the flowers); recently it became as bright as day in the darkness in front of me (even if only in a small spot). Usually, however, they are only small, strongly phosphorous dots (which sometimes grow into large flames). They are best compared to fireflies, as they fly around between the bushes during the long days in July. Our joy in fireflies perhaps has its unconscious reason for being similar to the appearance of the 'higher world'.

I now bring before my soul the meditation of the rose cross and the colours to my mind with great clarity in every moment and every situation, in fact it has always been present to me. The things of external life continue on their own. The attempt to lay hold of the 'I' leads to strange results, I don't know whether I'm doing it correctly. This 'I', which can otherwise come into such sharp contradiction with its surroundings, shows a tendency to merge into others. In meditation other Imaginations flow into it of another higher 'I' which at certain rare moments plays into life, and all of these conscious moments of life speak very vividly in the memory. There are also certain things that I cannot find in the memories of my current life. It flashes in, only immediately to disappear again. And I have known this experience for a very long time. Incidentally, I have not yet come to terms with the fact that I fully understand the 'I' and 'reincarnation' (I now mean more than just an intellectual understanding), these are the most difficult problems for me. I don't think it would be possible for me to stop with theosophy; theosophy is just a gateway to occultism for me, something in me that has been longing it for a long time.

The work of the Byron lecture was hindered by an influenza-like malaise, to which earlier on I tended to succumb every year. This time I quickly got over it by trying to work on the blood through meditation (this effect was already intense in my first attempts at meditation). I'm thinking about what is the occult cause of the illness mentioned. There are worse things one has to overcome, but this shouldn't be there either, at least it seems rather unnecessary.

Instead of 'Manfred' I talked about Buddha (similar to Nuremberg). The main purpose of the lecture was to illustrate what is said in *Knowledge of Higher Worlds* ... about the rhythms of the Buddha texts and the effect on the ether-currents through examples of the original text. I was a bit self-conscious because I believed that the unknown language would tire the listeners, but to my surprise this particular thing was well received and in enthusiastic agreement; people showed themselves to be receptive to the specific etheric effect that can be triggered by the rhythms of the Buddha texts. So in a certain sense I found a much greater understanding of these Indian things among the theosophists than among my specialist colleagues, who have no idea about rhythm (let alone about etheric flow)—none of them can really read Pali—and it gives me a deep satisfaction that I can talk about many things in theosophical circles that would be impossible to say at the University.

The trip to Nuremberg, which I had already given up, can now be made possible. It depends on the organizers at the lodge whether I can give the lecture. It's a matter of finding the day.

I will probably still be in Berlin on April 3rd and 10th. However, it is possible I will be passing through Erfurt on April 13th or 14th.

I remain
your devoted
Hermann Beckh

---

27 October 1913

Highly esteemed Doktor!

Since as you know I have carried the wish in myself for a long time to ask you several things regarding the exercises, I hope that it will be possible for you with your many engagements possibly during the course of the next months to grant me the favour of a conversation. I held on with the exercises during the summer, in all situations. The phenomena, too, that earlier on I described to you remained faithful to me with a few interruptions, at least the colours and light appearances, the flowers and similar formations. But occult figures (as during last winter, with the exception of the cross) have seldom shown themselves. During the summer I was able to call up the phenomena at will (and dismiss them again). Yet this power of will has certain limits, for example, I have had no influence on the red colour (which, however, comes up in mere meditation as well as the other colours do). The distinction between real appearance and the mere Imagination is also evident in this circumstance and deception is impossible.

At times, especially in the stillness of the night, the flooding ether-world appears to me not only in a burst of colours, but also quietly sounding, and in quiet moments I feel as if worlds of higher hierarchies were dawning before me. Such impressions (as I have had many in my earlier life) show particularly clearly through the difference how much everyday life is still dominated by Lucifer and Ahriman. But I make an effort to become aware of these influences, in particular upon waking up in the morning is often not what it should be, one is often far removed from the mood in which one would like to be. Is there any exercise that is suitable for this time and can be particularly effective here? At this moment I usually try to concentrate on the opening words of John's Gospel, but this attempt in particular shows how difficult it is to maintain the right concentration through the night's rest. As before, minerals are still an aid to me in meditation (in my early youth I already felt something like a feeling of friendship to them). In addition to pure mountain crystal, rose quartz has recently become important to me; it has a strong effect on thoughts, especially when the light shines through it.

The musical tones prescribed for the meditation exercise work better since I have used the 'voice of silence', the sequence of seven different types of voices. The last one in particular, the quiet rolling of thunder, is very suggestive and reminds one of what was explained in your lectures about the occult connection between the thunder in the outer air and the thoughts inside the human being, in the microcosm. Those sounds can probably be understood as the echo of the 'unspeakable word', also of that path of *unceasing* deepening into the communications of spiritual research, which you mention in *Lucifer Gnosis* (p. 118), particularly about the incarnation of the final planet.

Like a fruit of the efforts that had previously been devoted primarily to understanding ♃ ☉ ☽, this time it was the Earth's development that seemed to brighten up more than before, first of all the time in Paradise. Even if the path given to me initially requires an *understanding* of these things to be striven for with patience, it can still be the case that every now and then at least a faint inkling of seeing arises and, it is a huge thing, one sees all the Earth's dimensions and a tableau that far surpasses earthly notions. This I want to work out, even if only now and then individual pieces of this tableau brighten up (the earliest, for example, is the section O[c-cult] S[cience] (new edition) pp. 180-184 on the change of the Moon's sunny periods), and if it is a real beholding, I still feel it as something in which I already live in a certain sense and which contains a deeper reality than the earthly external world. Of most invaluable worth to me in these exercises were and are the lectures that you gave in Berlin several years ago about ♃ ☉☽, and which I will forever regret not having heard live. In these lectures, when you point out how the description of occult science are still steeped in Maya in many respects, one could probably say that the appeal of occult science lies precisely in the fact that one tries to get behind that Maya through the exercises and from what is hidden there in the webs of current thinking we try to keep out and enliven those sublime feelings and visions that were hinted at in those lectures. The key point seems to me to be the passage (actually two passages, one in the ☉ and one in the ☽ lecture) where Leonardo da Vinci's *'Last Supper'* is mentioned. I don't know any light or warmth in the whole world that is as strong as the light and warmth that emanates from this Imagination and from the words that come to my mind, and especially since this Christmas season it has seemed to me that here would be the point from which all real *seeing* begins. From here the farthest distances are illuminated, first the entire development of the Earth, then they enclose in a tremendous circle ☽, ☉, ♃, and finally here is the point where the light falls into the transitory from what is beyond all temporal development, still lying beyond ♃, ☉, ☽ in eternity.

Here is certainly also the centre of the Holy Grail (from which I already had in childhood, I no longer know where, the idea had or was taught that it was the last remnant of the glory of the primordial light that has shrunk into the Earth's darkness). In this sense, I would like to see the picture of Leonardo da Vinci and your works as the actual innermost centre of my theosophical search and work. And here is another strange thing, because of which I wanted to ask you (on one of the coming evenings): With the latter Imagination not only is there connected a wealth of light, the sunlight, but at the same time very clear musical tones and sounds; at the same time I felt that it had something to do with my blood, as if that picture acted directly on the blood. Does the music of the spheres have anything to do with blood circulation? It does seem so to me. Can one hear the pulsating blood, as well as the process of seeing sometimes as a stream breaking forth from the eyes (especially in the morning when awakening)? Everything I have perceived in colours, etc., seems to me to be connected with this objectifying of the visual process.

In deeply warm devotion,
esteem and gratitude,
Hermann Beckh

———————————————

24 March 1914

Highly esteemed Doktor!

It doesn't concern an actual request, but only a few questions that you may answer me in just a few words, perhaps on Thursday after the lecture or on Friday, or you may just listen to them if you think that is better. What makes me pick up the pen are but certain difficulties with which I have been struggling recently—others, too, as you told me, have fared in like manner; it seems because of the attacks sometimes in the air, especially at the end of February or early March, for me almost every year is a critical time. Might this also be linked with the development of the year, the feeling of the time in esoteric development? First of all, the difficulties I spoke of seem to have been overcome.—Perhaps they also take place in connection with the Christian esoteric exercises that, as I told you earlier, I tried to live, although such an attempt in the midst of an eventful Berlin life almost borders on the impossible. One can meditate some necessary solitude, such as a mountain retreat, but that's not always so easy to achieve.

In the first half of John's Gospel (up to and including the Lazarus chapter) I had the calm, even experience of a power and growing light that had not been experienced in this spiritual way until now. In the second half it was after Christmas, the turning point of the year was the limit here, too—this experience was interrupted by experiences of a different kind and sometimes disturbed for a long time. There was also no lack of moments of strong brightness, especially on the day when you gave your last Berlin Lodge lecture, when I experienced the glow of a new life in nature (in the etheric body) through the Christ-forces of the etherizing Blood on the cross, like a vision that lasted the whole day. On other days too similar experiences came in connection with the cross and suffering meditation. But at other times it was as if demonic forces were unleashed through the exercises and even some apparent coincidences of external life seemed to be in league with these forces. Now, is that a bad sign? Or does it just prove that through such exercises one is burdened with all sorts of tests, tests that one only has a chance of passing through by a serious strengthening of the 'I'? Also during the entombment, I had remarkable experiences, which at one time seemed to me to be the 'correct' one, while at other times they were turned into their opposite.

That's how it goes with meditation in general, for example one experiences a warmth that one certainly recognizes as the correct density of the warmth ether, at other times it is a kind of luciferic heat that comes from within and shouldn't be there. You feel it like an illness.—I perceive as something very valuable a certain coldness that seems to come from the depths of space, a cold etheric stream that is full of life.

I simply want to continue the Christian exercises, initially through meditations on the other gospels—in the sequence Mark, Luke and Matthew—in such a way as to create a basis for the future undisturbed success of the exercises with John's Gospel. I know of no other means of combating the challenges, which are not a few, flowing from the materialistic nature of my philological environment, no other means of help than a most energetic strengthening of the theosophical-esoteric exercises. For a time, it seemed as if my external profession with its various demands wanted to force me to sacrifice for other things the evening hours that until now I have always devoted to theosophy and spiritual paths. But I can't do that; I would become ill and lose all security. For me it is theosophy of which I have to say: without it,

> *ist Trauer nur für mich, Entsagung, Leid*
> *im Erdenfeld zu finden,—und der Tod —*

['Without him—there remains for me
But sorrow on the earth —
renunciation—suffering—and death'.
R. Steiner, *The Soul's Awakening*, Scene 8, Egyptian woman]

Finally, a request: would it not be possible for the lecture-cycle *Theosophy of the Rosicrucians* to be republished? (The *Gospel of St John* has also been issued in a second edition.) It contains so much that is important and especially in the last lectures, a lot that, as far as I can see, has not been repeated elsewhere. Many people would certainly be grateful for that.

With the most grateful devotion and veneration,
Hermann Beckh

23 Feb. 1915

Dear Doktor!

Would it be possible for you at this time to arrange a short interview, this time not with me, but with my sister, who has long had such hopes and is currently visiting me? Both the days here in Berlin and the following Nuremberg days (March 11-14) could be considered, whichever suits you better; because my sister is happy that she has the opportunity to hear the lectures not only in Nuremberg but also here in Berlin.—I, too, would occasionally have thought to ask something about the occult signs and about Dornach (where I would have liked to come in the spring, if the military authorities still allow me to do so). But my sister's request takes precedence over mine.

With full veneration,
Dr Hermann Beckh

---

10 June 1915

Highly esteemed Doktor!

This time it is initially something quite physical, about which I may possibly be able to ask you for advice, possibly this evening after the lecture, namely a disturbance in my hearing perhaps caused by a cold, but the etheric body could also be involved. The condition has already got better, but still changes. You may possibly tell me if I could do something about it; to consult a doctor, for example, is questionable. Deciding on the latter is not very easy if you have never had to be with doctors your whole life. It doesn't seem dangerous to me; I don't want to miss anything that is not only important for the outer profession, but also for theosophical striving.

Apart from this physical (or etheric?) disturbance, the other things are going much better than for a long time, especially since I followed your last advice during meditation. Also the attempt to harmonize the intellectual side of my outer profession with theosophical strivings, as it were, to 'jump' on the back of the Sanskrit lion—if the expression is allowed—works much better than before, and the work with the books is progressing. Hopefully the war will come to a good end. It seems to me that especially through the evil, now experienced with such horror, wonderful and subtle forces are being drawn from people, especially from the German people, and it seems to me with this, most recently since Italy's participation in the war, it would have increased.

During this time I had gained much, very much from the lectures in Dornach, especially from the Good Friday and Holy Saturday lecture (which I also read here in the lodge) [April 2 & 3, GA 161]. The Baldur lecture already reveals all sorts of miracles through the musical rhythm of the language. In addition, I am obliged to give you a reference to Jakob Böhme's writing, *'De incarnatione verbi'* (for this was the title, if I rightly recall). Without theosophy one won't gain much from Böhme, but if you approach him from theosophy, one finds great things, especially Imaginations, for example the comparison of Adam's rib, from which Eva is taken (Gen. 2:22) and the spear wound on the cross on Golgotha (John 19:34) is a tremendous picture. In addition, there is the heartfelt magic quality of the language. This magic exists only in the German.

During my exercises with *Occult / Esoteric Science*, I get ever further into a sacred, still twilight-like experience of the Ancient Moon period. In the loneliness of nature one could, of course, come further with these things. In this present time I gain much strength from the attempt to concentrate myself in the sense of your recent lectures in Neuchâtel on the etheric body of Christian Rosenkreuz (to which I feel drawn in my deepest being). I also feel I can relate to this certain experiences of earlier times.

In one of your recent Berlin lectures, you spoke of the astral body which during sleep gnaws at the roots of the plant world of the etheric body. Does the old Germanic serpent dragon Nidhogg, who gnaws at the roots of the Yggdrasil, have anything to do with this?

In the deepest warm veneration and gratitude,
Hermann Beckh

---

12 Dec. 1915

Highly esteemed Doktor!

The question I wanted to address to you refers to the 'Six Attributes', or rather Six Exercises, whose practical importance I am increasingly aware in the course of time. Especially difficult is a passage in *Occult / Esoteric Science* (p. 313 of the first edition, 327 of the new edition) relating to the sixth exercise (the harmonizing of the five attributes), which in the choice of words is somewhat difficult: 'the necessity to practise them simultaneously in pairs, or three and one, and so forth, in order to bring about harmony' [tr. Monges p. 289; tr. Adams

p. 250; tr. Creeger p. 316]. How is that done in practice? Moreover, can the striving for the attributes always be connected with the concrete exercises given in *Occult / Esoteric Science*? Or do these exercises only intend to support the striving for the six attributes in certain separate periods—of course, to be determined throughout life? What seems particularly important and difficult to me is the exercise of the will (No. 2), which leads to some tragic self-knowledge. Lately, I've been trying to do it with increased intensity, and from the very first few days I felt a positive effect going from the head to the heart, but later states of tension set in that could lead to physical pain, and the exercise wasn't always successful. It also happens that the exercise is successful to a certain extent, but in life the opposite of progress is noticeable in the qualities that the exercise is intended to develop. Perhaps you can give me some advice on what to focus in the six exercises in my case.

An obstacle to many things is also a certain inability to get rid of physicality in sleep, which is then either too dull or too light and becomes more difficult through enhanced wakefulness. It happens that at night the soul seems to receive instructions from somewhere—e.g. recently about something with light and darkness in the sense of Manichaean esotericism—and cannot retain anything because sleep is not as it should be, waking up too early or it does not occur in the right way. Finding the right balance between Lucifer and Ahriman is, it seems, even more difficult for some people while they are sleeping than when they are awake.

Your lecture on Austrian spiritual life was of the highest value to me—quite apart from the sympathy for Austria, which I have always had and which I feel particularly strongly in this time of serious testing—also in theosophical, especially in theosophical regards, one could feel that deep and intimate information about the Christ-principle and the twelve-petalled lotus-flower of the heart and its relationship to the upper centres was given. The content of *Knowledge of Higher Worlds: How is it Achieved?* has rarely stood before me in such direct vividness. The lecture gave a lot of sunlight, which is particularly needed at this time, a feeling that many certainly had.

In my outer profession a certain progress can be seen which I owe exclusively to theosophy. Whereas for years earlier on I suffered from the divide that I felt between the ahrimanic academic profession and my spiritual strivings, now I increasingly experience how theosophy makes my outer profession easier and enlivens it, so that these things too—at least at present—are much more enjoyable for me than they were earlier. I also feel the receptivity of the listeners has grown, as if the interest for spiritual questions in these circles too is increasing at least somewhat, especially most recently I believe something like an increased vitality.

Theosophy also helps me a lot for external studies itself. So it is especially the Veda with its abundance of images, with which one could otherwise do so little, and which now opens up completely new revelations. Also for the mantric side, which is present in the sequence of the individual sounds and words, in the rhythm, etc. one gains a completely different ear and completely different understanding through theosophy. Official academia still for a long time will not understand these things.

The little book about Buddha (two volumes in the Göschen series), about which you were gracious enough to enquire during our last conversation, has already been finished during the course of the summer and will soon go to press. Of course, I endeavoured to incorporate spiritual elements at least as far as possible in the context of such a necessary ahrimanic, external academic work, but it is only a weak initial attempt. Hopefully, however, it will be possible to continue to build on this in future to achieve more in the indicated direction when the fruits ripen of the tremendous efforts of the present time.

In deep veneration,
and gratitude,
Hermann Beckh

---

24 January 1916

Dear Doktor!

Even though an actual public advocacy for spiritual science will have to be reserved for a much later period of life, given my entire karma and the spiritual laws that govern these things, I would still have been sorry if in the recently mentioned book, that should now be published, there would have been no reference at all to the spiritual power that is uniquely given to my life—and thus indirectly also to my professional work—and to which I owe everything. Actually, theosophical— as much as it lies between the lines on the subject of Buddha, it could not be included in the context of the Göschen Series and in such a work that is initially purely philological and often quite scientifically sober. The only thing that could come into question was a reference to your work, which is rightly called upon to build a bridge from the material thinking of the present to the more spiritual thinking of a future development, but which, with forethought, still stays within the sphere of thinking, because of thinking. The exit must be taken—I mean the book *The Riddles of Philosophy* [GA 18]. The reference was introduced at a point in the second volume, where we talk about how in ancient India the transition took place from the old mythological-pictorial ideas to the later, more conceptually abstract forms of thinking. If anywhere, it seems to me that a reference to the *Riddles of Philosophy* is appropriate for this problem, indeed that it is required by the entire culture and current of the times. I have the feeling that it will not be without meaning for the entire karma of the book (my little book) that I have included this reference. But I think that the spiritual researcher's view of this matter goes further than mine, and so I dare to speak to you about the matter modestly, because I do not want to do anything that I am not sure is in your interest. It is not enough that something is done with good intentions, but rather that everything is done at the right time, in the right place and in the right way.

The thirteen [Holy] Nights, to whose experiences you urged me to pay attention, showed me a strange alternation of light and darkness. This time the actual 'Christmas spirit' seems to me to be strongest and most beautiful for me on those two evenings before Christmas when you were with us. On Christmas Eve itself I experienced that indefinite horror in a strangely strong way, as I always felt the presence of the (Lower) Guardian of the Threshold. This time it emanated not only from me, from my own phantom, but also from my surroundings, and the darkness spreading over the entire current events also wanted to play a part (as I later found out, a younger theosophical acquaintance at the front was particularly fired up that evening). I still lack astral vision, but I do feel the presence of that being. The impressions of the following day, or rather Holy Nights, were all the brighter. The starting point of my exercises is always how the other two parts of the exercise show a clear relationship, firstly to the 'unrevealed light', secondly to the 'consciousness without knowledge of an object'.

The feeling of the inner light has increased greatly through the continued exercises. It was sometimes like experiencing a strong (but not always equally strong) blinding brightness, so that when I opened my eyes I felt, and still feel, the brightness of the day like a heavy darkness, like a transition from light to darkness. Especially during the summer, this feeling of heavy darkness in the midst of daylight was almost depressing.

I have recently got into the habit of meditating in the evening in complete darkness because I find that the inner light develops more easily. As something new, in addition to the previous exercises, I have recently (only three weeks now) taken on the meditation of John's Gospel, in the way that, as indicated in your first cycle (and elsewhere), after the meditation of the first five sentences of Chapter 1, I meditate each chapter daily for a week. I have become extremely fond of this exercise, which I always do in the morning following the Rosicrucian signs [accompanying sketch], and I feel that it has a strong effect on the mind and body.

The special power of the opening words of the Chapter 1 always came strongly to my consciousness earlier in life when I knew nothing of Rosicrucian theosophy, and the impression was especially alive when once on a walk in the Tyrolean Alps I came to a mountain chapel lying high and alone on a steep rock face, and found there the beginning of John's Gospel opened up on the altar. At that time with those words, I felt cosmic life and cosmic light, the primordial cosmic light, which I now endeavour again in meditation to raise out of the soul's depths. It seems to me as if those words—especially *'et lux in tenebris lucet, et tenebrae eam non comprehenderunt'*—appeared strange in Latin, but perhaps this impression only derives from the fact that I have them in Latin before me. How did these opening and primordial words sound at the very beginning?

The exercises with John's Gospel are also a good thing for forming a harmonious counterbalance to the professional work (which is not particularly intensive this winter); at the moment it mainly involves an intimate immersion in the Buddha legend. As you know, this concerns the production of the two volumes on *Buddhism* for the Göschen Series. I did not make much progress with it during the summer, but now the work gives me great joy and I realize how what I have absorbed through your writings and lecture-cycles is also invaluable for deepening Indian studies. Connections that I could not have imagined before become clear to me. Even if it is not a question of allowing anything theosophical to flow directly into the book, its essence can still be hidden between the lines, and esoteric points of view are decisive, above all for the selection of the material. In any case, there will be a big difference whether a completely materialistic thinker or a theosophically inclined author writes something like this, even if for all sorts of reasons, he has to conform to a certain extent to the prevailing mode of expression and materialistic, ahrimanic logic. The feeling of responsibility that the theosopher should develop in itself is undoubtedly put to the test by such work, because appearing in a popular collection, it is likely to be read not only in narrow groups of specialist readers but also in wider groups. It is hard to say whether everything will succeed, as I would like. Your consent would be more valuable to me than anyone else's. You will certainly sympathize with me on this matter, and I would feel it strengthening for my work if I were allowed to say a few words to you about it. I would also like to ask you a very specific question about a Buddhist topic. It concerns the Buddhist formula of causal connection (*Pratityasamutpada*) the series of Twelve Deeds, about which at some point you supposedly have communicated something.

In the *Fragments* of Novalis (p. 125, 126. p. 201) I found a mystical-algebraic formula. Am I right to believe it relates to what is said about the secret of the flame in the Egyptian scene of your latest [fourth] Mystery Drama? I spent the week after the Munich Festival in Switzerland, particularly meditating on these things and about the Rose Cross Mystery. I was also in Dornach, although I knew nothing about the laying of the Foundation Stone [of the First Goetheanum]. If the inspiration in question had come to me five days earlier, I would have been published in time for the celebration. My impressions of the charming Dornach area are that it is highly suitable for the temple and [to house] the Mystery Dramas. I am really looking forward to hearing the drama in this environment.

In gratitude and respect
Your ever devoted
Hermann Beckh

---

23 February 1916

Highly esteemed Doktor!

May I venture to ask you for an interview in the near future, since you yourself were recently kind enough to offer me the prospect of the realization of that hope in the not-too-distant future? But everything depends on whether you consider the right time for the intended interview to have already come and are not too preoccupied with other things.

Of all the questions that I still have on my mind, none is so important or so urgent that it alone could justify the request for a personal interview. I believe there is something else behind that wish: a deep longing, heightened by the tragic gravity of the time, for esoteric impulses, for that esotericism that has a dissolving effect on everything that still exists in the soul in terms of thoughts and feelings and prevents them from confronting the abyss of nothingness in the way that is necessary for a serious meditation, which 'boldly from destruction wrench new life' [Maria, *The Guardian of the Threshold*, Scene 8, concluding line], and wants to find Christ behind what is expressed by Buddha as a negative, *Nirvana*. I also feel as if there is a search for esoteric trains of thought, perhaps more importantly: a desire to clothe oneself in certain trains of thought and esoteric experience in the soul. Especially in sleep, in dream experiences— but the waking consciousness does not yet have the power to shape and hold on to what comes from the etheric body; it disappears the moment you want to take hold of it. I am confident that it only takes a few words from your mouth to take me a few steps further in that direction.

Your last public lectures in particular should call us to most serious contemplation. It is actually something incredible that such things can and have now to be talked about. And at the same time one feels that there is something like a crown of thorns, especially in the public lectures, a kind of martyrdom so large and unique that never or rarely has an occultist ever taken on the like for the progress of humanity and into which to be allowed to participate and moreover we listeners are in a certain sense honoured.

The *Faust*-lecture has impressively integrated itself into the basic idea of this year's lecture series, and I—and many with me—have gained a completely new light on Goethe's *Faust*. Without spiritual science, an understanding of these things is simply unthinkable. *Faust* and Goethe are among the many things were given back to me by you as if they originally belonged to the soul but were later torn away from it by Ahriman.

[Regarding] the previously mentioned impression that occurred to me when I delved deeper into *Occult / Esoteric Science* (especially the passage on pages 180-184 of the new edition), like a spiritual vision of the [Ancient] Moon experience as a Sun-dream, as a dreaming reflection of the Sun experience [cf. *Language of the Stars*, TL 2020, IX, p. 127ff]. Does it not strangely resonate in Novalis? [In *Heinrich von Ofterdingen* in the description of the rising Moon, p. 64 in Beusche edition, Chapter 5, Eng. tr.]:

> The Moon shone mildly over the hills, prompting strange dreams in all creatures. Itself lay like a dream of the Sun, above the introverted world of visions, and restored nature, now living in its infinite phases, back to that fabulous olden time, when every bud yet slumbered by itself, lonely and un-quickened, longing in vain to expand the dark fulness of its immeasurable existence.

It is a question that has been close to my heart for years, to find all the numerous threads that run from Novalis—not only from the *Fragments* but also from his entire poetic work—to your spiritual-scientific work and *Occult / Esoteric Science*. Processing the richness of the material could seem like a worthy task, but too often things had to be touched upon that simply cannot be talked about in public. Are there not secrets linked to Novalis that must remain unspoken for the time being?

Music, which had long taken a back seat to the other spiritual pursuits in my life, as if due to an inner necessity, has recently sought to assert itself as an occult question. As in the entire realm of occult sign-language, the world's secrets must somehow also be hidden in the proportions and masses of music, in the tones and intervals, harmonies and rhythms, all of these things must have a reflection of the great harmony of the spheres—perhaps deflected by Lucifer and Ahriman. But perhaps it is better to let the problem go for now and suppress any impressions that arise? I have only one wish: to find the path, as spiritual science shows, better and more correctly, and to subordinate everything else in life to this one pursuit. Should not the encounter with spiritual science and its teacher be perceived by all of us as the outstanding experience that can give the entire memory of life direct strength and support, the backbone, so to speak, through which the ego-consciousness no longer needs to disperse 'to all the winds', but rather that the soul really gains the opportunity to find itself as an 'I' beyond the portal of death—in the sense of Novalis' beautiful word—cannot everything that has passed in life, even all the sad past things, be saved and ennobled through that one experience? [See Editor's Note below.]

Because of the request indicated at the beginning of this letter, may I perhaps speak to you briefly after one of the public lectures? The time is so rich in experiences that the longing to talk to you will seem understandable. The seriousness of the fateful events, the impact of which many are certainly feeling particularly strongly at the moment, may also excuse the request.

With deep devotion and respect,
Hermann Beckh

Editor's Note:

A note seems demanded to suggest the relevance of this astonishing paragraph to Beckh's subsequent life and work. To his questions regarding what the spiritual situations the musical element can bring, or can express, Beckh was soon to find some concrete answers in the artistic developments unfolding at the Goetheanum, CH-Dornach. He had already recognized the potential of eurythmy to reveal in art the creative side of speech, the mantric quality, termed by Jakob Böhme *Natursprache* and by Novalis as 'genetic etymology' to complement 'pragmatic etymology'. Beckh may have already been involved in the early performances of eurythmy; cf. the eurythmy programme of pieces in ancient languages, including Sanskrit (Berlin, 20 March 1914. GA 277a, p. 57).

Music eurythmy itself had been initiated in Dornach, 1915; actual developments only began from 1919, initially with children taught by Fr. Hollenbach (GA 277a). Professor Beckh, astonished at Steiner's musical ear, was himself to contribute significant musical studies in the context of cultural renewal. His major findings relate to the 'cosmic rhythms' of the natural year, the starry environment and ritual expression (H.B., *Collected Articles*, No. 47 [1930], TL 2023). In a ground-breaking lecture to his fellow founder-priests (Breitbrunn, July 1922; Eng. tr. *The Essence of Tonality*, TL 2022), Beckh explains that the natural year (12 months) of the Northern Hemisphere and the circle of musical keys (the 'circle of fifths' with 12 key centres) are intimately related. Beckh repeated his lecture in Stuttgart, probably October 1922, in Rudolf Steiner's presence. A few weeks later, in a unique lecture (Dornach 2, Dec. 1922, in GA 283), Dr Steiner describes the seven planets visiting in turn the twelve starry regions. He suggests cosmic names to the 7 days / notes and 12 months / key centres, which result in a product of 84 meditations. Hermann Beckh, in his 'contributions to a new star wisdom' (1930-1932; Eng. tr. *The Language of the Stars*, TL 2020), more than once claims that pursuing musical studies became his way to explore the cosmic rhythms, for example, in the gospels (*Collected Articles* No. 29 [1926]; publication of *Markusevangelium* 1928, and *Johannesevangelium* 1930).

On his deathbed (1937), wanting to write something more 'for the future', Beckh again took up the theme of music with *Die Sprache der Tonart* (Eng. tr. *The Language of Tonality*, Anastasi 2015, TL forthcoming), expanding his treatise by adding separate sections on Wagner's use of the musical keys. The basic concept, however, is independent of Wagner. Interestingly, one eminent Wagnerian

Steglitz, 12 May 1916

Highly esteemed Herr Doktor!

Now with 'Snow White' I had another brainwave with regard to the laces and the comb that completely fits into what I believe I have already recognized before as the meaning of the fairytale and attempted to sketch for you in the previous letter. Of course, I do not mean that one can say directly that Snow White accomplishes a Mystery of white magic, but that that which in the real Mystery is the overcoming (transformation) of the black evil (of the layers of the earth) through white magic that this is here shifted into the childlike sphere of the human being, where the sublime

---

scholar, Stewart Spencer, writes in a letter to the present writer that he was 'out of sympathy' with the basic concept, yet could not deny that the author makes 'significant observations'. For this final study, published posthumously, Beckh left off finalizing his lectures on music. The MS draft of that book only recently came to light: Eng. tr., *The Mystery of Musical Creativity* (TL 2019).

Further studies are included in this volume. The rhythms to which Beckh gave their traditional and familiar cosmic names are ably explained by him as the experiential moods summarizing all human development, individual and collective. On the basis of the above ref. to GA 283, a musician is justified to speak of Rudolf Steiner as the greatest unsung musician of the twentieth century. This specific claim is supported by detailed work showing how Steiner followed his own advice on 'style'. He gave specific clues to his own musical practice, to reveal the sentence rhythms in all his written books (actually few in number). The basic books all concern human development, 'to guide what is spiritual in the human being to what is spiritual in the universe' (see article below).

From 1912, after hearing Rudolf Steiner speak, Professor Beckh studied anthroposophy as a whole and in detail. In Dec. 1913, when present at the Leipzig lecture course, *Christ and the Spiritual World: The Search for the Holy Grail* (GA 149), he asked what he should read on astrology. 'Nothing,' came the answer, 'only anthroposophy.' Beckh kept to this advice. This universal scholar indicates how anthroposophy could enliven every branch of research. His lecture of 30 Nov. 1921 (Eng. tr. in *The Source of Speech*, TL 2019, 181-207) explains why he was leaving the prestigious Humboldt University of Berlin (despite a personal request from the Prussian cultural minister to reconsider) in order to work as a freelance lecturer for anthroposophy. He experienced the inner call to join the Movement for Religious Renewal (1922) as the goal of his life, serving it for 15 productive years. 'He is one of its co-founders,' observes Rudolf Meyer (*Neue Wege zur Ursprache*, 1954, p. 5). 'Without him our beginnings are inconceivable.'—A.S.

appears in a diminutive childlike measure, similar to how the Valkyrie in 'Briar Rose' has become a sleeping child. Thus there probably stands behind the 'seven dwarves' of the fairytale of 'Snow White' something bigger, which in the fairytale imagination has been made smaller into the dwarves, analogous to everything else in the fairytale. The stepmother's magic mirror points quite clearly towards 'black magic', and when it is said of Snow White that she is 'a thousand times more beautiful', this means that she is still something immeasurably more sublime than the power embodied in the beautiful queen, and this can then only be the highest, the white magic, i.e. she has to be the fairytale shadow and diminution of that which in the original Mystery is the embodiment of that highest magic. But also in this, that this embodiment of highest magic in the fairytale has become an innocent child, there again lies something precisely immeasurably profound and appealing. The highest which is unreachable by the beautiful queen appears embodied in a child.

If now Snow White's 'death' is not directly the Mystery of the Entombment, yet perhaps one could call it a childlike, fairytale shadow or mirroring of this Mystery, in the way I tried to explain in my previous letter in more detail, and with this the question of the laces and the comb solves itself. Of course, I am not saying the story with the laces is the initiation level of the Scourging and the comb the one of the Crowning with Thorns, nevertheless perhaps one can say: the Scourging and the Crowning with Thorns show certain processes in the etherbody, which were beheld in the Mysteries, already before the Mystery of Golgotha had worked on the physical plane, or in the Imagination of the thongs of the Scourging and the Crown of Thorns. From this Mystery Imagination the thongs of scourging in the childlike diminution, or the diminutive childlikeness, has become the picture of the laces of the fairytale Imagination, and likewise the Imagination of the Crown of Thorns has become the picture of the poisoned comb.

And so, if all this is true, the fairytale of 'Snow White' itself, although not directly presented, yet would contain a childlike mirroring of the Christian stages of initiation of the Scourging, the Crown of Thorns, Entombment and Resurrection.

II

And the fact that poor Snow White did not avoid the Crucifixion, for this those interpreters of the fairytale take pains to present her as a fool who succumbs to the seductions of the lower nature of desire and as a being who has lost any contact with the eternal! (I did not know this interpretation when I received my interpretation, but only read it afterwards with some shock, I feel it as a spiritual insult to sovereignty.) But the fairytale itself speaks of the innocent heart of Snow White, and of the fact that the wild animals (the evil desires) cannot harm her. For she is 'as white as snow', that is, pure, not succumbing to the lower nature. Her allowing the stepmother to enter her sphere, in the sense of my attempt to interpret a fairytale-like, mirrors the divine resignation of the white Mystery. With the poisoned apple, the sign of the 'I', she sees its value ('Snow White desired the beautiful apple') and thus in the sense of the white Mystery she takes on evil in order to transform and to conquer it—the hunter, I thought, is perhaps the power through which the beautiful queen tries to bar for the child entrance into the spiritual worlds; through the lower desires he is to lay hold of her astral element (lungs and liver), but because Snow White's heart is pure, he cannot carry this out. One could also think of the 'Guardian of the Threshold' or also of the Grail Knight in Wolfram's Epic ([*Parzifal*] Book IX), who steps in Parzival's way in order to bar his access to the Grail Castle. But this I will leave as such, because it is not directly experienced. But the other things I have actually already felt indeed as one of my strongest experiences. It came to me as in a super-earthly blissfulness and at the same time I felt my body as if penetrated with sharp needles throughout a whole night. Under these circumstances I look forward to your communications about the Buddhist matters in all calmness, but the comments on 'Snow White' I anticipate with a certain anxiety. For I feel, that here something is woven with my innermost being. I hope you will forgive me that I turn to you in this matter, but I could not discuss it with anyone else.

In gratitude and respect, your devoted,
Hermann Beckh

---

11 June 1916

Highly esteemed Herr Doktor!

The fairytale of 'The Crystal Ball / Sphere' [Grimms' Fairytales, No. 197] which during our last conversation you kindly pointed out to me contains such depths that what I believe to have found probably at the most can only concern an initial beginning, yet as such there is already so much that is so surprising that I would most humbly dare to put some questions to you, only in order to know whether the direction in which I was searching is more or less correct, for the 'questions' themselves one partly feels actually should not yet be asked, because it seems to me this fairytale touches on those Mysteries about which today nothing is yet communicated.

The fairytale seems to belong to those which, like 'The Golden Bird', 'The Water of Life', 'The Six Servants', 'The White Snake' and some others, describes in symbolic pictures the path into the spiritual world and the dangers encountered on it. But what surprised me so much with 'The Crystal Ball' is that here it almost appears as if the most modern Rosicrucian path is presented; it could appear as if here one of the main thoughts from your lecture-cycle on fairytales *Secrets of the Threshold* [Munich, 24-31 August 1915, GA 147] is translated into the pictorial language of fairytales. I mean that what is said in lecture 5 of this cycle about the relationship of meditation to the 'lonely thinking' on the one side, to the outer perception and outer listening on the other hand:

> thinking, the inner imagination, can again be looked at. The inner imagination, the working up for oneself the Mysteries of the world, is the one thing, the second is the pure perception, the pure listening ... In the lonely thinking lies the luciferic temptation, in the mere listening, in the mere perception, lies the ahrimanic element. But one can achieve a middle condition, as it were walking in between these ... Meditation is a middle situation ... The meditating human being who lives in his thoughts in such a way that they become alive in him, are present as perceptions, lives in the divine stream—on the right side he has the mere thought, on the left the ahrimanic element, the mere listening ... and he knows that the luciferic and ahrimanic element here in meditation have to be measured and be kept in balance.

In this sense the fairytale right at the beginning emphasizes as an essential point that the three brothers love each other as brothers. The early clairvoyance, in which consciousness still lays hold of the reality of the world, has dwindled, is enchanted through the enchantress, the luciferic-ahrimanic power. The bewitched consciousness of today no longer creates reality and yet stands to that old consciousness of reality (which through the Christ-Impulse is newly enlivened) in a new meaningful relationship. (Here I mean especially what is described in the lecture-cycle *Man in the Light of Occultism Theosophy and Philosophy*, GA 137. [Christiania (near Oslo, Norway), 2-12 June, 1912.] Thus, the lonely thinking of philosophy gives shadow-pictures of that which the occultist perceives as the reality standing behind them. (Of all the important, great thoughts of the philosophers whichever played a role in the world, the occultist can always name the original source. The philosopher only sees the shadow-picture, the thought; the occultist sees the real, living element standing behind it.) In the same way the tableau of perception, of the outer consciousness of objects, relates to a higher reality as far as the occult reality contains it, through which that reality can again be deciphered; outer consciousness produces a kind of reflected image of the spiritual world (see *The Threshold of the Spiritual World*, Germ. ed, p. 43), an image that nevertheless through the ahrimanic beings is magically transformed into an autonomous life. Thus the power, in itself valuable, that lies in thinking succumbs to the luciferic enchantment (the Eagle who lives in the rocky mountains [the brain?]) and the outer perception of the ahrimanic enchantment—the Whale who lives in the deep ocean—the deep ocean as symbol of the lower world which the ahrimanic beings take as their most active realm (in contrast to this, the luciferic Eagle in the upper world, the realm of the air). What does it actually mean that each of the two, the Eagle and the Whale, for two hours each day take on their human shape? This obviously not unimportant point of the fairytale is still quite obscure to me.

The third son seeks to get beyond the enchantment by seeking the spiritual world ('the Castle of the Golden Sun') through the path of meditation, the divine streaming, and nevertheless in the right manner holds on to the relationship to his brothers that connects him on the one hand with the Eagle of thinking and on the other side with the Whale of perceiving outer objects. Because his 'heart is without fear', a main prerequisite of success of the good of the spiritual world is fulfilled in him. Why are those who have sought before him without success exactly 23? Is here the zodiac somehow indicated? or the 24th hour as the great midnight-hour, in which the higher spiritual world of the 'I' is indicated? But I do not want to speculate. The 'great forest' is in any case exactly as in 'Snow White' and other fairytales, also in Wolfram von Eschenbach, the threshold to the spiritual world. In the same way as it was repeatedly developed in the public lectures of last winter, the third [brother] adds to the concentration of the thinking-forces and the concentration of the forces of will, for the story with the 'wishing hat' seems to relate to that. But who are the two giants who fight over the hat? Clearly two powers who want to grab the will for themselves. It would be comfortable to think again of Lucifer and

Ahriman, but this is not at all appropriate here, also the stupidity of the two giants does not fit. To what does this stupidity relate?

It is obvious that the spiritual world presents the lower element, itself standing in the bondage of enchantment, initially having to appear in distortion, in a distorted enchantment. As in an evil enchantment, the true form of the spiritual world, for human beings is turned into its opposite (the ugliness of the enchanted princess); the sadness of the princess reminds one of the sadness of the Beautiful Lily in Goethe's Fairytale. But the mirror shows the reflection of the most beautiful maiden, cf. Novalis, *The Novices at Sais* [1. The Novice]:

> I have fully understood what the second voice uttered at one time. I, and I alone, am cheered by those heaps of objects … as though they were all of them mere images, surfaces, and ornamental flourishes collectively comprising a single of wondrously divine picture, a picture that always remains uppermost in my thoughts. I do not seek them out, but into them I often enter seeking. It is as though they are intended to show me the way to the place where the maiden whom my soul longs for lies in deepest sleep.

But to the unprepared soul the esoteric truth never appears as something that evokes shocks and grieving, the spiritual world as a world of wild havoc. Initially the forces of the lower nature (the Bull) have to be overcome, or rather transformed, if one wants to penetrate to the higher Mysteries. Does the 'spring' at which the Bull stands directly indicate the sexual forces, the source of life? Everything else then lies in a very high sphere about which only some indications can be attempted. I think about the VIIth seal, the Grail Seal, where also the Bird, the Dove, hovers above what grows up out of the forces of the lower nature. I think of the Rosicrucian meditation in *Occult / Esoteric Science*: 'I think how through this in myself the lower element in these drives and passions can be overcome and can be raised again to a higher level'? The actual right to ask: What is the egg? What is the crystal-ball? and so on, can only be gained through the fact that the one who asks has successfully achieved in himself the struggle with the Bull. And the fairytale does not without reason emphasize that this struggle is 'a long struggle'. It is excellent in this fairytale how every little word carries a deep meaning (this to a high degree also in 'Show White'?). By the way, what does the word 'crystal' mean? When crystal is meant, the fairytale otherwise speaks of 'glass' (cf. 'Snow White'); 'crystal' means here more than 'crystal'; one would like to think of the diamond that opens up the spiritual world

(Mystery of the eight-sided stone), or of the philosopher's stone. In any case the whole thing lies high in the sphere of the Mystery of the Grail.

It is an especially fine trait of the fairytale, as already mentioned, that the treasure of the spiritual world contained in the glowing egg cannot be gained, or rather not really be laid hold of and be retained did not on the one side the Eagle of thinking come to help, hindering the firebird from flying away. And on the other side, the Whale of the solid perception of objects, having a cooling influence on the all-consuming glow of the spiritual inspiration, thus makes possible the gaining of the crystal-ball hidden in the egg. Moreover, in *Occult / Esoteric Science* we read, 'The person gets farthest who besides the faculty to withdraw into his inner being is also able to remain open to all the impressions of the outer world.'

But is it not very surprising that the old storytellers already could come to such things? At the moment I am surprised that I was again tempted to doubt the whole interpretation of this fairytale. Consequently, I would be very grateful if in some way or other you could give me a handhold for judging the matter and for the whole direction [of thinking].

In deep and warm veneration
and yours in gratitude,
Hermann Beckh

---

11 July 1916

Highly esteemed Herr Doktor!

May I add a few things more on 'Snow White', things which during the course of time have come to me. Almost every lecture-cycle [of yours] in one way or another throws new light on the questions in particular of this deeply meaningful fairytale.

Regarding the Imagination of the drops of blood on the snow, I would like to connect what in lecture 10 of the cycle on Karma has been said about light and love as the two components of all earthly existence:

> everything of soul nature of the Earth = genuine, good love,
> everything material [=] condensed light,

whereby in the human being the element of love is clouded over by the Moon-like luciferic element, the element of light is darkened through the ahrimanic darkness. When the Queen sees the drops of blood shining on the snow, she beholds Imaginatively the essential beings in whose earthly part the one element of love connects with the pure substance of the light, without the ahrimanic darkness and the Moonlike luciferic cloudiness coming between. For snow, as all matter, is condensed, crystallized light and this relationship of matter to the light, this 'weaving and essence of the material' can indeed in the best way be experienced meditatively with snow (*Spiritual Beings in the Heavenly Bodies and in the Kingdoms of Nature*, GA 136, Helsingfors / Helsinki 3 April 1912, lecture 1). That is, in this Imagination of the snow the substance of the pure light, the blood, expresses the element of pure love (also with Wolfram von Eschenbach, for Parzifal in beholding the drops of blood on the snow, a similar Imagination is involved). Moreover, what was said in the Hannover lecture-course on blood [GA 134] may be recalled: that with a being that has not come under a luciferic influence it would have come with a mere flashing up, shining up of the substance of blood in the matter; blood should have only come to the beginning of materialization. It should actually be something spiritual. And so, with the Imagination of the drops of blood in 'Snow White', an Imagination that relates to a being [Snow White] in which the Moonlike nature takes no part.

In the fairytale nearly every word is wonderfully meaningful. Thus when it says, after the meeting with the hunter: 'Now the poor child was all *alone* in the big forest ...', this is just the loneliness which is always mentioned in ascending into the spiritual world, when the soul has left behind everything sensory and begins to experience itself in its astral nature, or when it finds itself at that abyss of seeming nothingness, before entering the actual spiritual world. (Cf. *Mysteries of the East and Christianity*, lecture 1, p. 6.) Through this one arrives at the meaningful experience—it is a directly penetrating experience, 'You are alone in the world ... you are completely alone in the world' and many other similar places.

I have had to ponder much about the sleeping of the seventh dwarf with the six others. Here there certainly lies a Mystery. According to the fairytale, the seventh dwarf is the Mercury dwarf ('Little Cup') which would lead to the Mystery of breathing, working with the philosopher's stone, and so on. I am thinking of the Christiania-cycle, where according to the seven planetary forces, seven streams of forces in the ether-body correspond:

movement of the uprightness ♄
movement of thinking ♃

movement of speech ♂
movement of the blood ☉
movement of breathing ☿
movement of the glands ♀
movement of reproduction ☽.

Here the seventh force belongs to the Moon, to the realm of sexuality: in 'Snow White' I would also like to think of the seventh dwarf as the Moon-dwarf (could it not be possible that the Moon and Mercury are occultly exchanged as otherwise Mercury and Venus are?). This would then result in a beautiful meaning that in the place representing the Moon-forces, the pure virginal Snow White has stepped in (the sleeping of Snow White in the bed of the seventh dwarf), through this those forces are, as it were, 'redirected' (as this takes place in the Mysteries) and those forces then flow towards the six other forces of the organism as a life-strengthening force.

In 'The Crystal-Ball', too, that Mystery of the redirected sexual forces seems to me to play an important role: the firebird that rises out of the conquered Bull. With this I also think of the seventh 'Grail Seal'. What results out of the meeting of the two snakes (masculine and feminine force) and what otherwise as the fire of sensuality makes its impact downwards, and when the forces are employed as the sacred fire of offering upwards towards the spirit.

[ending page/s missing from *Nachlass* portfolio. Written July 2017—*A.S.*]

Berlin, Steglitz
30 July 1916

Highly esteemed Herr Dr!

To my joy it was still possible to hold the lecture. For on Tuesday 1 Aug., it would not have been possible for I had to return to war service, but Herr Walter had the kindness to organize an extraordinary Society meeting. Unfortunately, many could not be informed in time, but I hope that the course of outer events will make it soon possible in the not-too-distant future to return to that theme with a bigger audience. I feel how I myself have still to work further inwardly on it. The important communication of what has been found is sometimes more difficult than the finding. By the way, I was very happy that 'Snow White'[30] received an affectionate interest from so many friends. May it give to many people the strength that we need so much in this time. I am so grateful to you for everything that I have received especially during the course of this summer for the understanding of these things through you, and I feel how it also gives me strength for that which the near future demands from me. Also with the book [*Knowledge of the*] *Higher Worlds* I experienced something wonderful in this regard. I believe to have had with regard to this book always some special close and intimate relationship to this and with special preference appropriated in times of calm and tranquillity. And now, reading it again under such changed outer circumstances I quite unexpectantly experienced as if it were written for the war-like life-conditions of the present. This is a surprising experience; one sees just how the book is drawn out of the true depths of the spirit, and consequently fits in a truly practical way to all circumstances of life. Through this book the breath of eternity passes, something that relates to all conditions of time (similar to 'Snow White'), whereas I feel your new book *Riddles of the Soul* in the most eminent sense a book of the present and future (similar to 'The Crystal-Ball', a fairytale for the present and the future). It is also written in a completely new futuristic manner and has to be read in such a manner. May also in what are called scientific circles, the number of those who imbue themselves with the thinking that relates to reality demanded in that book, soon increasingly grow in number. May hopefully the time soon come when one can speak again in greatest calm and under [more] peaceful relationships than is now the case.

Looking forward to seeing you again
I remain in deepest warm devotion
and gratefully
yours,
Hermann Beckh

[Written in pencil]
In the field
26 Nov. 1916
Herrn Dr Rudolf Steiner, Dornach

Highly esteemed Herr Doktor!

In spite of the turmoil that surrounds me, I seek to direct my thoughts towards the spiritual as much as possible. In this war one is entangled as in a fairytale experience, with ever new pictures, new experiences and sufferings, and, above all, the charm of distant romantic landscapes (far down in the south-east [of Europe], precisely at a point of the decisive events in which fate has placed me). A certain substitute for the theosophical studies which are so painfully and longingly missed is also offered by fairytales, where all the great problems are presented in a narrow and reduced space. It was not without meaning that just before my departure I was concerned with Snow White; it inwardly accompanied me everywhere, I always carried it around with me.—The events of the war do not allow great fairytale research, but for something quite small there nevertheless remains time: No. 7 of 'Legends for Children' [Grimm], 'Our Lady's Little Glass': 'Once upon a time a wagoner's cart which was heavily laden with wine, had stuck so fast that in spite of all that he could do he could not get it to move again.'[31]

With the wine here too the relation to the 'I' (compare the marriage in Cana [John 2]) at first the lower 'I', the cart of life of the lower ego, which became stuck through egoism (and does one not, especially in this war, experience how thoroughly the cart of our life is stuck through the lower egotism). 'Now the Mother of God came, and when she saw the need of the poor man, she said to him, "I am tired and thirsty, give me a glass of wine, and I will set thy cart free for you."' This means that the 'I' is to be Christened, as the lower 'I' it should be sacrificed to the higher 'I' of the Mother-God and rendered serviceable, then the carts of our lives will become free again. 'Gladly,' replied the wagoner, 'but I have no glass in which I can give you the wine.' The lower man has not yet a worthy vessel in his bodily organization with which it can offer something to the higher hierarchies.

Only grace from above: 'Then the Mother of God plucked a white flower with red stripes, called field bindweed that looks very like a glass, and handed it to the driver.' The bindweed [? something like a Pisces sign crossed out] in its modesty, symbol of the influence of the higher hierarchies, of everything that is completely free from Lucifer and Ahriman, cf. Helsingfors lecture-cycle, especially in the windings and forms of the bindweed are mirrored the law of the spheres (the Spirits of Movement, the Spirits of Wisdom, and others). When hiking in nature, I have meditated much about this flower, and enjoyed unique experiences through this, which now return to me in deepening this legend for children. It is only a softly sounding harmony of the spheres. It is wonderful in the fairytale, the Christened feeling for nature, the cosmic infinities prevailing behind this most unpretentious of all flowers. 'He filled it with wine [that is, he pours his lowly being into the vessel of humility and devotion to the higher hierarchies], and the Mother of God drank it [the higher 'I' takes the lower 'I' into itself], and at that moment the cart became free [already Buddha speaks of a liberation] and the carter could drive onwards.' The flower is still called *Muttergottesgläschen* ('The mother of God's little glass'). One can meditate this name and then find everything I wanted to sketch here as a fairytale experience. May also such weak and lowly spiritual efforts serve that the theosophical friends may soon meet again together, and may peace, the redeeming Christmas, and the speedy completion and opening of the Building [the Goetheanum] take place. Day and night all our thoughts are directed with longing to this end.

In deep heartfelt devotion
and grateful veneration,
Hermann Beckh

---

8 Dec. 1916 [in the *Nachlass* list, but not found in my records—*A.S.*]

In a letter that he wrote ('In the field, the Balkans, December 1916', quoted in Beckh's biography by G. K-B, p. 151f. (also *Die CG* Nov. 1939, p. 192), Beckh describes a Christmas experience:

> I will not forget the beautiful, still moonlit night. At the entrance to the village we found an empty house, very small but 'indescribably dainty and neat'. An old Madonna picture, full of atmosphere (under which I slept), hung on the wall, and with everything a mood prevailed as in the high mountains, on the lonely heights of a pass. It was really a Snow White experience, completely the mood of Christmas. Perhaps it was spiritually my Christmas evening this year. At last, one was out of the hustle, away from all commanding officers, from all official stuff, alone with oneself in the freedom of nature. I slept so wonderfully as I had not done for months. At last, during the night one really was in the spiritual world.

---

18 Feb. 1917

Highly esteemed Herr Doktor!

Also during the further course of troop movements, spiritual research of fairytales has helped me over many sad or embarrassing hours, and before I return home, which should happen soon, involving a call to

Kiel—I would like to return to 'Snow White' in which I begin to find ever new depths in the solitude of a Romanian village, remote from the world. Recently there occurred to me as an occult impression the picture of the glass mountain and of the bush. The 'bush' is an indication towards the Mystery of the ether-body with its cosmic spreading ether-forces; it seems that the 'glass coffin' contains an indication of the Mystery of the physical body. Glass is here also 'crystal' and as a meditative observation of the plant-world leads to the etheric nature, towards the ether-body, so in a corresponding manner one can also immerse oneself into the mineral realm, especially into the world of crystals, and come then to the true nature of the physical body, which indeed is something quite different from what people usually assume, I mean, something quite supersensible, possibly still more supersensible than the other human members. The physical body, too, is filled with streaming light, but according to my impression, in quite a different way from the ether-body, whereas with the ether-body, one feels like a streaming-out into the cosmos, into the abundance of space and time; it is with the physical body, more like a raying-in from cosmic widths, the rays too are quite different, with the ether-body a weaving and waving, which is symbolized through curved lines as shown in the plant world, whereas with the physical body everything is more [arranged in] straight lines as in the crystal. The light-rays of the physical body surround the hollow space of the physical form (glass coffin) in a much more decisive way than the ether-rays flowing with the cosmic element of the ether-body. Thus, with the ether-body, perhaps: a raying-in from the Sun's centre into the etheric-form and through again a raying-out into the cosmos; with the physical body a raying-in out of the cosmos into the physical form, which through this is surrounded by a certain rigidity.

[sketch]

phy. body	ether-body
(glass coffin)	(bush)

The 'black earth' (into which the dwarves are not able and do not want to lay the dead Snow White), as it were, presents the ahrimanic element (the ahrimanic enclosure into the physical body is erroneously taken for the real physical body, by those who cannot recognize it), whereas the 'glass coffin' contains an indication of the true element of the physical body and with it of the Mystery of the whole Snow White initiation, which here too takes place in the sense of a Christian initiation.

For it has to do with that true physical body, with that element which through Ahriman is obscured and which through the Myst[ery] of G[olgotha] was brought to the light of day.

Through touching the bush, the living ether-forces spread into the cosmos, the physical body re-awakens to life. The lid of the glass coffin is opened.

Such a way of viewing the essence of the physical and etheric nature, as attempted here following the fairytale, leads me from another side also to meditate the eurythmy verse [source untraced]:

> Seek, O Soul,
> in stones the raying,
> in the blossom the light,
> and you find yourself.

What is here called 'the raying in the stones' and which can be laid hold of through a certain occult impression is no doubt the true physical body of the stone, the stone of those who know, the knowledgeable ones, the philosopher's stone, whereas that which otherwise is taken as the physical body of the stone is only the ahrimanic element, the darkness of the stone, of the 'not-knowers'.

It seems to me remarkable that fairytales, as in [Grimms'] 'Allerleirau—All-kinds-of-fur' and 'The True Bride' the Sun-dress, the Moon-dress and the Star-dress—in 'Allerleirau' are packed into a nutshell, are consequently not crudely material but of a supersensible nature and thus show the supersensory sheaths and certain corresponding levels of consciousness. The Sun-dress would then be the ether-body (in the same way as in 'Allerleirau' the mantle of animal skins is the crude physical body), the Moon-dress = astral body, the Star-dress = 'I'-sheath, 'I' (as higher Self). If one takes this terminology of fairytales together with that which arises out of the lecture-cycle on John's Gospel as the meditation: Body, Life, Light, and Love, then there arises the following meditation:

> physical body = earthly dress of the body
> ether body = Sun-dress of life,
> astral body = Moon-dress of light,
> 'I' = starry dress of love.

This 'starry dress of love' is today still quite in its first beginnings; this is realized in this war quite clearly, and the most painful experiences are those which flow from the above-mentioned fact. Moreover, I had the good fortune to be led wonderfully by the powers of destiny and was allowed to see and experience many interesting things. In my experiences a certain unifying element was at work; my being called up coincided with the beginning of the victorious advance in Romania, and now as it begins to quieten down, I am called back home. May I be able then to work for the spirit! The image of Dornach and the aims of our spiritual work always kept me firm and upright also during the most difficult times.

With deep heartfelt veneration
and gratitude,

Hermann Beckh

Kiel
4 March 1917

Highly esteemed Herr Dr!

Due to the wartime conditions, it is unfortunately impossible for me to stay in Berlin in order to hear the lectures. I do hope at least to be able to spend the Easter days in Berlin, but it seems it cannot be on any Tuesday. During this serious and difficult time I did seriously wish at least as regards outer meetings to see you once and to be allowed to speak with you. Consequently, if it is not too inconvenient, it would be a great joy for me if you are able to grant a conversation during one of these days, Good Friday or Easter Saturday or even Easter Sunday itself. In the case of a positive answer, you would be able to confirm with my sister who hopes to be again in Berlin on Tuesday before Easter and will appear at the Society meeting. (Perhaps you would also give her the joy of a short conversation, for every now and then she needs some strengthening and enthusing.) It is not impossible that I could come to Berlin on Saturday 11th March, though only for one night. Unfortunately, the train connections do not allow for me to arrive in time for the lecture in the Architects' House, but I would hope to come at least to the end of the lecture to see and speak with you for a moment.

About my experiences of the war in Bulgaria and Romania, I have told you at the time from the field. The letter was sent to you (or Frau Dr Steiner) in Dornach via my sister. I hope it reached you; in the face of the insecurities at the border it is never certain. The letter was sent from Sistov on the Donau where the big troop crossing had taken place. It discloses amongst other things some observations on the legend of 'Our Lady's Little Glass' in Grimms' *Fairytales* (with which I am much concerned during the war. I become strongly aware today of the strengthening and enlivening effect of everything Imaginative). Here I also looked up a connection in the Helsingfors lecture-cycle (on what was said about bindweed and the hierarchies) [GA 136].

At this time, I have been called to Kiel for some war service, but it could be that I am called in again (by the military) towards the end of April. The activity here brings much joy to me, although it is completely turned towards the outer 'practical' matters (having to do with the 'Institute for Sea Traffic and World Economy'). I experienced how much it is possible through spiritual-theosophical striving and the exercises also to enliven and penetrate this sphere with lively interest and to gather for outer work the necessary strength out of the spirit. What comes about is much more alive than for example philology (where of course especially the spiritual viewpoints can and should be brought in, but here the materialism of the ruling habits of thought makes it quite hopeless; I only find a dying tradition). A valuable help in living into the present 'practical' activity was offered me through Herr Meebold's book,[32] which I have read with great interest, with great inner involvement.

During the journey home from Romania the city of Vienna (which I had seen for the first time through this occasion) made a wonderfully sublime impression on me. Is it not, as it were, to us like an outer symbolism, that connection of head and heart, of thinking and the feelings in proper meditation—which now has increasingly to flow into the spiritual development of German culture and of humanity—through the combination of the new German regime and the old, dignified Austria, from Berlin (thinking) and Vienna (heart)? But the main thing of the actual central organ is and remains the heart (where indeed all these streams, which at first were situated further up in thinking and have to be developed, finally flow together, where they have to be relocated from the head). I had such an experience regarding Vienna on my journey with respect to the outer impressions (despite the strict military restrictions, I was allowed to walk freely through the city). In the impressive buildings and streets, as well as the whole being of the people (who through the war are now strangely in a serious mood, but nevertheless joyful and hopeful) one felt touched by the breath of an older culture, of something eternal, ever green, which will also withstand the storms of this difficult time. A mere glance at the more strictly German realm with its capital city (which embodies the whole non-culture of the present-day, of course its energetic spiritually progressive drive) could never awaken in me such reliable hopes and expectations for the future as was awoken in me during that single day that I was allowed to experience in the city of Vienna. One may hope that the coming together of the two realms so important for the well-being and development of the whole and of humanity will ever more surely come about. I was especially pleased outside and had a good feeling (and a recuperation in a certain sense) when we met Austrians.

In the loneliness and outer seclusion in which I live here I am at this time especially involved with Goethe's *Faust,* hereby seeking to digest all the stimuli deriving from your various lectures and writings on this theme. (In the already-mentioned book by Meebold, the importance of the poetic work *Faust* for the present and the future is impressively pointed out in many places in the sense of these stimuli.) What you said once during a lecture in the Architects' House on the question of Homunculus in his relationship to Wagner and Mephisto on the one hand and to Faust, Helena and Euphorion on the other hand at the time was especially light-bringing, but the details I have lost again as it is often the case with occult matters, thus with Homunculus I still have some difficulties. A valuable help is the place in Meebold on p. 36 below, but it is still not enough for me for all the threads of understanding to flow together. Perhaps you will be able, if the powers of destiny allow the requested conversation, to give me, regarding Homunculus and so on, some kind of pointer to help me again to that which I am not yet able at this time to bring to the surface out of the spiritual substrata. This, next to meditation, would be the main subject with which I would like to converse with you.

As we move towards the Festival of Easter, the memory is re-enlivened in me of those unforgettable spring days which I was allowed to spend two years ago during Eastertide in Dornach; more than anything else this memory holds me up during this difficult time, filling me with joyful-serious hope. With this it is something like a white light arising out of all the colours in my inner experience. May the day be no longer far off when all this, which is now held through dark powers as in an enchanted sleep, may experience its sacred resurrection. With these thoughts I look firmly to Dornach

and am in deep, warm respect and gratitude,
yours truly
Hermann Beckh

Kiel, 17 March 1917

Highly esteemed Herr Doktor!

When some time ago I had the pleasure to talk with you about 'Snow White' you pointed out to me the relationship of the seventh dwarf— whom initially, because of the 'little cup', I erroneously wanted to take as the Moon-dwarf—to Mercury. This relationship, which initially was not yet immediately transparent is now confirmed for me in a most beautiful manner, if I understand you correctly, through the occult script. At that time I asked: why is it precisely the Mercury-dwarf, in whose bed Snow White finally stays, after all the other six did not suit her? But one only needs to contemplate the Mercury sign ☿ (with the Sun-'I'-point[33] in the middle, as it is outward[ly] placed by Mee- bold), and one will recognize, how especially this dwarf mirrors Snow White's whole being in the most complete manner, and how the 3 com- ponents of the Mercury-sign clearly relate to the three basic character- istics of Snow White's nature. The purity, which she possesses in think- ing, 'as white as snow' is the Moon turned upwards, changed into the Grail-chalice, the upper part of the Mercury-sign. The solar quality of her [Snow White's] feelings, wherein passion is extinguished and love is raised towards a higher level—[']red as blood['] in the sense as said in *Occult Science* with the rose-cross meditation of the 'rose'—lies in the Sun-sign ☉ in the middle. And the third part of the Mercury-sign, the cross below, points towards the third of the three rose-cross qualities, the sense of sacrifice (sulphur) in the *will*, with Snow White: 'black as ebony', or like the burnt wood of the cross (and it is also the black *cross* within the window frame[34] that Snow White's mother sees before her when she sees that Snow White Imagination). Black is also the colour of Saturn,[35] and that third lower part of the Mercury-sign can be imag- ined to have arisen out of the Saturn-sign, only that the Moon turned downwards is missing, because it [the Moon] is used as the Grail-chal- ice opening upwards [and it has] moved to the top of the sign, just as Snow White has removed from herself the lower lunar nature, the ele- ment of passion. (The Jupiter-sign ♃ with the Moon already moving up but not yet transformed into the Grail-chalice would present itself in this regard as a transition stage between the Saturn-sign and the Mercury-sign, most likely = Venus.) The 'little cup' of the 7th dwarf is then nevertheless the Moon-Grail-chalice, but not because that dwarf would be the Moon-dwarf, which is not the case, but because espe- cially in the Mercury ☿ the Moon is contained and is changed into the

Mercury-chalice. Now one also understands without more ado why none of the other beds suits Snow White. For each of the other six dwarves, or rather planets, are part of her being, but precisely only this part and not the whole, only in the seventh, in Mercury is her whole being mirrored, in the same way as the Mercury-sign contains all the other planetary signs. The fairytale is truly tremendously deep in meaning; I am always amazed afresh about it and I admire how each word in it is almost a symbol of the occult script.

Thus in the three parts of the Mercury-sign the relationship is given to thinking—the feelings—the will (it thinks me—it weaves me—it makes (*wirkt*) me), and thereby also connected to this, to Manas—Buddhi (*addition*: also astral body, ether-body, phy. body, generally the 3 trinities of spirit, soul and body lie in the ☿ [dot in circle])—Atma or wisdom—life—power; also hope—love—faith (in that order), also the Rosicrucian salt—mercury—sulphur, or with Snow White: white as snow[,] red as blood etc. Also the three stages Imagination—Inspiration—Intuition are certainly to be imagined here and are contained in this sign, and finally, as I assume, possibly also the trinity of the animals who weep for Snow White by her coffin, the owl, the raven and the dove, who correspond to three different levels of initiation; the little dove—the Grail-dove!—belongs most likely to the chalice of the Grail ('white as snow'), the raven belongs to the cross ('black as ebony'), or is it the other way round, the dove to the Christian cross? (I thought that first, but the other is certainly correct.) I would also place the Saturn = cross—will—to the consciousness-soul, the Moon = Grail-chalice— the higher thinking to the sentient soul. But now in the initiation the consciousness-soul transforms into the Imagination-soul (raven?), the sentient soul into Intuition-soul (dove!), the dove 'white as snow' must indeed belong to the Moon-Grail-chalice. The raven, then, belongs to the black cross, to death, which through the initiation is transformed into life (here something has become clear to me in writing this). (It is strange that in the fairytale the owl first appears, then the raven; one expects it the other way round.)—In the sense of these interpretations, the raven is the Imagination; also that still has to do with the personal element, and has to be overcome in order that the higher, the Inspiration (owl) and Intuition (dove) can unfold, as it is described in *Occult Science* (extinguishing the Imagination, p. 316), 'In the attained Imaginative world, one has to erase *oneself*—this then corresponds again to the black cross. Meebold describes, if I understand him rightly, the same experience Imaginatively on p. 56 above: 'Finally it was truly the raven who brought me tidings that a decisive battle was won. For this he then gave his life. With outspread wings he lay down and passed away, after he had communicated his silent word. From then on the owl took over his [the raven's] office, the bird which flew around Pallas Athene and can see in the night.' For a long time I inwardly wrestled to understand this passage and all of a sudden here too the meaning seems to unfold out of the deepening in Snow White in connection with the ☿ sign and *Occult Science*. Thus it often transpires in spiritual studies, that what is sought suddenly comes about of itself.

Above all I strive to look at all these Snow White questions and the Mercury-sign in the light of the rose connecting to *Occult Science* (p. 300),[36] and the rose in the light of ☿ sign as it is given by M[eebold] p. 294, 'If with the rose one can apply the found numbers in the right way, then they give a certain connection of the powers of the Sun with those of Saturn, Moon and Mercury ... The meaning of the crown of thorns ... if here one lays hold of the above-mentioned forces where they are working together in a certain way. This they do in the plant-world in the rose, and in the human realm in the Son of man who goes towards the death on the cross.' (*Addition*: And in fairytales—one could add here—they do it in Snow White with the crown of thorns and this also can be shown in another form in the other levels of the Christian Mystery.) Should it not rather say correctly: 'The connection of the Sun-forces with those of Saturn and Moon *through* Mercury' not as something autonomous *besides* Saturn, Sun and Moon, but as the unification of these three, of the one who couples 'Sun and Moon', who in the sense of the ancient Rosicrucian verse given to me by yourself. This then leads to the connection of ether-body and astral body, the Tree of Life and the Tree of Knowledge, in initiation the actual true Yoga-Mystery, whose highest Christened expression is the union of Mother and Disciple at the cross. In the physical realm, on Golgotha, the union takes place *under* the cross, in the spiritual realm, accordingly also with the ☿ sign, *above* the cross because death in overcome, trans-formed into life.—In 'Snow White' that yoga-union of Sun and Moon leads us through Mercury to the 'Mystery of the 7th dwarf' about which we have already mentioned earlier (transformation of the lower forces into the higher ones, of the Moon—in a quite specific narrower sense—into the Grail-chalice). Only then does one rightly understand the 'red as blood', the meaning of the purely earthly element (or Sun-Earth element) in 'Snow White'. Hereby all this is to be recalled that is said in *Occult Science* concerning 'the red of the rose that may become a symbol for us of such a blood that expresses purified drives and passions, which has shed the lower element and in their purity manifest in the same way as those at work in the red rose'. One then sees the whole rose in the sign of Mercury, in the sense of that threefold meditation, which came to me once out of the 'it thinks me, it w[eaves] me, it m[akes] me': miracle of the light, light of the rose, the miracle of the rose.

Unfortunately, I could not come to Berlin yesterday and speak with you in the Architects' House. Hopefully this can happen at Easter.
In deep respect and gratitude,
Yours
Hermann Beckh

---

27 March 1917

Highly esteemed Herr Dr!

The fairytale of 'The Crystal-Ball / Sphere' [Grimm, No. 197] I also recently sought to read out of the occult script in the light of the 'Mercury sign' and perhaps I may write briefly to you about this. I'd like to commence from the lower part of the sign, from the cross. This expresses the 'depths of death' and thus at the same time the 'source of life', that 'source' mentioned in 'The Crystal-Ball' where the youth struggles with the bison and overcomes it 'after a long struggle'. As the 'raven' in 'Snow White' points to the depths of death, so the 'bull' (or 'wild bison') points towards the 'source of life'. Both consequently belong to the cross yet are both quite different. One also thinks immediately of the 3 animals in the 'Paradise sequence' of the Hague lecture-course [*The Effect of Occult Development*, GA 145, March 1913, lect. 6-10], where we also have below the bull, and they most likely also correspond in a certain sense with the 3 parts of the Mercury sign? In the Crystal-Ball the bison living at the source of life initially expresses certain lower forces that first have to be conquered, transformed. Then there arises out of the bull the firebird—the higher element is thus already hidden in the lower—and it soars upwards, towards that region corresponding to the upper part of the Mercury-sign, the Moon–Grail-chalice. Because the bird still contains in itself the 'glowing egg' it does not appear here as the dove 'white as snow' above the Grail, but as the firebird. It seems to be the same being, whose luciferic form or enchantment we meet in the fairytale as the eagle, dwelling in the 'rocky mountain', the hard skull of the brain, of the thinking not yet transformed into the Grail chalice. In the Paradise Imagination, too, the eagle is above. In the

Oriental fairytale, the phoenix corresponds to the 'firebird'. For the golden Sun-egg, which the firebird drops, we do not have to seek long, for in the Mercury-sign—it is always endowed with the Sun-'I'-point, ☿ [dot in the circle ☉], it is to be imagined—in its middle part we have the egg directly before us and in its centre the crystal-ball, that Sun-'I'– point (if this is the right expression). This dot (that is, the crystal-ball), one would like to believe, expresses the supersensory, magical 'I'-forces, the forces of that 'I' that with normal people slumber in deep sleep. Of these higher, magical ego-forces one may be allowed to say that they stand in a direct relationship to the forces of the supersensory-physical [element] (Stone of the Wise), to those forces symbolized in the cube or also in the octahedron, in the diamond. Consequently, in the fairytale we have the crystal-ball, whereas related so closely to it, the 7th seal (the Grail seal) the cube. The 'I' relates in the initiation towards the supersensory-physical element as the purified astral body—the Tree of Knowledge—then relates towards the ether-body, the Tree of Life—John who takes the Mother to himself [John 19:27]. Through the Crystal-Ball, the supersensory-magical 'I'-forces, the youth then breaks the power of the black magician, who only works out of the astral element, and which only covers with deceptive illusion the true reality that can only be recognized with the 'I'.

In Snow White, those higher, magical 'I'-forces are the King's Son, before whom the glass coffin of Snow White opens up, after he had come into contact with the bush, the outspreading cosmic living ether-forces.

Many things in the fairytale of the Crystal-Ball are still unclear to me, e.g. the 'fisherman's cottage by the sea'. Everything else, too, which I write here in the form of certain sentences, should initially be taken only as humble guesswork or questions. For one has to seek in order to penetrate ever deeper into the understanding of these things, and the actual true vision is hard to obtain in these difficult times, to wrestle through; for some days everything is covered as with a veil.

Wonderful results seem to arise with this sign ☿ [with dot] also with verse 'to behold the Sun at the midnight hour (☉), to build with stones' etc. … with 'decay' and 'night of death' there is again the +, the 'creation has a new beginning' is ♃, whose Moon-part in the Mercury-sign turned upwards. 'The heights reveal the eternal Word of the gods', this is the Moon-Grail-chalice, the upper part of the sign; 'in the depth shall shelter' etc., again the cross below. At the end 'no spiritual joy' belongs to the whole ☿ sign.

Perhaps I shall be fortunate at Easter; I might hear you or speak with you during that time. I arrive in Berlin on Thursday; my sister will attend the branch meeting already on Tuesday.

In deep respect and gratitude,
Hermann Beckh

Kiel

10 June, 1917

Highly esteemed Herr Dr!

While still standing with my *feelings* completely under the impression of what I experienced in Berlin, I now seek to digest the very depressing events with my *thinking* in the hope that finally everything, also the unpleasant can bear fruit for the world. Many things seem to be explained through this, that today in general many longingly desire occultism—or what they understand as occultism—but in the depths of their souls reject or even hate the Christ-Impulse which alone is able to provide the right support and sustaining power, without being conscious of this fact, for which it seems an experience of one's own self, a meeting with the Guardian of the Threshold would be necessary.

The soul does not have the forces to find the way to Damascus [ref. to Acts 9:3], and yet everything depends on finding it in the right way. Does not everything in our time become understandable from this point of view, e.g. the case of Nietzsche, how strangely in his commencing derangement the Crucified One stands before him, to Whom as it seems he could not find the way in his bright, clear consciousness. (Frequently, especially regarding Nietzsche as a true soul-experience and not only as speculation, the question came to me whether such personalities would not have helpers in the spiritual world, helpers that further their development towards the indicated direction.) Yet to return to the current events: the case of Seiling [Max Seiling, 1852-1928] one would honour much too much by placing him on a level with Friedrich Nietzsche or name him in the same breath. The essay in [the journal] *Psychische Studien* ['Psychological Studies'] is not only unsympathetic, ungrateful and vicious, but also strangely arrogant; it also misses—apart from higher Christian impulses—any clear traces of occult points of view; one wonders how such a person who has already concerned himself with so many occult questions can write something like that. Cannot he, one asks oneself, truly not understand why and from what viewpoints the spiritual researcher has stood up for Haeckel and several others, which the mere church Christian would not stomach, and is he not able to see the deeper plan, which like a thread runs through the whole of spiritual science? One would have thought, even a beginner in theosophical things should be able to divine something of the connections existing here. And how wrong he is concerning Goethe and the book *Goethe's World-Conception* [GA 6].

Thanks to a happy coincidence I have been occupied for some time especially with this book, and was deeply impressed, which earlier on I would not have been, for I see now how important this book is. It contains not only no contradictions with what comes later, but in noteworthy fashion connects up with later matters, moreover, particularly the latest book *The Riddle of Man* [GA 20] (I am thinking particularly of the chapter 'New Perspectives'). To discuss a 'pre-theosophical' book has basically little sense; those who know how to read between the lines already find there the whole plan of the later spiritual science. There is more 'occultism' smuggled into this book than it initially appears to be the case for a superficial reading, as that of Seiling. Indeed, precisely on the deepest occult questions, it seems to me, a fair amount is smuggled into this book, e.g. on p. 18 [Germ. ed.] when the discussion concerns the 'original sin' of Western thinking, or p. 13 concerning the 'two paths' (i.e. Lucifer & Ahriman); when on p. 33 we read that to him—Goethe—the interaction of idea and perception was like a spiritual breathing, or p. 50 we read how, in the process of gaining knowledge, a person strives for the balance of two forces that approach from two sides—so here and in many similar places, it everywhere concerns the three crosses on Golgotha, the question involving Lucifer, Ahriman and Christ in the sign of the Scales. Or the last sentence on p. 47:

> The human being doesn't simply exist to make a picture of the finished world; no, he himself collaborates with the world as it comes into being.

This is precisely a basic sentence for the whole of spiritual science. Only when one has assimilated a lot of theosophy, can one sense, or begin to sense, the scope of this sentence. Or how full of deep occult significance is p. 44, with the splendid quotation of Goethe on granite; all sorts of things are contained here, which in other words is said in the lecture-cycles; I am thinking first of all of a specific passage in the cycle on the folk-souls [*The Mission of the Folk-Souls*, GA 121]) concerning the wielding of the hierarchies, the Thrones, the Spirits of Movement, the Spirits of Form, etc. In reading one feels how the spiritual researcher out of his conscious knowledge feels the nobility that for him lies in the quoted words of Goethe:[37]

> So lonely ... as I look down this completely bare peak and ... for the person who but wants to open his soul to the oldest, first, deepest feelings of truth. Indeed, he can say to himself: Here on the oldest, eternal altar, which is built directly on the depths of creation, I bring a sacrifice to the being of all beings.

Cosmic Mysteries ring out through these words, but Seiling hears nothing of them, and what the spiritual researcher wants to say with the citing of such passages passes him by without a trace. Moreover, he understands even less of what on p. 73 is said concerning morals, ethical freedom and love as the motives for action—and this is one of the worst things about the entire essay by Seiling—he even confuses external coercive morality with the true, thoroughgoing morality based on moral freedom, which the spiritual researcher means. Because the categorical imperative and the like is rejected, the writing, according to Seiling, is supposed to be anti-moralistic, whereas in that rejection precisely the true, higher morality is expressed, of which Hofrat Seiling has absolutely no idea. Something similarly bad is his egotistical, self-convinced interpretation and exploitation of the theosophical teachings on *karma*, which can be read between the lines. All this is still haunted by the whole materialism of Du Prel's school of thought, a materialism that in many respects is worse than that of external science, and all the more dangerous because the adherents of each school are mostly unaware of it. This also applies to Seiling when he accuses the spiritual researcher of materialism with regard to certain passages in earlier writings. Their own materialism is not acknowledged. The case of Seiling shows once again how difficult it is for followers of Du Prel's direction to find the true path to the spirit. Du Prel's meritorious striving should not be denied, nor the nobility of his character—of which, however, there is nothing to be found in Seiling, at least no longer in this last regrettable essay.

What has been said about the book *Goethe's World Conception* is also just as valid for the books *The Philosophy of Freedom, Truth and Science,* etc. I and many others would be happy if the, as such, sad occurrence would lead to a new edition of these books. Earlier, I repeatedly read *The Philosophy of Freedom*, but since I do not possess this book myself— it was already out of print—I could not enter it with such peace of mind as I would have wished (only possible with one's own book), and now I see myself through my whole theosophical striving as has occurred up to now, directly facing the necessity to catch up with what I have missed, and of course I will now be able to experience much deeper things than was possible at that earlier time. I am now aware that through such immersion into such books something is directly done and created. One also may hope for a new edition of the books *A Theory of Knowledge* [GA 2] and *Friedrich Nietzsche, Fighter for Freedom* [GA 5]. One is of the feeling that these are all books for the future, books that contain and present from ever new viewpoints the great future impulse, the Christ-Impulse; only now is the world maturing to understand this.

This impulse for the future also pulsates particularly vividly in the *Fragments* of Novalis, which have become a main topic of work in my leisure hours here in my loneliness as a war exile in Kiel. Aren't these *Fragments* a programme, so to speak, the execution of which is represented by spiritual science? There are very specific, clear relationships that one encounters at every turn. Taken alone without theosophy one would probably never have properly understood these sayings in their full implications. But if one has theosophy—spiritual science in its Christianized, Rosicrucian form—one can find it in many details again in these *Fragments*; one can experience the *Fragments* of Novalis as germs, seeds of the spiritual science of his time. What lies in Novalis' sentences, such as the following, to cite just one of countless examples:

> View of the whole world through the moral sense. Deducing the universe from morality; all true improvements are moral improvements, all true inventions, moral inventions, progress' [p. 575 in Heilborn; on the same page, 'Uniting sleep and waking in one state,' etc. etc. (*Novalis Schriften*, ed. Tieck u. Schlegel, Part 1, Berlin 1837, p. 245)].

It is an extremely captivating work that also stimulates meditation (there is something in the *Fragments* that demands lively thinking and meditative experience) to arrange and compile all the rich material here according to certain spiritual-scientific points of view. I feel how this work demands much more internal [application] than did the more historical-philological work on Buddha during its time, and the only question is whether and to what extent a work dealing with the *Fragments* of Novalis (and subsequently also his other works) can and may be the subject of a publication. Because with the intimate nature of the subject very specific limits are drawn here; it would in any case be a matter of finding a tactful form in order so to express everything just as it is, as can be given to the public today. But if the right occult caution is taken here, then it can only be a good thing, in this materialized and edgy present, in which such severe tests are imposed on the German spirit, the true greats of the German spirit—and Novalis also belongs here in the first instance—to put in there as a counterbalance to Kant, and so many other things that the present suffers from. How grateful and worthwhile is, e.g. the mere reference to everything that the *Fragments* contain about Goethe and Kant, how the relationships to our spiritual science are given here.

When working through the book *Goethe's World Conception*, these enrichments can always be repeatedly brought to consciousness. This book—*Goethe's World Conception*—repeatedly shows itself as a new guide and viewpoint as an eminently esoteric and truly occult [= 'hidden '] book, a book in which a lot of 'occult' things are really hidden, and in which one can experience deepest matters everywhere. I have tried to give only a few examples today. And there is always something new to discover, which also stimulates Indian studies.

So today, during the presentation of Goethe's *Farbenlehre* [a teaching known as] *Theory of Colours* (p. 178 of the book), I suddenly realized the true meaning of the Indian teaching of *Sattva, Rajas, Tamas*, which no philologist had understood until then. How meaningful are the different meanings of *rajas*, which means dust, cloudiness, atmospheric element, air space, and then also the red colour and in general, then transferred to the soul—passion, activity, etc. These are hints; I must reserve them for another opportunity. I've been thinking about what you said to me about including or not including self-awareness in Buddhist meditation. The expressions *saññāvedayitanirodha* ('extinction of the sensation of consciousness') and *nirvana* already show that the highest level is not experienced here in full self-awareness, in the noontide of the soul. Perhaps I should have pointed this out more clearly in my work. I hope that it will only be possible to get full clarity on this point in an oral debate. Since 'contemplative awareness' is also important in Buddhism—but it is probably only taken to the entrance gate, not into one's inner being—the problem is complicated.

Hoping to see you in Berlin in the near future,
With deep heartfelt devotion and veneration,
Hermann Beckh

Kiel, 1 July 1917

Highly revered Herr Doktor!

May the separation and external loneliness imposed by the abnormal circumstances of the time justify the student at times seeking the way to spiritual life not only in thought but also in the written word, even if that which was touched by spiritual problems can only be answered in a later future, under different external conditions. The one stimulus drawn from your book *Goethe's World Conception* (the mentioning of which certain outer occasions recently gave me the opportunity) has now also opened up access to Goethe's treatise the *Farbenlehre* itself [first translated as *Theory of Colours*]. Does not the Rosicrucian initiate speak here more than in other Goethean writings? One can understand that a book that allows us to look into such deep esoteric contexts is not understood by our age; only a complete inner change and reversal (which Goethe wanted to bring about as an educator of his age) could here unlock the access. You go through something educational yourself when you immerse yourself in the *Farbenlehre*; it has a purifying effect on every possible access to yourself (even into the physical body, you begin to sense the value of 'colour therapy' or rather already practically experience it). It is certainly also very useful for meditation, indeed, everything in Goethe's *Farbenlehre* seems somehow to have a relation to meditation; new light and clarity is thereby brought into the colours of meditation. And an even deeper esoteric meaning is brought into it; you gradually learn to recognize the spiritual connections that you touch on through this colour scale. Certain appearances and colour phenomena also become clear to you, which could already be experienced earlier as a result of meditation. Actually, they are not yet Imaginations, because they are still completely on the border of the physical, really like outer colours, only floating detached in space. Through Goethe's description of the 'physiological colours' much becomes clear here. It is never like experiencing the process of seeing colours detached from external objects. And how much is taught by a sentence when it is thought through to the end, as with the one sentence that the eye doesn't actually see forms, but only colours. The scales fall from the eyes; there is something in such sentences which creates access to the spiritual world, here specifically to the Spirits of Form.

Incidentally, the word *rūpa* is taught to mean colour and shape in the Indian [Sanskrit language], and that the meaning of colour must be the original one. I tried to indicate earlier that there are deep connections between the primal phenomena of Goethe's *Farbenlehre* and the Indian theory of *sattva*, *rajas* and *tamas*. It was worthwhile to make this question the subject of a scientific investigation. Philology was completely helpless in the face of *sattva*, *rajas* and *tamas*; it was all so nebulously abstract, but the Goethean reflection brings light and colour into it. One feels something of the spirit of the early Zarathustra in the whole *Farbenlehre*, which, on the other hand, is also permeated by the spirit of the future, Christian esotericism. How strange is e.g. *'Paradoxe Seitenblick auf die Astrologie'*, 'paradoxical side view of astrology' (Didactic Part XXXII),[38] that is almost like a hint at the question of a new astrology, which was touched upon in your Leipzig lectures at the time [GA 149], the transformation of the old astrology through the Christ-Impulse. In the Novalis *Fragments*, too, constant reference to Goethe, the *Farbenlehre*, etc. is pointed out; one believes that a certain Rosicrucian thread is to be found in these studies, through which one is then led ever further as if through subterranean passages, up to the 'Fairytale of the Green Snake' and the Rosicrucian dramas.

And is there not also a strange, almost mysterious connection to the fairytale of the 'Crystal-Ball' from a philological point of view? The suggestion that you had the kindness to give me in this direction at the time has in the meantime led me to many things. In addition to what one already thought one understood, many other things still remain obscure, e.g. the story with the 'fisherman's hut' in the 'Crystal-Ball' despite long meditation. But now I think I understand that there is a relationship between this 'fisherman's hut' and the 'ferryman's hut' in Goethe's *Fairytale* (in which many other things are reminiscent of the 'Crystal-Ball': the dying youths, the mourning of the Lily and the mourning of the king's daughter, the forest and the river, the overcoming of the bison and the self-sacrifice of the snake, the soaring bird, and above all the thought of the harmonious interaction of the soul-forces; also the relationship of the 'golden egg' to the Sun—cf. the Mercury-sign ☿—and in Goethe's *Fairytale* the sunlight caught up by the hawk). Even Buddhism in a strange way seems to be able to contribute a building-block to the understanding here, not without one also becoming aware of a difference that governs between Buddhist and esoteric-Christian considerations. In *The Portal of Initiation* the Spirit of the Elements speaks: 'The human soul only sees me when the service I render to it is over.' Is one not reminded here of the role played by *samskāra* in Buddhism as the power that brings the human soul over from the supersensible world to the physical, and the words of the Liberated One referring to him: 'Housebuilder, you are beheld, you will henceforth no longer build this house.' The 'ferryman's hut' in Goethe's *Fairytale* as well as the 'fisherman's hut' in the 'Crystal-Ball' consequently have something to do with the formative forces, the archetype of the physical body in the supersensible world. In Buddhism it is a concern that the 'hut', that model of the physical body, is simply destroyed and no longer built in the future, whereas in the 'Crystal-Ball' as well as in Goethe's *Fairytale* the hut is especially protected just before the threatened annihilation; with Goethe the hut is transformed into another one made of nobler material. The hut becomes a temple, or an altar in the temple (probably also in the sense of the Pauline: *nicht entkleidet, sondern überkleidet werde*, 'not that we would be unclothed, but that we would be further clothed'.[39] So it would be the resurrection Mystery, which of course is still missing in Buddhism.

For a long time, I was inwardly concerned with the words on the cross, 'I thirst'.[40] Three things here, I believe, brought me understanding. The first was an indication which you gave me personally one year ago, during a consultation. The other was an indication through one of your lectures last winter in the branch meeting, on the meaning of the words 'It is fulfilled'[41] with regard to the power of the soul which corrupts the body, which is overcome on the cross of Golgotha. To these two indications, which for a long time worked concealed, now a third one was added: Buddhism, with that corrupting power of the soul *trsnā*, thirst. But especially here, Christianity is much more powerful, deep and full of life, for in Buddhism the overcoming of thirst is only talked about, but on the cross of Golgotha it is accomplished through the Deed and it is not only called 'overcoming', but thirst is taken from the world—thus you explained it at the time to me, and I can feel it in my innermost being—the Christ takes it upon Himself; this is an

Imagination, going far beyond any Buddhism. Consequently, I do not believe that Buddhism here brings something foreign into the gospel. It can rather help that the connection of 'It is fulfilled' with the previous quote 'I thirst' can be especially deeply felt. There are also other passages in the gospel where Buddhism is taken to account, as it were, e.g. the incident of the fig tree [Mark 11].

Do not the fairytales we were talking about have a connection to the most topical events of the present time? Especially that of the Green Snake, are we not experiencing it right now? Even an English statesman, who knows nothing of this matter, calls the present war the 'greatest calamity' since the Deluge—does not something from our inner theosophical [view] answer with deep but hopeful sighs, 'For the time is at hand!' And even the giant's shadow, which threatens to cause all sorts of confusion at the end, don't we also experience this with our efforts, as if it had to [experience] that everything is fulfilled? How deep must the revelation be from which Goethe drew. That episode with the giant seems to give a real key to the case just discussed. Herr Seiling perhaps intends to seek the 'arch of the serpent at noon', but what he really sought was always the 'shadow of the giant', and it was exactly the same in the case of Gösch and Haugen. May it continue with this 'shadow of the giant', as in the *Fairytale*, the time may not be far off when those who now have to stay farther away are allowed to participate fully in our community life again, and we, too, would like soon to be able to experience the 'greatest misfortune' in our Fatherland and beyond as a harbinger of the greatest happiness— because the time has come.

In deep grateful admiration and devotion
Yours, Hermann Beckh

Kiel, 23 July 1917

Highly esteemed Herr Dr

I have often wondered what the mirror in the 'Crystal-Ball' means, which shows the enchanted, ugly king's daughter in her true beauty. I think I can find the answer in the words of Theodosius in *The Portal of Initiation*, Scene 5: '*Love* will strengthen the soul so that it can become a *mirror* wherein is to be perceived what happens in the spirit-world.' In connection with this, my sister reminds me of the saying of Paul in the chapter on love: 'For now we see only a reflection as in a *mirror*; then we shall see face to face' (1 Cor. 13:12).

Much that is surprising (besides the obvious) can also be found in comparing Goethe's 'Fairytale of The Beautiful Lily' with the Rosicrucian dramas. The Lily, whose eyes deprive living beings of their strength, and whose touching hand kills, speaks of how every reed they break and plant on the grave of a favourite one immediately extends green shoots and mounts up high. In the language of the Rosicrucian dramas, this becomes the words of Benedictus to Maria ([*Portal of Initiation*] Sc. 3)

Der Geist in dir, er wirkt in allem
Was für das Reich der Ewigkeit
An Früchten reifen kann im Menschenwesen
Ertöten muss er darum vieles
Was nur dem Reich des Zeitenseins gehören soll.
Doch seine Todesopfer
Sind Saaten der Unsterblichkeit.
Dem höheren Leben muss erwachsen
Was aus dem niedern Sterben blüht.

The Spirit in you works in everything
which in man's being can grow ripe
as harvest for eternity.
Therefore much must be killed by it
which should belong only to temporal being.
And yet these deaths of sacrifice
are seeds of immortality.
There grows into a higher life
The blossom from the lesser death,
[Tr. Adam Bittleston, *The Four Mystery Dramas*, RSP 1982, p. 55]

(The green shoots of the Beautiful Lily)?—The mirror also plays a role in Goethe's Fairytale (with the hawk); one can probably interpret it there as in the Crystal-Ball?

With the key to *Faust* that you once pointed out to me, I think it was something like that (according to Jakob Böhme) [sketch]. I put a lot of effort into it. Does one get the right idea when one thinks of the eye, the prism, Goethe's *Farbenlehre*, and everything to which the *Farbenlehre* opens up access?

Finally, because of the deep impression I received from it, I would like to cite a saying from Novalis, a thought that has the effect of an occult sign, probably already approaching what Novalis calls the 'magic limit':

> Earth's specific gravity is almost that of a diamond. So, it is very probable that the earth is a diamond internally—which is also very probable for other reasons.

> The Earth and especially the precious stones are the most scorched bodies? Consequently, so water-like ...
> Burning much makes you more and more combustible.

With feelings of grateful devotion
your devoted
Hermann Beckh

Kiel, 31 August 1917
Kirchenstrasse 9.

Highly esteemed Herr Doktor!

Forgive me for picking up the pen again, but I feel compelled to speak out about something that was only touched upon briefly at the last meeting in Berlin but not fully addressed. I mean the case of Dessoir [Max Dessoir [1867-1947], philosopher and psychologist]. That this man, after all the infamous things he has done in his book (which I have only just seen) could allow himself to quote the two 'small volumes' on Buddha's teachings with a kind of patronizing benevolence, depresses me greatly; and even if I am subjectively blameless in the whole matter from the ordinary, trivial point of view, deep down I feel it as a serious reproach, an objective guilt, and I would gladly do everything to wash this stain out of my existence. I do not feel flattered by Dessoir's concoction, but rather hurt in the most severe way, especially one of his comments—I mean the one where something is said about 'smell' etc.—is the absolutely meanest and dirtiest thing I have come to know and experience in my whole life, compared to which everything that one knows in the so-called lower spheres of life in terms of dirt and meanness can be called harmless. Such meanness cannot be explained by being a professor alone, but only by the fact that Dessoir pursues his own lower occult aspirations under the guise of his academic position, which then leads him to look with enmity on higher aspirations, towards everything that has to do with Christ. As far as I can tell, D[essoir] is not particularly well respected among his colleagues and, as far as I know, they are quite dismissive of his efforts. It is understandable that an academic, if he is completely stuck in the materialistic-mechanistic thinking of the present, does not acquire 'occult science', cannot do anything with [Ancient] Saturn, Sun and Moon, because he does not want to muster the necessary soul-work, he will then, if he calls a remnant of distinction his own, just let these things lie to the side and let it be. But to trespass on it in such an impertinent and foolish way as Dessoir does deserves a thunderbolt from above; one really must be deserted of all good spirits to be able to contrive to speak of the most sacred affairs of mankind in such a tone. There is not a word to be said about the superficiality and instability of Dessoir's working method; it is the worst thing that has ever happened to me in this way (also the way in which he copies and writes out the two little Göschen volumes about Buddha is a pure annoyance). And how bad and disgusting is the whole style of the book. It is a shame for the university; you almost feel it is an impertinence still to strive for an academic position. Perhaps for higher reasons it is nevertheless good and necessary to do such a thing, because after all it could and should also have a positive effect. So, a higher sense of duty will have to decide here. But I don't need such positions for myself; I could imagine that after the war I would find a job that would correspond to my current occupation more focused on the external, practical side, and that I would feel just as comfortable or more comfortable with it, and would be entirely there for theosophical striving; it would not matter with any outer activity, because that continues in every case. I have found that an outer activity directed more towards the periphery of life is even valuable here in a certain sense, because the concentration on such opposites creates strong will-forces that can then be transformed again, bringing benefits and flow to the spiritual [matters]. Novalis also expresses himself in a similar way in one of his *Fragments* and it is not too difficult to make a practical test of all this. Especially my current time in Kiel has been extremely rich in practical results in this direction; I have never experienced such strong evidence of direct contact with the spiritual world; it went as far as the incidents and entanglements of the physical plane. This gives one great confidence for one's personal destiny as well as for the destiny of the world. I have only one wish that I may once again be able to work wholeheartedly on our spiritual endeavours, regardless of whether this work is done on the basis of an academic, an economic or any other profession. I have to fight so hard for all things in life and would have to fight hard for this too. But at some point, the time will come when cooperation—also in the higher sense of the word—will be achieved.

In the deepest and warmest
grateful respect and devotion
Hermann Beckh

---

10 Aug. 1919

[From G. K-B, *H.B.: Life and Work*, TL 2021, p. 115:]

Until now I was only connected to the dying spiritual life of the university. How I would like to serve that which wants to grow and develop! Yet I'm still far from it.

[From G. K-B, *H.B.: Life and Work*, TL 2021, p. 119:]

In my answer I pointed to meditation and eurythmy (considering the roots of Sanskrit and Indo-Germanic languages roots in the context of eurythmy. The revelation of the visual content of the individual sounds through eurythmy has already appeared to me as a grateful task of research for a long time); the concrete task wished for by Herr Hahn, however, I could not establish because he has not yet indicated with what he is concerned. If it were possible for him to give some specific indications, it would be a pleasure for me to be able to serve him with the results of my studies (as far as such were possible within the intellectually stifling atmosphere of the University). How grateful I would welcome this if it were possible for me on this path to receive guidelines indirectly through you for an anthroposophical orientation of linguistic studies. For precisely an occult understanding of the *word* perhaps more than anything else could lead into the depths of the spirit-realm. 'In the primal beginning was the word ...', still before I knew anything of meditation and anthroposophy, with this saying something of the essence of meditation opened up when I experienced it in the loneliness of the mountains.

Stuttgart
13 January 1924
Urachstr. 41

Highly esteemed Herr Doktor!

Still full of the impressions of the consecrated experiences for human-ity in Dornach at Christmas, I cannot help but ask you now to grant me admission to the First Class of the School of Spiritual Science in Dornach. After all the serious twists and turns of destiny, especially in the last few years, my life has come to the point that it can only feel meaningful if it is allowed to sacrifice itself to the spirit and put itself in the service of human work, as is being striven for in Dornach. Whether I will one day be allowed to work in Dornach is a question that probably does not need to be discussed today. For the time being, I am grateful for the guidance that brought me to Stuttgart, where I can hope that I will always succeed, besides the religious work also increasingly to grow into the anthroposophical work (as you have already begun with the Class lectures at the Waldorf School during the last trimester). I find the possibility of spiritual exchange with everyone involved in anthroposophical work to be indescribably valuable. And I have the feeling that these people, like those who work for our cause in Dornach and elsewhere, but first and foremost you, dear Doctor, have my whole love.

With deep gratitude,
devotion and respect,
Dr Hermann Beckh

Stuttgart
13 March 1924

Urachstrasse 41

I would like to add just a few lines to the short letter from my sister, who, after surviving a difficult operation, is still unable to use her right hand and sent you her request for admission to the First Class [written] with her left hand. I wrote to you a long time ago about my request for admission to the First Class. I very much hope that when I come to Dornach with my sister at Easter, we can take part in the work of the Class and in the evening lectures. In addition, I would like to ask for advice for my further anthroposophical (literary and lecture) work, perhaps also a criticism of my little work on the Imaginations of Gen-esis, which I will probably have published by then, the Foreword for which I presented in Dornach.

Finally, when I come to Dornach, I would like to ask you for advice on how I can shape my collaboration in the religious movement most fruitfully for the advantage of both movements, since their mutual relationship could and should always be much more harmonious. Many, including myself, still have a lot on their minds in this direction.

With deep respect,
Dr Hermann Beckh

———————————

Stuttgart
6 June 1924

Most esteemed Herr Doktor

May I dare to hand you the small, light green book that has just arrived from the press, the proofs of which you have already seen in Bern. Nothing essential has been changed, only in the chapter on the Fall of man a naming has been removed that could have hurt somebody who is still living. Certainly, much of what is said in the book and the manner in which it is said can be criticized. I would be grateful if you have the opportunity, to give me a hint about this, perhaps through Herr Steffen. It is precisely the recognition of our mistakes that helps us further. Inspired by the desire to integrate my work into the overall anthroposophical work, I suffer from the inadequacy of previous attempts. I have had so much in life—law and philology, State and University—*behind* me that I would like to have something *before* me now. It is depressing for the soul not to find the real full connection to the longed-for spiritual work. For me, the whole meaning of my future life lies in this possibility of working together properly. Is it immodest in this situation if I ask you, dear Doctor, to give me certain hints and advice, as you have already done with many others, on how I should best integrate into the overall work all the karmic aspects of my work for anthroposophy and The Christian Community? Is it right to stand as a priest in a predominantly scientific or literary work, or should more outer priestly work be sought? So far, for Rittelmeyer in Stuttgart I have been working more in a literary capacity, but at the same time, out of a certain inner urge, I've also been active as a priest in some of Heisler's[42] congregations. My relationship to the *word* also resulted in my relationship to the ritual and priesthood as a result of destiny. At the same time, I felt and I feel that it was more natural for me to continue working in the anthroposophical field. In the little book, *Der Ursprung im Lichte* [*Our Origin in the Light*], which I have now published on behalf of The Christian Community, anthroposophical viewpoints and those of worship come together. The Foreword tries to give an account of this.

And here, where it is a question of scientific-literary work, anthroposophical and religious work, I would like to dare to ask you to point out certain *topics* to me, the pursuing of which you would consider appropriate and fruitful from a spiritual point of view. I want to work in a direction that is in the spirit of the new Mystery Centre, [a direction] which from there is felt to be right for me and for the cause. I do not want to lose the great impulse of the Christmas Conference, which I experienced so strongly at the time. Perhaps it is at least possible for you to say something orally to me at some meeting in the near future, or to have something communicated to me through others, perhaps Herr Steffen, in whom I have always had such great confidence. It has long been on my heart to ask you such things. Because it is just terribly difficult to find the right thing, standing so lonely and apart without the advice of the spiritual teacher. I have always sought the relationship with others from within myself. With the Waldorf School [Stuttgart] in particular I am linked through many threads of spiritual connection and personal friendship. It is my wish and my longing to find the outer connection here with regard to future work and collaboration in much larger numbers. From this point of view, wouldn't it be possible to be allowed to take part in the sessions on the Dornach Class Lesson, in which the other local priests are now also taking part? Priests and teachers would thus come into ever more intimate communion. After I had the privilege of being admitted to the First Class around Easter and experiencing a large number of esoteric lessons— the full text—in Dornach and Bern, the desire to stay in some further connection with this work is more obvious. Is it wrong to express this wish in this way? Anyway, it is hard not to carry this wish in one's heart.

In grateful and reverent devotion,
Dr Hermann Beckh

CELEBRATION: APPRECIATIONS

Memories of Hermann Beckh
On the 30th Anniversary of his death (1967)[43]
Rudolf Meyer

On the evening of 1 March 1937 our colleague, Prof. Dr Hermann Beckh departed from us. A peaceful death released him from his sickbed he occupied for several months. He was the first of the founding group of The Christian Community who passed over the threshold of death. But he was not only known as a priest of a new Christianity, but in further parts of the scholarly world he was also known for his brilliant spiritual gifts and his publications.

It may be permitted to sketch a picture drawn from personal memories of this important scholar and courageous searcher for the spirit. It was Easter 1918 when I heard his name for the first time during the holidays from my studies. 'The way you experience anthroposophy always reminds me of the private tutor Dr Beckh,' someone said, whom I met in a gathering. 'You definitely have to meet him; he works at the moment in Kiel.' I answered, 'I actually have to travel back to Kiel in order to sit my theological exam. Somehow I might be able to bump into him.' When I had returned to Kiel I was at first not able to find his address. One day, in a bookshop I met a gentleman who asked the young man serving, 'Can you order for me the complete works of Novalis?' 'Yes,' said the bookseller, 'I will send them to you, Herr Doktor.' After he had gone, I asked the bookseller who the gentleman was who had ordered the Novalis. 'That was Dr Beckh, university tutor from Berlin.' I asked for his address and visited him in his modest accommodation. Whoever knew Hermann Beckh knows what the name Novalis meant for him. It was a cue, or clue, through which we found each other in a big town without any other point of connection. I believe that with this cue we will meet again in future on this or another planet.

Hermann Beckh at that time appeared as a small, very ascetic appearing scholar (photo, H.B. 1919). In the Institute for 'Shipping and World Commerce' founded by Bernhard Harms he had to carry out during the latter part of the War a kind of inland service for he was not

Meyer, 1922

fit for service at the Front. Thus he sat from morning to evening in the office and had to extract financial reports and statistics from Scandinavian papers. Because he was able within a short time to learn on demand any language, he was useful in that internationally oriented concern for business economics. In a very short time, he had to adjust to the Nordic languages, which hitherto were completely foreign to him. And he succeeded. In his free hours, beside this he learnt Hebrew. He already confirmed during our first conversation what a deep happiness he felt in experiencing this language. Until then he only knew the Indo-Germanic group of languages, especially everything belonging to its Indological subject. 'I have made a great detour,' he confessed to me. 'Actually, I have failed in my profession,' he said in a painful mood. He had given himself to the study of Sanskrit, 'because I was searching in the *East* for the true light'. This was after he had given up a promising career in law, because he had to pass sentence according to the book of law, against which his conscience rebelled.

But he was just beginning his teaching career when he experienced in Berlin how this 'true light' had arisen in direct proximity, in *Middle Europe*. He told me of a lecture that Rudolf Steiner had held in December 1911 in the Architects' House before the Berlin public on 'The Prophet Elijah in the Light of Spiritual Science' [in GA 61]. This lecture brought for him the inner decision. The figure of Elijah, the herald of the ascending Christ-Impulse in human history, signified for Hermann Beckh the turning point of his spiritual striving. From this moment he longed for a profession that might lead him completely to the research and proclamation of the wisdom of the Bible. Outwardly there was initially nothing like this; he envied me my theological studies, as he always said. Yet he was involved in another occupation at that time, and how could he at 43 years old once again change profession!

At that time his two Buddha-books appeared in the Göschen Series [1916]. They presented a first attempt to carry the light of Western spiritual research into the sacred traditions of Eastern wisdom. And in such a way that which was presented would also be acknowledged by the representatives of academic Sanskrit research. It was also acknowledged in many fields at the time and appreciated by the professionals. (*Buddha und seine Lehre* was published in a new edition by Verlag Freies Geistesleben 1958/1998/2012.)

And yet Beckh's inner striving turned now to the sources of the Old Testament and the Christian Bible. 'It is the happiest time of my life,' he confessed to me in those days. A rich world inwardly belonging to him opened up ever more tangibly before his restlessly searching spirit. We led the most fruitful conversations. I picked him up at lunchtime from the Institute and we walked part of the way home together. Also, during the evenings when we met with friends, one evening remained unforgettable. Before some friends he for the first time illuminated 'Snow White' through spiritual science. The inner feeling of the spiritual experience when he spoke of those pure paradisal childlike forces of the soul to which the name Snow White points was for us deeply impressive. The inner mobility with which he was able to lead into the understanding of the fairytale pictures, as well as in general into the Imaginative life, in itself possessed awakening force. I am indebted to this evening for significant impulses. To me it was as if the world of fairytales that I loved so much started from now on to speak. From that autumn 1918 my own fairytale research began which in a special sense became the gate into spiritual realities.[44]

In those days Hermann Beckh already lived deeply in the picture of John's Apocalypse. The outer events of the time drew us to interpret life in apocalyptic terms. For we experienced in Kiel the collapse after the First World War. A great spiritual earnestness, as if out of a deep depression ever again raising itself towards victorious spiritual light, gave its own stamp to the whole thinking and speaking of Dr Beckh in those destiny-laden times.

Soon after his outer activity became significant when he began to hold lectures on linguistics in the context of spiritual science conferences. In autumn 1920 we met again when we were both invited to give lectures to the opening of the first Goetheanum in Dornach. His Sanskrit lectures, the way, for example, he developed those Indian primordial words *brahma* and *atman*, compared to the usual philology appeared to me as a freeing gesture. In the same way the later individual lectures on etymological and genetical language were in part published. (They have been republished by me, three lectures collected under the title *Neue Wege zur Ursprache*, Stuttgart: Urachhaus 1954. [Eng. tr. *The Source of Speech*, TL 2019].) I know of many young students of those years, how much stimulation and enthusiasm of the experience and research into language they gained through those lectures. One could again become a real lover of the 'Logos', that is, of the Mystery of the word, a 'philo-logos'! And one could feel the world-creative formative forces of the sounds and syllables. Could one now not be able to believe again that the Word has created all things? Through this Beckh's language-research flowed into biblical research. The lecture 'Let there be light' ('*Yehi ôr*'), which is also printed in the above-mentioned book, about the original language forms the introduction to this.

During that time Prof. Beckh, who in the meantime had been offered a Professorship for Tibetan studies, extracted himself from the official University career. He who seemed so much pre-destined for the academic activities no longer found in these years of the urging spiritual renewal the inner possibility to allow his forces to be enthralled in an abstract concern with scholarship. What he strove for in everything that he had begun to present of new thoughts that came to him in abundance seemed to come to fulfilment within the Movement for Religious Renewal. At the beginning of 1922 he met the group in Berlin who were preparing the founding of The Christian Community. As a 'lover of the Word' he gave in deepest earnestness all his forces of devotion to the new word of the ritual. His priestly activities received a unique effect through the mantic strength of the language as it was carried out by him. The primordial power of his experience of language, the truthfulness for which he strove so intensively in laying hold of the spiritual content, penetrated the spiritual word. Through this fullness of revelation, one always felt enriched. From his fullness of wisdom, a first generation of priest candidates could draw the strongest stimulations, especially when during the courses at the Priests' Seminary, Stuttgart, he presented the great harmony of all religions and attempted to awaken in his listeners the organ for reading the spiritual documents of humanity. As the ripest fruits of these activities, we still have today the two translations of Indian texts: *The Departure of the Perfected One* and *The Hymn to the Earth* (a kind of song of praise from the Atharvaveda, witnessing to a primordial Aryan confirmation of existence). Professor Beckh was concerned to bring to light the precursors of the revelation of Christ and with this to give Christianity itself a universal stamp.

If one had the possibility to listen to this genuine sound in his word, then many other things that sometimes disturbed the one or other listener appeared inessential. It seemed as if the bodily vessel was not quite able to contain such abundance of wisdom and weight of experience. And Hermann Beckh suffered tremendously at times finding it difficult to be able to incarnate

Meyer in later years

his spiritual individuality into the culture of our time. It was consequently redemptive and a blessing for him when he was able to pass over from the power of experience of the word into experience of musical sound, into the realm of music. My last meeting with him in Urachstrasse 41—there he dwelt humbly in the attic flat—brought us a peaceful, beautiful hour when he sang for me in an indicative manner at the piano his setting of 'The Roses of Damascus'. In the symbolism of the seven roses that blossom out of the wooden cross all his spiritual striving is contained. The Mystery of Christianized blood, as it is also represented in Wagner's *Parsifal* that he experienced so deeply and explained, he wanted to reveal in music by setting the poem by Conrad Ferdinand Meyer. All seriousness of his spiritual strivings, all the tenderness of his world of feelings, flowed into those verses that seemed to him to glorify this Mystery of the Christian path. He sang the verses of 'The Roses of Damascus' as a true pupil of the Rosy-Cross.

Mit Rosen will ich drum zu Tisch, mit Rosen schlummern gehn,
Mit Rosen steigen in die Gruft, mit Rosen auferstehn!

So will I die with roses and slumber with roses,
with roses descend into the grave, with roses resurrect!

A Memory of Hermann Beckh

Harro Rückner

Die Christengemeinschaft. 33. Jg. Nr. 1. Jan. 1961. 30f. On the occasion of the reissue [1960] of *Der Hingang des Vollendeten* and *Hymnus an die Erde*.

It was 1925. On the Dornach hill, in a truly paradisal garden full of trees, a group of mostly young theologians gathered. Seeing them sitting there in the grass in the Paryanka position, holding themselves upright with effort, the older ones using apple trees to support their backs, one could be reminded of the words of Gautama, with which the Tathagata greeted the meadow of Vesali. 'Charming, Ananda, is Vesali, charming the sacred grove of the rising daylight, charming the sacred meadow of Gautama, charming the grove of the seven mango trees …'

But most of the theologians gathered there did not yet know these words, yet they were to get to know them now, for, after studying some serious questions of the history of religion a short breathing space appeared. Out of the group of 'apprentices of a new priesthood', appearing very young, there arose a man of middle age who, with a somewhat abrupt movement of his arms, pulled out of his voluminous pockets a bunch of papyrus leaves—well, no, they were printer's proofs of a book about to be published—and with a booming voice proclaimed he had to give us now some wisdom from a unique product of the human spirit, of a work of extraordinary beautiful language and primordial power, of a document of highest wisdom and deepest humanity.

The leader of the gathering enthroned under an apple tree like a teacher of wisdom, a certain Lic. Emil Bock, allows a softly resigned, mildly excusing, yet friendly smile on his Jove-like countenance, commanding indulgence. Encouraged by this, without properly waiting until everybody had settled themselves on the grass and placed themselves again in Paryanka position, our dear Professor Beckh began, not in German but in resonant Pali, to recite the third chapter of the *Hingang des Vollendeten* [*The Departure of the Perfected One*] with the same booming voice with which he had made his announcement, bringing to sound the magic, mantric quality of this solemn text with its rhythmic emphases.

Whereas initially you understood not a word, apart from some names, you felt a mighty primordial stream of words flowing over you; it was suddenly as if a veil would be torn away. You realized the good fortune of witnessing a miracle of language; now the German translation had the effect of a direct unveiling of the original, and like a mysterious song, better said like a bardic song, sounded in our receptive ears, 'Charming, Ananda, is Vesali, charming the sacred groves of the rising daylight, ...'

Suddenly Beckh's voice changed a little, without, however, losing the streaming rhythm. And so there sounded now a stern admonition, 'Whosoever, Ananda, awakens in themselves and develops the four elements of supernatural power through meditation, who knows how to move in them, realizes them essentially within himself, who masters their methods, has become strong through exercise in them and has completely mastered them, if he only wanted, could constantly remain for an age of the world on the earth, or for the rest of the world ages ...'

Thus Prof. Beckh read the whole passage in order, speaking in the same intonation, speaking on as though allowing the Pali-Sanskrit to sound, to show how at this place the Christ-Impulse and the Buddha-Wisdom meet very closely, but how precisely in this narration of Vesali the tragedy of Buddhism is revealed. The great world-teacher can point to the secret of change; he knows the law of renewing substance, but a Greater than him was to come, Who was not dependent on whether an Ananda understood Him or not, but out of His divine freedom decides to sacrifice Himself on Golgotha.

Some of the 'Vesali-apprentices' on that occasion wanted a repeat of this reading with Prof. Beckh. After 35 years, as one hears of the announcement of a new edition of *Hingang des Vollendeten* from Urachhaus, there appears in recollection to the writer of these lines that image of the wish that this work would be available to relate to a later generation something of the Mystery—'Buddha and Christ'. He rejoices to see that the publisher has included as an Introduction a substantial part of Beckh's *From Buddha to Christ*. Now it is up to the reader to create a Vesali-occasion, in which he can receive the key to understand in the Introduction and Afterword, and to bring the [Pali] text of the Mahaparinibbanasutta itself to sound for himself and others.

This method of 'making it sound aloud', however, also applies to another work of Prof. Beckh's from the same publisher, appearing in time for Christmas, with the *Hymnus an die Erde*. In this unique work, Beckh himself gives us an illuminating Introduction. Moreover, Dr Lauenstein takes the opportunity in an Afterword to sketch an exceptionally impressive picture of Prof. Beckh's personality and spiritual calibre. He also shows by comparing the translation of the Orientalist and the poet Friedrich Rückert, how Beckh's translation is a first-rate linguistic creation.

The present writer is impressed, alongside the Hymn itself, mostly by the deep devotion with which Hermann Beckh ponders on Christ's Being and Name, and how he finds in the Sanskrit a spiritually related word that expresses this title in Greek at a still deeper level. In truth, our dear, unforgettable Hermann Beckh has presented us for Christmas 1960 with the most beautiful gifts for which we could wish. They appear in a very beautiful outer dress, and it only rests with us to make use of this extraordinary gift.

From Memories of H.B.

Eduard Lenz[45]

 … As a priest, Beckh searched especially for the super-earthly Mysteries of Christ; he wanted to know how Christ had descended out of starry heights to the Earth in order to unite with suffering humanity. His two books on *Mark's Gospel: The Cosmic Rhythm* and *John's Gospel: The Cosmic Rhythm—Stars and Stones* are completely penetrated by this striving for knowledge. They also show his love for the stars, which meant more to him than physical balls of gas.

But besides this, Beckh was also enthused by a special inclination towards music. He wrote the important study concerning the spiritual essence of the musical keys, which gave rich stimuli to many lovers of music, but here too it was the Christian element he sought in the realm of musical sounds. Rudolf Steiner's remark that the deepest being of Christ in the future can only be expressed through music[46] pointed him towards this realm. And so Beckh mainly followed the Christian impulse in the life's work of Wagner. His book on Wagner's *Parsifal* eloquently witnesses to these strivings. And his last work looking at the development from Bach to Wagner that he wrote still on his sickbed concerns his beloved music.

For months Beckh patiently carried the pains of his illness. When he was allowed a few minutes of quiet contemplation, he continued writing his book. It is wrested from pain. Still during the last days of his life he read through the proofs. As an active, creative spirit right to the end, he went through the portal of death.

Masaryk once said that he hoped to meet in his life after death the spirit of Plato and Goethe to speak with them on the Mysteries of the other world. In this sense we could quite well imagine that the soul of Hermann Beckh will find the genius of Wagner to whom his love in the field of music was devoted. Perhaps the two spirits of a sublime order will exchange their divining how in the future of human development the divine Mystery of Christ, which they are allowed to behold face to face, can be conveyed through the power of musical sound.

Memories of H.B.[47]

Reinhardt Wagner

If I think about when in my life I have especially strongly experienced the personality of our dear Prof. Beckh, then three pictures stand before my soul. The first is in Berlin, the Conference of The Christian Community in February 1935. Beckh is speaking about Zarathustra. Before him sit some elderly gentlemen, obviously from the University. Prof. Beckh spoke. While he is speaking, he looks constantly to these old gentlemen, especially when he emphasizes that this or that he was already able to proclaim during his time as a Professor. Here was a scholar driven by inner fire, who had pulled himself out of the deadness of the institutional side of the University, now looking back with a certain sadness to his previous colleagues, who are now, however, so distant to him, because they were not able to go with him on his courageous path into the new world.

The second picture took place in the Priests' Seminary, Stuttgart, in those days still on the ground floor of Urachhaus. Beckh spoke about Buddha and mentioned his little book that had just appeared, *The Departure of the Perfected One*. At our request he read for us a passage of the original text. What one did not believe possible—the completely strange language sounds extraordinarily effective, directly proclaiming the event of which they speak. Later I heard that Beckh would have been the only European scholar who could rhythmically read Sanskrit and Pali in the original. Consequently, in 1928 the Schopenhauer Society had called him to Dresden. This, however, was not his strongest moment, but something different. We experienced there a scholar who was so modest that we were not always quite aware of the disparity between us, especially because he showed a slowly increasing absent-mindedness that almost became embarrassing for us. One day we experienced Beckh entering to celebrate The Act of Consecration, his hands clasped before him. In the session that took place the same morning he referred to this event. He said, that during the last weeks he must have given an impression unworthy of a priest and an a. [= anthroposophist—since the Anthroposophical Society had been forbidden, this word was not written in full—*Note by the German editor*]. This is connected with work of the deepest nature. During that morning, all this culminated in an unspeakably real experience of 'the Chalice', so that he entered the room with the quite real feeling of carrying a chalice in his hands. Since then I can say we not only admired Prof. Beckh, but also loved him with the feeling that he has given us something quite holy.

The third picture is of a Memorial Service. It was the first I experienced; [with it] that quality of Beckh that certainly many are grateful to him about which in the normal course of life one does not speak but only where together one remembers such a dear friend. When he spoke the inserted words, it was as if one would be taken up into the world about which they spoke. What it means really to be led to the portal of death, on the wings of a masterly crafted speech out of the mouth of a spirit-imbued mouth—this was the gift of this first Memorial Service.

When last Saturday I held the Memorial Service for him all this became alive in me and I knew: this friend will especially strongly help us in everything that will lift up our souls into the other world in which he now dwells.

In Memoriam: Hermann Beckh (1875-1937)

Alfred Heidenreich[48]

A year ago, on 1 March, 1937, Hermann Beckh, priest of The Christian Community, passed into the other world in his 62nd year. Of the forty-five original priests, who in 1922 founded The Christian Community, he was the first to cross the threshold of death. If we write in memory of him, we must describe a life that showed in a very remarkable degree along what extraordinary paths and ways someone may be led to find the spirit.

The Scholar

In his youth he was a very brilliant lad. He had received the rare distinction of receiving his education at the 'Maximilianeum' in Munich where the twelve best students of every year, together with a small group of specially selected sons of the old aristocratic families—at the expense of the state—were trained for a public career. Beckh specialized in law, soon acquired the degree of a Doctor of Law and, still very young, was appointed a junior judge. His office, however, increasingly became a source of great worry to him. He had to sentence when he wished to help. Eventually the tension of conscience was too great. He resigned and began to devote himself completely to a world which had increasingly become his real interest—ancient Asia. With his thoroughness of mind, he started again from the beginning. He went back to University as a student, took a degree as Doctor of Philosophy, and soon his second career promised to be as brilliant as his first. He became in turn lecturer and then Professor of Oriental languages at the University of Berlin. In those years he also spent some time in England, studying Tibetan manuscripts at the British Museum, in connection with the first Tibetan dictionary that he had begun to publish. From these occasions, which were his first and last visits to England, he treasured a great interest in all that was English.[49]

About the same time, shortly before the War, he also met Dr Rittelmeyer [the first *Erzoberlenker* of The Christian Community]. In an appreciation which he wrote on Beckh's death in the German journal of The Christian Community [*Die Christengemeinschaft*], Rittelmeyer says that he found Beckh disappointed with organized Christianity and very suspicious of it.

He was, however, full of original knowledge in the most varied provinces of scholarship. This knowledge was not so much gained on the well-trodden ways to an ambitious academic goal, but on the paths of an untiring and original search for truth and, above all, the living spirit. This combination of recognized and acknowledged scholarship and a quite personal striving for the living spirit was characteristic of him. In this respect nobody in Germany, near and far was comparable to him. For the sake of his spiritual aims, he learned, even at an advanced age, and with an amazing energy, Persian, Egyptian, Syriac and Hebrew in addition to the languages with which he had been familiar from his student days: Latin, Greek, Sanskrit, Tibetan, French, English and Italian. Everywhere he strove for the highest—the revelation of the spirit in its earthly reflection. He followed up the traces of the light of the spirit in all races and nations.

About the same time as Rittelmeyer, he found Rudolf Steiner. He was deeply drawn into anthroposophy and became one of Steiner's personal pupils. It was through Steiner that he learned to see the meaning and reality of Christianity. 'It is quite certain,' says Rittelmeyer, 'that he would not have found Christ without Rudolf Steiner, but he found Him through him in a magnitude that made the whole world translucent.'

When the first preparations were made for the foundation of The Christian Community and Beckh heard of them, he was almost annoyed that he had not been invited from the very beginning to take part. We, on our part, did not think, of course, that 'the Professor' would come and join us. But he did ['I belong with you,' he said. He joined] with all the zeal and enthusiasm of his character. When it became clear that the priesthood in The Christian Community required the whole of a person's work for the rest of his life, and consequently involved for him the resignation from his position at the University, he did not hesitate for a moment. It meant, of course, also a complete financial sacrifice. He had no income besides his salary as a professor, which ended with his resignation. Whatever private means he may have had he lost, as all Germans, through inflation of the Mark. His resignation left him literally penniless, with an aged mother and a sister dependent on him. He took the risk, in the full confidence of the full necessity and momentous significance of the new Movement.

When the time for his resignation from the University came, he discussed with Dr Rittelmeyer the best form it should take. They both came to the conclusion that it would be the right thing for Beckh to announce a lecture at the University and give a full and public explanation for his decision. Beckh had just published a two-volume work on Buddhism, *Buddha und seine Lehre* (1916. Eng. tr. *Buddha's Life and Teaching*, 2016), in a somewhat popular form. These volumes, which are still reckoned among the standard works on Buddhism in the German language, had considerably enhanced his esteem among his colleagues, and had also made him known, for the first time, to the general public. One should have expected, consequently, that Beckh's lecture would have attracted a great and interested if not sympathetic audience.

What actually happened was tragically typical of the academic life of Germany at the time (1922). Beckh's lecture was boycotted. Not one of his colleagues attended. The audience consisted of several students, a few casual listeners, and members of the Anthroposophical Society. To speak publicly for Rudolf Steiner in those years meant to be morally struck off the register of the intellectual society of Germany. Beckh henceforth was labelled and ostracized. Although he was not the only one who had to suffer this fate—the way in which Dr Rittelmeyer was treated was very similar—it was at times more difficult to bear than the legal prohibition of certain anthroposophical activities in recent times. And few who saw through the intolerance and conceit of the leading academic circles of Germany after the War, could doubt that sooner or later fate would wield an iron broom.

Dr Rittelmeyer[50] writes of this event:

Beckh's lecture was a noble and magnificent challenge to the scholars of the première German University. But it was as if he had been held in a desert. In the future such an event will be regarded, practically unnoticed at the time, as a great historical question, a solemn test, a kind of decisive judgement over the intellectual and spiritual life of Germany at that time. The intellectual and spiritual life of Germany has failed and must bear the consequences. From then onwards Hermann Beckh was no more listened to. For them he was dead. All the more so, as he now began to live and write entirely out of his new knowledge and no longer cared for what the reactions would be. Among the many hundreds of scholars at the time he was the only one, the solitary one, who had found the way to the new spirituality; among the followers of Rudolf Steiner, he was the only scholar with an officially established reputation, and in particular with an unparalleled authority on the spiritual wealth of ancient India. This was his historic part and will be his for all time.

The Man

Those who know him only from his books may find it difficult to form a picture of the man Beckh. In his books he is the scholar and sometimes the prophet. But in his private life he had a great deal of the proverbial peculiarities of the German Professor. It was quite natural that to his death he was always known as 'Professor Beckh', even among his fellow-priests in The Christian Community, and invariably addressed as 'Herr Professor'. Shrewd as he was in general management of life, he was at times quite oblivious of circumstances and surroundings. It has been pointed out that this is only the other side of a life of great concentration. With him this certainly was the case, but it added greatly to the sometimes-bizarre charm of his personality. Many amusing stories were current of him. It could be rather embarrassing at times, to sit with him at a table in a restaurant or in a railway compartment where he would suddenly begin to lecture with a thunderous voice on his latest discoveries on Zarathustra. At his lectures he often had a pile of books on his desk, and those who knew his ways were always prepared for the moment when after a sudden enthusiastic jerk, the whole pile would tumble to the floor and Beckh make frantic efforts to collect them again. I remember him coming to a lecture with considerable traces of his supper of fried eggs still on his lips and chin. When this was pointed out to him, he began to lick and wipe his face with tremendous energy completely forgetting that he stood already on the rostrum. Rumour has it that when he once preached at Stuttgart his biretta worried him; and after several attempts to put it right he hurled it from him. Without, however, for a second stopping the magnificent flow of his address.

If one made deliberate fun of him, and at times this was very tempting, one would somehow regret it afterwards. He did not take offence, but he seemed curiously helpless in such moments. One loved him all the more for this because one would then suddenly have a glance into the great loneliness of his soul. He was not only a bachelor, but he was also at bottom a stranger almost to everyone in contemporary society.

At the depths of his being, he was like one of the wise Rishis of ancient India suddenly transplanted into completely uncongenial civilization. His nearest friends were little children and the mountains. In the first house of The Christian Community at Stuttgart he occupied three tiny attic rooms, and it was deeply moving to meet him occasionally in his study, with a baby of one or two years on his arm, explaining to him in the sacred tongue of ancient India the beautiful pictures of the Himalayas that hung round the walls. He knew the mountains not only from pictures. True to his Bavarian origin, he was a competent and fearless mountaineer who to the last year of his life would always go alone. After a difficult passage in the Bernese Oberland he was once overtaken by a storm and had to spend the night on a glacier. When he spoke of this experience one felt that he was happier among the giants of frost and snow than among human society.

You could receive the greatest impression of him as a lecturer when he read from the Holy Scriptures of the East in the original and in his translation. Of what is called the 'gospel of Buddha's Death', he published a German translation of very great poetical beauty. After this translation had appeared he went on a lecturing tour. He spoke on the 'Departure of the Perfected One' and recited the important passages in the ancient language and in his translation. I have heard once or twice in my life a cultured Indian singer recite some of the great texts of his religion. In comparison, Beckh had all the incantation and delivery of a native guru, but in addition to it also the clear vision and knowledge of the 'consciousness-soul'. To listen to him on such occasions was indeed an unforgettable experience.

His Work

A short review of his literary work will show that this extraordinary man possessed still other qualities. Such a review will best take its start from his two-volume [later editions one-volume] work on Buddha's life and teaching, mentioned above, his first work outside the precincts of the ordinary specialized academic periodicals. The success of this work was due to the different treatment of Buddhism which no one could fail to notice. Buddha's teaching was revealed as proceeding from the reality of a meditative life. Beckh proved even to the critical scholar that the Buddha never intended to develop a speculative system of metaphysical truths to answer 'ultimate questions', but that he wished his followers to pursue a path of inward experience where such 'ultimate questions' either lose significance or can only then be rightly put. From this viewpoint many things that Buddha said become clear, and why he left many things unsaid. Beckh's work displayed not only the competent knowledge of the scholar, but also a personal first-hand experience of meditative life which is normally strange, and even incomprehensible, to the ordinary Western mind.

After reading Beckh's *Buddha und seine Lehre* [1916/'28/'58/'98] one was tempted to become a Buddhist oneself. How tremendously real seemed the spirit of which the Buddha knew and spoke, compared with the anaemic spirituality of contemporary Christianity! But Beckh did not join the ranks of those who in despair over the decline of the West emigrated spiritually to the East. In less than seven years after the appearance of this fascinating presentation of Buddhism, Beckh became a Christian priest.

This was a representative deed. I do not know whether it ever occurred to Beckh himself, but this fact stands there in the spiritual history of our time as an opposite landmark to Annie Besant's [of the Theosophical Society] conversion to Hinduism, and to the change which the one-time Anglican priest Leadbeater made from Christianity to Buddhism. If Leadbeater later had himself again consecrated as a Bishop of the Old Catholic Church, it was not done from conviction but for other purposes.

Beckh's step from the Orientalist to the Christian priest was a process in reality. He achieved in himself the development which he had recognized as the spiritual order of evolution and which is the spiritual order of evolution. He saw Christ as the fulfiller of the Mysteries. The essence of this progress is contained in a volume entitled *Von Buddha zu Christus* (1925) [the English complete edition, *From Buddha to Christ*, TL 2019, replaces the earlier heavily abridged version by A.H.]. It is a small volume but indeed full of meaning. If one reads it one wonders at the ways of Providence. Had this book appeared in the English language, and outside the circle of what is still wrongly labelled as a 'sect', it might have become an event in the history of Oriental scholarship, and no doubt it would have had reactions in the East. One need only think of the many Christian missionaries who feel called to convert Buddhists into Christianity and are increasingly driven into the defensive, and of the many Indians and Chinese who look with a bewildered apprehension and suspicion and yet, in spite of everything, still with a secret expectation to the West. Here is a book written by a Western scholar who not only loved the East with a true and enthusiastic love but knew its sacred writings and understood their esoteric and even occult significance. And he showed the way from Buddha to Christ which he himself had gone. Providence has ordained that it remained comparatively unknown. Perhaps The Christian Community would not yet be strong enough to deal with the practical effects it might have, and to fulfil in practice the expectations it might arouse. And surely there is no other Christian body that could do this. Beckh himself did not see the missionary side of his work, I think. This was outside his province. In that respect he was just the German professor. To him, the East-West problem was a problem of consciousness and spiritual evolution. He knew all about Buddhism as a religion, he knew a great deal about the geography and spiritual climate of the East, but he knew hardly anything of the Indian people of today. I wonder whether they even interested him. In this attitude we have a striking example of the difference of the German and English genius which so obviously need each other as mutual historic supplements.

Heidenreich in 1972

After he had finally found his place in Christianity, Beckh turned to the study of other pre-Christian religions. He traced in them the cosmic reality of Christ in His approach to the earth and to incarnation. A monograph on *Zarathustra* appeared, followed by a book on Egypt, *Aus der Welt der Mysterien* (1927), [both contained in Eng. tr., *From the Mysteries*, TL 2020], with an especially impressive chapter on the figure of Isis and her relationship to the Virgin Mary. It was a matter of course that now he should also include the Old Testament in his studies, which until recently was the only recognized prophecy of Christ. If I remember rightly, the first public lecture which he gave, at the invitation of Rudolf Steiner, at the first public Conference in the first Goetheanum[51] was on the single sentence from Genesis, 'Let there be light'. He described certain primeval elements of sacred language, uniting philology and esoteric knowledge. Later he wrote a book on the hieroglyphic picture-language of Genesis, from the creation to Noah's rainbow, *Der Ursprung im Lichte* (1924), ['Our Origin in Light: Pictures from Genesis', in the triple volume *From the Mysteries* TL 2020]. His last work in connection with the Old Testament is a translation of the 23rd Psalm, done with extraordinary vision and beauty, which he himself also set to music. This little gem anticipates prophetically the future union of scholarship, art and religion.

This, however, is by no means the complete list of Beckh's works nor even a complete list of the provinces of learning in which he moved and was at home. In 1926 it was suggested to him that he speak at the International Summer Conference of The Christian Community at Freiburg on the true nature and significance of the cosmic rhythm in Mark's Gospel that Arthur Drews and others had discovered. This led Beckh to an investigation of the 'wisdom of the stars' which soon became a subject of absorbing interest to him. At that period Beckh hardly spoke of anything else, even in private conversation. The result of his exploration in the new land appeared in three successive books, *Der kosmische Rhythmus im Markus-Evangelium* (1928) [*Mark's Gospel: The Cosmic Rhythm*. Anastasi 2015, rev. tr. TL 2021], *Der kosmische Rhythmus, das Sternengeheimnis und Erdengeheimnis im Johannes-Evangelium* (1930) [*John's Gospel: The Cosmic Rhythm—Stars and Stones*. Anastasi 2015, rev. tr. TL 2021] and *Vom Geheimnis der Stoffeswelt: Alchymie* [*Alchymy: The Mystery of the Material World*. TL 2019]. Beckh succeeded in describing and proving down to small details how the composition of the gospels, particularly Mark's, is determined through the relationship of certain stellar constellations, in the main through the progress of the Sun through the zodiac. There are lines of indications in the New Testament which show that the sequence in which the events are described reflects the sequence of the positions of the Sun in its relationship to the signs of the zodiac. Drews had discovered the principle of it but drawn from this discovery the hasty conclusion that therefore Christ never existed historically and that the gospels were only 'astral myths'. Drews never reckoned in reality with a spiritual world which would manifest itself in the constellations and which would also as its own essence send Christ to the Earth. Beckh showed how the life of Christ was like a sacrament celebrated according to the ritual book of the heavenly constellations. Consequently, the gospels were books both of earthly and heavenly history, of historical and cosmic truth.

It may sound strange after all this that Beckh's last and most original province was music. He was not only a very good pianist who would play for hours his three great favourites, Bach, Wagner and Bruckner [as well as symphonies and other works arranged for piano duet with his friends, including Emil Bock, Rudolf Frieling and Alfred Heidenreich], but he was right when he once said, 'In all other respects I stand on the shoulders of my predecessors in scholarship, and my particular viewpoint I owe to Rudolf Steiner; but in music, I feel I am really breaking new ground.' Rudolf Steiner himself said of him in this respect,

'Beckh ventures into provinces which I have not yet had an opportunity of investigating myself. And there is a great deal in what Beckh says about them.' There are not many people of whom Rudolf Steiner would have made such a remark.

His first publication in the realm of music was on *Das geistige Wesen der Tonarten* (1922/25) [*The Essence of Tonality*, TL 2022] which soon ran into more than one edition. It was followed by *Das Christus-Erlebnis in Wagners 'Parsifal'* (1930) [The 'Parsifal' Christ-Experience, in the double volume with *The Essence of Tonality* and by his posthumous work, *Die Sprache der Tonarten* 1938/77/99, [*The Language of Tonality in Music from Bach to Bruckner*. Anastasi 2015, TL forthcoming]. This last work shows Beckh as a man who knew all the works of the classics, from the smallest Prelude to the great symphonies. He read the proofs for this book during the last weeks of his life and said once to a friend how happy he was 'to pass over with such wonderful realities'.

During the last years Beckh began also to write music himself. Several compositions of songs appeared, mainly of his favourite poems. Already on his sickbed he completed a series of compositions for The Act of Consecration of Man, following the seasons of the year, which can be performed either on the piano or by a small chamber group. His compositions are extraordinarily 'conscious' works, with a very deliberate use of the symbolic significance of key, interval and rhythm. They are nevertheless very 'musical' and not a bit artificial, which shows that this analysis of the essential musical elements was a discovery of realities.

Besides the scholar, he was a great 'character', who left besides his great works many small and quaint notes and jottings of a quite humorous and original nature, often found in letters to his friends. I shall venture to give a sample here which is actually contained in his last letter to me. He wrote it in the summer of 1936. The first signs of his illness appeared then but it was not yet established as malignant. Beckh sought recovery in his beloved Bavarian Alps. From there the letter is dated. One day, he says, his mind got fixed on a quotation from Wilhelm Busch, the great humorist and cartoonist dear to every German big and small. And one morning in bed, he hit on the idea of translating it into English. And now, this is characteristic of Beckh, he turned it over and over—he could 'ponder' over a thought—and made no fewer than seventeen translations. Here is the original German:

> *Ein Schlüsselloch wird leicht vermisst,*
> *Wenn man es sucht, wo es nicht ist.*

And here are the 17 translations:

1. A keyhole is missed easily—O great fatality when it is sought where you can't find it in reality.
2. An unsuccessful man, deceived by distance, looks for a keyhole there where it has no existence.
3. Who obstinately seeks a keyhole in wrong place, a man like this remains in all his efforts lacking grace.
4. A silly man is disappointed soon when he for earthly things is seeking in the Moon.
5. It will oftentimes for you a great distress when seeking nightly for a keyhole you can't find the place.
6. When after many efforts broken-hearted he could not find the keyhole, he at last departed.
7. All things are ordered well in time and space you never find a keyhole outside of its place.
8. O stupid man, how will you ever find a keyhole if you are for earthly matters blind.
9. Where is the keyhole now? It's really no jest, To be or not to be—this the great request.
10. It is a world of tears, you never must forget, when you are searching for a keyhole which you cannot get.
11. There is no help against. It's really all in vain, when you are searching for a keyhole which you can't obtain.
12. No problem is so difficult as this, when you are trying for a keyhole, and you try amiss.
13. I think it is a very hopeless game when with the keyhole you don't reach your aim.
14. For any keyhole—mind the solemn truth—will never try in vain a skilful youth.
15. The night was very cold, no keyhole could be found; the other morning lay a dead man on the ground.
16. The end is very sad and full of fate, a keyhole must be found before it is too late.
17. At last, for consolation take this principle, for an attentive man no keyhole is invincible.

Here you have a first-hand side-glimpse at Hermann Beckh, thoroughly thorough, even in making fun.

His last days

But this is not how we should take farewell of him. We must return once more to the centre of his personality. We cannot do this better than by quoting the concluding passages of what Dr Rittelmeyer wrote about him (*Die Christengemeinschaft* 1937), referring to the last days of Beckh's life.

> An exceptionally versatile and spiritually mobile man, ever active, living entirely in his own searching and striving, though allowing his friends most willingly to share it, he had now the task to lie still under pain, and to watch slowly his own death. With a vitality and strength of mind, which was incomprehensible to us, he studied for weeks while he hardly slept more than a quarter of an hour at night, the essential books which he had come across in his life. 'Either I shall die,' he said; 'then this is the best preparation, or I remain alive, then it is also the best I can do.' If one found him groaning and restive, tossing himself about on the pillows one need only touch on a subject which interested him, and at once he would begin with a voice, completely unimpaired, to speak and to extemporize almost a small lecture—and in the end he would say that his pains are now no more there. Only in the very last days this was different. Then he lay still in his bed and had texts of Rudolf Steiner, or the ritual of The Christian Community read to him. In the depths his thoughts, however, were occupied with himself, his own being and life, his relationship to people, his relationship to Christ, and we were allowed to listen at times to words of self-criticism but also of his passionate link with the spirit. We believed we saw something of the guidance of his angel, when, after a life of indefatigable activity, these hours of inward reflection were vouchsafed to him before his transition into a higher world.
>
> After suffering greatly for months, the passing was quiet and peaceful. When we celebrated the last rituals at his deathbed and at the coffin, it was as if a spirit full of peace filled the room. A unique scholar, a rare spiritual fighter, an inspired messenger of the spirit had finished his life and had written his name for ever into the stormy history of our time.

•

What prompted me to write this article was not only the pious duty to say at the first anniversary of his death something in memory of a fellow-priest and a great scholar. I felt that a picture of this personality, which is inseparably united with the foundation of our Movement, would show something of the compass of The Christian Community.

In this country we are in some ways separated through the barrier of language and geographical isolation from the whole of The Christian Community. This is inevitable but it might lead us to form our vision of the Movement only from what we see close at hand. That would obviously be incomplete. It is right for us that we should remind ourselves at times of the potential greatness of our Movement. We find this greatness indicated, in the first place, in the spiritual content of it, but it announces itself also in a tremendous variety and wealth of human character and human destiny which has flowed and is continually flowing into it. Last summer, at the 'World Conference for Faith and Order' in Edinburgh, the thought flashed through my mind that the foundation of our Movement is like a replica, in principle and on another plane, of what was attempted there. The aim of the Conference was to prepare the way for a reunion of the many historic sections of Christianity. The historic significance of The Christian Community with a view to the future is the fact that numberless currents of historic Christianity have at its foundation flowed together into one pool, as it were, and out of this inward amalgamation the nucleus of the united Church of the future has grown. Not only did the founders come together from the most varied sections of historic Christianity; it might even appear—if for once we may think in terms of repeated earth-lives—that men and women have united now who in another age were themselves the protagonists of separation. Hermann Beckh added to this union another and unique reality. In him those have joined us of whom it is said in the words of The Act of Consecration of Man that God received once 'the offerings of those who had not yet Christ'. Beckh has made room for them. May what was potentially contained in his life and work, and what has become part of the being of the Movement, come once to a glorious realization in the future life and activity of The Christian Community.

Decisive Experiences through Hermann Beckh

Wilhelm Hörner (1913-2013)
(*Die Christengemeinschaft*, March 1987, p. 104f.)

After the death of Prof. Hermann Beckh on 1st March 1937 [fifty years ago], some students of the Priests' Seminary helped to clear his flat. Each helper was allowed to take one of his books. The secretary chose the complete edition of Grimms' *Märchen*, the Fairytales. Still today, as my wife, she reads almost daily from this volume. I chose *Geheimwissenschaft im Umriss* [*Occult Science: An Outline*] by Rudolf Steiner. The book contained an abundance of marginalia, especially astronomical and alchemical signs and symbols; in addition, many pressed gentian flowers and rose petals.

This book accompanied me from the first day of the War 1939 in the field. I also took it with me to Crete. On the return journey of the South-East Army through the ravines and passes of the Balkans only the most essential things could be carried. In the hard winter of 1944/45 nearly all transport vehicles were inoperative. In the deep snows of the Karaula Pass, in order to be a good example I decided to lighten the load on the last transport vehicles, also to sacrifice the beloved book of Hermann Beckh's. The pressed gentians I took out and added to my Breviary carried on my person. Then I threw *Geheimwissenschaft* into the snow as far as my strength could reach. But when I saw this unique book lying there I had quickly to pick it up again. Once more I threw it far off; again, I took it up and for the third time I threw it out of the fast-moving vehicle. The separation from the valuable piece of memory stimulated an even stronger connection to the being of Hermann Beckh and his work.

At Beckh's coffin I had an experience that was decisive for my life. Coming from a study of theology at the University, I opted to join the wake. During the night from 2nd to 3rd March I was alone for some hours with our dear departed, who was lying in his flat in Urachhaus. Around the wall the scholar's high bookshelves reached the ceiling; where there were no books pictures covered the walls so closely that the walls were completely covered. But at his head there hung in a large reproduction his favourite picture, Botticelli's *The Birth of Venus*.

In this Beckh always saw the heavenly, virginal side of Venus-Urania. Through the heavenly beauty his inner experience was akin to what Goethe puts into words at the end of his *Faust*: 'Eternal Womanhood leads us above'.

In his book *John's Gospel: The Cosmic Rhythm*, Hermann Beckh describes this as follows [2015, 81; TL 2021, 55]:

> Nowhere does the connection of the Mysteries of Christianity with the pre-Christian Mysteries appear more deeply and significantly than where we look from the revelation of the sea of Venus-Aphrodite to *Mary*, the '*star of the sea*', where, in and behind the Christian Mary, the Christened Isis-Venus-Mystery is gently announced—the Mystery that in Rev. 12 has found its strongest, most revealing expression.

With these words the whole of human becoming is indicated. The mood of this event hovered as an inexpressible, tender and deepest breath of life in the room softly lit up by peaceful candles. Carried by such a mood I dared to make two simple sketches of the sublime countenance. But the decisive element of these hours was the real experience that all existence contains its deep meaning, humanity's aim, which includes each individual person with his/her pre-birthly and post-mortem existence. The decision to become a priest—concerning myself—was taken here.

As someone who still knew all the founders of The Christian Community in person, I too was graced by destiny to experience Prof. Hermann Beckh in his last seminars and lectures. He lectured with an enthusiasm appearing with almost childlike innocence and totally unencumbered. During his lectures on 'Tristan and Isolde' or 'Parzifal' there had to be a piano at hand. He played not only the main motifs of Richard Wagner's works, but when his own verbal explanations, when language appeared to him as an insufficient means of expression, he passed over into musical improvisation. It then served, as it were, as a continuation of the verbal lecture. 'With words one can't pursue it further, but musically somewhat like this. ...' Thereby he turned his head to the audience in order to secure the undivided attention of his listeners. A spark of enthusiasm with such presentations kindled all those present.

The presentation of the cosmic rhythm in Gospels of Mark and John had struck a chord with me, the tone of which had already been stimulated by Rudolf Frieling. Consequently, with his words of Hermann Beckh's literary work I will here conclude my experiences.

It is always one and the same attitude of soul revealed in all these writings. They all bear the character of 'experienced knowledge'. You feel the strength of devotion, of meditation as of a tangible substance. You perceive the sonorous sound of a full-blooded soul-life that in all its primeval strength and vitality *is love towards the spirit*.

Hermann Beckh: on the occasion of his 100th birthday, 4 May 1975[52]

Kurt von Wistinghausen[53]

When Professor Beckh—his university title had become his first name—after excruciating suffering closed his eyes on 1 March 1937 at the age of not quite 62, there appeared on his countenance the greatness and clarity of his being; nothing could be seen any more of his somewhat child-like, ludicrous world-estranged character.

This highly gifted graduate of the Maximilianeum in Munich coming from Nuremberg, originally studied law, but he baulked already in his first placement as a judge from the non-existence of compassion in the world of legal practice. He quickly decided to change course and, in addition to the classical ancient languages that he knew, studied Oriental languages, especially Sanskrit. As Dr jur. et phil. he became a private tutor in Berlin and learned the Tibetan language. At times he was the only person at the University of Berlin who was able to read the ancient manuscripts kept there. Soon he was developing a lively, scholarly publishing activity of Oriental documents in large, formatted volumes, which today have become quite rare. Amongst them are the writing of Kalidasa. The First World War interrupted this work. Because of his knowledge of languages (it was not difficult for him to learn in eight days the basics of a language), Beckh was called to the '*Institut für Seeverkehr und Weltwirtschaft*' ['Institute for shipping and world commerce'] in Kiel, because he was otherwise 'not suitable for war service'. Looking back, he called it in jest '*Institut für sehr verkehrte Weltwirtschaft*' ['Institute for very wrong world commerce'] … Here he encountered anthroposophy and met his friend Rudolf Meyer. Immediately after the First World War he taught again—now as a.o. Professor [*außerordentlicher Professor*— extraordinary Professor with no chair—*Ed*.]—mostly a very small group of students in Berlin, and he published his highly recognized and today still valid work (now published by Verlag Geistesleben, Stuttgart [Trs. are published in Japanese, Dutch and English—*Ed*.]).

Anthroposophy and the writings of Novalis, however, led him to Christianity.

At the initial Class Conference for the opening of the First Goetheanum in autumn of 1920, we see him holding deeply researched lectures. All too easily they went on too long, so that Rudolf Steiner has to pull out his pocket watch. In spring 1922 he hears of the imminent founding of The Christian Community. This ignites his enthusiasm; he knows with inner surety against all objections that he belongs to the group of priests. Once more Professor Beckh changes course, he becomes a theologian, by far the most learned one amongst us. He takes part in the founding of The Christian Community with the agreement of Rudolf Steiner and the co-founders.

After this he is found engaged in extensive lecture-tours, or in his three tiny attic rooms in Urachhaus, Stuttgart. There he becomes a special friend of the children growing up until they were three or four years old (and *this* is the Himalaya. 'The Himalaya.' And this *is* the Matterhorn. 'The Matterhorn.' And this is the *dear*, good Dr Steiner. 'The *dear*, good Dr Steiner'). Behind the thin walls, the neighbour hears him explaining his pictures to the young, elder daughter of Emil Bock, in the exalted voice of an Oriental reciter.

In Breslau 1924, during the time of the Agriculture Lecture-Course a eurythmy performance took place in the Lobe Theatre. At that moment the volume, *Die Ursprung im Lichte* [*Our Origin in the Light*] on Genesis had just been published in the series of small volumes *Christus alle Erde* ['Christ of all the Earth']. At this opportunity we were immediately able to give a copy to Rudolf Steiner who was heartily glad and carried the light green volume—we still see it—placed under his left arm throughout the performance. How happy Beckh could be to hear such news.

There was hardly an opera by Wagner that Beckh did not attend. For this highly musical man was able to say by heart, of every motif every instrument, where and when it plays and what function it has. It was immediately explained on the piano. Just to add, his book *Die Sprache der Tonart* ... [*The Language of Music in the Music of Bach to Bruckner*]—pulped by the Gestapo—was his last. He corrected the proofs on his deathbed.

There were many occasions to laugh with Prof. Beckh and sometimes about him. This universal genius found it difficult to cope with daily demands. He wove with his soul in a fairytale mood. One day, bronzed on his return from his spring tours in the Alps, he could announce that he had met 'the Easter hare in person'. But one can imagine that the landlady in Dresden was not delighted when Prof. Beckh, although he took on to clean his shoes himself, included the soles with the black shoe polish, endangering the carpets. Also, he never quite mastered how a telephone, a tool of Ahriman, had practically to be used.

Rittelmeyer was sometimes in mild despair about his highly learned colleague. But Emil Bock loved him especially and via humour always found a way to his mysterious soul.

That a figure like Hermann Beckh—in its way unrepeatable—found its way to anthroposophy always appeared to us quite natural. However, it was also a rare gift of grace with which the early years were blessed.

Hermann Beckh (1875–1937) A Sketch of his Life's Motif

Edzard Clemm, Basel

> He who speaks truly is imbued with eternal life, and His scripture
> appears to us to be miraculously affiliated with authentic mysteries,
> for it is in accord with the symphony of the universe.
>
> Novalis, *The Novices of Sais*

Overview

Hermann Beckh (4 May 1875–1 March 1937) not only mastered more
than a dozen ancient and modern languages; his translations from
the Persian Avesta and from the ancient Indian Pali language are still
unsurpassed in their artistic and creative stylistic character. His interests and the broad horizon of his knowledge encompassed, amongst
other things, the early cultures of humanity, music—especially the language of tonality in its variety, alchemy as the transformation of substance, the ethers, the world of fairytales, and the starry aspects of the
gospels and the Apocalypse. He researched these subjects as a pupil of
Rudolf Steiner and a member of his First Esoteric School.

After he retired from his work as a judge, in what was for him a
very characteristic fashion, he became internationally known as a
most thorough and respected expert in Buddhism as a Professor of
Sanskrit and Indology. In 1922 he withdrew entirely from his academic career at the University and threw himself energetically into
The Christian Community which he had co-founded. The two dozen
books he wrote—all pearls—are at present almost all out of print in
the original German.

Heaven and Earth

If we enquire after the motifs of Beckh's life and the central veins of his
many-sided creativity and activities, two main lines become visible:

The arc of this rich life, with its many renunciations and new creations, reaches from his early spiritual experiences as a child in the
mountains, which enabled him to re-experience his own pre-birth
existence, to his experience of after-death inspiration from his sister
with whom he had been very closely connected in writing his book on

cosmic rhythms in John's Gospel (as is evident from the Foreword).

His spirit—rich, broad, and overflowing in all directions—had the power to rise up from mountain heights and heavenly distances to the stars and the harmonies of the spheres, to live in the pure light of these heights, and at the same time to unite himself in love to the Earth and its world of matter, researching its depths and transformations— entirely in the sense of the words of Novalis,[54] whom he loved and mentions in every single book:

> I do not know whether anyone already understood the stones and the celestial bodies, but if he did, he must certainly have been a sublime being [Novalis, *The Novices of Sais*].

Speech and Music

The rhythmical languages of the early high cultures of mankind were Hermann Beckh's natural element. They enabled him to dive into their mysteries, especially into the most ancient mantric speech of the Gathas of Zarathustra, ancient Indian poetry and the world of ancient Egypt. In their contexts and in the light of the ethers, the polarity of the Tree of Knowledge and the Tree of Life was for him a very deep concern. His struggle to comprehend this continued right up to the manuscript book that most likely stems from his last years. To date only a few extracts of which have appeared in print—*The Mystery of Musical Creativity: The Human Being and Music*.[55] In it he writes:

> Earlier people still possessed or looked for the experience of the sound-ing of the spheres. Recalling the relationship of the 'higher kinds of ether', sound-ether and life-ether, with the biblical 'Tree of Life' ..., we can also say, the true original, primary cosmic element of music is the *sounding cosmic starry Tree of Life*, the harmony of the spheres connected to the cosmic life.

This book has a universal human significance. With his legacy, and again basing himself on Novalis and Rudolf Steiner's spiritual-scientific research into the ethers, Hermann Beckh created something both fun-damental and contemporary for music and the experience of musical sound—half a century after the onset of the Age of Michael [began 1879]. It compares with what Goethe did in his way over a hundred years ear-lier when he gave to the world his *Farbenlehre*, his *Theory of Colours*.[56]

Hermann Beckh received his strongest musical impetus from the music of Bach, which he and his sister loved throughout their lives. In his youth his deepest impressions came from a performance of

Wagner's *Parsifal*, and later from *Tristan and Isolde*. He remained deeply attached to Wagner's work for the rest of his life. Indeed, he even composed himself.

> (...) my soul had an intimate relationship to what sounds in the world, to that which lives most inwardly as the eternal harmony in everything. Already in my early years I could hear this sounding of the world also sounding in my soul.[57]

The Transformation of the Earth and Resurrection

His lively spirit of research was always directed in this etheric universe at the Earth transformed by the Mystery of Golgotha. We consequently read in *The Mystery of Musical Creativity*:

> In the book *John's Gospel: The Cosmic Rhythm—Stars and Stones* it is shown in the John's Gospel itself how aspects of cosmic music and the cosmic word are linked with the alchemical (chemical) aspects of metamorphosing the Earth, of the transubstantiation of what is the Earth. Again, Novalis is the poet and thinker in whom chemical-musical viewpoints of John's Gospel are called to life again in more recent times. In the *Fragments* that are so instructive concerning musicality, he has given the subject conceptual expression.

Hermann Beckh saw his profound little book *Alchymy: The Mystery of the Material World* as the direct continuation of this tremendous book. The 4th edition of *Alchymie vom Geheimnis Der Stoffeswelt* was published by Rudlof Geering Verlag, Dornach 1987. Today it is completely and unjustly forgotten.

Among the fairytales, he mused for decades over the story of 'Snow White'. In its images he saw the transformation of the Earth and the Mystery of resurrection expressed in a completely new and fresh way.[58]

Another forgotten work, which includes so many of his artistically gifted insights and the actual concerns of his heart, is the poetic work *The New Jerusalem*.[59] It appeared in 1925, the year of Rudolf Steiner's death, and contains a wealth of experiences: from the world of the high mountains, from the alchemical-Rosicrucian vision of 'Snow White' and the Tree of Life in Paradise to knowledge of the most profound depths of the Holy Grail. On this last motif, and after experiencing the Rudolf Steiner's lecture-cycle *The Mysteries of the East and Christianity* (GA 144), Beckh wrote from Steglitz (9 Feb. 1913) to Rudolf Steiner:

(…) after the last lecture cycle [on 6 Feb. 1913] (for which I am eternally grateful to you), for here with the Parsifal and Grail motif you have touched my innermost soul, the thought in which I live already since early childhood, without which I would never have found the way to you (this is a completely assured fact).

On the lecture-cycle Steiner gave after Christmas in Leipzig in 1913, *Christ and the Spiritual World and the Search for the Holy Grail* (GA 148), Beckh wrote in his memoirs, 'that I could attend belonged to the most beautiful, unforgettable memories of my life'.

The Departure of the Perfected One

At St John's Tide of that year, 1925, Hermann Beckh published *Der Hingang des Vollendeten. Die Erzählung von Buddhas Erdenabschied und Nirvana* [*The Departure of the Perfected One. The Story of Buddha's Departure from Earth and Nirvana*, TL 2023]: it was his contribution to work through the passing of a great personality.[60] This rhythmical and musical Pali text had been for him 'an inner companion for decades'. This and his other translations on the Buddha in the light of Christ seem to be pervaded by the Christened breath in close proximity to the paradisal world of the Tree of Life and to the Buddha who is united with it.

Concerning the polarity between heaven and earth mentioned above at the beginning—who, then, provides the balance? It is the Christ Who has passed through the Mystery of Golgotha. Hermann Beckh, whose spirit was as broad as the starry heavens, experienced all his own creations and works, including his work in The Christian Community, in the light of Christ and the light shed by Rudolf Steiner. He was united with Rudolf Steiner in deepest gratitude and never published a book without acknowledging his teacher in the Preface. Before his birth and after his death he is firmly united with the spiritual community around Rudolf Steiner.

[My special thanks go to Richard Ramsbotham for the translation of Hermann Beckh's profound mantric texts, and to Terry Boardman for translating the article (ed. A.S.). First printed in *Der Europäer*, Vol. 20, No. 5, March 2016 (German), and *The Present Age*, Vol. 2, No. 1, April 2016 (English), both Perseus-Verlag, Basel. Reprinted with kind permission—E.C.]

*

Psalm 23
German translation by Hermann Beckh

Der das Ich in mir spricht,
Ist mein Hirte.
Es wird mir nicht mangeln.
Auf frischem Grün läßt er mich ruhn.
Zum Lebensstrom führt er mich hin.
Meine Seele läßt er genesen.
Den Weg der Wahrhaftigkeit läßt er
mich wandeln.
In seines Ichwesen waltender Kraft.
Ob ich auch ginge im Abgrund
Der finstern Todesschatten,
Fürchte ich nimmer des Bösen Gefahr,
Denn du bist bei mir.
Dein Stecken und Stab sind mir Stütze
und Trost.
Im Angesicht meiner Feinde deckst du
den Tisch vor mich hin,
Mein Haupt salbst du mit Öl.
Meinen Becher schenkst du mir voll.
Ja, schenkende Güte, sie trägt mich all
mein Leben.
Und im Haus des Herrn,
Der das Ich in mir spricht,
Will auf immer ich ruhn.

[The One who says 'I' in me
is my Shepherd.
I shall not want.
On green pastures he lets me rest.
He leads me to the stream of life.
He restores my soul.
He lets me walk on the path of
truthfulness
in His 'I'-being's governing power.
Even though I walk in the abyss
of the dark shadow of death
I never fear the dangers of evil,
for You are with me,
Your rod and staff are my support
and comfort.
In the face of my enemies
you laid a table before me,
My head you anoint with oil.
You fill my cup full.
Indeed, bestowing goodness
supports
my whole life.
And in the House of the Lord,
Who speaks the 'I' in me,
I will rest for ever.]

Hermann Beckh's version was first published in: *The 23rd Psalm of the Holy Scriptures. Newly translated from the original and set to music by Hermann Beckh. Op. 7. For voice, accompanied by piano, organ or orchestra* (Sulze & Galler, Stuttgart 1935).

*

From: THE GATHAS OF ZARATHUSTRA (Yasht 19, 89)

To the ether aura of the Sun in glory
Bearer of the mighty, kingly promise to the world,

Born from the Father in eternity,*
We pray,
Who will unite with the most victorious of the saviours,
And with the others, his apostles,
Who will bring the world forwards,
Enabling it to overcome old age and death,
Corruption and decay,
Helping it to flourish evermore,
To gain free will**
And life eternal—
When the dead will arise again,
When the one appears who will livingly overcome death,
And when the world, through its own will, will be brought forwards on its path.

From: Hermann Beckh, *Zarathustra* (Stuttgart, 1927. Eng. tr. in *From the Mysteries. Seven Essays.* TL 2020).

   * This line is only rendered in *The Original Sacred Texts of Zarathustra* as a footnote.

   ** In *The Original Sacred Texts of Zarathustra* ('To gain the rulership of its own will') is added.

*

The BEGINNING of GENESIS (The Biblical Story of Creation)

   In the spirit-thought of the primal beginning
   The creative being of the Elohim
   Wove the heavens and the earth,
   And the earth, potential and unformed, was a being in becoming,
   And darkness held sway over the world-deeps,
   And the spirit of the Godhead, who breathes through the sacred winds,
   Brooded upon the primal waters.
   And then the holy Word of Worlds spoke: Let there be Light!
   And there was Light.
   And the divinity of the Elohim beheld the beauty of the Light.
   Then the creative thought of God separated the light from the darkness
   And named the light day and the darkness night.
   Thus it became evening in the world—and then morning –
   The first day.

H. Beckh's rendering was published only in the Appendix to the first edition of his translation of *The Hymn to the Earth—from the Sanskrit Atharvaveda* (German ed., Stuttgart 1934); Eng. tr. see p. 65.

*

From JOHN'S GOSPEL (17:3)

> But this is the life of eternity,
> that they recognize You (Father), as the Divine
> resting in the omnipresence of never-extinguished consciousness,
> and the One as the Christ, the Saviour Jesus Who is sent, arisen out of your star-radiance.

From: Hermann Beckh, *John's Gospel:The Cosmic Rhythm—Stars and Stones.* Anastasi 2015, 117; TL 2021, 83.

Memories of Prof. Beckh

Gertrud v. Hohnhorst, geb. Klein[61]

[Typescript held in the Zentralarchiv der Christengemeinschaft, Berlin. Pub. in *Rundbrief* A186, S. 18-21 with tiny omissions, here restored. Eng. trans. M. & A. Stott, 2023.]

It certainly did not happen often to Prof. Beckh that he was addressed on the street by a female, but this was how we met. He loved little children very much and became enthusiastic about a picture of my daughter which he had seen and wanted to meet her. I became interested in his work, so gathering my courage, I told him who I was, and this began a friendship lasting until his death. This occurred at the conference in Freiburg, Summer 1924 or 1925. In the Autumn 1926 he visited us and in 1928 and 1932. A part of his book on Mark's Gospel was written here. Above all he enjoyed a spring in the forest and a fountain at our place. Early in the mornings he walked regularly to this spring, only dressed in a trailing dressing gown over the 'Grail meadow' (his name for the area), to take a cold shower and hold a dialogue with fairies, gnomes, undines and sylphs. A fairytale arose at this time, which had this landscape and experiences as its background, 'The Story of the little Squirrel of the Moonlight Princess and the little Rose'.[62] During the course of the morning he went for a second time to the place where I often joined him. Then the Sun shone through the fir trees into this hidden part of the valley and conjured the most beautiful colours of the rainbow out of the dispersing water from the fountain, a view that repeatedly delighted him and inspired him in his work. He often tried also to see there a Moon-rainbow, but never succeeded. He very much enjoyed drinking the spring water, for the water in Stuttgart was not at all to his liking. Of course, studies on the stars were also undertaken. Unfortunately, he was not able to see the Morning Star from his room, having always to enter another room for this. Nevertheless, he never missed one morning. When the star could be seen especially beautifully, he could not do otherwise but wake the children to show this to them. Fortunately, he did not notice that in his enthusiasm they sleepily did not show the same feelings as he did.

In 1928 we travelled together to the inauguration of the Goetheanum where Prof. Beckh also had to hold a lecture, which filled him with great joy. He experienced the days there inwardly moved as in a festive, celebratory consecration, but one had to protect him from becoming unbalanced. Following this, we undertook with other acquaintances a trip to the *Jungfraujoch* mountain. He felt especially connected to this mountain and loved it above all others. There he felt close to the Mystery of the Ice-maiden, Isis etc. We had to overnight in Lauterbrunnen and next day made an expedition to the mountain. On the next morning, he appeared at the breakfast table with the enthusiastic announcement, 'Last night the *Jungfrau* [the Virgin] was simply wonderful!' And when malicious people started to laugh, he could not understand what was funny about it. I have seldom seen him so open and full of joy as in the mountains. It was as if the equivalence of the basic elements of his being and that which lived in the mountains had a beneficial effect, as if the burden of his body, which he always found as too heavy, was removed and he felt rejuvenated and light. This beautiful tour with conversations about the gospel books I will never forget; it was a true 'climax', which later I often experienced— how freeing it was for him when a person in his vicinity could offer him some light remark in outer life-situations. He often told me how he was tormented by dreams, when he stood in the middle of a confusion of train tracks, having to find a direction or a connection, or had to find something that was lost and could not find it. He could then be beside himself with despair, or helpless like a small child. Then it was much better not to brush aside such seeming obstacles, but to help him with some light comments to see them in their proper proportions. A joking word at the right time could often rectify things for him. I recall a nice anecdote I didn't experience myself; it was told me by acquaintances. When he moved into his room in Urachhaus, he wanted to unpack all his books. He sorted them into different piles according to the subjects, not noticing in his zeal that they were getting ever higher until finally he was surrounded by a wall that held him prisoner, not knowing the way out.

These experiences of the heights were often followed by some adventurous plunges into the depths. Some years later, in 1932, I was a guest together with Prof. Beckh at Eva. v. Schlözer in Dresden, where he held his first lecture-course on the stars. From there we travelled to Freiberg to visit a mine. It was all more difficult that we thought. We had to travel for a long time in the car, the way not easy to find. There was no miner available; for many years it had been out of use, not prepared for visitors. But we did not give up, until the miner's wife promised to guide us. Dressed in old coats, kitted out with miners' lamps we set off. One entered through a trapdoor and had then to descend on a narrow ladder that was wet and slippery. To right and left water trickled on the walls. It could be heard rather loudly. These were the only sounds. One false step and disaster would have occurred. It made a great impression. Of course, we could not tell how deep we had descended; a little farther we entered a passage, but it became too difficult, too low, uneven and slippery, moreover, there was a ditch full of water to one side. The ascent was still more arduous than the descent and I was quite relieved when Herr Prof. Beckh had happily landed again above ground, for I felt responsible for the outcome of such excursions. Afterwards, we still visited a wonderful collection of minerals in Freiberg, where especially a gold crystal, certainly a great rarity, repeatedly attracted him. With all this it had become late and we had misjudged the way from this place to the station. It was the last train for Dresden, where just on this evening a lecture was to be given in the Community. All running would have been senseless and threatened to lead to a catastrophe on the street. Then I saw a car parked before an inn (there were no taxis). With the courage of despair, I asked the owner whether she might drive us to the station; we urgently had to reach the train. She was so very nice and all the waves of excitement became smooth again. This visit to Dresden for him was an indulgence in experiences of stone, star and flower as probably never again to occur. A few days still in the *Erzgebire* [Ore Mountains], with another, more harmless visit to a mine made a nice rounding-off.

In the following year he asked me to Stuttgart to help him through some difficult days. He had taken on a lecture, in fact the opening lecture, and two talks at the Astrology Congress. He was somewhat apprehensive about the whole thing. From his listeners, he always required a certain patience and openness to relate to him. This goodwill was like the nourishing ground on which his contributions could grow and flourish. And it was a help for him to know at least one person, from whom he could expect this. Too much admiration or devotion was to him rather a hindrance. It had to be something like the way children listened to him. I believe he particularly liked to talk to them simply because for him they had the right way of listening. I still must smile today when I see myself sitting there as a guest of honour, yet I could not protect him from a pain caused by a letter from the Executive Council in Dornach, which expressed some concern regarding his lectures before this audience. But he only said what he thought he was able to attempt, fully responsible towards Dornach, for his inner responsibility for the spiritual good of anthroposophy was the highest maxim of his life. He then did not give the second talk; for him it was a deep sadness. Consequently, it was a greater satisfaction a year later, after he had for a long time been reconciled to Dornach concerning the incident, approximately around the same time during a summer conference, to give a lecture in the Goetheanum on difficulties in studying the stars.

The last time I saw Prof. Beckh for a longer time time was during the Winter and Spring of 1936 in Oberstdorf when he was looking for recuperation and healing from his sufferings that were beginning. Already then, he could only walk with difficulty and with great pain. But the mountains there still made things possible. We went on a beautiful trip to Mittelberg with a walk to a lonely farm, where earlier he had enjoyed spending several days. He loved the view of the Widderstein. Often his eyes looked longingly from the balcony in Reute for the *Hohe Licht*, the 'High Light', a mountain he especially loved, and which he had climbed. There was something wistful over that whole time, although he certainly did not think he was there for the last time, and that it was actually a farewell to the mountains forever. A walk over the meadows covered with Spring flowers was ever again a memorable experience for him. For anyone who accompanied him it was a double experience. One evening was unforgettable for me when he spoke of Bruckner's Ninth Symphony and of its experiences of death and the threshold, as in a premonition of what will come, in an arresting power and reality. At that time, he played lots of music. Music, by the way, is an old love of his. I possess two songs by him, composed around the turn of the century. The one is called 'Young Werner', the text taken from 'The Trumpeter of Säckingen'; the other one 'Die Ilse' to a poem by Heinrich Heine, from *Die Harzreise*. I am happy to pass them to anyone interested. There is no point to give the publisher, for they are either out of print or were pulped long ago.

In Oberstdorf he also met up with the poet Talhoff, but it led to nothing. He still enjoyed one evening, when he was invited to the Crown Princess, played for her and read from his books. The last time I saw Prof. Beckh was after Christmas on his sickbed. I was shocked by his appearance, which spoke of all the sufferings and struggles. A beautiful and final memory are three nights during which I held watch there. It was as if, already freed from anything disturbing, a second human being was awake. During this hour he attempted beyond all pain to be strongly present with his best qualities. And he was grateful if one did not torment him with compassion but stood at his side and made oneself aware of what this time of difficult illness meant.

When Dr Husemann asked me to write down something of what I had experienced with Prof. Beckh, I was taken aback. But I face it in gratitude for this human being. Only the fact that I owe him so much helped me overcome my shyness. I got to know him as a selfless advisor and a faithful friend. That I did not experience with him so many humorous episodes was possibly because I made it my specific task to let everything carry on as 'normally' as possible and to protect him from any mishaps. But every described meeting was important for him and his work. Other meetings, when I got to know his touching hospitality in the Urachhaus, have been omitted. If these lines can help round out the picture of his human, personal side, then its purpose has been fulfilled.

[*Note in the RB*: Gertrud von Schwindt von Hohnhorst, maiden name v. Staudt (1902-1972) was the daughter of a general and an anthroposophist [mother]. Her sister Elisabeth married Gerhard Klein, and another was married to the composer Otto E. Crusius. She contributed greatly to the creation of The Christian Community in Saarland and was chairperson of the local Red Cross—*F. Ht.*].

Prof. Dr Hermann Beckh

Johannes Lenz (Berlin)

According to the gospel, as Matthew 16:13 reports, Peter matures as a disciple (a student, as the Greek text says, who searches for *mathesis*, knowledge) in order to utter the confession: 'You are the Christ, Son of the living God.' Then Jesus Christ answers this with a beatitude: 'Blessed are you, Simon, son of Jonah, for this was not revealed to you by flesh and blood, but my Father in the heavens. And I tell you that you are Peter, and on this rock [Peter means 'rock'—*Ed.*] I will build my Church.'[63]

This key-sentence of Christ says, firstly, that He Himself intends to build His *ecclesia*. The builder of the Christian Church, the Community of those called, is the Lord Himself. And [secondly] the impulse to build hopes that people as seekers for knowledge wake up to the will to learn. The faculty arises to deepen knowledge towards wisdom and intensify it towards confession. The confession becomes possible when the knowledge bound to the body ['flesh and blood'] is deepened to a body-free wisdom. With this, the spiritual world of the Father-God can enter; as revelation, it can reach the consciousness of the human being. On this bedrock the building of the *ecclesia*, the Church, is possible.

The renewed Christian confession only becomes possible again after 1922 after the emergence of anthroposophy, the science of the spirit, has become a present reality helping people to feel the call from their destiny so far to become a community of professing Christians.

A glance at the personalities of the founders of The Christian Community from 1922 is always a moving experience. It makes one grateful for the life-decisions and sacrifices that were necessary to enable the creation of communities. There were personalities, on the one hand, some from the Protestant Church in Germany, like Dr Friedrich Rittelmeyer and Lic. Emil Bock who could link the old and the new. With Eduard Lenz and Dr Doldinger a Catholic wing of the Christian Church was involved in the Movement for Renewal; striking examples representing the Youth Movement are Wilhelm Kelber and Dr Alfred Heidenreich, and for the scholars Prof. Dr Hermann Beckh and the chemist Gottfried Husemann.

In Beckh's biography it is clearly shown how the call from the spiritual world came to him as early as childhood and youth. In the lonely mountain world (Einödsbach in the province of Allgäu) he experiences the spiritual world. He is aware that he comes from another world. He experiences his prenatal existence. Later, in the renewed sacrament of baptism, he experiences again that the human soul stems from the world before birth. The baptized Christian is to find it again in love on the Earth. After his time at the Maximilianeum in Munich, Beckh's path leads through a study of law to a career in the higher Civil Service. He encounters a human couple whom he has to sentence for stealing some firewood. Humanly he cannot do this, so he pays the fine himself. He meets anthroposophy and becomes a pupil of Rudolf Steiner. The explorer of ancient languages teaches Tibetan and Indology at the Humboldt University in Berlin. He is led from Buddha to Christ and meets the group who found The Christian Community. The fundamental renewal of the seven sacraments including ordination of priests becomes possible. In the service of the word of worship, he experiences the fulfilment of his search as a scholar for the spirit-filled word. Already at his ordination, he feels the Logos according to John's Gospel, that the WORD was at the beginning of all creation. He proclaims it on the day of his ordination. Hermann Beckh found the goal of his career and ideal of life. He served the word of the renewed sacrament. The close human connection to Dr Friedrich Rittelmeyer who ordained him and Lic. Emil Bock was another factor that pointed to his remaining in Stuttgart, the centre of the Movement.

A major donation of the Swedish engineer Ruth, who through his inventions had built factories in Scandinavia and had invited Rittelmeyer to Uppsala, makes it possible to acquire a vineyard on which a house could be built in which Rittelmeyer lived with his family and Beckh moves into a garret. On the ground floor a chapel is established; a priests' seminary founded, and the Professor begins his teaching. He travels to give lectures in the communities, helps in founding and developing communities, participates in conferences. He belongs to the core-group of founders who cultivate the life of the renewed sacraments of a community of a renewed priesthood including women as priests.

He completed his earthly life and died on 1 March 1937 in Stuttgart. He now belongs to the souls that will strengthen the sacramental life from the world beyond death when their memory is sufficiently fostered.

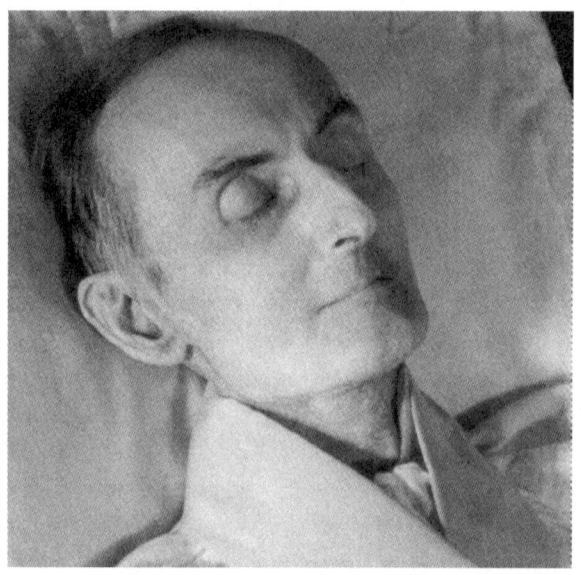

Hermann Beckh on his death bed

ESSAYS IN HONOUR OF HERMANN BECKH

Introduction to *Festschrift* (2016, rev. 2023)

Neil Franklin, Ph.D., General Editor of the 'Collected Works' in English

 In 1932 Hermann Beckh wanted to make one point very clear. Referring to the mysteries of Christianity, the Gospel of St John, the stars and alchemical traditions, he simply stated:[64]

> Only the patient and devoted meditative work opens up the depths of its content, the richness of its Mysteries, the abundance of its contexts. As with astrology and alchymy in general, which basically can never be made into academic book-knowledge—which is why all the literature in this subject is questionable and critical—only the intuitive [process of] knowledge, in devoted esoteric-meditative work, as far as the conditions given by destiny permit, gradually permits an opening.

On arriving at Felpham in Sussex in 1800, where he was provided with a small stone cottage, William Blake went out for a stroll in the surrounding countryside. He heard a young lad call out, 'Father, the gate is open.' Blake dissolved in rapturous tears of joy—it was an auspicious omen for his new life. Nearly two hundred years earlier Jakob Böhme—whose translated works Blake had on his shelves—had repeatedly prefixed significant passages of Christian wisdom with the phrase 'An Open Gate'. Without any doubt, Hermann Beckh had something of the same experience. Of what value is the Pearl (Matt. 13:46)? Beckh did not hesitate to give up his career as an Assistant Judge in Bavaria. Refusing the offer from a government minister to make him Außerordentlicher Professor in the University of Berlin, he chose to become a freelance lecturer for anthroposophy. These were enormous sacrifices at a time when inflation was rampant in Germany, moreover, with no savings or income, and he was carrying responsibility for his mother and sister.

In his lecture of November 1921, intended for colleagues in Berlin, Hermann Beckh sets out plain, cogent reasons why the academic world, in its various departments, is at a dead end.[65] This should not be taken lightly. The choice is between belief in academic respectability and the conviction that *only* an 'intuitive process of knowledge', in the strictest sense of the word, can be *meaningful*. For Beckh in 1921 such intuitive knowledge had to follow the guidelines set out by Rudolf Steiner. Not one of his colleagues attended the lecture. It is not one's life-situation which is the decisive factor, it is how one makes *one's choices*.

Had he been born in Britain—an argument he would no doubt have thrown out of court—Hermann Beckh would most likely have taken up the legacy left by Blake, Coleridge and Wordsworth. As it was, we find him in a bookshop in Kiel, towards the end of World War I, purchasing the complete works of Novalis.[66] From this time on these writings appear most often in his own publications, elegantly sustaining the results of meditative Imagination. In Novalis'[67] words:

> The imagination places the world of the future either far above us, or far below, or in a relation of metempsychosis to ourselves. We dream of travelling through the universe—but is not the universe *within ourselves?* The depths of our spirit are unknown to us—the mysterious way leads inwards. Eternity with its worlds—the past and future—is in ourselves or nowhere. The external world is the world of shadows—it throws its shadow into the realm of light.

To this one may compare Blake's well-known letter[68] to the Rev. Dr John Trusler (author of that most popular book *The Way to be Rich and Respectable*) from the same period (1799):

> But to the Eyes of the Man of Imagination, Nature is Imagination itself. As a man is, So he Sees ...To Me This World is all One continued Vision of Fancy or Imagination, & I feel Flatter'd when I am told so. What is it that sets Homer, Virgil & Milton in so high a rank of Art? Why is the Bible more Entertaining & Instructive than any other book? Is it not because they are addressed to the Imagination, which is Spiritual Sensation, & but mediately to the Understanding or Reason?

Hermann Beckh would have agreed with Blake, certainly he appreciated Novalis, yet, with the help of Rudolf Steiner, he further understood, as they did, that such Imagination or 'Spiritual Sensation' does not mean being swept away into a world of uncontrollable dreams, spirits, séances and mediums. Nobody more than W.B. Yeats understood better what that meant—realms of deceptions, lies, mistaken appearances and falsifications. Imaginative knowing comes through the 'I' in full self-consciousness; as a development of the 'I' it is subject to the tests of logical consistency. On one occasion Beckh addressed this as '*Ich-Prüfung*', 'testing of the "I"'.[69] It is what Jakob Böhme meant by the 'narrow gate'. What is striking here is the suggestion that the discoveries of Imagination are as real and authentic, as the commitment to a personal choice made in full responsibility.

In contrast to what Beckh calls the zero-point of the 'I' and as its complementary opposite, the territory of 'spiritual sensation' that fell within Hermann Beckh's reach is vast. His approach to the starry heavens recalls what Paracelsus discovered about the *'astrum'*,[70] and his own love of observing the Morning Star or a specific constellation is well documented.[71] No less grandiose and refined are his investigations of the tonal system in Western music from Bach to Bruckner, his studies of Wagner, and his own compositions. Back in 1612 Böhme, too, passed through the open gate and encountered the world of musical sounds. Regarding the origins and development of Indo-European languages and their different cultures, Hermann Beckh was in his professorial element; he could draw upon extensive studies in philology. Böhme and Novalis also found that the gate opened beyond musical sounds into the native ground of speech, and the Kabbalah became transformed into the European tradition of *Natursprache*. Ultimately the realms of harmony, musical sounds and speech opened to the last great Mystery of substance, its origins and transformations. With Jakob Böhme and Rudolf Steiner, Beckh stands before the fact of the Christian Eucharist. The highest I AM, passing through different manifestations, is revealed as the substance, that is *hypostasis,* of Divine Love.

On the one hand we have all that has so far been unveiled of the life of Hermann Beckh, and we are beginning to appreciate how his publications form an organic whole directly related to Rudolf Steiner's *Knowledge of the Higher Worlds: How is it Achieved?* and indirectly related to Böhme's comprehensive vision. As a counterweight, astronomy continues to be purely quantitative; music has been threatened by intellectual, atonal developments; linguistics has long repudiated the idea that a speech-sound has any intrinsic meaning. Among the theologians, form criticism reduces the gospels to inchoate fragments reflecting cultural presuppositions; I-Thou traditions tend to cut out all that shapes the middle of our rich life-experience.[72]

Nevertheless, the present section 'Celebration' testifies to the undeniable fact that a number of well-informed writers *have freely chosen* to contribute essays in honour of Hermann Beckh. All contributors, I believe, have been impressed not *simply* by the range of his knowledge and the sharpness of his acumen. With the earlier memoirs, biographical material, and contributions from Beckh's literary estate, we also find substantial appreciations of both the 'intuitive process' of knowledge, cultivated in the most disciplined and loving earnestness, and also his findings to which the open gate gave access.

As Beckh himself said,[73] the Buddhist writings were very close to his heart, and this volume publishes contributions acknowledging his major publication from within the university world: *Buddha's Life and Teaching* (1916). Dr Katrin Binder, the first English translator of this work, presents here her assessment of what Beckh achieved in the context of the ensuing one hundred years. Manfred Krüger contributes a consideration of the sage Asita who prophesied the coming of Gautama Buddha. It is doubtful whether any approach to Hermann Beckh could be truly substantial without such knowledge of Buddhist traditions.

With the essays by Susana Ulrich-Alvarez Ulloa and Oliver Heinl we are introduced by experienced researchers to the Hermann Beckh who investigated the origin of speech: it appears that the theory of *Natursprache* and its development into eurythmy is fully justified. For Beckh's work on music we are grateful to Alan Stott, who presents Beckh's contribution to the Western classical tradition grounded in the cycle of musical keys—an approach most dear to Beckh's heart that he called 'my theme'. The latter part of this volume is dedicated to what we have come to know and love of Hermann Beckh, the man. None of this would be possible without the personal memories of the Bock children who knew 'Fesser Beckh as the wonderful man at the top of the stairs in Urachstrasse 41.

There is nevertheless work still to be done once the extent of Beckh's achievement begins to be recognized and loved from the centre of one's 'I'. What were his contributions to The Christian Community conferences which were held during his lifetime? Moreover, Beckh's correspondence awaits exploration. And we are only starting to discover Beckh's lectures to groups outside The Christian Community.[74]

Why should there be such an endeavour? On one hand there is the issue of finding a balanced assessment of Hermann Beckh's work in comparison with what was achieved, for example, by Emil Bock and Friedrich Rittelmeyer—different personalities, different priorities and therefore different styles. Yet above and beyond this, Beckh gave all that he had to enrich the life of The Christian Community and to share the results of his discoveries with the world at large. It may well turn out that, since Rudolf Steiner, no one had more to offer between 1916 and 1937. The perceived value of the Professor with his knowledge of Tibetan, Sanskrit, Pali and Avestan, his mature understanding of music, his devotion to the eucharist, is indeed steadily growing. The least we can do is to try to make his work better known by offering our contributions in his honour.

Buddha's Life and Teaching One Hundred Years On

Katrin Binder (translator of Beckh's *Buddha und seine Lehre* into English)

 The following are some thoughts on Hermann Beckh's *Buddhismus* [*Buddha und Seine Lehre*]. I attempt to speak here from the heart, as a practitioner of Buddhist meditation, as someone with a deep interest in Buddhist scriptures and traditions, who has immersed herself in Indian culture and ways of life. But I would also like to speak here, as it were, as a 'colleague' of Beckh, having studied Indology to Ph.D. level and taught the discipline at several German universities. Working on the translation of Beckh's *Buddha* for me has been one of life's amazing invitations to delve deeper into a dear subject while providing unexpected opportunities to learn and broaden the horizon.

Finding Hermann Beckh

Beckh's commissioned work on the Buddha's life and teaching, *Buddhismus*, first appeared in two volumes in 1916 in the series published in the Göschen series by Walter de Gruyter Verlag, Berlin. It was exceptionally well received at the time, and its author was held in high esteem by his academic colleagues. All this changed when he started to speak openly for anthroposophy and when he left his university job to devote his time fully to lecturing and writing for anthroposophy. Diether Lauenstein, the editor of two of Beckh's translations, reports a conversation during World War II with a leading Orientalist at the University of Berlin:

> When Beckh published his little book on Buddha in 1916 we read him with great joy. It is the best thing written in the German language on Buddha. But when Beckh then turned to Rudolf Steiner, we didn't read him anymore.[75]

The public lecture Beckh gave when he left the University sealed his intellectual fate:

> To speak publicly for Rudolf Steiner in those years meant to be morally struck off the register of the intellectual society of Germany. Beckh

henceforth was labelled and ostracized. Although he was not the only one who had to suffer this fate—the way in which Dr Rittelmeyer was treated was very similar—it was at times more difficult to bear than the legal prohibition of certain anthroposophical activities in recent times [written 1938]. And few who saw through the intolerance and conceit of the leading academic circles of Germany after the War, could doubt that sooner or later fate would wield an iron broom.[76]

From then on Hermann Beckh was not heard any more by official science. For them he had died. All the more because from then on he did no longer consider his scholarly position. He lived and created in a completely new way and was not afraid of clashes. Of the group of many hundreds of scholars in Berlin, he was the one, the very only one who had found the way towards a new spirituality; he was on the other hand in the group of listeners around Rudolf Steiner, the only one of eminent recognized professional standing—especially in the realm of the oldest and richest spirituality of India. This was his very special historical position which will remain his for all time.[77]

Hermann Beckh's ostracization from the academic world appears to have been rather thorough. When I studied Indology at the University of Tübingen in Germany between 1998 and 2003, his name appeared neither on any reading list accompanying general lectures, nor on lists of recommended study materials for the intermediate and final exams. This may have been different had my place of study had a stronger tradition of Tibetological Studies or had I chosen to attend Tibetological classes.[78] As it is, not even does *Einführung in die Indologie. Stand. Methoden. Aufgaben* (ed. by Heinz Bechert and Georg von Simson, Darmstadt: WBG 1979), still in use as an 'undergraduate guide', mention any of his Tibetological works, nor his seminal Buddha book.

Diving a little deeper, however, one begins to find footprints. A small volume which did appear on a reading list for an introductory lecture on Buddhist philosophy I attended, Moriz Winternitz' *Der ältere Buddhismus nach Texten des Tipiṭaka* (Tübingen: Mohr/Siebeck 1929) significantly refers to all those works on Buddhism by Beckh that had appeared by that time. The first reference occurs in Winternitz' summary of the canonical Buddhist scriptures known as the *Tipiṭaka* ('three baskets') where he lists Beckh's 1925 translation of the *Mahāparinibbāna-Sutta*.[79] Winternitz further provides references for standard introductions to Buddhism at the time. Among those is Beckh's two-volume work on Buddhism in the Göschen series[80] which is also referred to in the context of discussions of the teaching of *paṭiccasamuppāda* (Skt. *pratītyasamutpāda*, dependent or conditioned arising). The most important reference is again to Beckh's translation of the *Mahāparinibbāna-Sutta*, as Winternitz choses to follow Beckh's translation of a problematic term.[81]

An online search on googlescholar brings to light an astonishing number of contemporary reviews of Beckh's publication. These reviews continue into the 1930s as the original two volumes saw several subsequent editions.[82] What is most remarkable is the fact that these reviews were not only published in magazines and journals dealing with the expected subjects of religion or philosophy, but journals with a wide range of interests took notice of Beckh's work. Although we may struggle today to imagine the context of the times of its first appearance,[83] we may be able to appreciate why Beckh's *Buddhismus* was welcomed as an accessible introduction to the Buddha and Buddhism amongst a rising number of publications on Eastern religions and philosophies.

The earliest publications on Buddhism in European languages faced the problem of limited access to original sources and even to the necessary language skills. While this situation had improved markedly by the time Beckh studied Indology, academic approaches to Buddhism were still influenced by a nineteenth-century bias for the search for the 'original'—i.e. the 'original' texts and oldest strata of a tradition in question. For many scholars at the time, this implied accepting only Theravāda (Hīnayāna) sources as valid and denouncing texts and commentaries from the Mahāyāna. Beckh does not accept such a limited approach but draws freely on several Buddhist textual traditions. He, too, is interested in capturing the Buddha and his teaching in their 'original' truth. Working from a sound philological basis, he is able to argue, however, that it is not necessarily the actual age of a text as it appears today that tells us all about the information we can obtain from it. 'Later' texts that may appear full of interpolations and hagiographical material may rest on much older strata of tradition, and even 'overgrown' legends may contain pictures and metaphors that point us to 'original' facts and truths. Beckh argues all these points convincingly and in a scholarly way which at the same time reflects his warm-hearted interest and involvement.

Beckh's contribution

What can be considered the lasting contribution of Beckh's work on Buddhism? Apart from those aspects already hinted at above, the most striking characteristic of Beckh's *Buddha's Life and Teaching* is the fact that in his delineation of the Buddha legend in particular he remains very close to his textual sources from within the Buddhist traditions. Bringing his inner connection with the subject fully to bear on his writing, he finds a beautiful, adequate language in German. The reader feels as if he is reading an original text. At the same time Beckh sometimes achieves a vividness that allows the reader to get very close to the events and teachings. Thus, we may say that in a way unusual for the early twentieth century, he allows the sources and the associated tradition *to speak for themselves*. To me, this was not only a radical step then, but remains so now, making the publication all the more relevant.

In his thoughtful and well-placed comments, Beckh does not pass sweeping judgements or confront us with startling generalizations. Where necessary, he provides gentle aids to understanding for the general reader. Here again, we come across a unique characteristic of Beckh's writing on Buddhism. Not only does he work from a basis of inner understanding but indicates directions for accessing the *meditative truths* behind the Buddha legend. While the reader is left with the task to verify these truths for him/herself, pointing them out itself allows Beckh to assign the texts the legitimacy and value due to them.

The section 'Buddha as a human being and spiritual teacher' also appears to be particularly important. Here Beckh gauges the extent of what we (are able to) know about the Buddha and explores how we can approach his person ourselves. In this context he stresses the significance of the 'poetical element' of the Buddhist canon. Beckh's insight into the deeper meaning of seemingly superficial outer characteristics of these texts is unique indeed. In contrast to many other descriptions of the Buddha legend, Beckh allows this element to penetrate his own writing, and he knows how to justify his approach in academic terms. No other publication I know has taken the significance of the particular textual forms into account. Winternitz (see above) is a good example for the tendency to cut out extensive parallelisms and repetitions. Beckh realizes the significance of the images and parables as a necessary counterweight to the 'abstraction of the sequences of technical terms' (p. 108).

In his Introduction to the 1958 reprint by Verlag Freies Geistesleben, Stuttgart, Heimo Rau writes (p. 11):

> The task [of writing the Buddha book] affords particular satisfaction to the linguist and religious historian, since he was concerned with characterizing Buddha and his teaching in such a way that reading it would

serve the German reader as a basis for his or her own fruitful engagement with the most significant personality in the spiritual history of
Asia. Whatever he did, he did from the heart. And thus, he achieved a
portrait which fills the scholarly material he so diligently acquired with
life and warmth. And yet the objectivity does not suffer. He chooses to
stay close to the original scriptures and brings the poetical beauty of the
Buddha legend to its legitimate position. Descriptions of this kind stand
in enlivening contrast to his academic observations. His sense for the
poetic word and the rhythm and musicality of the language [...] were of
decisive assistance to him. His enthusiasm and the inner fire with which
Hermann Beckh used to present his thoughts will remain unforgettable to those who have known him. They are equally effective in these
printed lines. In this form characterized by thoroughness and artful por-
trayal, this work enthrals the reader over and over again and remains
safe from becoming outdated.

It is in no way surprising that the Indologist Tilmann Vetter writes in
1988: 'The first volume of *Buddhismus* by H. Beckh (Berlin 1916) is still
a good introduction to the Buddha legend.'[84]

Beckh proved his linguistic scholarship in works that reach far into
his later anthroposophical output. His works are beginning to be reap-
praised today, for example in this volume. The fact that Winternitz in
his collection of texts from the Buddhist canon explicitly mentions his
debt to Beckh for the translation of a problematic term (*nimitta*) just
serves as a proof that his contemporaries recognized his philological
and linguistic knowledge and sensibility.[85]

Concluding remarks

Like other works in Beckh's extensive *oeuvre*, his *Buddha's Life and
Teaching* appears to be at once unique and typical. It is unique among
his scholarly Indological works in its general appeal and accessibil-
ity. Although standing before his explicitly anthroposophical master-
pieces, the work foreshadows these by its concern for humanity and its
stringent coupling of rigorous historical-philological methods with the
author's inner, meditative insights. And in this, it is 'typically Beckh'
and may allow those of us who are just starting to discover his work an
ideal starting point.[86]

Daniel Simeon and the Sage Asita

Manfred Krüger (Nuremberg)

 On 2nd January 2011 the news came—the sixteenth grandchild has arrived. The little lad is called Daniel Simeon. The choice of this name evoked in me spontaneous enthusiasm. It spoke to me, and I said to myself and then to others: This name-giving is for me the stimulus to write a new book.

Daniel [the prophet] had prophesied the Son of Man, and the wise man Simeon was the first human being to recognize him: after forty days at the Presentation in the Temple [Luke 2], not only Messiah as Saviour of Israel, but the Son of Man as Saviour of humanity. He announced it to the parents, Joseph and Mary, witnessed by Anna the seeress, and Luke later told the story.

Simeon was old and could only die after he would recognize the Saviour. This had now occurred.

I thought immediately of Rembrandt, who throughout his whole life painted, drew and etched the wise Simeon with the Child [pic. previous page]. When he died, his last piece of art was not quite finished. His artistic testament: Simeon with the Child, is also the title of the book that appeared in 2012, *Rembrandt und der weise Simeon—Die Erkenntnis des Menschensohnes* (by Manfred Krüger. Roderer, 2012. ISBN 3897837463, 9783897837461).

Simeon! I recall that Rudolf Steiner recognized[87] the wise Simeon the old-Indian seer Asita. Asita *redivivus*—Asita reborn! Who was Asita? What better than look up Hermann Beckh's book *Buddha's Life and Teaching*? Beckh tells the story of the wise Asita, who clairvoyantly perceived the process of birth around the Bodhisattva who was to become the Buddha. Through the 'air' he arrives at the palace of Suddhodana, Prince Siddhārtha's father, who receives the wise one in the figure of a common mortal. Hermann Beckh[88] writes:

> When the *ṛṣi* [sage] makes his wish known to see the newborn child, the king asks him to have a little patience, for the child was just sleeping. But the seer responds, 'It is not the habit of such great persons to sleep for long, their natural condition is waking', and directly the Bodhisattva effects his own awakening in order to pay his respects to the *ṛṣi*. The king offers the child to the seer. As the latter beholds the '32 signs' of the *mahāpuruṣa*, he falls at the feet of the Bodhisattva, calling out, 'Verily, a wondrous being has arisen to the world' and he venerates him in reverent awe. He then suddenly breaks into tears. The king, fearing a calamity for the child's future, asks the seer worriedly why he is shedding tears. Asita responds that he was not crying over the prince, but over himself because he was now an old man and aged; the prince Sarvārthasiddha, however, would certainly become a Buddha and 'initiate the movement of wheel of the norm' (i.e. proclaim the doctrine) for the salvation of gods and men.
>
> Just as, O great king, a flower of the Udumbara fig tree only arises over a long course of time, a holy Buddha only arises in the world after long world periods. The prince, however, will certainly awaken to this highest enlightenment of a Buddha and then save innumerable beings from the ocean of the cycle of rebirth (*saṃsāra*) and lead them across to the other shore, to the place of immortal salvation (*amṛta*). Because I will now, O king, no longer behold this gem of a Buddha (i.e. no longer witness the moment when the Bodhisattva becomes the Buddha), I am crying now and feel sorrowful in my heart.

The king, highly filled with joy, allows the *ṛṣi* to part from him after entertaining him lavishly.

Asita saw in the child of the great King Shuddhodana the Bodhisattva who is to become the Buddha, the human being who redeems himself. As Buddha he will no longer incarnate. Simeon recognized in the forty-day-old Jesus-child [the one]who becomes the Christ Who redeems humanity. And he praises God:

> Ruler of all,
> now dost thou let thy servant go
> in peace, according to thy word;
> for my own eyes have seen
> that saving power of thine
> which thou hast prepared
> in the sight of all nations.
> This is the light
> which shall give revelation to the Gentiles,
> this is the glory of thy people Israel.
> [Luke 2: 29-32. Knox version]

Both, Asita and Simeon, are old, very old. Youth does not seem to be wise. But exceptions exist: the twelve-year-old Jesus in the Temple, and the thirty-year-old Baptist John. The seeress Anna is also old, who reports to everyone expecting 'the redemption of Jerusalem' with the arrival of the Redeemer.

The child, who becomes the Buddha, has many earthly lives behind him. The child who becomes the Redeemer is only once on the Earth for thirty-three years.

Buddha has pointed humanity to the Path, the Eightfold Path with which each individual soul can approach perfection. Hereby, the soul leaves the physical body behind, which ultimately keeps the wheel of incarnation in movement; for 'all obligations are rectified on Earth'.

Christ is the Way, that unites the Truth with the Life. Whoever goes on the Way of Christ has part in the resurrection even of the physical body. On Golgotha the physical body is included in the redemption.

Asita takes the child in his arms and weeps, for he can no longer experience the rise of the Bodhisattva to the Buddha. Simeon takes the child in his arms and full of joy speaks God's praise. He can now die in the consciousness: In death this Child brings new life.

Hermann Beckh: The Search for the Lost Word

Susana Ulrich-Alvarez Ulloa (Öschelbronn)

 The work of Hermann Beckh is concerned with themes that on the one hand arose out of his investigations into Oriental culture, and on the other hand out of his inner connection to the world of speech and of music. In this contribution we concentrate on his studies on speech. I would like to preface it with a personal story that shows the significance of my relationship to Hermann Beckh's work.

On a journey to India, I heard a group of yoga students reciting their opening prayers. Most of the students were of Indian origin. Although I did not understand a word, it was immediately clear to me that this was not Hindi, which, since 1965—alongside English—has been the official language of India. The recitation produced a strange effect on me and through its sound I realized it had to do with a very ancient language. Later I became aware that the yoga students were reciting Sanskrit mantras.

This experience left a lasting impression on me, confirming my decision to study Indology. My interest in language is due to my work as a eurythmy therapist, as eurythmy,[89] an art of movement in the widest sense of the word, originates in language.

Through dealing with this ancient culture, I hoped to better understand the origin of language. Questions arose, such as: What meaning did language have at that time and how did the people perceive language? In order to answer these questions, I had first to undertake a demanding study of Sanskrit and its still older form in the Vedas.

In the midst of my studies, which were partly like wandering in the desert, the purpose of this great effort becoming increasingly distant, my singing teacher Ursula Koepf, who closely accompanied my steps, put into my hands Hermann Beckh's little book, *Neue Wege...* ('New Ways to the Source of Speech'). Reading the three lectures in this book, strengthened my decision to see to the end the path I had chosen. From then on Hermann Beckh's thoughts and insights were a great support to me, helping me to overcome moments of weakness.[90]

The three lectures held in 1921[91] belong to a time of emotional turmoil for Hermann Beckh. In the previous year, he had requested, from the Faculty of Philosophy of the University of Berlin, a sabbatical from his teaching position in Tibetan Philology, which was granted him until the end of the summer term 1921. Then he had to make an important decision for himself and his career.

After hearing Rudolf Steiner give a lecture in Berlin in 1911, he increasingly took part in the anthroposophical life. Full of devotion, he turned towards the task, which Rudolf Steiner had suggested to him, of renewing the approach to linguistics. He presented the results of his research to the public in the above-mentioned lectures. He writes[92] about this situation in a letter of 15 February 1921 to Ingeborg Stegemann:

> My own strength is at present completely taken up with preparations for Dornach, where I [will be engaged] in extensive studies to found a spiritualized linguistics that will draw the living element out of the word and language, a linguistics as Novalis had already imagined it and as Dr Steiner expected from me. What will become of it in the future remains to be seen. From this it also depends in the autumn—not before—whether I return to my activities in Berlin, or whether I find elsewhere the people with whom to work that will connect me with intimate tasks for humanity. At the moment everything is in transition and preparation.

Hermann Beckh did not return to his academic teaching, but his relationship to India remained unchanged throughout his life. In meeting anthroposophy, he was not only led to a deepened understanding of Indian culture, but also a new relationship to Christianity.[93]

On 21 August 1917 he writes concerning his two-volume work *Buddhism*, I. *The Buddha*, II. *The Teaching*:

> Buddhism as everything Indian is hereby not yet the highest, there also exist 'Mysteries of Christianity' (the saying is from Novalis), which demand an even deeper penetration.[94]

From now on he devoted himself to this new task of research with enthusiasm. This finally led him to participate in the founding of The Christian Community.[95] Also, in the field of linguistics, new viewpoints opened up for him. Novalis, whom he mentions in the above-quoted letter, was for him a special source of inspiration. In the first lecture 'Etymology and meaning of sounds in the light of spiritual science', we read:[96]

> The simple saying in Novalis' *Fragments*: 'Etymology is differentiated: genetic and pragmatic', is one of those unassuming future seeds that, on the basis of spiritual science, we can nurture to grow. It truly contains a comprehensive programme for linguistics of the future. Already with the investigations today, it will be shown what service for researching the deeper questions of language can be achieved by differentiating genetic and pragmatic etymology.

The quoted *Fragment* consists of five words without further explanation. Anyone else would perhaps have overlooked it, but for Hermann Beckh it opened a new field of research.[97] In it, he saw a 'seed for the future' and willingly took up the task of helping this seed to unfold. This development corresponds to Novalis' concern, as he saw his *Fragments* as stimuli and motivation to think further. He himself described it as the 'beginnings of an interesting train of thought—texts to think over', as he writes in a letter of 26 December 1798 to the magistrate Just, who later became the biographer of Novalis.[98] One of his well-known *Fragments* reads: '*Alles ist Samenkorn*'—'Everything is seed'. What Hermann Beckh produces out of this 'insignificant' seed is really remarkable.

His lecture 'Etymology and the Significance of Sounds in the Light of Spiritual Science' begins as follows:

> Already in the world 'etymology' from the Greek ἔτυμος 'true, genuine, real', lies the fact that the conventional meaning of the word does not mean for us the ultimate and highest, cannot yet say the actual truth about language. We have to penetrate more deeply into the origins of words in order to recognize the true meaning, content and value of words out of these origins.

Novalis points to this fact as the difference between pragmatic and genetic etymology.

While *Pragmatic Etymology* (from πρᾶγμα 'what is done, what has happened, the deed') investigates the origin of words that have already been created, with reference to the changes of those words over the course of time, such as the sound shift, *Genetic Etymology* (from the Greek γένεσις 'origin') is concerned with unlocking the primal original of the word. The way to this is not free of obstacles. One can trace a word right to its root, but then one asks the question how this particular sound relates to that which it expresses. How does a particular content connect itself with the individual root and out of this to the produced word? That is, how does the related concept arise?

There are different theories in linguistics such as the 'Kling-klang' theory, the 'A-ha' theory, the 'Wau-wau' theory and so on. Others proceed from an arbitrary ordering.[99]

Hermann Beckh was not satisfied with this. He had mastered several ancient languages: Avestan, Vedic, Sanskrit, Tibetan, Hebrew, Old Greek and Latin. His vast knowledge of languages offered him a wide, diversified basis to be able to approach this theme. A further important viewpoint came into consideration: it would be instructive not only to investigate the connection between sound and meaning, but also to test whether human consciousness, in relation to language and its meaning, had changed during mankind's development.

Beckh found out that language in all cultures was regarded as something extremely sacred. He turned his attention to the reasons that engendered such a respect for language—in the conviction that one from it can gain something for the future.

> In order to reach this experience of the speech of the future in the right way it is not without significance to look at those languages of the past of humanity which stand more closely connected than our modern languages to the origin of the human race. Different from modern European languages, ancient Sanskrit, ancient Avestan and ancient Hebrew allow us to approach those living origins of the word, that genetic etymology which we can only find in an incomplete manner in the word of today.[100]

However, we must not believe that it is possible to gain a correct understanding of the spirit that governed those far-off times if we look at it with our present point of view. It is no simple task to enter into the level of consciousness of the people of that time. Just at this point, language itself comes to our aid, for the mentality of the speaker is revealed through the word and through the language. The attitude of the people of earlier ages is reflected in the writings that have come down to us. In this consideration, the language of ancient India stands in the centre, the language of the Vedas, which plays such a great part in Beckh's descriptions.

The Veda (Sanskrit, वेद, veda: knowledge) contains, according to the root of the word, the knowledge of that time. We are speaking of an age difficult to date. For the composition of the Vedas, the academic view arrives at a timeframe from 1500 to 1000 BCE, whereas relevant Indian traditionalists claim this period is too late, since the written version of the Vedas does not coincide with the period of their composition.[101] It is seen as the highest human task to guard this knowledge, revealed by those wise seers, the seven holy Rishis[102] (Sanskrit, ऋषि, ṛṣi from dṛṣ: to see), in verbal form. Since then, it has passed on from generation to generation. The transmission of the received wisdom takes place exclusively orally, by word of mouth. Any other method would be regarded as unseemly. Moreover, recitation is necessary in order to preserve the strength contained in the words. Not only is the language with its semantic content important, but also the sound of this language, (being its phonological expression), which is intrinsically linked to it. The exact pronunciation of a word is of great importance; small deviations having devastating consequences in the ritual in which Vedic Hymns are used.[103]

The deeply felt reverence of the early Indian for language is founded on the belief that the universe has arisen out of the word, understood as the 'utterance of God'. Originally the word 'Veda', even before the knowledge of that time was gathered and written down, was regarded as divine utterance.[104] According to this view, the entire creation was breathed out and revealed through being fashioned into form through Brahmān, who presents the principle of creation.[105]

The important grammarian Bhartṛhari (c. 425-520 CE) begins his work Vākyapadīya ('Concerning Sentence and Word') as follows:

> Without beginning and end is Brahmān, who presents the imperishable true being of the word, through which the birth of the world unfolds through development into objects.[106]

In his work, Bhartṛhari says, 'simply expressed, the teaching of speech is the primordial ground of being'.[107] His profound philosophy of language, even if difficult to understand, contains valuable observations on the views of language in the pre-Christian Indian tradition. In the first part of his book, which deals with language as an all-embracing phenomenon, the connection between word and meaning is established:

> This [word] initially conceived by the faculty for knowledge, at some time is connected to a [specific] meaning, and is taken hold of [by the listener] through the sound produced by the speech apparatus.[108]

> Word, meaning and their connection are hereby taught by the great seers as eternal.[109]

The connection between word and meaning is presented in detail in the course of the work. One soon realizes, in his way of arguing, the 'otherness' of his view, which for us causes considerable difficulties and is not easy to follow. The ancient Indian did not doubt that between word and meaning there is connection, which has endured from the beginning and will do so for all eternity.

This fact is also mentioned by the French Orientalist Andrée Padoux (*1920) in his work *Vāc*. With *Vāc*, language is meant as act, as speech. In the Vedas it appears as a goddess of the poetically spoken word. Padoux points out the importance of name-giving and emphasizes that a close link exists between the name and that which is named. In the moment we give somebody or something a name, the one who is named becomes real and his existence revealed. Expressed in Padoux's words:

> A formulation that from the outset points to a major role of the Word, that of placing of names, *nāmadheya*; and giving a name, in mythic thought (not only in India) gives being. For the word, the name, as early as the Ṛgveda, is the very being of what is named; it is immortal.[110]

The process of giving a name is mentioned in the Ṛgveda, the oldest of the four Vedas, which at the same time is the oldest surviving text of India.

The other three Vedas are the Sāmaveda, 'the knowledge of the songs', the Yajurveda, 'the knowledge of the sacrificial verses' and the Atharvaveda (added later), a collection of magic verses for the healing of illnesses and magical formulae to banish demons.

The Ṛgveda, 'the knowledge consisting of verses', consists of 1028 Hymns, which are mostly dedicated to invoke and praise the gods.

The Hymns are arranged in ten books (Sanskrit, मण्डल, maṇḍala: 'circle'). In the Ṛgveda some Hymns can be found that praise the goddess of speech, Vāc.

One of these Hymns seems to be of central importance: RV X.71. Karl Friedrich Geldner, in an excellent translation of the Ṛgveda, describes it as follows: 'The Hymn called by the Indians the Song of Knowledge or Wisdom speaks about the question of the sacred speech—only this interests the poet of the Ṛgveda—its discover and its Mystery.'[111] The first verse of what is called the Song of Wisdom is:

> 1. Bṛhaspati![112] This was the first beginning of speech, when they came forth for the name-giving. The best and purest of what they possessed, that which was locked up within, was revealed through their friendship.

The above refers to the holy Rishis, the seers full of wisdom, who formed language and have revealed it, as is proclaimed in the next verse:

> 2. Where the wise ones have fashioned speech by contemplation, purifying it like wholemeal through a sieve ... [113]

In the Indian tradition, the course of this event is a controversial subject. The older tradition assumes the clairvoyant faculties of the Rishis who, having beheld everything with the inner eye, conveyed it in their verses.[114] Yet, the later Indian tradition believes in transmitting through hearing. In each case the Rishis have directly perceived from the divine and proclaimed the sacred wisdom.[115] Consequently, this oldest account of humanity is called श्रुति, śruti, 'that which is heard', taking the highest place in the Hindu canon, whereas the more recent texts are called स्मृति, smrti, 'that which is remembered'.

In any case the extraordinary pictorial quality of the Ṛgveda is remarkable. The message of the Rishis is always clothed in splendid expressive pictures that veil their actual meaning and for this reason are difficult to interpret.

For Hermann Beckh the options at his diposal are not mutually contradictory. He releases the tension by including both sides:

> [...] when [the early Indian] heard the word, the sound, 'something took place within him', and he beheld that which arose in him in a delicate etheric picture. Such tangible pictures later became abstract concepts.[116]

The tradition of naming in India belongs not to the past, but up to today is firmly anchored in the life of the people. In an old Vedic ritual, the Nāmadheya,[117] the name of the new-born child is conveyed by a Brahmin.

In his lecture 'Anthroposophy and Linguistics' held in Berlin in 1922, Rudolf Steiner points out the relevance of this theme to understanding the early Indian consciousness. In a short account of the subsequent lecture held by Hermann Beckh on 'The Poetic and Musical Element in Language', Steiner explains:

> We may not take Sanskrit with the same feeling towards speaking, towards language, as we look at language today. [...] At that time, when something like the word *manas* was still inwardly livingly taken hold of, something existed which I would like to call the experience of the meaning of the sounds.[118]

This indication concerning 'the experience of the meaning of the sounds' is taken very seriously by Hermann Beckh. This remark underpins his own conviction and corresponds to the heart of his research into language. One month later, Beckh pointed out the following in the Dornach lecture mentioned above:[119]

The actual experience of speech-sounds, which in the primal language coincided with the meaning of the word, has sunk into the subconscious. Through this the meaning of the word has become conventional. From an original, not merely indicative but a directly effective means, language has moved towards a mere means of communication.[120]

The renewal of linguistics has thus the task to raise the subconscious experience of sounds of speech into consciousness. The necessary means to carry out this, he adds, 'are no other than the intimate cognitive living in, and feeling into, the elements of the sounds of the word and of speech'.[121] In order to attain this, a more discriminating, strengthened perception of speech than is usually the case is necessary.[122] Beckh proceeds courageously on this new path. Arriving at the word's root, he does not stop, but takes a step further. He persists with each single sound, attempting to research the characteristics and possibilities of the expression of each sound and finds in Sanskrit a valuable support for this:

> Observations on the significance of speech-sounds, proceeding from Sanskrit, is especially meaningful in so far as the early Indians, apart from the teaching of *sphoṭa*[123] and in harmony with it, place quite concrete meanings for the single sounds of speech themselves. [...] Everywhere it has to be noted, that the essence of a speech-sound can only be characterized from a particular side. Only by combining the many-sided viewpoints can a full light illuminate the object.[124]

Based on his solid knowledge of language, new viewpoints in researching language and its meaning opened up for him through focusing and investigating the individual sounds. He and all those who join him on this path become aware of connections that hitherto had remained undiscovered.

One of the words described in detail in the same lecture is the Indian word *manas* mentioned by Rudolf Steiner. Here is a short but impressive excerpt:

> And so, *man* is the root of *manas* 'strength of thinking, spirit-strength standing behind the thinking', …the strength through which the human being is a thinking being, precisely a human being. The words *Manu* (cf. the Gk. *Minos* and Egyptian *Menes*), from which derive *mānuṣa, manuyṣa,*

'human being', all lead back to the root *man* 'thinking' (Avestan likewise *man*). Thus we learn to feel the *m* in the Germ. word *Mensch* [and English 'man'] itself connected to *manas*. How expressive is the Gothic word for 'mankind': *manaseths*, which actually [means] *Menschensaat* 'seed of man', *Manas-Saat*, mankind as a seed of *manas*, the heavenly manna (Heb. *mān*).[125]

An old Brahmanical legend tells how Manu survives the Flood with the help of a fish. Similar to Noah he was to build a ship. When the Flood came, he entered the ship drawn by the fish and was the sole survivor—the first human being. We find a later version of the Manu legend in the well-known Indian epic, the Mahābhārata. In this version he does not enter the ship alone but is accompanied by seven holy seers. Unlike Noah, they are not to take in any animals, but all the seeds of the Earth. These seeds are an image of the concentrated strength, which under favourable conditions unfolds and is revealed. Even thoughts possess a similar characteristic, as the above-quoted saying of Novalis proclaims: 'Alles ist Samenkorn'—'Everything is seed.'

The Rishis became the prophets and carriers of the divine knowledge, which was guarded by the Vedic priests, the brahmins. Prior to this, the brahmins had to carry out the *upanayana*, an initiation ritual. The *upanayana*, which takes place around the age of seven, is described by most brahmins as one of the most important moments of their life. The ritual is based on the belief that the one to be initiated thereby attains the status of a dvija, someone twice born.[126] Upon completing the *upanayana*, he becomes worthy of schooling, known as the *upadeśa*. From now on he may appropriate the wisdom of the Vedas and guard it for the coming generations. The instruction of the teacher begins within the ritual, forming its centre. The first thing that is deeply impressed on the child and has to be learnt by heart is 'the Gāyatrī Mantra', the one most recited by the brahmins, a most highly venerated mantra. It is whispered by the teacher into the ear of the child and learnt by heart through an astonishingly precise imitation and untiring repetition.

Here we add Beckh's translation of the Gāyatrī mantra rendered into English. In a wonderful way he explains its meaning in his lecture 'The Physical and Spiritual Origin of Speech':

tat savitur vareṇyam / bhargo devasya dhīmahi / dhiyo yo naḥ pracodayāt //

The love-awakening light of the enlivening Sun-being, of the divine, let us receive into ourselves, that it stimulates our thinking to move forwards.[127]

The Hymn addresses Savitṛ, the Sun-god. The divine motivating strength of Savitṛ is to set our thinking into motion, the faculty that makes us human.

For the brahmacārin, 'he who is on the path to Brahmān' begins an ascetic life with strict discipline. The brahmin has to prove himself worthy of the sacred revelation of the Vedas through self-education. The unveiling of the sacred knowledge is made possible through the refined perception of speech, which a brahmin has to achieve.

The view of the early Indian rests on the fact that what we hear is but a part of speech:

> Speech is measured in four parts, known to the contemplative brahmins. The three parts, which are kept hidden, they do not divulge. The fourth part of speech is what people usually speak. [RV I.164.45][128]

Bhartṛhari probably relates to this saying about speech when in the above-quoted work he describes three of its areas in more detail, described as sounding, silenced and not-sounding. They present three stages in refining speech, from the sensory-audible to the spiritualized speech appearing in the form of light.[129] All the levels of speech are linked to each other and form a path from the audible part up to the sublime sphere of speech and, in reverse manner, from the ideal part, not perceptible to the senses, down to the physically audible expression of speech. As Bhartṛhari, however, indicates, the non-audible speech should be of far greater importance that the audible. The unspoken contains in itself a free space, in which every single word, as all words, together form a unity. Out of this stillness is created in the moment, in which the divine Voice resounds, the entire creation and with it speech in its most primordial form.

Hermann Beckh also presents the conviction of the early Indians that, in order to completely be able to lay hold of the essence of speech, one has to take into account, along with its physical manifestation, also its spiritual dimension. In his attempts to show us the path to this, the underlying intention is revealed, to cast light on the spiritual element of speech, that in our age is hardly considered. The certainty lived in him that we could come to understand or even arrive at the knowledge of the spiritual element of speech, when with full application we attempt with our conscious and active will to connect with the spirit.[130]

This thought of Hermann Beckh's becomes clearer in a passage further on in the same lecture:[131]

What has been said about genetic etymology and the meaning of speech-sounds is never to be understood as though the application of spiritu-al-scientific methods to the phenomena of language could only lead to reading the meaning of *each* word out of its sounds. Yet we learn through these methods, which in a certain manner are also presented in eurythmi-cal presentations of the words and speech-sounds, to consider individu-ally the value of words, to differentiate from the less expressive ones, an expressive or, as Novalis says, a *'rightig fortpflanzendes' Wort*—a 'rightly propagating' word. We learn to decide the choice of words not only according to their conventional meaning, but according to their genetic, expressive value. [...] In that the word and speech-sound through spiri-tual-scientific methods become Imaginations for us again, we experience with words something that points us directly towards a spiritual world. Out of this world have flowed thinking and language, as well as man with his speech organs and man's whole sensory-cosmic environment.

Because of our blind striving for progress, we have increasingly lost sight of our origins and thereby left out of consideration that today's progress is only possible thanks to past millennia. By not including this aspect of history, we shall never attain the breadth of view necessary to really become global citizens. One can, however, observe, that based on a lack of interest in our own roots, the consciousness for the meaning and the purpose of our past will become increasingly lost. Interest in the early cultures and especially in the early languages is becoming rare. The following thought of Bhartṛhari, although it originates centu-ries ago, has not for this reason lost its relevance:

Science does not smile on those who neglect the ancients. [Bhartṛhari][132]

Hermann Beckh, who on the one hand carefully approached the begin-nings of human culture and on the other hand, pointed to the future, opened up new ways of understanding and comprehension, which with his far-seeing gaze can serve as a model for us. This contribution only shows a tiny fragment of his activity as a researcher, seeking the spiritual source of speech. This search was a central concern of his and formed the basis for a renewal of linguistics. We close with his own words:

In an especially deep sense, in a sense that at the same time brings us closer to the questions of speech that we have mentioned, we can name that which humanity has lost, had to lose through its development, as the 'lost word'. Rudolf Steiner once said that all spiritual science is in a certain sense nothing other than a search for the lost word.

Bibliography

– Beckh, Hermann (1916): *Buddhismus—I. Der Buddha, II. Die Lehre*. Sammlung Göschen. Berlin und Leipzig. One-vol. ed. *Buddha und seine Lehre*. Stuttgart: Urachhaus 1958/98/2012. Eng. tr. *Buddha's Life and Teaching*. TL 2019.

– Beckh, Hermann (1954): *Neue Wege zur Ursprache*. Verlag Urachhaus, Stuttgart.

Consists of three lectures:

– *Etymologie und Lautbedeutung im Lichte der Geisteswissenschaft*. Dornach, 7 April 1921.

– *'Es werde Licht'—Schöpfungsurworte der Bibel und Urbedeutung der Laute im Lichte der Geisteswissenschaft.'* Zürich, June 1921.

– *'Der physische und der geistige Ursprung der Sprache'*. Stuttgart, Sept. 1921.

– All three lectures originally pub. individually, Stuttgart: Verlag Der Kommende Tag. All in Eng. tr. in *The Source of Speech*, TL 2019.

– Bronkhorst, Johannes (1989): *Veda*. Annals of the Bhandarkar Oriental Research Institute 70. 125-35.

– Heinl, Oliver (2013): *Einblicke in das Wesen der Sprache*. Verlag epubli. Berlin.

– Kačer-Bock, Gundhild (1997): *Hermann Beckh Leben und Werk*. Stuttgart: Verlag Urachhaus. Eng. tr. *Hermann Beckh Life and Work*, TL 2021.

– Geldner, K. F. 1(1923) (2008): *Rig-Veda Das heilige wissen Indiens*. Hrsg. und eingeleitet von Peter Michel. Wiesbaden: Marix Verlag.

– Mauthner, Fritz (1912): *Zur Sprachwissenschaft*. http://www.textlog. de/31001.html

– Mukhopadhyaya (1999): *Importance of Sound in the Tradition of Vedic Chanting*. Indira Gandhi National Centre for the Arts: New Delhi.

– Lommel, Hermann (1964): *Altbrahmanische Legenden*. Zürich u. Stuttgart: Artemis Verlag.

– Lutzker, Peter (1996): *Der Sprachsinn. Sprachwahrnehmung als Sinnesvorgang*. Stuttgart: Verlag Freies Geistesleben.

– Padoux, Andre (1992): *Vāc*. Delhi: Sri Satguru Publications: Delhi.

– Rau, Wilhelm (2002): *Bhartṛhais Vākyapadīva*. Stuttgart: Franz Steiner Verlag.

– Schulz, Gerhard (1981): *Novalis Werke*. Studienausgabe. München: Verlag C.H. Beck.

– Sivaramamurti, C. (1981): *Rishis in Indian Art and Literature*. Delhi: Kanak Public.

– Steiner, Rudolf (1994): GA 81. *Erneuerungs-Impulse für Kinder und Wissenschaft*. Basel: Rudolf Steiner Verlag.

– Stenzler, A.F. (1876-78): *Pāraskara: Indische Hausregeln.* Leipzig: Brockhaus.
– Stevenson, M.S. (1920): *The Rites of the twice-born*: London: Oxford Univ.
– Zimmermann, Ursula (2013): *Eurythmie. Skizze einer neuen Kunst.* Dornach: Verlag am Goetheanum.
– Witzel, M. (2007): *Rig-Veda Das heilige Wissen.* Deutschland: Verlag der Weltreligionen.

Ill 1: The oral teaching of the Vedas. Sivaramamurti (1981)

Ill 2: Teaching the Vedas today
http://www.unesco.org/culture/ich/RL/00062

Prof. Dr Hermann Beckh: Pioneer Linguistic Work in the Light of Christ

Oliver Heinl (Oldberg)

Partial views and holistic vision

Each detail of the constellation and the events that one encounters during one's earthly life can be viewed in the most varied ways. This experience belongs to the most important and partly possibly most difficult insights. It is relatively unimportant which kind of viewpoint one prefers to assume; it is important to understand that one is able to recognize the limitations of a single viewpoint. It is erroneous to live in the belief that a valid aspect of a viewpoint could encompass the whole truth. This only applies to the profane life and private concerns, but this knowledge is eminently important for the whole world of contemporary science. Every honest researcher understands this ancient wisdom and more or less respects it in his daily work.

This article is concerned with such a researcher who throughout his life did this, always striving to reach a complete view of things. Hermann Beckh worked untiringly for anthroposophical spiritual science inaugurated by Rudolf Steiner. Besides his passion for the research of Far Eastern wisdom-teaching, Beckh was also a pioneer in the realm of spiritual-scientific linguistics, not least thanks to his great talents and tremendously sensitive perception. As one of the first, he understood how to implement the impulses that Steiner introduced into the realm of research of the word. He sowed the seeds for a future, necessarily contemporary approach to linguistics. So, today too, nearly 80 years after Beckh's death, the world's linguistic scholars can receive valuable supplements to their views that often appear very one-sided.

Not only Hermann Beckh, but also scholars of the Eastern mysteries who preceded him have emphasized that a main concern of the historical Buddha was to bring the limitation of earthly viewpoints before the eyes of his pupils and followers. Buddha was concerned with a soul-understanding of a higher kind, able to go beyond a merely logical recognition.[133] For this the Buddha used, for example, that parable which illuminates the difference existing between the higher knowledge he taught and the taught opinions of the various speculative systems. He compares the followers of the diverse speculative directions who quarrel over all the metaphysical questions, with some persons born blind who explore an elephant. Each of these blind people touches one body-part of the elephant: one the foot, another the trunk, the next the tail, and again another an ear of this animal. Accordingly, each of these blind people, because of the limitations of his senses and limited field of touch, gives a completely different description of the elephant. He is initially completely convinced that what he perceives is the truth. Indeed, having touched, felt, and experienced it, he can consequently describe his own experience of the elephant's make-up. The ensuing difference of opinions leads to a quarrel and finally a brawl.

With this parable something characteristic for the philosophy of Buddhism is taught. It has to do with the fact that to Buddha each worldview is justified, because each one in their—although limited—realms pictures in the right way the reality to be experienced. The views and opinions uttered by all the blind people consequently present a certain lower and limited viewpoint of the whole composition of the truth. The mistake of the observer lies solely in not recognizing this limitation of one's own standpoint, of one's own experience, and of defending one's own opinion so drastically and emphatically as if it already would entail the full reality. Buddha was concerned to lead the soul of his pupils to that higher standpoint of the 'knowledge that beholds'. This cannot be reached by a lower thinking bound to the senses. For such a knowledge that beholds, all those who alone hold on to a sensory thinking, seeking to fathom the world-contexts, appear like those described in the parable as born blind.

Differentiating in linguistics

Such basically easily understood teachings of leading human personalities are today often neither understood nor taken up with the necessary respect and earnestness. In the age of technology and rapid developments, one feels beyond such philosophical pictures. Instead of the demand for a holistic overview, on which only a few scholars and people in general orient themselves, the demand has stepped in to find 'the devil hiding in the details', as the German saying goes [= 'study of the small print'—*Tr.*]. Only, what does one expect on finding this devil? An examination of this leading thought can and should lead us to a collective vision, the leading picture of a *new symbolism* to be created through this commemorative volume, not the demand of—this word to be taken literally and not as an evaluation—a diabolical concern.

The syllable '-bolic' stems from the Old Greek *ballō,* or the Greek *bállein* (to throw). In connection with the syllable 'dia', which in its numerous variations always describes separation, doubting (*Zweifeln*—notice *Ent-Zwei-en* 'divide into two'), dividing into parts, forms the word *diabállein,* which is usually translated as 'to divide' and 'to slander', but actually means 'to throw apart'. I do not wish to use this naming as a criticism, but only to characterize the difference between various approaches. Many themes today are taken apart and described and interpreted in increasingly complicated detail, nevertheless at the price of no longer recognizing the whole. Here the frequently great use of such approaches should in no way be looked at negatively. On the contrary, without a conscious study of the details, indeed, without directing attention towards the single part and know the devil in it, he, the devil, cannot be recognized in it. Ultimately each research has to do with the will to acknowledge. But when this to a certain extent has been achieved, one always has to return to the greater whole in order to survey how the detail stands in relationship to the whole context, how it fits into the whole and therein makes its effect. Hermann Beckh fully possessed this strength and talent to such a comprehensive beholding, especially on the path of anthroposophically-oriented linguistics.

The means using spiritual-scientific methods to research words, however conceivably simple to state, are nevertheless a completely new manner to behold the life of the word, indeed life as such. Consequently, the anthroposophical method not only takes place on the outwardly chosen path of the search for knowledge. It is aware of the simplicity of the venture, to intend to explain and trace the facts of speech—words—alone to their earlier forms. The connection of the essence of a speech-sound and its meaning, the living element of language, repeatedly crosses the path that only explains what is directly perceptible and can be evidenced—what is called pragmatic etymology. Only an etymology of sources that characterizes, searches for these new paths and methods. One of the most brilliant and most talented personalities of early Romanticism, Friedrich Freiherr von Hardenberg (Novalis), was the first to differentiate, as he called it:

- a *genetic etymology,* that is, research of the origin of speech-sounds and of words that illuminate the connection between the becoming sound and its meaning, and

- the normally employed manner of *pragmatic etymology*, one of [studying] the [word as] deed, what is done; it traces back the destiny of the word in space and time, that is, its historical development.

Novalis and Beckh

Novalis was a great artist and spiritual researcher and thanks to his great talent was early in the position to achieve such a comprehensive vision of the expressions of language. Linking to his theses and clothed with the necessary spiritual equipment, Hermann Beckh went on the search to discover the origin of words and formulated the necessary means and methods which are suggested in order to make possible an holistic research of speech.

> The means here are no other than the intimate cognitive living in, and feeling into, the elements of the sounds of the word and of speech. Amongst the twelve senses of which spiritual science speaks, besides the sense of hearing, or the sense of sound, there exists the actual sense for language, the sense to perceive the characteristics of the word and its meaning, as distinct from the mere perception of the sounds.

Hermann Beckh spoke these highly significant words during his lecture held in Dornach on April 7 1921, 'Etymology and the meaning of speech-sounds in the light of spiritual science'. From someone who had behind him his own research journey lasting many years through the world of Far-Eastern wisdom-teaching and languages, and already in 1916 had produced the masterly *Buddha's Life and Teaching*, Hermann Beckh here sketches the path which in future will be the human being's own path of becoming, his own development in language—ultimately recognizing that it has to be travelled. It is the path of feeling oneself into, thinking into and immersing one's will into the spiritual connections that lie as the basis of the world and its physical revelations.

> The word, too, of which linguistics today only knows, as it were, the outer physical body, possesses an ether-body behind the physical manifestation. In an especially magnificent way, this super-sensory element, this auric element of the word is felt in Avestan, the ancient sacred language of Zarathustra. Zarathustra himself speaks of this, of how the essence of the word, as it were, relates to the divine, with the great cosmic aura, with Ahura Mazdah ('Ahura' has become 'aura' in Persian). [...][134]

The elevating security with which Hermann Beckh here announces the aura of the word allows the question: from whence could he find this security? Who was this Hermann Beckh and what contribution can the study of his publications—regarding linguistics—limited to a few pages offer? In this *Celebration* no doubt Hermann Beckh's career is dwelt on sufficiently, so at this juncture we need only indicate the most relevant points of this unique human being.

Beckh's career

The necessary faculty for his later knowledge, as mentioned above, was laid in his cradle. The talent to receive sense-impressions, moods of nature and sounds formed in the soul of the child a very pronounced ability to differentiate. According to his own account, already early on he experienced something supersensible, convincing him that behind the material world a far more open world is hidden through which the human being passes before [his birth] and after his death.

After his school finals Beckh's fellow students talked him into studying law, which he concluded with a work that earned a prize.[135] Following this Beckh worked until 1899 as an Assistant Judge. Nevertheless, he ended this path after having to convict [in a case] that heavily injured his feelings for justice. Through this he finally felt that convicting was against his nature. Instead, he was inclined to achieve something fruitful and constructive for society. So he began to study Indian and Tibetan mythology, graduated, and through this became one of the few, excellent experts in the subject. He taught for some time as a private tutor in Berlin, and then in 1911 through a lecture of Rudolf Steiner he became aware of anthroposophy. From then on, a new fire was kindled in Beckh's life; after personal meetings with Rudolf Steiner and Friedrich Rittelmeyer, he dedicated himself extensively to study the basic writings of Steiner and he joined the Anthroposophical Society. After the appearance of his work *Buddha's Life and Teaching* he had to enter War service in 1916. Soon after was called to the 'Institute for Shipping and World Commerce' in Kiel, where he had to evaluate the business reports in the Scandinavian papers. For this he had to learn the Nordic languages. Since then, besides the languages learnt in his studies, he was able to speak English, French, Italian, Greek, Latin, Hebrew, Egyptian, Syrian, Sanskrit, Tibetan and Avestan and on top of this the languages of the north-Germanic branch.

During his life Beckh held lectures on diverse themes to the Anthroposophical Society. Alongside spiritual-scientific linguistic studies and themes, including the Eastern traditions of wisdom, Beckh began to concern himself with questions about music, the essence of the musical keys and its connection with the starry forces. He gave himself extensively to this study. Beckh sought to find the cosmic laws of the forces of the zodiac reflected in their various manifestations in all realms. Thereby he connected his knowledge of the ancient languages with the knowledge concerning the language of the speech-sounds and tonality in music, the colourful circle of fifths of the musical keys. In a later period of his activities, he expounded two of the four gospels according to the above-mentioned points of view.

Arnold Wadler

Without Hermann Beckh's work Dr Arnold Wadler would not, or at least not so early, have met with the anthroposophically-oriented spiritual science of language, which would possibly have hindered or delayed his considerable deed for humanity, the work *Der Turm zu Babel*. Wadler already in 1919 read a brochure by Beckh which deeply impressed him. In this publication we cannot pursue Dr Wadler further. This will be followed up more extensively on another occasion.

Beckh's lectures on speech

The publications of Beckh's lectures on speech are significant in this connection. Besides the already-mentioned report on the lecture 'Etymology and the meaning of speech-sounds in the light of spiritual science' these are the writings: 'The Physical and the Spiritual Origin of Speech', and the write-up of a lecture Beckh held in June 1921 in Zürich, as well as the write-up of the lecture 'Let there be light' of 7 September 1921, held in Stuttgart [all reprinted together in *Neue Wege* ... Eng. tr. in *The Source of Speech*]. Alongside important interpretations of connections to the primordial root-language, Beckh pointed in particular to a still more important characteristic of an holistic striving in linguistics.

What has been said about genetic etymology and the meaning of speech-sounds is never to be understood as though the application of spiritual-scientific methods to the phenomena of language could only lead to reading the meaning of *each* word out of its sounds. Yet we learn through these methods, which in a certain manner are also presented in eurythmic presentations of the words and speech-sounds, to consider individually the *value of words*, to differentiate from the less expressive ones, an expressive or, as Novalis says, a *'richtig fortpflanzendes' Wort*—a 'rightly propagating' word. We learn to decide the choice of words not only according to their conventional meaning, but according to their genetic, expressive value. We gain another, more active attitude to the word and speech. This leads beyond Mauthner's assumption, as if words only contained abstract concepts in a conventional manner, or as if only confused, dim memories of sense-impressions would be grasped through them. In that the word and speech-sound through spiritual-scientific methods become Imaginations for us again, we experience with words something that points us directly towards a spiritual world. Out of this world have flowed thinking and language, as well as man with his speech organs and man's whole sensory-cosmic environment. We gain an organ for the individual element, hence what are called synonyms that delineate the same concept of different words of the same language or of different languages. In this element of individual differentiation, we learn where on the one side the spiritual origin of speech has been obscured, and on the other side we glimpse an enrichment.[136]

The word for 'human being' and 'light'

Thus far for the words of a true priest of the Son of Mankind, of the Cosmic Word. Beckh recognized in his hitherto unique manner how the choice of words, especially of the early peoples, leave their spiritual traces crystal clear to this day. Thus, he places the word *Mensch*, the human being, in all its greatness before the observer, by pointing out that the human being is a thinking, spiritual being. Behind the thinking, the essential power of thinking governs, as in Sanskrit *manas* (spirit, meaning, understanding), *man* (believe, think, mean [an opinion]), *manu* (human being), *mani* (jewel) or in Ancient Indian *mánas* (human being, thought, soul, spirit). In Ancient Greek *Ant^{h}ró-pos* (human being) Beckh sees rather the soul aspect of the concept 'human being', the one who looks to the heights; he perceives the glowing, upwards striving emotion expressed in the soul (*ant^{h}rakia$^-$*= glow; *ant^{h}os* flower). In contrast to these words striving towards the heavenly sphere, Latin shows more the aspect turning towards the earthly element, of naming the earth, *humus* (earth), *homo* (the human being), also in Hebrew *adámâ* (earth) and *ádám* (human being). Beckh points, as Steiner before him, towards the balancing gesture of the sound M, which between the H striving towards the heights and the S inclined towards the Earth, shows itself as the connecting balance. Thus, the word *humus* that contains this triad is placed significantly before our soul.

With such descriptions Hermann Beckh in his works points characterizing and explaining the completely different feelings of the peoples expressed in their choice of words. Already purely from this aspect there arises a completely new, much more careful manner of approach towards the etymological study of words, not to mention the manner of approach to the laws of metamorphosis of speech-sounds.

Thus I, too, have to thank this splendid man that he helped the light, which previously Arnold Wadler had already kindled in me, to continue to shine. And precisely to this *light* and its varied facets I would like again to allow Dr Beckh to explain:

> We meet a special richness of expressions in speech when we look at the word 'light' in the various languages. A variety reminding us of the conditions of the original, root-language is shown us here by the Vedic Sanskrit. It is as if the early Aryan Indians, far removed from being satisfied with the general, abstract concept for 'light', still felt the most varied nuances of the light and would have expressed this quite tangibly. And yet it is possible, by surveying the Indo-European realm of speech on the one side and semitic Hebrew on the other, to pick out four large, main groups for 'light' and pursue their development in the various realms of language.
>
> (1. Early Aryan) A first main group is formed by the words leading back to the early Aryan root for 'light' $\sqrt{d\bar{\imath}}$ from which, besides the main words of later classical Sanskrit for 'light', also the words of the Gk., Lat. and Germanic languages are derived. In this root $\sqrt{d\bar{\imath}}$ the bright vowel *ī* is expressively connected with the sound *d* indicating the clear contours of the outer world beheld in the light of the senses. (Originally *dī* means 'to fly', that means, the tangible appearance of the flying arrow with which the arrows of light of the Sun are compared.) The Aryan thinks with 'light' especially of the physical, tangible, bright daylight. And so from the root $\sqrt{d\bar{\imath}}$ we have Indian *dyu*, Lat. *dies* the day, Eng. *day*, Indian *Dyaus* (genitive *Divas*) the bright sky of day, Gk. Ζεύς (genitive Διός), *Dyaus-pitar* 'Father (heaven)' (the god of Light of the early Aryan Indians) = Lat. *Jupiter* (genitive *Jovis*). In one part of these words *d* is already transformed to *div* 'shining' of which *deva* 'god' (actually a shining, raying being), Lat. *deus*, and Gk. δῖος 'divine' are derived. Further developments of the root are Skr. *dyut* and *jyut* 'to shine', then *jyotis* (spoken 'djotis'), the main word for 'light' in later classical Sanskrit.
>
> When the aspirate, the spiritual *h*, is joined with the *d* to the root 'light' *dī*, the word *dhi* 'the thought' arises. The light painting the contours of the outer world then becomes the light of thought that reflects spiritual contours; the word *dīdhi* derived from *dī*, or *dhi*, in classical Sanskrit means 'beam of light', in the earlier Vedic language it also means the spiritual

beam of the light of devotion and contemplation. … The spiritual connection of light and thought in the relationship of *dī* and *dhī* receives in
speech a significant expression. The mantram on light of the Rig-Veda
(III 62, 10), is completely tuned to this relationship that speaks to the
early Indian of how, through receiving it within, he has to transform the
outer sunlight into spiritual light, the light of thought.

tat savitur vareṇyaṃ
bhargo devasya dhīmahi
dhiyo yo naḥ pracodayāt

'The love-awakening light of the enlivening Sun-being, of the divine, we
will take up into ourselves in order that it give our thinking a forward
impetus.' […]

[2. Hebrew] The root √*dī* and everything deriving from it speak in
some way of the physical daylight, which allows us to recognize the contours of the sensory world, whereas the Hebrew root √*'h-v-r* (spoken as
'ôr') 'the light' leads us back completely to the spiritual origins of the
light, 'and the Godhead (the community of the Elohim) spoke: Let there
be light! And there was light': *vayomer Elohīm vehi ôr vavehi ôr*. The *'h,*
aleph, is the potential, the impulse to create still lying in the spirit, *v (vau)*
as the mystical sound of the Hebrew alphabet, profoundly discussed by
Fabre d'Olivet (*La Langue Hébraique restitué.* Paris 1815).[137] But it is still
not yet recognized in its ultimate primal meaning, as so to speak the
primal sound itself, the cosmic Being which expresses itself in the music
of the spheres, in the cosmic weaving. Rudolf Steiner says of the primal
word *vha*—it is a matter of convention whether I transcribe the Indian
व Hebrew ו written sounds as *v* or *w*, the pronunciation stood in many
cases closer to the English *w*, and in others closer to the *v*—(Indian *vāc* =
λόγος, Lat. *vox, voc-em* = Indian *vācam*):

> the Indian called what lives as forces in the universe *wha* … When
> the Indian pupil rose into the spiritual world, he perceived through
> the music of the spheres and the word of the spheres how the primal
> spirit Brahman is divided through evolution, and he hears this out of
> the primal word *wha*. This was the designation of the primal word of
> creation which the pupil heard, and in it he heard the whole evolu-
> tion of the world. The word divided into seven members; the primal
> word of creation was active in the soul of the pupil, the primal word,
> which he described in the same way as we today would describe our
> world-evolution … and this description we find again in what was

called the Veda, or in German *das Wort* [or English 'the word'] [Rudolf Steiner, *Egyptian Myths and Mysteries*. GA 106. Lecture 4. Leipzig. 5 Sept. 1908].

Veda is the knowledge, that is primal knowledge, from the root √*vid* 'to know', in which the two sounds of the root of light connect with the primal sound *v*, the symbol of the primal word; *vid* is also the reversal of *div* 'to shine', so that also from this side the connection of the physical and the spiritual light is expressed through the language. In the Hebrew word for light *ôr,'h-v-r*, the divine-creative primal power '*h* (aleph), the impulse of creation still in the spirit relates to the primal sound *v* and this connection leads to *r*, towards the emanation of the light. The primal sound (*v*) is connected to the primal light (*r*); the Hebrew *ôr,'h-v-r*, already out of its speech-sounds means 'out of the divine-spiritual ('*h*), expressing itself in speech (*v*), is the light (*r*)', consequently the mantric power of the *vayômer Elohim vehi ôr vavehi ôr.* [And God said, 'Let there be Light'.] The sound *r* (in Sanskrit √*r* means 'to move') means the movement of propagation, emanation, in the highest sense emanation of the light, of the light-waves; the speech-sound *r* is related to the human eye (or in a certain spiritual sense to the place between the eyes), consequently the Hebrew root √*r'h-h* (*râ*) 'to see' (still to be found in Eng. 'ray', ray of light) is one of the primal words of humanity. [...]

[3. Greek] In the Greek *φῶς* we find another primal-light word that lies a step lower in the sensory [world] than the Heb. '*h-v-r* אור]] the most spiritual of all words for light. The *φ* stands still close to the *v*, the *ς* (s) lies already in the sensory appearances. In Sanskrit the root √*bhās* 'to shine', as noun *bhās* 'the light', corresponds to the Gk. *φῶς* (in the sense of strict scientific 'pragmatic' etymology). In an especially remarkable way, the etymological connections of this word allow us to experience indirectly the relationship of primal light and primal sound, as it gives itself to the clairvoyant and presents itself *directly* in the Hebrew primal word '*h-v-r*. In those regions where we have to seek for the origin of the word, light and sound stand closer to each other than in the outer, physical world. And so we find an inner connection between the Greek *φῶς* 'light' and *φωνή* 'sound, voice' (where in place of the *s* that relates to the sensory and visible, the more resonant *n* has appeared), and the same relationship as between *φῶς* and *φωνή* exists in Sanskrit between *bhās* 'to shine, light' and *bhan* 'to sound, to speak'. Even with keeping the sibilant in Sanskrit, there has arisen, besides *bhās* 'to shine', a verb *bhāṣ* (spoken 'bhash'), 'to speak', *bhāṣā* 'language'. From the Vedic Sanskrit numerous words could be listed that at the same time would designate appearances of sound and light, and in the Hebrew besides a root *halal* 'to shine', there stands the same-sounding root *halal* 'to rejoice', cf. the Germ. *hallen* 'to sound' and *hell* 'bright', both visible and audibly.

[4. An internalization] A fourth major group of words for light is finally the one out of which in New High German the word *Licht* 'light' itself derives. As a primal seed of speech, a root at the base in which the *r* of the emanating movement, of the emanation of light, is connected with the creative *k*, which in Sanskrit in many cases has already become palatal, and consequently appears as *c* (spoken 'tsh'), √*rc* 'to radiate', from which *arka* 'the ray', 'the Sun', *arcis* 'ray of light', or with the transition of the *c* into the tender *j* (spoken 'dsh'), *rj*, or *arj* 'to shine, to ray'; from here derives *arjuna* (spoken 'árdscoona') 'white, light', and as a name Arjuna, the bright hero of the *Bhagavadgita*. Also, as a noun, *rc* means 'splendour, light', at the same time 'poetic hymn', from which Rig-Veda, the 'Vedic hymns'. The *v* of the mystic primal sound or primal word, of the primal weaving, connects with the *r-c*, to *r-v-c*, from which derive *varcas* 'splendour of light', and with the vocalizing of the *v* the root √*ruc* 'to shine', *ruc* 'the light' derive, hence *rukma* 'glistening', *rukṣa* 'glistening, radiating' and other derivations, Avestan *raoco* 'light', *raokhšna* (spoken 'raochshna'), 'bright, glistening'. (The expressive vocalizing with the words of Avestan allows the element of the feelings, the reaction of the soul, to come more to the fore, whereas in the more consonantal words of Sanskrit, the element of thought predominates which mirrors the contours of the outer sense-impression.)

In Latin, the Sanskrit word for light, *ruc*, with a significant transition of the *r* into *l*, appears as *lux, lucis* 'the light', to which in Greek the adjective λευκὸς 'white' is added. In Sanskrit, too, the transiton from *r* to *l* takes place in *lok* or *loc* 'to see', *āloka* 'the seeing', 'the light', *locana* 'the seeing, the eye', *loka* 'the realm of the visible, the world'; it is remarkable that in the earlier Vedic Sanskrit, the consonant *l* is still rare, and the *r* predominates. In Avestan, which stands close to Vedic Sanskrit, that *l* is entirely missing, substituted by *r*. In later Sanskrit we find that the *l* increasingly emerges at the expense of the original *r*. One should not draw the conclusion that *l* is everywhere nothing original or does not belong to the primal language; but in Avestan and the Veda it had already fallen into decadence. Between *r* and *l* a similar polarity exists as between *j* and *v*. Spiritually taken, *r* lies more within sight, *l* more in the region of the heart.[138]

Sufficient of this somewhat extensive passage from Hermann Beckh's pioneering lecture. A detailed study of his short explanations will establish that Beckh possessed the ability to portray in the briefest space a closely packed amount of information. Beckh never dreamt of using an unnecessary word. From his descriptions a clear picture results of a future, complete etymological research. A new approach to the origin and significance of the metamorphosis of words stands before us. Hermann Beckh places in our hands four main groups to name the light, which prove fruitful. He gives four main terms for light, the words *di*, *ôr*, *p^hōs* and *arc*. This results in the following. From each of the four groups of speech-sounds,

> dental or teeth sounds (D, T, TH, S),
> labial or lip sounds (B, P, F, M, W, V),
> velar or palatal sounds (G, K, H, CH, Q, X),
> lingual sounds and glottal sounds (R, L),

we receive a word. The designation *di* clearly belongs to the dental sounds, to the palatal sounds the word *arc*, to the lip sound *p^hōs* and out of the fourth group, the throat or lingual sounds, we find *ôr* appearing to Beckh as the earliest appearing designation for light.

Using a databank that I have provided and a conceptual numerical key a possible allocation of sounds results, which fully supports Hermann Beckh's account, though here only a beginning can be made. Each of the four named classes of speech-sounds, each according to how many consonants a word is to possess, has a specific number of possible combinations of sounds. So, with a word of two consonants there are 21 possible variants of the basic sound. As will be shown in a later treatment, with the help of this key it allows a glimpse of the prototypes of the art of constructing human language. Thus, one day it could be possible to reconstruct actual primordial words of a primordial language that at one time existed.

How can it be stated here—proceeding from a word with two kinds of consonants—that there result 21 possible combinations of sounds? This can be indicated. Take, for example, a word beginning with B, followed by a vowel. This could be an A. We arrive at the syllable *ba.* Should we work towards a word of two kinds of consonants, this syllable can be added to four kinds of consonants.

Ba + labial sound,	example: *BaB*
Ba + dental sound,	example: *BaD*
Ba + palatal sound,	example: *BaG*
Ba + lingual and glottal sounds,	example: *BaR*.

A further fifth possibility would be to add nothing or attach one further vowel. Then for our example *Ba* from the Labial classification of speech-sounds, five possibilities result for an expansion of the basic root. This extended to all four classes of consonants results in 4 x 5 possibilities. Nevertheless, there also exist words completely without a consonant, consisting only of vowels (e.g. the *Ei*, 'egg'). This is the additional possibility. Thus, we have the 21 [(4 x 5) + 1] basic sounds, which for each word are available as [their] original potential. Using this key, we come directly to realize how Beckh's four main groups come about. Thereby it becomes clear how perfectly and conscientiously Beckh worked in his day. For from the above description the following pattern results:

R/L	= R, L, HR, HL etc.	here:	*ôr*
labial	= B, P, PH, F, PF, M, W, V etc.	here:	*pʰoš*
palatal	= G, K, CH, H, Q, J etc.	here:	*arc*
dental	= D, T, TH, S, SCH, X etc.	here:	*di*
vowel	= all words without consonant	here:	no example

What follows is worth noting:[139]

language	word	meaning	class of sound
Sumerian	*bu*	light, sheen, to illuminate	labial
Sumerian	*ku*	bright	palatal
Sumerian	*ud*	light, Sun	dental
Sumerian	*di*	to shine	dental
Sumerian	*ilu*	god	glottal/lingual
Sumerian	*ri'a*	Sun-god	glottal/lingual
Sumerian	*rà*	bright, to illuminate	glottal/lingual

In Beckh's lifetime the Sumerian language was already known, and the first publications appeared about it, nevertheless this oldest known language of mankind did not lie within the area of Hermann Beckh's research. Today, we possess an established and rich quantity of data, with which we can include into our comparisons and analyse the language. The following list contains all four main types, which Hermann Beckh describes. The Sumerians in addition use further variants of their basic roots. These come about in words of two or three consonants. Here is a small selection of Sumerian roots for 'light':

Basic root labial—*e.g*: *bu* = light, sheen, to illuminate

language	word	meaning	root
Sumerian	bar	become bright, to be, illuminate	B-R
Sumerian	par	bright	P-R
Sumerian	babbar	Sun, bright, Sun-god	B-B-R
Sumerian	pirig	shining, raying, bright	P-R-G

Basic root palatal—*e.g*: *ku* = bright

language	word	meaning	root
Sumerian	gàm	to shine	G-M
Sumerian	gin	hell	G-N
Sumerian	ĝir	hell, to illuminate	G-R
Sumerian	gug	illuminate	G-G
Sumerian	guru	illuminate	G-R
Sumerian	ḫaad	to shine, to illuminate	H-D
Sumerian	kár	to illuminate	K-R
Sumerian	kug	bright, to radiate	K-G
Sumerian	kun	to illuminate, become light	K-N
Sumerian	giššir	light	G-SH-R
Sumerian	gazibu	ray	G-Z-B

Basic root dental—*e.g*.: *ud* = light, Sun; *di* = to shine

language	word	meaning	root
Sumerian	nu	light	N
Sumerian	si	light, ray	S
Sumerian	utu	Sun, light, Sun-god	T
Sumerian	uzu	sunset	Z
Sumerian	dag	bright, shining	D-G
Sumerian	dalla	to illuminate, ray	D-L
Sumerian	adus	ray	D-S
Sumerian	dutuè	sunrise	D-T
Sumerian	nuru	light	N-R
Sumerian	sud	light	S-D
Sumerian	sen	bright	S-N
Sumerian	ùsun	Sun	S-N
Sumerian	ašme	Sun disc	SH-M
Sumerian	šeer	to be bright, light	SH-R

Sumerian	*tán*	light	T-N
Sumerian	*azag*	bright	Z-G
Sumerian	*zal*	to illuminate, to ray, light	Z-L
Sumerian	*dadag*	hell, to ray to ray, to illuminate	D-D-G
Sumerian	*diĝir*	godhead, bright	D-G-R
Sumerian	*ñišnu*	light	N-SH-N
Sumerian	*saĝdu*	a ray	S-G-D
Sumerian	*šamaš*	Sun-god	SH-M-SH
Sumerian	*šeerzi*	light	SH-R-Z
Sumerian	*zalag*	to shine, light, bright	Z-L-G

Basic root glottal/lingual—*e.g.*: *ilu* = god; *ri'a* = Sun-god

language	word	meaning	root
Sumerian	*el*	bright	L
Sumerian	*lá*	light	L
Sumerian	*ara*	bright, to illuminate	R
Sumerian	*ùr*	a ray	R
Sumerian	*ùru*	light	R
Sumerian	*rà*	to illuminate, bright	R
Sumerian	*lach*	light	L-CH
Sumerian	*alad*	godhead	L-D
Sumerian	*lah*	light, become bright	L-H
Sumerian	*lal*	light	L-L
Sumerian	*ilati*	goddess	L-T
Sumerian	*rin*	bright	R-N

Conventional research cannot conclusively answer the question why in the Sumerian language there exists such an abundance of terms for 'light'. On the other hand, spiritual-scientific methods are able reliably to solve this without the help of a walking-stick, for it has sufficient knowledge, at the latest since Ernst Moll with his *Die Sprache der Laute* and its further influence. Thanks to the spiritual-scientific views it can now be recognized that earlier human beings, based on their perception of the connections to the world, felt it necessary to name the light in its varying stages and manner of appearance. An abstract name for light for all the various characteristics of light-phenomena as we imagine it doesn't come into question. They could not see the light abstractly through a cool understanding, but into their souls was built in a concrete manner a tangible reflection of the light, of the spiritual word, which they directly rendered, that is, expressed, in language.

In addition to the depicted designations around the *light aspect* and their formulations in Sumerian, there also existed with the Sumerians a purely vowel variant for the word light: *u*. As far as the example for the palate sounds *arc*, which in principle is a late variant of *ôr*, the series from Dr Beckh is found to conform completely with what is found in Sumerian. Unfortunately, Hermann Beckh probably did not know, or he overlooked the ancient Greek variety *augé* (gaze, ray, light, eye). With this word from the area of the palate sounds the series Beckh gives is completed. Thereby all Beckh's characterizing use of letters are justifiably confirmed. Also, in the Sumerian depictions one finds the types of the sensory-perceptible light, right up to the primordial form for naming the divine, which was probably still clearly seen by the Sumerians. So it is no wonder that *uzu* with its Z making for the material element refers to the sunset, whereas with its primal sound for light R and the light vowels A and I, the concept *ri'a* is possibly one of the oldest words of humanity for the Sun-god, the sublime Being of the Sun. The clues which in his day Hermann Beckh already glimpsed, today with the help of modern techniques of analysis can be better pursued and over wider areas. Beckh's great cognitive-spiritual deed, however, consists, firstly in the way he can bring the most varied obscurities into the brightest light, and on the other hand always to awaken and retain a kind of sacred awe in those who study his accounts. He brings the spiritual heights of the early civilizations in a masterly fashion before the eyes of the observer, giving him the possibility, carefully and at eye-level looking with the consciousness of the time, at that which is essential for a new understanding of our honourable predecessors of humanity. So it is possible only thanks to the conscious beholding of the spiritual speech-aspect through Hermann Beckh and before him Rudolf Steiner, to come today a step nearer to the Mystery of speech.

With this summarizing and surely inadequate attempt to begin to appreciate the tremendous life-work of Hermann Beckh from the aspect of his investigation of speech, the writer hopes to have humbly contributed to give the interested reader of this volume an inner incentive, alongside Hermann Beckh's invaluable activities within The Christian Community as well as in the realms of Indology and musicology, also to recognize him as a pioneer within the sciences. This would and could lead us, to fathom that which was in the primordial beginning. For in the primordial beginning was the *Word*.

Hermann Beckh: Musician—on the Occasion of the Newly Discovered MS *The Mystery of Musical Creativity*

The element of soul-and-spirit in music of the past and the future with special consideration of Wagner's *Tristan and Isolde*

From the handwritten MS left unrevised at the author's death.

'Beckh ventures into provinces that I have not had the opportunity of investigating myself …'—Rudolf Steiner

Lost for decades, the manuscript of Hermann Beckh's final lectures about music present fundamentally new insights into its cosmic origins. Beckh characterizes the qualities of musical development, examines select musical works (that represent for him the peak of human ingenuity), and throws new light on the nature and source of human creativity and inspiration. Published here for the first time, the lectures demonstrate a distinctive approach founded on the raw material of musical perception.

Beckh discusses the whistling wind, the billowing wave, the song of the birds and particularly the theme of longing. Never losing the ground from under his feet, he penetrates perennial themes: from the yearning for real spontaneity and the 'Mystery background' uniting heaven and earth, to spiritual knowledge that can meet the demands of the twenty-first century. Out of the cosmic context, Beckh writes to the individual situation. From there, he seeks again the re-won cosmic context. He does not write as a musical specialist and then turn to universal human concerns; rather, Beckh writes from universal human concerns and reveals music as of special concern to everyone.

In addition to the transcripts of fifteen lectures, this book contains a valuable introduction and editorial footnotes. It also features appendices including Beckh's essay 'The Mystery of the Night in Wagner and Novalis'; reminiscences of Beckh by August Pauli and Harro Rückner; Donald Francis Tovey's 'Wagnerian harmony and the evolution of the Tristan-chord', and several contemporaneous reviews of Beckh's published works.

Beckh himself wrote a year before he died:

> Initially the *lectures on music* demand my whole concentration. I hope in my suffering condition I am still able to succeed at least satisfactorily

with these lectures. They are important for me in so far as they give me the theme for the *next book* that I now intend to write. The theme is simply the cosmic rhythm in the musical keys. This really lives in me; this is my theme [letter 26 January 1936].

From Chapter 6:

The Indian primal root '√ *wa*' as a common source of the two basic elements of music.

All creation goes through pain. When the world-creation descends from the spiritual-etheric into the earthly-physical realm, it also descends into pain and suffering, taking these into itself. This is something extraordinarily important, revealing cosmic backgrounds, when we believe we hear in the blowing of the wind a note of mourning, when we speak of the 'howling of the storm', and so on. This is a profound cosmic intuition of the genius of language when '*Windeswehen*'—'blowing of the wind' and '*Schmerzenswehen, Sehnsuchtswehen*'—'labour-pains, pains of longing' all meet in the word '*wehen*'—'blowing':

> *Sind's deiner Seufzer Wehen,*
> *Die mir die Segel blähen? —*
> *Wehe! Wehe, du Wind!*
> *Weh'! Ach wehe, mein Kind!*

> Is this your tearful sighing,
> Keeping the vessel flying?
> Waft us, waft us O wind!
> Woe, ah woe to my child!
> [Wagner, *Tristan and Isolde*. Act 1, i.]

This intuition of the spirit of language is not at all limited to the German language; we also find it especially in the Indian language that stands close to the archetypal language. There the root '√*va*' also means '*Windeswehen*' the 'blowing of the wind' (it is the same word as the German '*wehen*') as well as the call of pain '*wehe*'. In the lecture-cycle *Egyptian Myths and Mysteries* [GA 106], Rudolf Steiner speaks about 'the primal word *wha*' (this is the same root). And the name Yahveh (I-H-W-H), so significant for the Mysteries of Genesis 2:7, contains this root and all the air-breath secrets of the soul and of suffering.

If one looks at all these secrets of the Indian archetypal root √*va*— '*wehen*', one can find enclosed in it the primal motif of Wagner's *Tristan and Isolde*, that primal motif that finds its mantric, musical expression, in the longing motif that directly opens the Prelude. In so far as this motif of the air-element contains the 'wafting breath', with all its connections to pains of longing and painful woes, therein we feel what we have called the *secondary* element of music. That the *primary* element is not missing was emphasized earlier. And in this direction the Mystery of the Indian primal root √*wa* can lead us a step further.

This root signifies not only '*wehen*' and '*wehe*', the *Windeswehen* and *Schmerzenswehen* ('the blowing of the wind' and 'labour pains, pains of longing'), but there is *yet another* root √*va* (also from the grammatical viewpoint, presented as *ve*) meaning '*weben*—weaving'. In other words, in the primal root √*va* the German '*wehen*' with its overtone '*wehe*' (woe) and '*weben*' (weave) coincide. Already in the Indian Rig-Veda this '*Weben*' is throughout a picture of the creative cosmic weaving.

- Where does this creative cosmic weaving commence?
In the etheric realm, in the sound-ether.
- Where does *Weben* become *Wehen*, with its overtone of pain?

Where the creation is led down from the etheric spirit into the material and earthly, where the earthly element of dust and with it the earthly air-breath is imprinted into the creature, where the air-ether becomes physically breathed air. Where earthly air is breathed, suffering and death also begin. Our observations are to show how all this is not only a general truth, but also true in music and for the musical element.

From Chapter 11:

… This cosmic, supersensory element of music we could also call in the anthroposophical sense the *sound-ether element of music*. And because everything etheric is basically a star-element, it can be called the *star-element*. This at the same time is the *spiritual* element in music. On the other hand, recalling Genesis 2:7, we found the earthly, sensory element of music is at the same time connected with the air-element, the *soul*-element of music. This also carries the element of *longing*, the element of pain and suffering of music, the passionate element, the element of death. The *sigh* in music appeared to us as the observable connection between the breath of air and longing. Just this element of soul and longing of music, thus it appeared to us, could be that which a modern, contemporary music tries consciously or unconsciously to overcome. One day a true future music, today still lying in the future, will have found the means and the path to penetrate through this soul-element to the actual spiritual, to the cosmic, to the *starry element* of music.

Of this cosmic element of music, we also spoke of the billowing, surging sea of the ocean of world-music—the etheric, too, is pictured in the 'etheric sea'. The other, the soul-element of music, connected to the breath of the air, could appear to us in the picture of the wind, of the sighing breath of longing, the storm-wind of passion, and so on. *Wind* and *wave* became discernible pictures for us to lay hold of the two elements of music: the earthly and the cosmic.

In Bach's music we found dominating throughout the *wave*, the surging sea or cosmic music. The wind-element, the longing, beginning with *Mozart* as a gentle wafting air, as a tender childlike sigh, we then found already with Beethoven growing towards a *storm of passion*. A grandiose connection of the two elements of music, of wind *and* wave we experienced in Wagner's *Tristan and Isolde*.

The knowledge of the two elements of the musical element, discussed in anthroposophical writings and lectures, we saw, is already contained in Novalis' *Fragments*. It has also found a wonderful poetic expression in a dramatist whose works are marked throughout with a richness of spiritual insights, better said, the soul-feelings of the world-secrets, with August Strindberg [1849-1912], in *The Dream Play* [1902].[140] In this whole exposition we seek to connect the musical element with the world-secrets. This connection cannot be expressed more splendidly, and at the same time artistically and poetically, than it appears in Act 3 of Strindberg's play, in the scene where the daughter of Indra and the poet meet on the beach in Fingal's Cave. Already the introduction remarks to the scene, 'music of the wind, music of the waves' refer pictorially to that motif in our observations which we recognized as the secret of the musical element—the relationship of earthly to cosmic music as the essential matter.

A Title for Beckh's Manuscript?

Neil Franklin

(A contribution to the Musicians Conference, Dornach, 30 April, 2016)

When considering Hermann Beckh's work on the zodiac signs, the circle of keys and the examples that he provides from a range of music, by far the best thing to do, of course, is to immerse oneself in the music. This seems particularly favourable for music-lovers and players. At the same time, however, two other tasks come into view. Firstly, it appears valuable to survey the complete works, especially the newly transcribed manuscript *The Mystery of Musical Creativity; Man and Music*, as well as Mark and John, for what Beckh has to say, for example, on any one Sign and the related keys. Thanks to Alan Stott and his team, we do now very nearly have *The Collected Works* in English. Secondly, there is a considerable need to find a balanced orientation towards what the writer has said. It may be enough to depend on a musical sensitivity, or to call upon the considerable wealth of insights arising from Rudolf Steiner and the subsequent studies contributed by Hermann Pfrogner, Christoph Peter, Friedrich Oberkogler, and others. However, I suggest that this pursuit is enhanced by a process of triangulation. This is akin to the procedure necessary to tune-in a modern telescope: the best way to achieve a high resolution on a given celestial object is to first relate it to *two distant* stars.

Consequently, before attempting an inspection, as it were, of what Beckh has to say about the key of B-major and A♭-minor (Beckh gives reasons why he prefers this to the enharmonic and more usual G#-minor) in relationship to the heavenly sign of Virgo, we can establish two widely spaced points of reference and establish a stable context. As with the telescope analogy, the choice is very wide, but I have chosen a single line from William Blake's unfinished manuscript *The Four Zoas*,[141] and a theological article by Father Sergei Bulgakov. Both discussions will be kept brief—they are simply distant sightings to assist the principal task.

Blake's manuscript

The manuscript of *The Four Zoas* was considered by the Blake scholar Northrop Frye to be 'the greatest abortive manuscript in English literature'. On Blake's decease it came into his wife's possession. She presented it to the English painter John Liddell (one of Blake's most devoted patrons and supporters) who in turn left it to his son John Liddell Junior. All 144 loose-leaf pages languished in Liddell's substantial mansion in Redhill until they were carefully transcribed by W.B. Yeats in 1889, with pagination being unsure. The first publication followed in January 1893.[142]

With his own visionary powers in the late 1790s, Blake investigated the origin of phenomena and human faculties to create a dramatic form of what Jakob Boehme had seen as The First Mother, or 'Mysterium Magnum'—the empty mirror that reflects the transcendent Will of God and leads it into manifestation.[143] Blake's line is:

Mighty was the draught of Voidness to draw existence in.
[Night the Second, l. 18 in Keynes' edition]

Scholars of Blake since Yeats have shown that:

- Blake alludes to the experience of the draftsman before committing pencil to paper.
- The 'void' is an empty circle, the original representation of the Hebrew letter *ayin* ע.
- The empty circle of *ayin* עין represents an eye and also a spring or well.
- The first movement of divine creation is an 'in-drawing' (*anziehen*), repeatedly discussed by Boehme as the 'first quality' or first 'fountain spirit' (*Quelle*).[144]

There is no need here to go into various Kabbalistic and Neoplatonic sources; the simple point is that for Blake as poet (c. 1797) and Yeats as editor-commentator (1893) the starting point of creation, both cosmogonic and for the human spirit, is an in-drawing emptiness.

A second text

Our second text in the orientation process is Bulgakov's extraordinary article 'The Holy Grail' (*Sviatyi Graal*) published in the magazine *Put*, Paris, 1932. This is now readily available in an English translation by Boris Jakim.[145] It is enough to say that Father Sergei was the most significant Orthodox theologian of his time, working as Dean of St Sergius' Academy in Paris from 1925 when most Orthodox thinkers were in exile. We find Hermann Beckh producing the essay 'Richard Wagner and Christianity' one year later.

By 1932 Father Sergei had already accomplished a vast range of publications covering major areas of theology for the Russian Church and beyond. He was found to be always pushing at boundaries and having to prove that an opinion (*theologoumenon*) was consistent with the faith. Then, with *Sviatyi Graal* he went a great step further. The eucharistic elements, he argued, established at The Last Supper were to be distinguished, but not separated, from the body that was on the Cross and the blood and water that flowed from the side. The blood and water did indeed reach the Earth and were also held in the Grail cup.

We now find the proposition that the eucharistic elements are presented to and taken in by the communicants: a real and active pledge of everlasting life and renewed union with the Divine Ground of the World. But what of everyone and all things that do not receive the eucharist? As a complement to the eucharistic elements, he argues, the Divine-Human body as blood and water entered all the Earth *for the healing of all*.

> The blood and water that flowed into the world abide in the world. They sanctify this world as the pledge of its future transfiguration. Through the precious streams of Christ's blood and water that flowed out of His side, all creation was sanctified—heaven and earth, our earthly world, and all the stellar worlds.[146]

The whole of heaven and earth as the receptacle of what flowed from His side 'is the chalice of the Holy Grail'. Christ's *universal* 'power with its effectiveness' is acknowledged in a footnote to be 'The Christ-impulse according to the anthroposophists'.[147] Father Sergei accepts that the legends of the Middle Ages have kept this knowledge in their heart, despite the accretions of largely poetic and romantic fabrication. The *Sviatyi Graal* is:

> inaccessible to veneration; in its holiness it is hidden in the world from the world. However, it exists in the world as an invisible power, and it becomes visible, appears to pure hearts who are worthy of its appearance.

> .... this abiding is a *Mystery* [original emphasis], the world's great holy, divine Mystery, the world's treasure, holiness and glory—[148]

The article, already entering a new world for the Orthodox Church, then observes that the flowing of blood and water from Christ's side (John 19:34) is not specifically represented in the liturgical cycle. He recommends that a new 'additional celebration' would be most appropriate, a thirteenth festival, as it were, within the established cycle of twelve major feasts of the Church. Pondering an appropriate date for the proposed celebration, that is, The Celebration of The Holy Grail, Father Sergei notes that it should be close to the canonical Exaltation of the Cross and decides that the new liturgical celebration could well be on the first post-festive day after the Exaltation, that is, 15 September.[149]

Having taken two sightings, one from the West and one from the East, one can begin to focus on Hermann Beckh.

Beckh and music

On the north coast of Cornwall there are many West-facing coves and strands. Especially in late August and the first week in September one will find many families—before the school starts again—gazing westwards in the glowing light of the last hour of the Sun. There is usually some warmth left in the air and it has been a tiring day for many. The golden Sun is dimming towards the horizon and there is a very great feeling for this, a decided mood. The holiday, too, is coming to an end.

Other experiences, of course, come to mind: the departure of a beloved one whether through death or on a railway platform, at an airport. Yet the hour before sunset towards the end of summer is especially engraved on us for many reasons, including its regularity and the fact that one can experience the departure of the Sun affecting all of nature around us. On the coast there can be the especially powerful presence of the horizon to which the Sun declines: a clearly defined threshold.

W.B. Yeats spent most of his adult life in search of what he believed to be spiritual realities—these included, for example, conversations with those who had died, graphic visions, and 'Instructors' who could produce automatic writing. However, he was also sure from the 1880s that such realities included supersensory 'Moods' in man and nature. When Steiner considered the zodiac and eurythmy there appeared the 'Twelve Moods' presented in *Wahrspruchworten* (GA 40) and in English both separately and in *Eurythmy: Its Birth and Development* (GA 277a).[150] The choice of the word *Stimmungen*, 'Moods', is striking (*Stimmung* also means 'tuning').

It is worth spending just a minute or two on an attempt to clarify what Steiner and Beckh had in mind with '*Stimmung*' and similarly what Yeats meant by a supersensible 'Mood'. We might recall here that Steiner's *Weltendenken* refers to divine-cosmic thinking accessible to human thinking; consequently, at a higher level, what can be called *Weltenstimmungen* would refer to divine-cosmic feelings, spread out through phenomena and the cycles of time. Beckh observes such *Stimmungen* in the cycle of musical keys and the zodiac; Yeats decided there were 28 such *Gestalten* represented by the phases of the Moon,[151] Jakob Boehme described their formation out of the ground of seven archetypal Qualities, and Alan Stott has termed them 'spiritual situations' above.

One can simply collate the principal features of *Weltenstimmungen* in an overview of their general nature and being.

Moods:

- are encountered by the whole person.
- Do not sweep one away but centre / focus concentration.
- Have a strong conceptual content of conscious associations.
- Are an aesthetic perception-conception, with some resemblance to the experiences of nostalgia and expanded self-knowledge.
- Consequently, a Mood is one gestalt, or form, recognized aesthetically.

Beckh would have agreed with Yeats who claimed that a Mood is an expression of Divine Love as defined by Thomas Aquinas: 'Eternity is the possession of one's self, as in a single moment.'[152]

It seems to me that when Hermann Beckh wrote about music, especially in the unpublished manuscript of 1937, he was very alive to the certain open space that exists between the technical analysis of a score and its 'meaning' in the broadest sense of the word. Whereas the first can benefit from an established vocabulary, the second is more problematic. Most people will have recourse to the language of *description*, and this will usually entail some elements of symbolism and *metaphor*, calling upon a smaller or larger range of *connotations*. Hermann Beckh also does this regarding the cycle of musical keys (the circle of fifths), and in the first instance it is possible to collate what he said by way of description for a given key, and then observe the associated metaphors and connotations. By doing this for the key of B-major and its relative minors, and the associations with the sign Virgo, we can draw together a certain number of facets of a Mood, perhaps like the sides of one of the precious crystals always dear to Beckh himself.

Within all of Beckh's works on music, including the unfinished MS now edited and translated, there are four principal descriptions of B-major and A♭-minor:

- 'the hour before sunset'
- 'the end of summer'
- a 'mood of farewell'
- 'transfiguring'.

The range of music considered here by Beckh is quite narrow in compass, with most points being consistently refurbished between 1923 and 1937:

- Isolde's *Liebestod* at the end of *Tristan and Isolde* (B-major);
- the *Karfreitagszauber* in *Parsifal* (B-major);
- the A♭-minor Arioso in Beethoven's *Piano Sonata*, op. 110;
- the Funeral March movement in A♭-minor from Beethoven's *Piano Sonata*, op. 26;
- music associated with St Elisabeth in *Tannhäuser* (B-major);
- music associated with Midsummer's Eve in *Die Meistersinger* (B-major).

Between the publication of *Vom geistigen Wesen der Tonarten* (1923) and *Der kosmische Rhythmus in Markus-Evangelium* (1928) Beckh was sharpening his spiritual—or aesthetic—perception of the correlations between the cycle of keys and the cycle of the zodiac signs in relation to the Earth. The four fundamental descriptions now underwent a massive expansion, too large and well-known to be listed here in its totality. Central to the endeavour was, of course, the cycle of the Christian year and its principal festivals, especially within The Christian Community. Yet one should make a few observations.

The mood of B-major, A♭-minor

Firstly, the largest group of correlations for Virgo / B-major / A♭–G#-minor is *a feminine Gestalt* which includes images of the mother, the Earth, the maidenly soul and Isis. A second group is associated with an experience that Beckh nurtured from his earliest lecturing for anthroposophy and which he frequently addressed as '*the heavenly nourishment along the way*'. Here there are close links between Indian *soma*, Isis, the constellation Virgo dominated by the star Spica, and manna. A third group is constituted by the recognition of 'heavenly feeding' as the *Last Supper and the transfiguring of matter*—the earlier Mysteries become the Christian Mystery. This is regularly presented within the compass of both the Tree of Life and the Holy Grail.

With the major work on John's Gospel, published two years later (1932), Beckh confirms the overall *Gestalt* for Virgo while making the all-important distinction that Mark's Gospel displays a circulation or spiralling structure (associated with the circulation of the blood), whereas John is informed by a descending-ascending structure (similar to breathing). A comparatively small number of correlations were added—for example, Mary Magdalene, the Woman Taken in Adultery and the Mother with John at the Cross. Yet Beckh does make one most telling observation beyond anything that he had said so far: the transfiguration mood of Virgo is explicitly:

> 'where the Earth has remained Sun, in the human heart'.[153]

In the last year of his life, 1937, we know that he completed *Die Sprache der Tonart*; it appeared posthumously. In increasing pain and distress Beckh penned the MS 'The Mystery of Musical Creativity: Man and Music', now come to light and about to be published complete. In the former, the key of B-major is again exemplified from St Elisabeth, the *Liebestod* in *Tristan and Isolde*, and he also adduces Beethoven's Funeral March in A♭-minor from the *Piano Sonata, op. 26*. The *Gestalt* is now movingly described as 'the hour of dying light', and the Funeral March conveys:

> Here everything breathes the most painful mood of parting, the mood of the departing light, a leave-taking from daylight, from the light of life.[154]

More generally, the B-major experience is described as '*the light of the hour before sunset*' which is 'super-earthly and solemn', '*super-earthly and transfigured*'.[155]

In the unpublished MS Beckh now writes of 'this B-major of the Virgin', '*the Mystery of the Virgin*' and of '*nature transfigured*', while returning to Isolde's *Liebestod*. The MS will move on shortly to further reconsider St Elisabeth, the *Liebestod* again and the midsummer evening of *Meistersinger* before coming to a climactic conclusion with a study of *Parsifal* and the Christian Mystery. Yet before making this progress Beckh unexpectedly paused. Referring to Rudolf Steiner's observation that primary, spiritual being of music is 'between the notes' (repeated 28 pages later), the text characterizes this as 'the starry element' and 'the primary element'. In the context of Strindberg's *The Dream Play* (1902), he further clarifies the perception by confirming that this element is 'the sound-etheric ... which lies between the notes'.[156]

Hermann Beckh was never shy of extending the *Gestalt* of Virgo (B-major, A♭/ G#-minor) into vast cosmic and scriptural dimensions, nor did he avoid the attempt to be as precise as possible regarding what was meant by the sound-ether. All the same, in the last year of his life we find the Professor addressing some of the central questions of music. What is the transition from all that is sense-perceptible in music to that which is a spiritual and aesthetic experience? How do we hear the true music? How is an impression or a feeling raised to an archetypal Mood? In the manuscript Beckh considers this transition and finds the one answer: through a death and resurrection. He quotes Schopenhauer:

> My imagination plays (especially in music) with the thought that all human life and my own would only be dreams of an Eternal Spirit, bad and good dreams, and each death an awakening.[157]

Beckh finds the archetypal being of the B-major / A♭-minor keys primarily in the death of Isolde and secondarily in the story of St Elisabeth, who has died in Act 3, Scene 3 of *Tannhäuser*, in the Beethoven piano sonata with a 'Funeral March', and then finally in the *Karfreitagszauber* of *Parsifal*. Yet the Virgo *Gestalt* is not death itself (represented by Sagittarius / midnight / midwinter) but *the hour before sunset and the end of summer*. This has several broad implications.

In the daily cycle, evening comes before morning. In many Churches, including the Russian Orthodox, Vespers is the first service, leading through Compline and Orthros to the celebration of the Eucharistic liturgy on the following 'day'. In the Jewish world, evening prayers (*maariv / arvit*) is again the first service of the day, and Beckh would have been pleased to note that the prayers should begin with the first appearance of three stars (*tzeit hakochaim*) in the evening sky.

Again, for the Christian year the traditional Churches find a beginning under the sign of Virgo in early September; this is most decisively expressed in the Orthodox world with the first festival of the year: the Birth of the Most Holy Mother of God celebrated on 8 September. Here we find a continuity with the Jewish year which begins (*Rosh Hashanah*) on the first two days of *Tishrei* at sunset. These days are known as *Yamim Nora'im*, 'Days of Awe' and usually occur within late Virgo or early to mid-Libra. Such a beginning, for example, was found on 13 September in 2015.

Within the human constitution, the circulation of the blood is found to have such a beginning in the diastole when the depleted blood enters the right atrium. All four sections of the heart can be found to be linked to Beckh's 'Cross of the Son', or 'Etheric Cross' with the corresponding musical scales.[158] By the same argument, exhaling precedes inhaling.

Consequently, with regard to music there seems to be an unavoidable inference, especially holding in mind Steiner's well-known observation that the true spiritual-aesthetic experience of music is 'between the notes'. Now it can be claimed that silence, a pause, a rest, comes *before* a tone, and that such a rest is anticipatory. The same must hold true for stillness before movement in eurythmy? There must be at least as many *different qualities* of silence or rest as there are scales, chords, progressions ...

Certain problems begin to appear here. Obviously, most of us are little practised in listening to silence or comparative silence, and what might lie between the notes. Even if we hear, or rather experience, something semi-consciously a language for description is not common or readily available in everyday life. Anticipation, or an expectancy, for what is to come may be as far as we generally are aware. Furthermore, just as we usually assume that the day starts with sunrise or the Christian Year with Easter, Hermann Beckh within The Christian Community was fettered by the fact that there is no evening service preceding the eucharist on the following day. All that he describes as the hour before sunset as related to the key of B-major and its relative minors has no correlative in the festivals which he celebrated: there is no Birth of the Mother of God, and the other traditional festivals of Mary, including the Dormition / Assumption have been removed from the Church calendar with the exception of The Presentation, Candlemas, on 2 February. Beckh, as the vast majority of the founding priests, had been brought up in a Lutheran milieu.

Nevertheless, with the recovery of Beckh's final MS it now appears that he had a strong sense of what was needed. As the manuscript enters its last sections, he devotes what must have been most painful hours to consider a desired future of music. In just a few pages of Sütterlin handwriting Beckh explains that the future of music would do well to raise itself from feelings to 'a spiritual level' by discovering what lies between the notes. Considering both Wagner and Strindberg's *The Dream Play* such a level is described as 'the starry Mystery of the circle of keys' encompassed by a threshold or 'Mystery-experience': all of which had essentially been said before. But then he adds that Mozart's *The Magic Flute* is 'the first truly highly significant Mystery drama of the musical repertoire'.[159] This may not seem at first sight to be particularly original, yet I think that some vital content is implied *in this context*, hovering, as it were, in what is unsaid.

'The Magic Flute' and the Mystery of silence

Externally, *The Magic Flute* can indeed be said to be a 'Mystery drama' simply through the Masonic contents of trials, temple and brotherhood; Tamino is guided by the spiritual agency of the three boys. But internally the Singspiel finds its living heart in No. 8 Finale when Tamino is finally alone in darkness. *O ew'ge Nacht* is sung with the haunting transition to A-minor. The spiritual world *replies* through the invisible choir with the most resonant pauses in both *Bald, Jüngling, oder nie!* and *Pamina lebet noch.*

Christoph Peter commented on the first of these messages from the spiritual world that: 'The transitional rests intensify the tense awareness to the highest degree.' With *oder nie* 'It is as though one's heart stops still. Once again, a moment where the inaudible, the spirit, speaks.'[160] This is the heart of the Mystery drama, and furthermore bears a comparison with the three fermatas of the threefold wind chords at the beginning, making their great proclamation in the Overture. In this instance, the fermatas 'pronounce solemnity and create stillness': the rests solicit a calmness 'which an audience produces when wide awake and intently listening'.[161]

Hermann Beckh would have rejoiced in Christoph Peter's concluding sentence to the chapter devoted to exploring the taxonomy of rests and silence: 'All of them make manifest in music the world of stillness, that *foundation in which our inner being is at home.*'[162]

One may ask how or where did Hermann Beckh experience the Virgo *Gestalt* leading into the silence that awakens an inner listening to the spiritual mood of the B-major and its relative minor keys? Here we are fortunate to have been given his own autobiographical recollections, the most helpful biography by Gundhild Kačer-Bock, and the numerous memories of those that knew him well.

I think that it is fair to say that Beckh *found himself at home* most of all when by himself in high land or walking in mountains covered with snow, frost and ice. He repeatedly wrote about this and the clear air, the transfigured light. He frequently explained that the ice crystal was the clearest manifestation in matter of the etheric formative-forces, noting that the sound-ether was behind both music and the formation of substance. In his study at Urachstrasse 41, the Seminary of The Christian Community, he loved to recall such experiences by displaying his own collection of crystals and pictures both of the Alps and the Himalayas.

Equally important, though, is the Hermann Beckh who loved to observe stars and constellations appearing in the night sky. There are several distinct recollections of this in the collection of tributes held by Dr Wolfgang Gaedeke in the Berlin Archives.[163] It is in the falling darkness that points of light begin to cross the threshold of visibility.

On the following morning Beckh would often talk with the greatest enthusiasm of what he had observed during the night.

Stars and stones, however, were but secondary reminders of the central Mystery. One cannot avoid and should not understate the fact that Hermann Beckh was a priest of The Christian Community first and foremost. When addressing music, he was inexorably drawn to Wagner's *Parsifal*; when considering the stars and signs he found that Virgo represented the *Weltenstimmung* of The Last Supper. The central moment of The Act of Consecration of Man is the *silence* of the celebrant when s/he makes the threefold cross over the chalice.

One may observe that such a silence, as also in *The Magic Flute*, is *indrawing*, as Blake found around 1797. The hushed mood which comes over people on the Cornish coast towards sunset in early September is an expression of what Beckh discovered in relationship to Virgo, B-major and A♭-minor. Quite independently, at the same time in the 1930s, Father Sergei Bulgakov, theologically at the head of the Russian Orthodox Church in exile, found that the Church would benefit from a new major festival—that of The Holy Grail—to be celebrated on 15 September.

Hermann Beckh surely believed that the eucharist re-enacted or re-presented the fact of The Last Supper (echoed in the musical exempla from Beethoven and Wagner) *and also* that the silence of mountains, crystals and stars, the silence between the notes, the silence at the heart of *The Magic Flute*, were invitations to meet what Father Sergei Bulgakov called 'the sanctification and transfiguration of the world'.[164] It was, for Beckh, the silence that reigns between 3 pm and 6 pm on Good Friday, still palpable today. Jakob Böhme repeatedly and consistently confirmed the claim that the opus of God, as it were, has three movements.

- First movement, there is the beginning of creation through the emptiness of the Mysterium Magnum;
- second movement, the New Creation achieved on Golgotha and in the silence that followed;
- third movement, The Last Judgement.

It is most moving in Christoph Peter's *Rests and Repetition in Music* when the first section concerned with rests and pauses concludes:[165]

> And if we become engrossed in a rest in which the inner stream also comes to rest as in the rest of potentiality, or for moments in the corresponding transition rests, then we experience the significance and

importance of *an unnamed, creative force* which is effective precisely in this rest [emphasis added].

There is something magnificently honest and sensitive here as, for all the later taxonomy and analyses of music, Christoph Peter stands before a Mystery—that which commands a certain silence, a standing before the unknown. Consequently, at a certain moment in the reading, transcription and translation of Hermann Beckh's unfinished manuscript it became necessary to find another title for the work. This could only be to confirm Beckh's own suggestion—'The Mystery of Musical Creativity'.

*

Celebrating the Musical System: Bach and Chopin

Alan Stott

 This article, considering further discoveries since Beckh's day, attempts to approach his discovery of the archetypes present in the tonal system by focusing on the first major composition to celebrate the circle of fifths—nobody's creation, and thus no 'theory'; it is indisputably a basic fact to be explored.

Introduction

The music people like tells us a lot about them. A well-known BBC-radio programme invites personalities to select recordings with which they could imagine living on a fictional desert island. We learn about the personality being interviewed. If music tells us about ourselves, then composers are rightly treated as pioneer inner explorers who to various degrees question and interpret our human existence. The curious balance between what we want and what we need is reflected here. Getting what we *want* might last an hour, perhaps a week or two; entertainment, after all, is a part of life. If we hear something of what we *need* but can't always put a finger on, we find ourselves attracted or called to return. We find ourselves searching: will we find more treasure of self-knowledge in getting to know such pieces of music? It might be a particular composer who appeals. But how do they do it? Astute composers even take popular measures, a dance rhythm, say, and transform it into 'something rich and strange'. Bach (1685-1750) and dance suites, finding the Sarabande a vehicle for a deep soul-searching; Beethoven (1770-1827) speeding up the Minuet and creating the dramatic Scherzo, and so on.

Already we arrive at themes not only of illustration but also of transformation. This leads to the idea of an inner narrative. This is a well-tried way to hide, or rather transform, personal experience, for example, bereavement. A strange phenomenon appears here. The more authentic and private, the more it touches a chord in many people, illustrating the law of inverse proportion. Beethoven's 'Moonlight' Sonata (1801) made of longing a recognized theme for two centuries. He expresses the artist's predicament. Facing dilemma itself, the artist asks, 'How can I remain whole, without repeating myself, or coming to grief?' Gustav Mahler (1860-1911), writing symphonically of painful things in his life, strikes home to listeners a hundred or more years on. We, too, share the artist's situation, the search for answers to tragedy, and openness to transfiguration and vision.

J.S. Bach and tonality

In all this, it is assumed the composer is a craftsman. The above observations point to the source; how they use their craft to speak 'from the heart—may it again reach the heart', as Beethoven puts it. But we have already touched on genre and the techniques of composition. At some stage composers realize that these things are more than formalities. At the right time, the musical system itself will be celebrated. The major-minor system had already arrived when J.S. Bach composed not one but *two* explorations of every key. Exploration of all the keys was on the cards, so a method of tuning ('tempering') had to be devised to make that possible. The *Well-tempered Clavier (WTC)*, Book 1 (1722), seems to have begun life as a collection that became something rather more. Several techniques of composition appear, but the point to be made is the overall form of this work, that of progressing chromatically through all the keys.

The two books of Bach's *Well-tempered Clavier* are not cycles that develop or vary an obvious theme, a 'tune' consisting of musical notes. But halfway through Book I, the theme plus its answer of the F-minor Fugue No. 12 includes all 12 notes; the theme alone of the final Fugue No. 24 consists of all 12 notes—do these statements summarize his overall 'theme'? For years the *WTC* circulated amongst keyboard teachers, finally no less than three versions were printed 1800-1802. It was for long despised (or, to be fair, also recognized, as—praise the Lord!—in the case of Beethoven's teacher in Bonn, Gottlob Neefe) as 'teaching material'. It fared better than the 'technical exercises' that until the twentieth century summed up the general attitude towards the solo violin works and the solo cello suites! Most players and listeners assume that with his *WTC* Bach made a collection to show what he heard as the characteristics of every key. It is even felt that, as the first composer to write in all the keys, Bach has more or less defined tonality.

Others go on from this to suggest even more. By 1742, Bach had matured to write *WTC* Book 2 as a convincing *cycle*—we are taken on an inner journey. In the *Bach-Jahrbuch* 1951-52, Hans Nissen published evidence illustrating his hunch that for Book II Bach took the *Heilsges-chichte*, the Bible story of salvation, as his hidden narrative. This runs from the Creation to a *warning* of the Last Judgement (for *Prelude* 24, the same music is written twice in different note values, a choice for the player. The piece ends with dramatic, interrogatory pauses … as if to say, 'Wake up, before it is too late!'). One scholar dismissed Nissen's submission as a 'completely abstruse theological interpretation' (Hans Keller 1965). However, in 1985 Hertha Kluge-Kahn, with further evidence from the score, showed that Nissen was correct, except for one detail. She showed that Bach had hidden concepts for the structure of his late instrumental cycles (of the last 12 years), always with the holistic idea of unity—for example, the alphabet, the Creed, the Mass, the Rosicrucian verse.[166] Bach sat at the feet of the mystics and found a way of praising God when there was no text to be set. There is evidence that Bach even tried to find and use the laws of creativity themselves. Number was a major means at his disposal. He searched for any musical way through rhythms, proportion, numbers of bars, notes, intervals, time signatures and so on, to express holistic concepts.

Then Helga Thoene[167] more recently has analysed the works for solo violin. They are full of codes. Here one hidden concept is the Christian Year. There are hidden chorales in free rhythm—with their implied texts—for Christmas, Easter and Pentecost in the three pairs of Sonatas and Partitas for solo violin. The three Sonatas were already composed when destiny struck. Bach's first wife Maria Barbara died (1720) when he and the orchestra were away with the Court. Upon returning and facing the facts, he immediately began writing the Chaconne, part of the Partita in D-minor which celebrates Easter. Not only does Bach employ 12 chorales, but using the ancient technique of gematria he found a way to include his own bereavement and hope of resurrection.

It has been known for a long time that the simple number-alphabet comes up with 14 for Bach's name: B = 2, A = 1, C = 3, H = 8, together making 14. 'J.S. Bach' adds up to the reverse of the digits, 41. The letters themselves are musical names, in English: B♭, A, C, B. When he found out that David, 'the beloved' (King David, we know, was the 'sweet singer' [2 Sam. 23:1], the divine musician) in Hebrew also = 14, he must have swallowed hard.[168] Bach uses gematria but kept it secret. The Reformer Luther frowned on it, permitting its use only as a possible means of gaining Jewish converts. Steiner relates it to the sixth degree of initiation, the 'Sun-hero' (8 March 1924. GA 353. 64f.).

But the point of an *esoteric side to creation* has a deeper justification. It appears to add through inverse proportion a deeper authenticity to the obvious, surface meaning. A literary example that recently came to light is C.S. Lewis's Narnia stories (1950-1956). Why have these children's stories lasted longer than their author's apologetics and even his scholarship? To Lewis, the 'astrological planets are spiritual symbols of permanent value'. He kept even from his closest friends the knowledge that the seven planets of the Ptolemaic universe are behind the seven Narnia stories. Such an open secret was waiting for 50 years to be discovered (Michael Ward 2008). But it suggests the stories are given even more inner substance than the Christian allegory that is also present.

Chopin's Preludes, op. 28[169]

Chopin (1810-1849) also wrote pieces in every key; he was *the first major composer to take the circle of fifths and create a major work*, the cycle of *Preludes* (written 1831, 1838/39). Bach had proceeded chromatically: C-major, C-minor, C#-major, C#-minor, and so on. Chopin took over the polarity of a major followed by a minor key, but in his scheme the order is C-major/ A-minor, G-major/ E-minor, and so on. The pieces in major keys are generally more positive, extrovert, those in minor keys more questioning and introverted. Chopin's 'theme' is the simplest combination of musical elements:

  (i) rising third/ falling second and its inversion,
  (ii) the dotted rhythm, and
  iii) repeated notes.

A connection to Bach has been felt by many musicians, but to my knowledge never quite demonstrated.[170] Clearly, Chopin is not imitating Bach, but he is influenced by classical, or rather baroque notions of form (exploiting predominantly one idea/ key for a piece, with some notable exceptions to prove the rule). Although the results sound romantically spontaneous, this is belied alone by the composer's scrupulously written manuscripts, and, of course, by further investigation. Chopin forces nothing extraneous; he knew what he was doing in celebrating the art of music itself.

B-A-C-H as 'theme'

The four notes of the name occur at the very top of the basic scale of 'C'—which is how the keyboard is made—the degrees of major sixth, the two sevenths and the octave. They are intrinsically 'expressive'

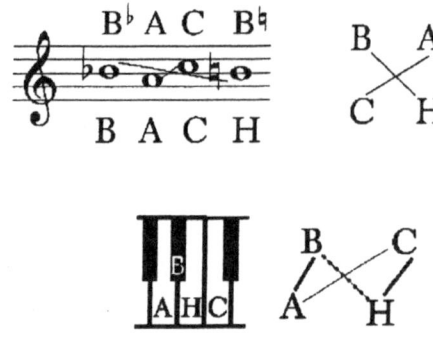

degrees. Add to this the fact that the order contains a cross in the notation—a mark of self-consciousness, the primordial symbol for 'the human being' and what he does to qualify as such. The descending second and rising third are already present in B-A-C-H. It seems to be the uniting 'theme'.

Moreover, the two last letters are shared with the name CH-opin.

I submit as *Thesis No. 1* that *Chopin employs the notes of the name B-A-C-H in a freely expressive or 'arbitrary' order whenever he could.* It becomes focused in No. 4 (E-minor) in 4/4 where the tune is employed of only these notes (notice b. 4: C-H-B-A).

When other notes *are* used (only from b. 8), the four notes appear in

the 'tenor' and 'bass' of the accompaniment. In the overlap of bb. 21-22 B-A-C-H overlaps, or 'crosses over' (CH-opin meets BACH?), from the tenor to the bass. Before the final cadence, the note B♭ again appears, which one editor[171] says 'should be A#'. The enharmonic B♭ (= B), though, gives a clue. A pause follows, before B♮ (= H)—but no player would make audible the missing A and C!

The *definitive quotation* of B-A-C-H comes once in the whole cycle, when you least expect it. In No. 19 in E♭, before the return of the theme there are 4 bars of chromatic writing. B-A-C-H appears three

times, first in the bass, then the 'alto' and 'tenor' in stretto. For the final bar (14 notes) C is heard twice, then A, then C♭ (= H), and finally B♭ (= B). Other freer moments occur (bb. 49-50 B-H-B-A, and bb. 51-52 B-C-B-A).

The *cross motif* appears in several *Preludes*, for example, in the accompaniment figures of No. 13 in F#-major, the seventh major key, where each figure contains at least one seventh. The initial melody is a 7-bar phrase; b. 8 contains 3 crosses featuring the major seventh.

No. 14 in E♭-minor, the seventh minor key, a hitherto rather 'enigmatic' piece, is, however, a study of the seventh. The range of every bar is a seventh. The cross finally appears in the last piece, No. 24, where the range here (the 12th minor Prelude) is a 12th (D to A); two figures of a 12th to the bar = 24. The characteristic runs span a 'compound' 12th (= 12th plus one or more octaves); the final run of 24 notes (b. 74) features Bb-A six times. There are 12 triplets of descending minor thirds. Bar 10-11 lightly quote A-H-C-B.

Composing the numbers

With this *Thesis No. 2* is already being described. *Chopin from start to finish composes the numbers of the 12 key-centres and some reference the numbers of the pieces (1-24).*

The time signatures of *Preludes* Nos. 1–4 progress from 1–4 beats in the bar (written 2/8, alla breve = 2/2, 3/4 and 4/4).

Further examples: No. 5 in D-major opens with a two-quaver motif that lands on the fifth degree (A) five times, echoed between the two 'verses' and at the end in a variation (bb. 33-6); b. 1 contains 5 x 2 = 10 notes for the two hands; the tune of this 'Song without Words' begins on b. 5.

No. 6 in B minor is written with 6 quavers to a bar; the initial B rises to C (b. 12), includes A# (b. 15) and eventually A (b. 22). The R. H. ends with 6 notes, the second beat of a single hemiola 3/2 bar (the digits 1 + 2 + 3 = 6, as do 3 x 2 and 2 x 3).

No. 9, the fifth major key, E-major: b. 1, 5 notes for the tune (beginning on the 5th degree), for the bass line and for each *beat* of the middle voice. Finger no. 5 plays most of the melodic line. No. 10 in C#-minor, the fifth minor key: each beat of the descending cascade consists of 5 notes. Each phrase is accompanied by 5 chords. The answering phrases (e.g. bb. 3 & 4) always consist of 5 beats. The final phrase reaches the 6th degree in anticipation of the next piece, the 6th major key, which it reaches over a melodic sixth (A—F#).

No. 11, the sixth major key in B-major plays with 3 x 2 and 2 x 3 in rhythmic alternation—the bars alternate 6/8 and 3/4—thus the three crotchet beats are 1 + 2 + 3 (2 notes to each crotchet beat = 6 notes). The transition bars 6 and 18, the only bars to contain 18 notes (6 x 3), amalgamate characteristics of both 6/8 and 3/4 measures (announced in b. 2); a triple cross is apparent in the notation. The final two bars are a neat unit: 12 notes, 3 note-names, 6 notes in the R.H. and 6 notes in the L.H. The piece consists of 27 bars (3^3), a well-known mystical number, suggesting divine harmony. No. 11—the number of the sacred, hierogamic marriage (6 + 5). The piece is a 'Song without Words' combining voice and accompaniment in 2 verses weaving together as a perfect marriage of Heaven and Earth. B-major is allotted to Virgo in Hermann Beckh's tone-zodiac.

The 'golden mean' of the number 24 occurs (rounded off) as No. 15, the famous 'Raindrop' Prelude and the longest. D♭-major is the 8th major key. There are 8 quavers to each bar, keeping up the famous repeated note throughout. The tune spans a 7th; when it returns it only twice touches the octave (plagal scale, here A♭ to A♭), b. 23 and towards the end, b. 79, played *smorzando*, 'dying away'. Eight is the number of resurrection (e.g.1 Pet. 3:20; 2 Pet. 2:5).

The treble of No. 17, the 9th major Prelude in A♭-major, beginning from middle C, is a melodic ninth from the B♭ that ends the previous piece. The opening tune (the first phrase consists of 9 notes) spans a ninth to D♭, climaxing on the 9th degree in b. 5, the highest note of the section, a ninth harmonically and reached by a melodic 9th (A♭–B♭). The two E-major episodes (the first from b. 19) link to the E-major *Prelude*, No. 9. The piece is written in 90 bars. Are the consistent crossed hands of the player a parable?[172]

(9 Tone)

(17)

A glance at genres is revealing. The rhythm of No. 7, the heavenly A-major mazurka (or possibly waltz; 7 notes in the L.H. of the first three phrases) becomes reversed for its opposite number in the circle of fifths; No. 20 in C-minor is a funeral march. Here one of Chopin's friends persuaded him to repeat the second phrase. Originally the eight bars of the 10th minor *Prelude* consisted of 10 major chords and 10 minor chords, leaving 13 discords. The notes B-A-C-H appear in the bass of bars 5-6: C-H-B-A. No. 11 begins with 11 notes in b. 1.

(18)

No. 18, b. 1 contains 9 + 9 = 18 notes, the highest note of the first motive (9 notes, emphasis on the 9th note) is the 9th degree and the first bass chord is a harmonic 9th; No. 16 with 16 semiquavers to every bar, … but perhaps enough examples have made the principle clear.

What does this attention to number amount to? If correct,[173] the evidence—admittedly cumulative, but that is also evidence—suggests the composer took number as a stimulus to composition. The numerical facts of music are in themselves sufficiently valid musical phenomena—is there more to say?

Chopin, precisely through the absence of a hidden narrative, has allowed the nuts and bolts of the musical system to speak for themselves. The 'classical' Chopin is revealed, celebrating the facts of the musical system through their disciplined exploitation. What results, though, is music as the expression of our make-up. As a homage to Bach (= 14), the *Preludes* (op. 28 = 14 x 2)[174] are, as it were, Bach revisited; he is the father of tonality, the representative creative researcher, the master. But there appears to be more.

A further suggestion

Further differentiation of the qualities of the progression of intervals can arise from following the composer as he concentrated on hearing the transitions *between* the stages, or degrees 1–12. A certain expansive breath pervades the whole work, which at the same time expresses other rhythms or breaths, the major/ minor alternation being a main one. Pictures may also arise.

—The first Prelude (written last) in C-major portrays the moment of spiritual birth, fleeting, one-in-a-bar (although written 2/8), traversing all the notes of the octave (bb. 12-21—10 bars; 10 = ordinal completion; 10 written notes to each bar), with a subtly disguised inversion of the prime—the R.H. octave-echo in every bar—till finally emphasized (spanning 3 octaves, bb. 29-32). The final bass C is heard 9 times (3^2), the final chord spanning a 10th in the final bar of the last phrase of 10-bars. Note the three-in-one (repeated notes of the tune) of the first three bars and elsewhere, and those four concluding octaves, as it were, squarely 'on the Earth', hinting at a 3 + 4 conception, the union of Heaven and Earth. The melodic line is played by the thumb; throughout finger no. 1 plays the 'tune' of Prelude No. 1.[175] A comparison with Bach's C-major Prelude (*WTC* I) has often been suggested. B-H-C-H-A is heard at the climax (bb. 20-23). Is it far-fetched to claim that by beginning with C-B (= C-H) in the bass (bb. 1 & 2) and echoing it at the climax in the treble (bb. 21-22) CH-opin is 'signing in'?[176]

—A beautiful spiritual climax comes in the 12th Prelude in the major, in the key of F-major (No. 23, a well-known esoteric number). In b. 4 (on the 14th beat) the notes of Bach's name (in other orders) appear in a highly concentrated form twice 'horizontally'—hiding, however, two definitive readings of B-A-C-H read 'vertically'. (The 10 notes—or 12, including an extra initial and final A—mostly emphasized through minor seconds.) The directions of this vertical reading are opposed, like the two Fishes of the 12th zodiacal sign. Writing the note-names on two lines (for the two hands, or the treble and the bass)

more or less in the order they occur and joining up the points makes a geometrical figure in two-dimensions, illustrating a three-dimensional cube—a traditional image for the end of a cycle (cf. Rev. 21:16). Complete self-knowledge can be attained. B-A-C-H can be read on 4 faces of this cube (the direction of reading on the same plane again pointing in opposite directions, peculiar to the sign of the Fishes). The piece, moreover, expands to the high notes A (b. 12), B (b. 13), H (b. 14), C (b. 15). This Prelude (of 22 bars) ends with the famous unresolved chord of F^7, which, however, links to the final piece in D-minor.

—The final piece No. 24 seems like a 'War of all against all' (Cortot: 'Blood, Passion and Death'), with a display of rockets and so on, concluding with three pounding, booming, deep bass Ds of utter destruction. However, op. 28 being a cycle implies the return, or resurrection—No. 1.

And analogy?

There seems to be no end of treasure in the details. The impression of Chopin's awareness of the quality of number can be further enhanced by analogy with other patterns of 12. (Is 'analogy' the correct term? A comparable situation was experienced by the poet S.T. Coleridge. As a seminal thinker, he spent most of his life trying to convince his contemporaries that with concepts such as 'organicism' the *same forces* are expressed in nature as are expressed in the images created in the poetic mind.) No doubt the traditional zodiac springs to mind here. But rather than 'directly' investigate this concept of the archetypes, another path could be followed. This is absolutely not claiming Chopin was illustrating any concepts beyond writing music. But neither was he writing simply only for musicians. He loved Bach and celebrated his name ultimately because *both composers* are like Tamino in *The Magic Flute*, of whom Sarastro said he is 'more than a prince—he is a human being'. In other words, celebrating the musical system, Chopin celebrates our humanity. He associates Bach because of his pioneer example. And like Bach, he is doing more than stringing together pretty, spontaneous pieces.

Suggestive titles have been made for the *Preludes*. Hans von Bülow (1830-1894), pianist, conductor and composer, made one series, and the famous French pianist and Chopin exponent Alfred Cortot (1877-1962) in his famous edition (Paris: Edition Salabert) suggested a poetic sequence that is widely known. Die-hard musicians only admit such things as 'useful teaching aids'. However that is, the exercise may indeed be incidentally helpful, yet as such does not reach beyond the concept of a collection of beautiful musical sketches.

Thesis No. 3: Any extra suggestion has to avoid subjective impressions if it is to correspond with Chopin's discipline. Points of contact might be discovered later. The proposition is this: *an accepted unity of twelve is to be found, then compared; finally, the experienced results are to be evaluated.* Note here, an arbitrary 'poetic' suggestion is *not* being made, but a strict comparison, actually of the same theme: the human being as the source of creativity. The point has to be emphasized as all my critics without exception ignore or attempt to falsify this claim.

 John's Gospel is known as the 'musical' gospel. Less well-known than the seven 'I-am' sayings are the twelve 'Verily, verily' groups of sayings. In 1879 Andrew Jukes (photo: left) lectured on them, and later wrote his definitive biblical study, *The New Man* (1882). The twelve sayings of the 'new man' can be summarized as follows (zodiacal signs are added for those who know Beckh's tone-zodiac). Like Bach's scheme, those *Preludes* in the keys of the relative minor depict the situation: loss of, or of striving for, that which is expressed in the *major-key series*:

1. *Prelude* 1 in C: the *Sphere* or *Home*—Heaven (Jn. 21:22) ♈
2. *Prelude* 3 in G: a *New Birth*—born from above (Jn. 3: 3, 5) ♉
3. *Prelude* 5 in D: the *Way* (Jn. 5:19-22)—is the life ♊
4. *Prelude* 7 in A: his *Food* (Jn. 6: 26-58)—bread from heaven ♋
5. *Prelude* 9 in E: his *Liberty* (Jn. 8: 31-35)—is His own to give ♌
6. *Prelude* 11 in B: his *Divinity* (Jn. 8: 48-58)—creator and creature are one ♍
7. *Prelude* 13 in F#: his *Service* (Jn. 8: 31-35)—as a shepherd gives all ♎
8. *Prelude* 15 in D♭: his *Sacrifice* (Jn. 12: 24-36)—has to die to bring forth fruit ♏
9. *Prelude* 17 in A♭: his *Lowliness* (Jn. 13: 1-32)—feet-washing glorifies God ♐
10. *Prelude* 19 in E♭: his *Glory* (Jn. 14: 8-14)—God is revealed ♑
11. *Prelude* 21 in B♭: (and 22 in G-minor)—his *Joy* and *Sorrow* (Jn. 16; 16-25) ♒
12. *Prelude* 23 in F: his *Perfection*—union of *Heaven* and *Earth* (Jn. 21: 15-23) ♓.

One example: the correlation of the grain of wheat dying that much life can result is a sublime concept corresponding to the 'Raindrop'

Prelude, with its middle section of 'death lurking in the shadows' (Cortot). Death-throes from bar 71 seem justified; the final swansong reaches the octave (*smorzando*, as noted above), is interrupted by the high B♭ (6th degree of the key) *forte*, sinking two octaves into a resigned and positive ending. The allocation of *Prelude* No. 15 to Scorpio in Beckh's tone-zodiac makes sense, but also a hint of the return to the Eagle, transmuting this double-sided, intense star-sign.

Jukes concludes by arranging the 'Verily, verily' (or 'Amen, amen') sayings into three groupings (1-4, 5-8, 8-12), which he notes (p. 287ff.) correspond to the threefold mystical path of probation, purification and union—in Steiner's terminology[177] 'preparation, illumination, and initiation'. The *Preludes* follow suit. Moreover, Chopin's own life is reflected in the *Preludes*, his authentic portrait, involving his:

- homesickness (he left Poland on a concert tour and never returned) that became transparent, a parable, for a spiritual *homelessness*,
- his especially sensitive nature was dedicated to the service of *beauty*,
- an earthly sickness was the counterpart of a spiritual *health*.[178]

A recently discovered photo of Chopin

Chopin's sufferings—suffering is often called the 'way of the cross'—enabled him to portray in his music what Rudolf Steiner (30 Dec. 1914. GA 275) calls the 'life of initiation'.

Conclusion

The journey through Chopin's *Preludes* is more than a pleasant diversion. The music has certainly to speak as music, regardless of the circumstances and any conceivable 'programme'—some people are tempted to say 'theory', or 'theory behind it'. If, however, to Chopin there is *no* 'theory'; if the composer has achieved the artistic ideal, a *union of form and content*; and if music itself really does take a step in self-recognition, then it is time fully to recognize Chopin's achievement. My own impression, for what it is worth, is that composers recognize in a flash patterns and relationships that can later be found in the score. The toil, or craft of composition, appears pre-eminently to concern a paring away to arrive at the succinct, 'inevitable' statement.[179] So-called 'improvisation' is always prepared. Explanations of musical creativity are protected from the danger of 'explaining things away' by the very nature of music itself. The critic can show—what the test of time also indicates—how human musicality transforms a technical exercise into something heavenly (Bach's four volumes of *Klavierübungen*, the violin *Partitas* and the cello *Suites*; Chopin's and Debussy's *Études*; Bartok's *Microcosmos* …); the artist's cooperation is repeatedly demonstrated. Certainly, no one has been able to *define* the basics—for example, rhythm. However, in the presence of mastery, we bend the knee in gratitude.

Many composers imitate Chopin's example, but none quite match him. I submit this is because his artistic discipline involved focusing—another word for meditating—on the musical elements, *including the tentative searching*. Only some details have been mentioned here, leaving much more to be discovered. Chopin links to Bach, yet also anticipates Bartok and Debussy in researching the rhythms of creation. The subject has opened up in recent years, as we try to catch up with composers. René Guénon (1886-1951), the French traditionalist, points out that the distinction between sacred and secular is formal, not ultimately real. Nevertheless, we know people have 'secular opinions', including the premature judgement that the subject here is all 'abstruse, esoteric moonshine'.

*

Bibliography:

- Hermann Beckh, *The Language of Tonality*. Tr. A.S., Anastasi 2015, TL forthcoming.
- Alfred Cortot, *Chopin 24 Preludes*. Paris: Edition Salabert (Fr. and Eng. editions available).
- Andrew Jukes, *The New Man*. London: Longmans, Green & Co. 1884[3] (download: archive.org).
- Hermann Keller, *The Well-Tempered Clavier by Johann Sebastian Bach*. London: Geo. Allen & Unwin 1976.
- Hertha Kluge-Kahn. *Johann Sebastian Bach: Die verschlüsselten theologischen Aussagen in seinem Spätwerk*. Wolfenbüttel u. Zürich: Möseler Verlag. 1985.
- Hans Nissen. Der Sinn des 'Wohltemperierten Klaviers II. Teil'. *Bach-Jahrbuch* 1951-52. 54-80. Online:

https://doi.org/10.13141/bjb.v19521567 (Some typos are apparent, e.g. numbers of bars.)

– Helga Thoene. helga-thoene.de/ To date, Frau Thoene has published detailed analytical studies on the G-minor Sonata (Cöthener Bach-Hefte 6, Veröffentlichungen des Historischen Museums Köthen/ Anhalt 19. Köthen, 1994), D-minor Chaconne (Dr ziethen verlag, Oschersleben 2003), the A-minor, (2005) & C-major Sonatas (2008).

– Michael Ward, *Planet Narnia: The Seven Heavens in the Imagination of C.S. Lewis*. Oxford: OUP 2008.

– Michael Ward, *The Narnia Code: C.S. Lewis and the Secret of the Seven Heavens*. Milton Keynes: Paternoster 2010 (a more popular account).

The Music of Freedom; Rudolf Steiner's 'Dry Mathematical Style'

Alan Stott

> The single day is the rhythm of the 'I'.
> Wilhelm Hoerner, *Zeit und Rhythmus.*

Basics—with help from 'analogy'

What are the basic facts that make up Rudolf Steiner's literary style, and specifically, what clues has he himself left? What relationship between form and content exists in Steiner's prose? Rather than be discouraged by the comprehensive context, we here attempt to focus on basic phenomena, hoping never to lose sight of the ground under our feet, that is, by exploring *method.*

This enquiry links directly with the researches of Hermann Beckh, in ways both apparent and less obvious. With his endeavours to trace the origin of speech, of music and of religious texts, Beckh sums up his approach by explaining the Sanskrit word *ṛta.*[180] Beckh repeatedly seeks ways to explore the Mysteries of *rhythm*, noted here in a threefold, comprehensive statement:

> For the old Indian word *ṛta* (pronounced 'rita'), for which, amongst other translations 'law, order, custom, sacred cosmic order, truth', we find especially a threefold meaning: firstly, the course of the year, which is, secondly, regulated according to the stars that move on the eternal ordering on their preordained paths, and finally the religious sacrificial ritual in harmony with the annual events of the permanent order of the stars in their courses.

To set the scene for an enquiry into Steiner's literary style, a parallel study of *music*, might prove most helpful, especially as music is Rudolf Steiner's own choice to illustrate his actual intentions as a 'writer'—his occupation, according to his passport.

Firstly, some advice in a preparatory word from the Professor. In introducing his essay on the musical keys,[181] which was initially given as a lecture to the founding-priests of The Christian Community at their preparatory meeting, Hermann Beckh writes in his Foreword (Breitbrunn, July 1922, emphases added):

> The facts and connections indicated here are in themselves not really new. Through the *method of observation* attempted here, they might be viewed in a new light.

The human story, Beckh claims, is where we can surely find answers to our specific questions. An inter-disciplinary approach is recommended; non-verbal, musical experience is confirmed by poetic experience and vice versa:

> He who is not only a musician with his ears, who carries the spirit of music in himself and appreciates it, will also find in poetry, the words of the poets, moods of keys and their differences [Beckh 2015, p. 232].

Beckh links musical and poetic experience; artistic 'moods' are something shared. We approach the region where opposites meet in a higher unity. Moreover, Beckh defines the word 'cosmic', which in German and English can also mean 'universal'. It is 'the revelation of the spirit in the earthly realm' (ibid., p. 59). The efforts to appreciate specific creative processes both of the natural world and of the human imagination involve tangible spiritual awareness open to everyone. The wider context is cultural advance and even planetary renewal. The poet who wrote the Atharvaveda XII, 1, 'The Hymn to the Earth', clearly knew this from experience:

> 1. The great cosmic truth,
> the sublime order of natural events and of religious life,
> the priestly consecration and the conscientious inner work of the spiritual contemplative,
> the sacred prayer and word, the sacrifice,
> they maintain the Earth upright on its course.
> This Earth, which for us governs everything that was and is still to come,
> may it create a wide space for our existence,
>
> 2. and that we may be uncrowded by people [living] in their midst.
> The Earth, to which belong the height and the sudden plummet, also the wide steppes,
> the Earth, which carries the various strengths and virtue of the herbs,
> may it stretch far for us and bless us.

Steiner and basics

To trace the human story, rather than take the history of musical art ('which reveals the laws of the "I"', primarily involving *decisions*),[182]

Rudolf Steiner (photo: left) pursued philosophy; he earned his doctorate in the subject and kept abreast of developments that came to fruition in a history of philosophy, *Die Rätsel der Philosophie*, GA 18 (1914/1918). But he was wise to lay the philosophical basis for cognition very early in his career. His holistic approach, nevertheless, is eminently musical. To the first edition of *The Philosophy of Freedom, Fundamentals of a Modern World-Conception: Results of Introspection according to the Methods of Natural Science* (GA 4), written in 1894, rev. 1918, Steiner concludes his Foreword (emphases original; bold font added):[183]

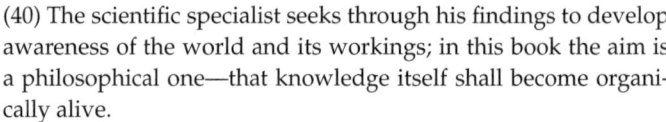

(40) The scientific specialist seeks through his findings to develop awareness of the world and its workings; in this book the aim is a philosophical one—that knowledge itself shall become organically alive.

(41) The separate sciences are stages on the way to that knowledge we are here trying to achieve.

(42) A similar relationship exists in the arts.

(43) **The composer works on the basis of the theory of composition.**

(44) This theory is a collection of rules which one has to know in order to compose.

(45) In composing, the rules of the theory become the servants of life itself, of reality.

(46) In exactly the same sense, philosophy is an *art*.

(47) All real philosophers have been *artists in the realm of concepts*.

(48) For them, human ideas were their artists' materials and scientific method their artistic technique.

(49) Abstract thinking thus takes on concrete individual life.

(50) **The ideas become powerful forces in life.**

(51) Then we do not merely have knowledge about things but have made knowledge into a real self-governing organism; our actual working consciousness has risen beyond a mere passive reception of truths.

(52) How philosophy as an art is related to human *freedom*, what freedom is, and whether we do, or can, participate in it—this is the main theme of my book.

(53) All other scientific discussions are included only because they ultimately throw light on these questions, which are, in my opinion, the most immediate concern of mankind.

(54) These pages offer a *'Philosophy of Freedom'*.

(55) All science would be nothing but the satisfaction of idle curiosity did it not strive to raise the *value of existence for the personality of man*.

(56) The sciences attain their true value only by showing the human significance of their results.

(57) **The ultimate aim of the individual can never be the cultivation of a single faculty, but only the development of all the capacities that slumber within us.**

(58) Knowledge has value only in so far as it contributes to the *all-round* development of the *whole* nature of man.

(59) This book, therefore, conceives the relationship between science and life, not in such a way that man must bow down before an idea and devote his powers to its service, but in the sense that he masters the world of ideas in order to use them for his *human* aims, which transcend those of mere science.

(60) One must be able to confront an idea and experience it; otherwise one will fall into its bondage.

Below, more light will be shed to explain the musical seven-sentence arrangement, the emphasized middle 4th lines and the added sentence-numbering of this Foreword consisting of 60 sentences. We have first to gather clues left by Steiner. They are all to do with *rhythm*, a phenomenon that can be described yet no one has ever defined.

Six Clues

Rudolf Steiner frequently spoke about his *Philosophy of Freedom*; in it he invested enormous energy and explains why he did so. Here we begin with this work in our search for clues:

Clue No. 1. He calls the book an 'organism', using *musical imagery* in the context of the seven stages of 'Christian initiation' and catharsis.[184] If the reader:

> holds the same relationship to this book [*The PoF*] that a virtuoso ... on the piano holds to the composer of the piece, that is, he reproduces the whole thing *within himself* ... [T]hen through the strictly built-up sequence of thought of this book—for it is written in this manner—catharsis will be developed to a high degree. ... [T]he book is a *logically arranged organism* and the working out of the thoughts in it has an effect similar to an inner schooling.

The emphasis is on inner work, structure and healing. The book, arranged as 'an organism', is read like a musical score. Why bring in the piano? The piano *keyboard* is constructed on the notes of the basic

7-note scale (called C-major for historical reasons), the white keyboard notes. The extra 5 black keyboard notes bring the total within the octave to 12 notes, which then repeat at different pitches. Modern 'tempered' tuning enables all the 12 keys to be played—a rather 'rock bottom' approximation to sensitive ears, nevertheless highly practical and a necessary historical stage. The question here, however, is how *the first two levels in our musical system stand in relation to spiritual training*:

- The 7-note (diatonic) *scale* is an existentially calibrated series, or degrees, comparable to the stages, or degrees of inner training (cf. Dornach 30 Dec. 1914, GA 275, *Art as seen in the Light of Mystery Wisdom*).
- Through the fact of 'tempered tuning' to equal semiquavers, the same pattern of degrees (the 7-note *scale*) can begin on any note, thus creating the possibility of visiting all 12 *musical keys*, or better, 'tonal regions' of the closed musical system (diatonic-chromatic level). This cycle is beautifully ordered according to steps of fifths, diagrammatically a closed circle, hence the well-known name, 'circle of fifths'.

Beckh's lecture (Breitbrunn, July 1922) was repeated in Stuttgart, perhaps in October, in Dr Steiner's presence. Some weeks later Steiner appears to have responded with a unique lecture, Dornach, 2 December 1922 (in *The Inner Nature of Music* ... GA 283, AP 1983). Here he uses cosmic names for the *7 notes and the 12 keys* and gives what amounts to the esoteric foundation of the musical professions.

Clue No. 2. To the *actors and speakers*, Steiner recommends[185] 'for *good style* in writing an essay', the first sentence should have something to do with the last, the second with the penultimate sentence, and so on, concentrating on the *single central sentence*. Of course, with a written piece consisting of an even number of sentences, there will be *two* central sentences. 'If the author has a true feeling for style in prose, he will have the whole essay before him as he writes.' The technique is called *chiasm*.

How would it be if, for example, the author wants to describe Earth-evolution? A footnote from the book *Christianity as Mystical Fact and the Mysteries of Antiquity* (GA 8) runs: 'Regarding the significance of the number seven, enlightenment may be gained from my book *Occult Science*.' Does this sentence only refer to what we already know, everything (stages, epochs, etc.) is arranged into sevens? However, if the author, a philosopher, is an 'artist in concepts', would he not attempt to follow his own advice and demonstrate through the technique of composition—by reflection in content *and form*—the composition of the universe? The alternative could merely amount to making empty or derivative claims. To this we shall return after reporting on the remaining clues.

Clue No. 3. Steiner gave another clue to the *eurythmic artists*. The lecture-cycle on music given for them consists of 8 lectures which follow the unfolding stages, or degrees, of the scale (prime to octave) and at the same time of initiation, with down-to-earth allusions (some are admonitions and some ostensible jokes) to the Eightfold Path.[186] This teaching promotes a balance of heaven and earth. At the sixth stage, the lecturer advises how to study spiritual-scientific works, reading 'between the lines ... even between the words'; he speaks of 'dreaming while being awake', of 'meditation', even of setting *Occult Science* to music. He confesses:

> [W]hen I described the progression of world-evolution ([Ancient] Saturn, Sun, Moon and so on), people thought the very things important that were unimportant to me. It is certainly correct that the processes on Saturn were as I described them. But that is not the essential point. The essential point is the *inner movement* that is described ...

For this, he claims, one needs to dream. For 'the dream is already a piece of music, ... you cannot write it down except in musical notation'. Then you really begin to understand a dream, not regarding its content, but 'by looking at it directly'. So speaks the craftsman, interested in 'how the *inner movements*' take place in living art, not in dry symbolism, for the 'musical element lives *between* the notes', phrases, voices and so on.[187]

Clue No. 4. To the *scientists*, Steiner speaks of mathematics, as experienced by Goethe and Novalis (from whom he takes the phrase the 'melos of mathematics'). 'In writing,' he writes,[188] 'I subdue what comes out of warmth and deep feelings into a *dry, mathematical style*, yet this style alone can be an awakener for the reader who has to allow warmth and feeling to awaken in him/herself.' Elsewhere, pointing to this response, he said:

> The pursuit of philosophy is actually impossible without a grasp of at least the spirit of mathematical thinking. We have seen what Goethe's attitude was toward this spirit of mathematical thinking, even though he made no claim himself to any special training in mathematics. Many thus would deny the existence of the very faculty I would like those who study *The Philosophy of Freedom* to acquire.[189]

Hermann Beckh wrote a magisterial essay[190] on 'Goethe and Star Wisdom'; again, there is hardly a contribution without a quotation from his beloved Novalis. Beckh was drawn to *The PoF*, yet it does not feature in his writings. Beckh's biographer writes:[191]

> The new expanded edition of Steiner's *The Philosophy of Freedom* appeared precisely in 1918 and he [H.B.] busied himself with it. He had written to Rudolf Steiner during the previous year (on 10 June 1917) how he looked forward very much to a new edition of this book that was first published in 1894, which in earlier years he had repeatedly read, yet would like to acquire in order now to work with deepened understanding and in greater peace. He described this book as *a future book, to understand which the world had slowly to mature*. Now he wrote to his friend in Kiel about this tremendously important but difficult book that requires a special concentration and devotion: 'At the moment it gives me an awful lot' [19 September 1918].

For Beckh, the human world aspires to reflect the order of the cosmos, to which the anonymous poet of 'The Hymn to the Earth' also witnesses as he begins his quite modern-sounding hymn. As mentioned above, Beckh writes eloquently on 'Rhythmic Events in the Gospel'[192] by explaining a threefold meaning in the Sanskrit word *ṛta*. To recap briefly: [i] the course of the year; [ii] regulated according to the stars that move on the eternal ordering of their preordained paths, finally [iii] the religious ritual of sacrifice in harmony with the annual events of the permanent order of the stars in their courses.

Upon this threefold basis of beginning, end and the transition between—or, the natural year, the ordered stars and the creative, sacrificial path to unite them—Beckh made significant contributions with his studies on the Gospels of Mark and John, not least his many articles and essays and his 'contributions to a new star wisdom', *The Language of the Stars* (TL 2020). If that work had been published at the time (1930-32), we would have a different astrosophy today, almost one hundred years on.

Clue No. 5: In 1924, Steiner speaks to the priests,[193] how someone initiated in the early Mysteries 'was expected … to think in accordance with … the secret of numbers'. 'The apocalyptist … like the musician … senses more or less consciously the secret of numbers.' The example of lightning is taken to describe how the initiate experiences in and behind nature; he 'quietens the thunder' in order to 'listen to it modulating, and [then] music will arise'.[194] When the divine Voice sounds the uninitiated speak of thunder (Jn. 12:27-33).

Prose method

Friedrich Hiebel (1903-1989; photo: left), who became Leader of the Humanities Section at the Goetheanum, a researcher of Greek culture, Novalis, Goethe and several other themes, wrote an illuminating analysis of 'The last Preface to *Occult Science*', Steiner's last prose work for the public (1925).[195] It reads, he says, 'like a testament'. By analysing the content, this researcher arrives at a sevenfold structure, and makes most valuable observations. However, Hiebel fails to notice the 1925-Preface (like that to the 1st edition, 1909) is composed of 77 sentences, and thus he just misses discovering the seven-sentence rhythm as such.

Clue No. 6: The direct hint (already touched on above) is given in the ninth endnote of Steiner's *Christianity as Mystical Fact*, GA 8: 'Regarding the significance of the number seven, enlightenment may be gained from my book *Geheimwissenschaft [Occult Science]*.'

The present introduction points to the down-to-earth *technique of chiasm*, which Steiner never did more than significantly hint at during his lifetime. Nevertheless, at least one, but very likely two simultaneous 'sentence-rhythms' have been found in all his written prose. A more detailed account, taking *The PoF* as an exemplary text,[196] follows up the simple formula $(\alpha \times 7) + \beta + (\alpha \times 7)$, where α = the number of septenaries and β = the number of central sentences (which vary with each section, chapter or article). With septenaries, Sentence 1 relates to Sentence 7, S. 2 with S. 6, S. 3 with S. 5, leaving S. 4 as the pivotal statement around which the interplays move, illustrated in the lengthy quote above. Beyond this, the septenaries are connected both 'laterally'—with 'recollection' and 'anticipation' constantly in play,[197] as with the notes any melodic phrase—and also across the centre point of the composition, as Steiner originally points out to the speech artists.[198] This key-thought leads one to appreciate how 'content' and 'form' can unite in a successful work of art. The basic equipment of literary and musical appreciation, or 'criticism'—the elements of language and the musical system, involving recognition of the *qualities* of number—work together.

The claims

The number 7, Steiner confirms, is 'the number of completion'.[199] By analogy—if that is the right term—the standard chiastic form of the seven notes, or degrees of the scale, is taken by Rudolf Steiner as his basic, *rhythmical sentence-structure*. To the best of my knowledge the form is exhibited in every marked section, chapter, or article of his *written work*—the form is even to be found in the addenda and longer footnotes. This claim is made of the *original German sentence-order*; translations occasionally differ in this respect. (To repeat, the specific claims are *not* made regarding the *lecture reports*.) The rhythms always reflect over a central sentence or point. These central sentences are especially significant. Other researchers do not appear to emphasize this. The chiasms appear at multiple levels: a group of 7, frequently 12 as well, with a centre and balanced outliers; a centre with outliers softly reflecting; a centre with very firm reflection and metamorphosis.

The chiastic form itself is known in literature[200] and in the Bible;[201] it is illustrated in nature (leaves, butterflies …) as well as in architectural and artistic forms. *The specific seven-sentence rhythm in Steiner's prose is one rhythm that satisfies all the clues he gives, noted above.* An organism is not a structure cast in stone, a pattern that would have been discovered long before now. Like experience of the 7-day week—an entirely human rhythm[202]—a 'logical *organism*' offers a remarkable possibility to develop *by reflection, correspondence, inner grip and change, metamorphosis* and many other essentially *musical* phenomena. Steiner chose to use it with persistent faithfulness when writing, starting from his expositions on Goethe's science, GA 1 (1883-1897) and GA 2 (1886) onwards.

The simultaneous presence of another chiastic rhythm, a 12-sentence rhythm, is also noted. This *cosmic* rhythm of 12—experienced initially as the monthly moods—was Hermann Beckh's acknowledged realm of research ('my theme'). The details particularly of a *sentence*-rhythm of 12 in Steiner's prose have yet to be explored. However, it is instructive to note what happens in longer chapters at the 'nodes' where the 7 and the 12 meet (sentence 84 and multiples thereof). Initially then, one concise passage, a written report, is offered as a highly suggestive Appendix (see below). The central 12 sentences of this report offer a powerful example. Steiner faces the strongest objections head on; with only a basic vocabulary he justifies artistic renewal.

The Tree itself

There is space for one further important clue from *The Philosophy of Freedom*. Chapter 4, occupying the centre of Part 1, consists exactly of 41 septenaries: 287 sentences = (7 x 41). The chapter-centre features 'the tree', which first appeared in Chapter 2 waving its branches 'out there', posing questions. In Chapter 4, central section, the reader becomes intimately acquainted with this tree; as a 'Tree of Life' it clearly holds the secrets of cognition. With C.G. Jung, we recognize it as a 'philosophical tree'.[203] The unique structure of the climax here is breathtaking. *PoF*, Chapter 4 arranged as a less obvious formula—but also present—in 12s, is $287 = (12 \times 11) + 23 + (12 \times 11)$. The central section with 'the tree' beautifully occupies 23 sentences, a significant number in esotericism. The mid-point, sentence 144, reads: 'This element I call my mental picture of the tree.'[204] This sentence, 144 from the beginning *and* 144 from the end, taken as the 'pivot' to two interlocking parts, points to the form: $(12 \times 12) + (12 \times 12)$, suggesting a cosmic whole. The addition of 'one', or a 'minus-one' formula, is precisely what the text seems to imply of the reader. With the structure of 7, moreover, we are initially reminded of the Menorah, the seven-branched lampstand in Solomon's temple that as a sacred almond tree represented the presence of the Lord and the embodiment of the heavenly Lady.[205] Number is a sacred science. The example of structure here might be compared to several others, for example, the penultimate section of Chapter 6 of *Occult Science*, namely, $180 = 84 + 12 + 84$, or $(7 \times 12) + 12 + (7 \times 12)$, and equally $(12 \times 7) + 12 + (12 \times 7)$, with nodes each side of the central group. The last section of Chapter 6 yields: $41 = (7 \times 2) + 13 + (7 \times 2)$, and at the same time $(12 + 17 + 12)$.

From this brief survey—foregoing detailed comment on 'sacred number'—it strongly appears that Rudolf Steiner purposely kept his method an open secret—the least said, the stronger the educational effect by the law of inverse proportion. *Rather than merely speak of the ideal, eventual union of science, art and religion, Steiner 'silently' worked towards it in every sentence he wrote—and the effort is re-lived in the reader's effort to study.*

Conclusion

The work of Hermann Beckh and Rudolf Steiner has been initially compared here concentrating on method and less by comparing the formal 'subject matter'. The important historical facts mentioned at the end of Clue No. 1 need to be reassessed. Attention was drawn to Beckh's lecture on the musical keys (Breitbrunn, July 1922) and its repeat in Stuttgart presumably that year, attended by Steiner. A few weeks later (2 Dec., Dornach), Steiner gave a single lecture on the origin of speech and music[206] with an Imagination of the 12 starry regions, visited in turn by the 7 planets = 84 meditations. In other words, he gave the cosmic names to the 12 keys and the 7-note scales of earthly music, qualitatively described by Beckh. The two systems, zodiac circle and circle of fifths have a lot to do with each other; one might say they are one and the same.

From what we have discovered of Steiner's written style, the question can now be suggested: Where did Steiner pour his musicality? To a comprehensive view, the sum of 7 and 12 may suggest more, as far as the body of '19 Class Lessons'—certainly the 7 main vowels and the 12 consonantal groups, and the 7-note scale and the 12 keys. We set out to show down-to-earth sentence-rhythms in Steiner's prose. At present, research into the context is still at an early stage, but files of the basic books arranged in the discussed sentence-rhythms have been prepared. Interestingly, the subtitle of *The Philosophy of Freedom* is missing in some editions, certainly in every online version. 'The basis of a modern world-conception', however, is likely to mean more—according to the *author's* concept of 'modern'—than its assumed 'specialist' meaning. But rightly understood, based on the author's indications beginning with the Foreword to the first edition—now relegated (as some historical 'curiosity'?) to the end of the volume—it implies that Rudolf Steiner could well qualify as the most significant unsung musical artist of the twentieth century.

Beckh describes the universal laws governing the musical system and the sounds of speech, leading to what he calls 'cosmic rhythms'. The mathematical structures in Steiner's prose also point to cosmic connections. Both researchers point to the stage known technically as 'Inspiration' and even 'Intuition'. Practically—to follow Steiner's recommendations—it means the study of spiritual-scientific *texts* includes, yet leads beyond, the surface meaning, including, but moving beyond, analysis.[207] More is contained in the union of form and content, on a par with studying *musical* scores, for what lives 'between' the notes, voices, and so on. On this path, the opportunity is given to enter into dialogue ('as far as meditation') with the creative powers (to add to the examples already mentioned, studies on Bach and Shakespeare,[208] and indeed Chopin—see previous contribution—need to be acknowledged). In down-to-earth terms, initiation into authentic audition of the inherent 'singing-speaking, speaking-singing' (Steiner's expression) can be practised. In 'ultimate' terms—to borrow a word from the third subtitle of *The Philosophy of Freedom*—initiation into actual being, whatever name (and she has many) by which she has been known: 'Musica', 'Anthroposophia', 'Wisdom', or 'the Lady' Who is seeking to reveal Herself to the patient, and thus worthy, lover.

*

> … By one pervading spirit
> Of tones and numbers all things are controlled,
> As sages taught, where faith was found to merit
> Initiation in that mystery old.
> [William Wordsworth][209]

Appendix 1: Rudolf Steiner on the Music Eurythmy Lecture-Course (GA 278); report from the Newssheet of 2 March 1924, arranged to show a sentence rhythm of the original German: (7+12+7).

(The sentences are numbered. The numbers in brackets may assist recognition of an overall chiastic relationship. The central sentences—in bold*—encapsulate the objection which is then answered directly in simple language. Two septenaries flank the central 12-arrangement. Zodiac-signs might suggest a meditative deepening; conceived as a circle, the 12 sentences relate e.g. in triangles and/or squares—A.S.)*

1. (26) Now in the Section for Speech and Music, of which Frau Marie Steiner is the director, it was felt intrinsically necessary to arrange a course on music eurythmy.

2. (25) The practicing artists and eurythmy teachers living in Dornach, and those living elsewhere who were able, took part, in addition the Council Members of the Anthroposophical Society and some personalities interested in music and eurythmy.

3. (24) So far as is possible in a corresponding manner, the content will be reported in a suitable way.

4. **(23) Here in only a few sentences the aims and intentions should be reported.**

5. (22) In the art of eurythmy, speech eurythmy has been developed to a certain extent.

6. (21) We are our own most severe critics, and realize that whatever we manage to achieve in this realm is merely a beginning.

7. (20) But what has begun must be developed further.

♈ 8. (19) Less progress has been made so far with music eurythmy, 'visible singing', than with speech eurythmy, 'visible word'.[210]

♉ 9. (18) So that the beginning which we have achieved can be continued in the right way, the stage at which music eurythmy is now practised had to be taken a step further.

♊ 10. (17) This was the purpose of the lecture-course.

♋ 11. (16) Consequently, the nature of the musical element had to be indicated, too.

♌ 12. (15) For in eurythmy, music is made visible, and we have to feel where music has its true source in the human being if its fundamental essence is to be made visible.

♍ 13. (14) Music eurythmy makes visible that which is invisible, but lives audibly, in music.

♎ 14. (13) It is just here that we are in the gravest danger of becoming unmusical.

♏ 15. (12) I hope I have demonstrated in the lectures that when music flows over into movement, the urge arises to reject all that is unmusical in music and to make visible only 'pure music'.[211]

♐ 16. (11) Those who hold the view that music ceases when the audible is carried over into visible movement will certainly have reservations about music eurythmy as such.

♑ 17. (10) This view, however, is not in the deepest sense an *artistic* one.

♒ 18. (9) For someone who inwardly experiences art must take delight in *every* extension of artistic sources and their forms.

♓ 19. (8) It is a fact that music, like all true art, springs forth from man's innermost being.

20. (7) His life can reveal this in the most varying ways.

21. (6) What wants to *sing* in the human being wants to be presented in forms of movement too, and only those possibilities of movement that lie in man's organism are called forth in speech eurythmy and music eurythmy.

22. (5) It is the human being himself who reveals *his* essence here.

23. **(4) The human form is only truly understood as arrested movement, and only the movement of the human being reveals the meaning of his form.**

24. (3) It may be said: Someone who disputes the justification of music eurythmy and speech eurythmy refuses to allow the human being to appear in his complete *totality*.

25. (2) Materialism does not permit the spirit to appear in human understanding, and the rejection of eurythmy as an art that can justifiably stand on a par with the other arts no doubt has its origin in a similar conviction.

26. (1) It is to be hoped that the eurythmists have received some inspiration from this course, and thus some contribution has been made towards the further development of our art of eurythmy.

Central 23-sentences of Chapter 4, mid-point of Rudolf Steiner, The Philosophy of Freedom, *Part 1.*

Chapter 4 consists of 287 sentences = 7 x 41, or also (12 x 11) + 23 + (12 x 11). The central section (below) is then revealed to consist of 23 sentences. This can be experienced as 12 + 12, with sentence 12 (sentence 144 in Chapter 4) overlapping. This overlapping integrates the two halves of the chapter, in effect: 2 x 144, or 2 (12 x 12).

*

1. [sentence 133 of Chapter 4] I perceive not only other things, but also myself.
2. The percept of myself contains, to begin with, the fact that I am the stable element in contrast to the continual coming and going of the percept-pictures.
3. The percept of my 'I' can always come up in my consciousness while I am having other percepts.
4. When I am absorbed in the perception of a given object I am for the time being aware only of this object.
5. To this the percept of my self can be added.
6. I am then conscious not only of the object but also of my own personality which confronts the object and observes it.
7. I do not merely see a tree, but I also know that *it is I* who am seeing it.
8. I know, moreover, that something happens in me while I am observing the tree.
9. When the tree disappears from my field of vision, an after-effect of this process remains in my consciousness—a picture of the tree.
10. This picture has become associated with my self during my observation.
11. My self has become enriched; its content has absorbed a new element.
12. **[sentence 144] This element I call my mental picture of the tree. [MID-POINT]**
13. I should never have occasion to speak of *mental pictures* did I not experience them in the percept of my own self.
14. Percepts would come and go; I should let them slip by.
15. Only because I perceive my self, and observe that with each percept the content of my self, too, is changed, am I compelled to connect

the observation of the object with the changes in my own condition, and to speak of *my mental picture.*

16. I perceive the mental picture in my self in the same sense as I perceive colour, sound, etc., in other objects.

17. I am now also able to distinguish these other objects that confront me, by calling them the *outer world*, whereas the content of my percept of my self I call my *inner world.*

18. The failure to recognize the true relationship between mental picture and object has led to the greatest misunderstandings in modern philosophy.

19. The perception of a change in me, the modification my self undergoes, has been thrust into the foreground, while the object which causes this modification is lost sight of altogether.

20. It has been said that we perceive not objects but only our mental pictures.

21. I know, so it is said, nothing of the table in itself, which is the object of my observation, but only of the change which occurs within me while I am perceiving the table.

22. This view should not be confused with the Berkeleyan theory mentioned above.

23. [sentence 155] Berkeley maintains the subjective nature of the content of my percepts, but he does not say that my knowledge is limited to my mental pictures.

Appendix 2

Occult Science—An Outline

Discovery of the sentence-rhythms began with questions about *The PoF.* After twice 7 chapters, why another, Chapter 15—which even has two titles: 'Ultimate Questions' and 'The Consequences of Monism'? Does it say anything new, perhaps 'ultimate'? There are 102 sentences, at first glance a quaternity. Every sentence of the second quarter contains at least one word relating to 'reality' or 'real', which words crop up less frequently in the rest of the chapter. The 'God who can be experienced', the 'universal primordial Being', is mentioned in sentence 64, marking the Golden Mean of Chapter 15. After initially skirting the periphery (*Zipfel*, 'coat-tails', mentioned in Chaps. 3 & 8), the book ends at the centre, answering the initial question involving 'the knowing doer' (Chapter 1, central sentence 66 of 132 sentences). In Chapter 15 the total 7-sentence rhythm emerges as 102 = (7 x 7) + 4 + (7 x 7).

In the penultimate 'Comment by the Author' to *Christianity as Mystical Fact* (GA 8), we recall: *'Über die Bedeutung der Siebenzahl kann man sich aufklären aus meiner* Geheimwissenschaft.' In English, this reads: 'Regarding the significance of the number seven, enlightenment may be gained from my book *Occult Science.'*

The author of *Occult Science* (*O.S.*), unusually, does not number the 7 chapters at all, nor does he add any subtitles. As *structural hints*, all he gives are single stars, asterisks, to divide the sections of the longer chapters. Comment on 'sacred numbers', e.g. 7, 12, 23, 84 (which with its multiples supplies 'nodes') is not elaborated here. It might be worth mentioning, however, that Steiner's early lecture on number reflects traditional wisdom (*Occult Signs and Symbols*, GA 101, but a short description of the number 6 is apparently missing). The positive value of 6 is balance between heaven and earth, cf. 'Solomon's seal'. In a 'workers' lecture', Steiner refers to number mysticism as 'superearthly'; he relates it to the sixth grade of initiation, the Sun-hero (Dornach, 8 Feb. 1924. GA 353).

Some people name repeated digits as 'angel numbers'. Is the sentence total for Chapter 3 provocative? In his 'thorough inquiry' *Mystic Numbers*, the remarkable Milo Mahan (photo: left) defines 6 as *'secular per-*

fection' or *'completeness'*. 666, he writes, 'I expect to prove is not a bad number in itself, but is simply "the number of man", that is of man in his human perfection.'[212] John Michell (photo: below, left) claims that 'the number 666 is the polar opposite of 1080, and it is also its complement and *partner.*

The number 1080 is the essential lunar number, applying to the world of imagination and the gifts of the holy spirit, whereas 666 refers to pure solar energy.'[213]

Michell devotes a section of his book on 'Twelve and Seven: The Supreme Numerical *Marriage*'. Now, to summarize the essence, it was mentioned above that one number (23) appears significantly

in the very centre of *The PoF* Part 1, where sentence 144 (= 12 x 12) appears in the centre, reading: 'This element I call my *mental picture* of the tree'—i.e. the Tree within. *By ascribing a dual function to sentence 144 (which is also 144 from the end*), a double 12 + 12 construction is completed.

The whole chapter 287 = (7 x 41) in chiastic twelves is (12 x 11) + 23 + (12 x 11). With the central sentence 'overlapping', or 'doubling', a formal perfection is apparent: 288 = (12 x 12) + (12 x 12). Now, eleven is not only 12 minus 1 or 10 plus 1, but 6 + 5, the number of the sacerdotal *marriage* of heaven and earth. Perhaps the reader is to supply this *single* adjustment—by entering the 'marriage' and perfecting the form? In other words, in affirming, or 'appropriating', the central statement, the reader *recognizes* s/he, too, unites with the thought, shown by the 'overlapping' of the numerics. One Tree, yet everyone has their own mental picture. Above, we have suggested to what 'the Tree' points, not merely a 'thought'; it actually goes by a variety of sacred names— including One 'Who caused to be and causes to be and will cause to be' or more simply 'was, is and is to come'. This is supported by what later in *The PoF* is called 'ethical individualism'; here it is shown to be the *uniting* factor in humanity (cf. Rev. 7:4, 14)—precisely not a threatened anarchy needing supervision and constant surveillance from outside. The implied, essential recognition is this: a free deed has to be lived, individually, and is to be repeatedly renewed. 144 represents the ultimately achieved organization. Similar to 11, 23 is also a penultimate situation of expectancy. It appears again in *O.S.* (see table below, e.g. final section of Chapter 5 and in Chapter 6), anticipating a completion to make 24. Is the intention behind Chapter 7 hidden in the numbers of the sentence-rhythm?

Attention has been drawn above to Friedrich Hiebel's article on the last Foreword to *Occult Science* (1925). Hiebel discovered 7 sections in the 77 sentences and thereby almost discovered the 7-sentence rhythm. Applied to the whole book, the German sentence-order of *Occult / Esoteric Science* appears simultaneously in chiastic rhythms of 7s and 12s as:

Preface 1925, in 7s	77 = 7 x 11 = (7 x 5) + 7 + (7 x 5)
Preface 1925, in 12s	77 = 7 x 11 = (12 x 3) + 5 + (12 x 3)
Preface 1920 in 7s	7 x 1
Preface 1913 in 7s	73 = (7 x 5) + 3 + (7 x 5)
Preface 1913 in 12s	73 = (12 x 3) + 1 + (12 x 3)
Preface 1909 in 7s	77 = 7 x 11 = (7 x 5) + 7 + (7 x 5)
Preface 1909 in 12s	77 = (12 x 3) + 5 + (12 x 3)
Chapter 1 in 7s	185 = (7 x 13) + 3 + (7 x 13)
Chapter 1 in 12s	185 = (12 x 7) + 17 + (12 x 7)

Chapter 2 in 7s $342 = (7 \times 24) + 6 + (7 \times 24)$

Chapter 2 in 12s $342 = (12 \times 14) + 6 + (12 \times 14)$

Chapter 3 in 12s $666 = (12 \times 27) + 18 + (12 \times 27)$

Chapter 3 in 7s $666 = (7 \times 95) + 1 = (7 \times 47) + 8 + (7 \times 47)$

Chapter 4

Introduction I $83 = (7 \times 5) + 13 + (7 \times 5)$

                               $83 = (12 \times 3) + 11 + (12 \times 3)$

Introduction II $65 = (7 \times 4) + 9 + (7 \times 4)$

                               $65 = (12 \times 2) + 17 + (12 \times 2)$

Introduction III $47 = (7 \times 3) + 5 + (7 \times 3)$

                               $47 = 12 + 23 + 12$

     Saturn $248 = (7 \times 17) + 10 + (7 \times 17)$

                               $248 = (12 \times 10) + 8 + (12 \times 10)$

     Sun $170 = (7 \times 12) + 2 + (7 \times 12)$

                               $170 = (12 \times 7) + 2 + (12 \times 7)$

     Moon $409 = (7 \times 29) + 3 + (7 \times 29)$

                               $409 = (12 \times 17) + 1 + (12 \times 17)$

     [Earth entire: $1001 = 7 \times 143$]

     Earth I: $855 = (7 \times 61) + 1 + (7 \times 61)$

                               $855 = (12 \times 35) + 15 + (12 \times 35)$

     Earth II: $146 = (7 \times 10) + 6 + (7 \times 10)$

                               $146 = (12 \times 6) + 2 + (12 \times 6)$

                               central sentences 73-74

Chapter V (11 sections)

I $107 = (7 \times 7) + 9 + (7 \times 7)$

              $107 = (12 \times 4) + 11 + (12 \times 4)$ *or*

              $107 = (12 \times 9)$ minus 1

II $371 = (7 \times 53)$

              $371 = 182 + 7 + 182 = (7 \times 26) + 7 + (7 \times 26)$

              $371 = (12 \times 15) + 11 + (12 \times 15)$ *or*

              $371 = (12 \times 31)$ minus 1

III $44 = (7 \times 3) + 2 + (7 \times 3)$

              (23 + 23 overlapping by 2)

              $44 = 12 + 20 + 12$

IV $53 = (7 \times 3) + 11 + (7 \times 3)$

              $53 = 26 + 1 + 26$

                      [= 27 + 27 overlapping by 1, *or* minus 1]

V	$109 = (7 \times 7) + 11 + (7 \times 7)$
	$109 = (12 \times 4) + 13 + (12 \times 4)$ *or* $(12 \times 9) + 1$
VI	$113 = (7 \times 8) + 1 + (7 \times 8)$
	$113 = (12 \times 4) + 17 + (12 \times 4)$
VII	$35 = 7 \times 5$
	$35 = (7 \times 2) + 7 + (7 \times 2)$
	$35 = 12 + 11 + 12$ *or* (12×3) minus 1
VIII	$170 = (7 \times 12) + 2 + (7 \times 12)$
	$170 = (12 \times 7) + 2 + (12 \times 7)$
IX	$44 = (7 \times 3) + 2 + (7 \times 3)$
	$44 = 12 + 20 + 12$
X	$31 = (7 \times 2) + 3 + (7 \times 2)$
	$31 = 12 + 7 + 12$
XI	$23 = 7 + 9 + 7$
	$23 = 12 + 12$ overlapping (*or* $- 1$)

Chapter VI

$$180 = (7 \times 12) + 12 + (7 \times 12)$$
$$180 = (12 \times 7) + 12 + (12 \times 7) = 12 \times 15$$
$$41 = 12 + 17 + 12$$
$$41 = (7 \times 2) + 13 + (7 \times 2) = (7 \times 6 \text{ minus } 1)$$

Chapter VII (nine short sections)

I.	$33 = (7 \times 2) + 5 + (7 \times 2)$
	$33 = 12 + 9 + 12$
II.	$11 = 5 + 1 + 5$
III.	$7 \, / \, 3 \, / \, 16 \, (16 = 7 + 2 + 7)$
IV.	$23 = 7 + 9 + 7$ *or* $23 = 11 + 1 + 11$
V.	$13 = 6 + 1 + 6$
VI.	7
VII.	$11 = 5 + 1 + 5$
VIII.	12
IX.	$13 = 6 + 1 + 6$

Total $141 = 33$, 16 (x 2), 13, 12 (x 2), 11 (x 2), 7 (x 2),

'Special Comments' (five paragraphs)
56 sentences—11, 5, 11, 6, 23

'Farther In!' Hermann Beckh: Passing Through Four Levels of Consciousness, 1916-1931[214]

Neil Franklin

'… that seemed to be the direction Aslan had meant when he cried out, "Farther up and farther in".' C.S. Lewis, *The Last Battle* (1956).

On first acquaintance Hermann Beckh appears as the learned Professor and one-time judge who had given up a secure position in the Friedrich-Wilhelms University in Berlin to speak for anthroposophy as a freelance lecturer. He then became one of the elder founder-priests of The Christian Community, where he served as celebrant and teacher for fifteen years (1922-1937) within the Stuttgart Seminary.

With a little more devotion to this extraordinary man, Beckh's works on the origins of language, the structure of music and then the studies on the Gospels of St Mark and St John begin to be uncovered as standing among the most erudite and perceptive publications within The Christian Community, indeed the whole anthroposophical movement at the time. Certainly, there was no one else who had Beckh's professorial knowledge of Tibetan, Sanskrit, Pali and Avestan (not to mention Hebrew, Latin and Greek and the nine modern languages) to bring to bear on the nature of Christ and Christianity.

However, over the last ten years an ongoing project to recover, translate and edit *The Collected Works of Hermann Beckh* (including over eighty periodical articles, previously unpublished typescripts, a book-size series of articles plus a major unfinished manuscript) has provided the opportunity to consider not only the vast range of his insights, which indeed struck his contemporaries, but also to begin to approach his *developing* vision. This is largely beyond the reach of a single person, but the years of research have shown that a small team working closely together may make some progress.

Given what we know about Beckh's life before his ordination, both from Gundhild Kačer-Bock's biography and the first-hand memories of his colleagues,[215] there is no avoiding the observation that Beckh was never a person who rested on his laurels or made an uneasy peace with dissatisfaction. Between 1901 and 1921 (age 26-46) he made three life-changing decisions to abandon acclaimed, prestigious posts to venture into the unknown. Something similar can be discerned in his published and unpublished writings during the second part of his life. Yet these now appear not as the wandering tracks of some kind of 'restless soul', but as an indication of a determined and assured spirit who wanted to press on further, ever more deeply into the Christian Mysteries. Moreover, there are distinct signs indicating or suggesting that Beckh's work between 1916 and 1931 follows a recognizable spiritual lawfulness that reflects his own deepening pursuits.

*

That said, this exploration sets out from the same point of departure as Beckh himself in 1912. Within ten years, to 1922, the judge became the Professor of Indology and then the priest serving at the altar, increasingly able to call upon Tibetan, Sanskrit, Pali, Avestan, Hebrew and Koiné Greek to support fundamental insights. On the whole Beckh became somewhat frustrated by the traditional academic approaches to ancient languages and sacred texts—comparative philology and cultural comparisons were indeed necessary but left a void. Beckh had found what he felt he had always been looking for on hearing Rudolf Steiner speak concerning the prophet Elijah on 14 December, 1911.[216]

As a member of the newly born Anthroposophical Society and soon after the First Section of the Esoteric School, Beckh read as much as he could of the publications and lectures, attended lectures when work permitted, and corresponded with Rudolf Steiner: at least 34 letters are still held in the Dornach *Nachlass*, plus a correspondence with Marie Steiner. Without any shadow of doubt, when he was working intensively with Tibetan and Sanskrit texts for the Friedrich-Wilhelms University in Berlin, Beckh reached the conviction that the Sanskrit texts, the Pali Buddhist Canon and the Zend Avesta provided a clear testimony for the evolution of consciousness and of supersensory perception.

Yet Beckh did not want some kind of antiquarian knowledge. Sacred traditions and footprints in the snow were fine as far as they went, but what was their relevance as Europe plummeted towards the Great War? As Blake had argued in 1789,[217] if there is one humanity then there is one underlying spirituality, something that had to be founded in absolutely universal human experience, the real common ground. As with many such things (it is perhaps their most common feature) the reality was plain and simple, staring one in the face all the time, but so ubiquitous as to pass notice. For Beckh it was inescapable that there were *four states of consciousness* in addition to everyday waking thoughts and feelings. There was the borderland of waking and dreaming, full dreaming, sleeping, and something that Beckh had personally experienced first as a five-year-old: a pre-natal or post-mortem condition of consciousness. Given this *universal fact*, he would argue, there must be some traces in the sacred texts.

Hermann Beckh the judge would be the first to ask for some documentary evidence as background to the argument in hand. Our first testimony is St Paul, who wrote in the second letter to the [2] Corinthians 3:18:

> ... beholding the glory of the Lord, [we] are being changed into his likeness from one degree of glory to another, for this comes from the Lord who is the Spirit.

The Greek text has 'from glory unto glory' (ἀπὸ δόξης εἰς δόξαν) and is so expressed in the Authorised Version. Luther wrote '*von einer Klarheit zu der andern*'. Yet what the RSV translators clearly recognized was that 'from glory unto glory' is not an expression of a package trip around a series of equally interesting sites but a progression of an *intensifying experience*, ever farther in. We may not be entirely happy with 'degree' with its Masonic connotations, but the attempt at clarification in 1881-1885 RV and RSV 1971 is most welcome. Paul was clearly aware that there was more than one threshold.

Our second witness is the author (if such sources may be so expressed) of Exodus 31:3, usually presented to the public as the venerable E—the Elohist tradition. This evidence addresses the master craftsman Bezalel 'God is protection',[218] who was appointed to be the overseer or overall constructor of the Tabernacle in the desert.

> ...and I [the Lord] have filled him with the Spirit of God, with ability and intelligence, with knowledge and all craftsmanship, ...

It is helpful to tabulate the translations of the four qualities:

RSV	'Ability'	'Intelligence'	'Knowledge'	'Craftsmanship'
Hebrew	hokhmah	tebunah	da'ath	mᵉlekah
	המכח	הנובת	תעד	מלאכה
LXX	sophias	syneseos	epistemes panti ergo	
Vulgate	sapientia	intelligentia	scientia in omni opere	
A.V.	wisdom	understand-ing	knowledge	all manner of workmanship
Luther	Weisheit	Verstand	Erkenntnis	allerlei Geschicklichkeit

For the craftsman who was to build the image of heaven on earth, the Spirit of God (Elohim) leads to a progression of gifts in what may be called *a descending order*, from the exalted Sophia / Wisdom / Hokhmah right 'down' to what we might call applied, practical skill, but at the same time this 'lowest' or 'outermost' gift is still seen as something supra-earthly: *m^elekah* also represents a feminine angelic being.[219] All four are Divine faculties *closely corresponding* to the four 'levels' of the 'descent' of the Divine Nature through the Kabbalistic Sephiroth as represented, for example, in the Zohar[220] and in the four-fold division of space with the Tabernacle.

Comparable to Bezalel in Exodus is the *precise description* of the 'Elect One'[221] in 1 Enoch 49:3:

> In him dwell the spirit of wisdom, the spirit which gives thoughtfulness, the spirit of knowledge and strength, and the spirit of those who have fallen asleep in righteousness.

The four terms can once again be tabulated:

C'worth 1983	the spirit of wisdom	and the spirit which gives thoughtfulness	and the spirit of knowledge and strength	and the spirit of those who have fallen asleep in righteousness
Ge'ez (Ethiopic)	መንፈሰ ጥበብ	ወመንፈስ ዘየሀቡ	ወመንፈስ ተምህርት ወኀይለ	ወመንፈስ እለ ኖሙ በጻድቅ
Tr'scribed	mänəfäsä ṭəbäbə	wämänəfäsä zäyalebu	wämänəfäsä təməhərətə wäḫäyələ	wämänəfäsä who nomu bäṣədəḳə
1821 R. Laurence	the spirit of intellectual wisdom	-	the spirit of instruction and of power	and the spirit of those who sleep in righteousness
R.H. Charles 1912	the spirit of wisdom	and the spirit which gives insight	and the spirit of understanding and of might	and the spirit of those who have fallen asleep in righteousness

Here once again the first three terms are generic, akin to the O.T. *Hokhmah* (Wisdom), *Binah* (Understanding) and *Da'ath* (Knowledge) in the Zohar system, but the last term pertains to post-mortem and pre-natal consciousness.

Preparation 1912-1916: Buddhist Studies and Anthroposophy

In 1916 Hermann Beckh addressed the issue of Buddhist knowledge (*pañña*) in the Pali canon for his major (two volume) academic book, *Buddha und seine Lehre*.[222] With the aid of Gundhild Kačer-Bock's biography and a little further research, it has now become possible to appreciate the fact that Beckh was one of the very few Indologists in Germany sufficiently qualified in Tibetan, Sanskrit and Pali to undertake the demanding task for the publishers, Sammlung Göschen. The centenary of the publication has been celebrated in the UK with an English translation, updated and expanded, to mark the centenary of the German edition and accompany the issue of a *Festschrift, Essays in Honour of Hermann Beckh*, in English.

It is of the highest significance here that the translator, Dr Katrin Binder, prefaces the translation with the acute observation that Beckh's rendering of *pañña* as *Erkenntnis* poses questions for an English translator. Having worked as a lecturer for the University of Würzburg and Göttingen in Indology, and being personally experienced in Buddhist meditation, Dr Binder explains that *pañña / Erkenntnis* is best expressed in English as *'realization'*. Truth here is not something downloaded from external sources but has to be *created* afresh in meditation—it is *'realized'*, made real independently and originally:

> With Beckh I understand Buddhist *'Erkenntnis'* as knowledge or insight acquired in meditation. This inner process implies a 'making real' of the teachings, including the Buddhist 'truths' and imaginations. This is well illustrated by Beckh's discussion of the role of deities and supernatural beings in Buddhism. It also emerges from his discussion of the concept of *'schauendes Erkennen'*—realizing vision (or 'seeing realization', *ñāṇadassanaṃ*). This term implies not only the gradual acquisition of supernatural powers of clairvoyance through the practice of meditation (for example with regard to the memory of previous existences). It also carries the Buddhist image (resting on much older Indian ideas) of the 'blind' person who is made seeing by his insight, or realization, into the Buddhist truth of suffering.[223]

There can be not the slightest doubt that Beckh, having joined the new Anthroposophical Society and the Esoteric School in 1912, corresponding quite regularly with Rudolf Steiner, well understood that the older Buddhist *paññā* had a great deal in common with Imagination, Inspiration and Intuition. This should not be underestimated: we know from his biography that he was devoted between 1912 and 1916 to both *Knowledge of the Higher Worlds, How is it Attained?* and *Occult Science—An Outline.* Beckh could confirm what Steiner outlined and what the older Pali texts taught. In the simplest terms, knowledge (*paññā*) is *seeing and creating* in the supersensible for oneself. It is experiential, not learned from an outside authority.

Such personal realization, however, needs to be underwritten by the certainty of established *order.* When he left school in 1893 and won a scholarship to the prestigious Maximilianeum in Munich, Beckh took up the Law. He then became a judge within the Munich circuit, after composing a prize-winning essay on the Bavarian Code of Law for which he was awarded D. Jur. We can have no doubt that he possessed the acutest legal judgement. It is clear from his biography that he understood that 'natural law' had priority over state legislation—'positive law'—that the efforts of the French *philosophes* (Voltaire, Diderot and De Jaucourt) were not in vain. There is, absolutely, a natural law that all men and women are born free, for example, and that slavery is against such law. However, the natural law of the *philosophes* was historically a prelude to the discovery and elucidation of lawfulness in Imagination (1781-1820). From Goethe to Hegel in Germany, and from Blake to Shelley in England, the leading spirits of the time responded to a Divine call and demonstrated that '*schaundes Erkennen*' or *ñāṇadassanaṃ*, realized concrete Imaginations, have a universal, objective reality. A little later, in 1922, Beckh penned a fascinating article for the journal *Anthroposophie*, 'Zur Wandlung des Rechtsbegriffs in Menschheitsbewusstsein,'[224] where he argues convincingly that from the earliest Indian culture *lawfulness* is rooted in Sanskrit *ṛta*: the spiritual, cosmic *order* which is truly reflected in religious ritual. Within Buddhism, the perception of such lawfulness and regularity is the prerogative of the *atīndriyadraṣṭar* 'seer of the supersensible', or the one 'who saw beyond the sense-world'.

Threshold 1 1921-1922: The supersensible origins of language (Natursprache)
The borderland of waking and dreaming

It is clear from Beckh's own autobiographical writing that his great divorce from a promising legal career in 1902 was the first of three such dramatic life changes. Yet even then Beckh could rely on two sources of enduring strength. The first was the fact that he had directly undergone experiences of a pre-natal existence which were undeniable (recurring at important times in his life); and secondly, especially as a student in Munich, he had heard astonishing messages in Wagner's music. As a judge Beckh found that the law punished, it did not foster human potentials. On the other hand, performances of Wagner provided a divine sustenance for those who had ears to hear. Was there a link between the experience of a pre-natal Paradisal state and the structures of richly romantic music? Was there something of cosmic lawfulness, *ṛta*, in Mozart, Beethoven, Wagner and Bruckner? The threatening gulf between his old, well-trodden career in government service, now dismissed abruptly, and a new life studying Tibetan, Sanskrit and Pali—settling down in Berlin—could be safely traversed with the aid of music.

All the same, Beckh never wanted to take short-cuts. If there was a link between the great works of music and *Erkenntnis* in the Buddhist and anthroposophical sense, then it would have to be demonstrated— almost, one might say, to the satisfaction of a global jury. How could this be achieved? The process over the seven years 1916-1923, aet. 41 to 48, entailed two further sacrifices of career. Beckh first gave up his university position, despite a personal request from the Minister of Culture in Bavaria, and then abandoned his acclaimed work as a lecturer for anthroposophy to become one of the founding priests of The Christian Community, joining young Emil Bock and his own contemporary Friedrich Rittelmeyer in the new Stuttgart Seminary as one of the three leading teachers. Thus it was, in 1923, that Beckh found himself in the attic rooms of 41 Urachstrasse with his piano, an iron stove, and an imposing collection of authoritative books regarding the sacred texts of India and Tibet. At the time when the Russian civil war was still in violent conflict and Mount Etna erupted, making 60,000 people homeless, Beckh composed and published *Vom Geistigen Wesen der Tonarten*,[225] his first major book since the Buddha study of 1916. This was not some kind of personal whim or caprice.

In the two previous years, before becoming ordained, Beckh had responded to Steiner's personal invitation that he (Beckh) should develop both the understanding that the origins of speech should be sought for in *schauender Erkenntnis*, and that distinct traces of such an origin can be found through traditional, academic philology. For two years Beckh lectured and published as much as he could to build bridges between the primordial roots of Indo-European languages, with special attention to Sanskrit, and the inner Imaginative / Inspirational experience of speech-sounds. In this domain we find Professor Beckh moving fluently among the older sacred languages, including Avestan and Hebrew. The reissue of *Neue Wege zur Ursprache* in 1954[226] has contributed substantially to his growing reputation and it is true that Beckh stands today as a pioneering colossus in the anthroposophical approaches to speech and eurythmy. Yet in 1923, surrounded by a good deal of acclamation for his articles and lectures on language, Beckh chose to write on music and to leave aside his professional expertise in the oriental languages. It was time to move on.

Threshold 2 1923: Music and the Zodiac
Entry into dream consciousness

For Beckh this was an enormous step forward. If in philology there was a close tie between scientific research into word roots (Novalis' *pragmatic etymology*) and the supersensory *Erkenntnis* of the primordial meanings of speech-sounds (*genetic etymology*), then a corresponding connection may exist between the musical keys as played in classical compositions and a spiritual–supersensible source which we can call a 'mood', *Stimmung*.[227] Given that Rudolf Steiner consistently elaborated on the archetypal *Weltendenken* within cognition, there must also be higher *Weltenstimmungen* expressing archetypal *feelings*.

As an example, Beckh investigates, as an *atīndriyadraṣṭar*, the key of B-major and A♭-minor.[228] He describes the mood as:

- 'the hour before sunset'
- 'the end of summer'
- a 'mood of farewell'
- 'transfiguring'.

The range of music considered here by Beckh is quite narrow in compass, with most points being consistently refurbished between 1923 and 1937:

- Isolde's *Liebestod* at the end of *Tristan and Isolde* (B-major);
- the *Karfreitagszauber* in *Parsifal* (B-major);
- the A♭-minor Arioso in Beethoven's *Piano Sonata*, op. 110;
- the Funeral March movement in A♭-minor from Beethoven's *Piano Sonata*, op. 26;
- music associated with St Elisabeth in *Tannhäuser* (B-major);
- music associated with Midsummer's Eve in *Die Meistersinger* (B-major).

In 1923, however, Beckh had *realized*, heard for himself, that such passages, which had nourished him during many a weary hour of studying legal texts and hand-printed Tibetan characters, could not have been written in any other key. Once again, the task was to plummet universal *lawfulness*. Here the ocean was very deep and difficult to sound, but life as a priest of The Christian Community could confirm that the rhythms of the day, the week and the year expressed *ṛta*, the rhythmic cosmic order. Beckh must have deeply reflected on the seasons of the year and the Christian festivals. The inherent lawfulness of the musical keys was rooted in the rhythms of time expressed spatially in the zodiac, and this was far more difficult to access than the sources of speech. The Mystery of the musical keys belonged to an interweaving of *Weltenstimmungen* experienced in the seasons with the dark night sky becoming alive with stars. Where was the archetype of B-major and A♭-minor to be found? Beckh found that the 'mood' (*Stimmung*) of this key, especially in selected bars from *Tristan and Isolde* and *Parsifal* was that of late summer, perhaps the first week of September when light begins to fade, and people gather along the coast to bid farewell to the setting Sun and the end of the summer holiday. Such an experience of leave-taking, a 'mood of farewell' falls to the sign of Virgo. Some ten years later Beckh was to write in detail for the Priests' *Rundbrief* on the zodiac *signs* while Rudolf Frieling supported his findings and carefully extended the study to focus on the 12 signs and the 12 sentences of The Creed, also for the *Rundbrief*. Within Beckh's contributions, however, we now find that Virgo (the archetype of Isis and Provider of Nourishment, Eucharist) is accepted as the star-guide, presiding genius, of The Christian Community in its life and work.[229]

Between 1923 and 1930 Beckh was hard at work meditatively researching the starry archetypes which he encountered in music. For the time being, the emphasis moved from examples in music to the stars themselves, that is, as they are found to be in relationship to the Earth and its rhythms and seasons. There was a strong reason, or occasion, for this. When Beckh responded to Steiner's open invitation to speak about the origins of language it was understood that academic linguistics had fallen prey to the assumptions and theories of Fritz Mauthner.[230] In Mauthner's view, any observation on speech had to be supported by empirical evidence; introspection was unacceptable; there was no *psyche* as it could not be observed or measured by sense perception. Shortly after September 1920 Europe was further stirred up by the popular success of Arthur Drews'

Das Markus Evangelium als Zeugnis gegen die Geschichtlichkeit Jesu.[231] Drews had thrown down the gauntlet: the Gospel accounts of the life of Jesus were no more than a rehash of ancient myths associated with the constellations through which a non-historical, fictional Sun-God ran around his path three times in three years. There were riots outside Vienna Cathedral.

Expanding the Vision 1924-1928: from music to the gospels

The Faculty later met in Urachstrasse and concluded that someone had to reply to Drews, and it could only be Beckh. The principal problem here was that Drews had compiled an argument that had some vestige of the truth in it but had reduced the *Weltenstimmungen* of Beckh's approach to music to the crudest observations on zodiac and other constellations, not signs. Put in the simplest terms (as David Hume used to enjoy doing) Drews' argument was:

> The gospels are rooted in ancient and classical myths of the stars.
> Such myths are obviously worthless as history.
> Therefore, the gospels are worthless as history.

Along with the call to reply to Drews, Beckh now found himself living at a time, 1923-1928, when there was a dramatic explosion in Germany of popular and indeed academic interest in astrology. The principal authority on this subject, Ellic Howe, has shown that:

> ... the majority of some 400 astrological books and pamphlets were printed in Germany between 1921 and 1935; between 1926 and 1931 there were no less than 26 astrological year books or predictive annuals in production; by 1928 half a dozen specialist monthly or bi-monthly periodicals were available for practising astrologers in Germany.[232]

In these years Beckh had to contend both with Drews and with misapprehensions of astrology; also, as the threats from National Socialism and Communism grew apace. Neither Emil Bock nor Friedrich Rittelmeyer could take up the challenge. Yet we now find Beckh still moving on into uncharted waters, that is (still with almost unavoidable metaphors) deepening the meditative quest. The calling was now to extend earlier discoveries in the lawful structures of speech and music to the structures of the Gospels of Mark and John. Beckh found that realizations of the zodiac signs were the essential spiritual guide to both music and the gospels, but at the same time something more profound was just beginning to make itself felt.

In the early 1920s Beckh had to cross a first threshold, from academic erudition and skilfulness to the borders of dreaming where the origins of resonant word-roots could be inwardly experienced. Here there is a certain balance between sharp fully awake consciousness and something of a waking dream which is often found to be highly attractive in his writings on language and etymology: it is a broadly accessible area. With the progression to music in 1923, however, Beckh is more deeply within a dreamlike environment where the meanings of the zodiacal archetypes begin to shine forth as actively creative beings, and this is much harder to experience truly for oneself. One can say that an evening twilight brings forth a night that is radiant with stars, radiant with new meanings. Yet as time progressed from 1924 to 1930, Hermann Beckh also took further steps in meditation: it is as though (we are always encountering metaphors) he encountered a realm where the stars, constellations and planets disappeared entirely to produce a pitch-black night sky wherein there was no orientation. Here was a third threshold, between dreaming and sleeping.

Threshold 3: 1924–1928. Encountering The Divine Feminine Entry into Sleep Consciousness

In the later 1920s Beckh was blessed with two sources of support for the daunting task of crossing this 'deeper' threshold. On the one hand there was the continuing publication of fine anthroposophical studies. Günther Wachsmuth's *Die ätherischen Bildekräfte in Kosmos, Erde und Mensch* appeared in 1924,[233] to which Beckh had constant recourse; and then Albert Steffen's *Mani* was published in 1930.[234] Like Beckh, Steffen was well versed in the nature or substance of Paradise and came up with the glorious old term *'terra lucida'*.[235] On the other hand there was Mozart. Probably the most heart-stopping moment here is when Tamino, within the Temple of *The Magic Flute*, finds himself in total darkness, all lights are extinguished. The musical key changes to a haunting A-minor with *'O Ew'ge Nacht'* and Tamino's tenor launches out the great question to darkness and infinity, *'Ihr Unsichtbaren, saget mir / Lebet Pamina noch?'* Almost as an echo to the question, the invisible choir replies in what must be one of the most truly magical moments in the history of Western music, redolent with profound pauses: *'Pamina —lebet—noch!'* In the deepest darkness, almost at the edge of all extinction and hope, Tamino is assured that the Divine Feminine is still alive—the choir here is usually led by high female voices. Mozart achieves the astonishing task of portraying a true Mystery on the stage, something that Beckh could profoundly appreciate.

While Beckh confronted the extinguishing of all lights and the inner darkness without stars, with consciousness penetrating from dream to deeper sleep, we too have a very important threshold to cross. Beckh found between 1924 and 1930 that the darkest night sky, bereft of signs and constellations, became radiant with the Divine Feminine. In all probability we do not have an adequate language for this: even Steiner's communications on Inspiration are only waymarks. The darkest night sky becomes radiant with the presence of, well, what language shall we use? The Divine Feminine? Pamina?

There is no lack of options. The best of recent studies on the Old Testament (Margaret Barker D.D.) elucidates the 'Queen Mother' Ashratah or 'The Lady';[236] *The Zohar* points to a fourfold feminine from Hokhmah to Shekinah; other Kabbalist texts emphasize that Shekinah is found also to be the text of the Torah; Solovyov, and Bulgakov encountered Sophia.[237] The list of possibilities is almost endless, but one of the most helpful guides is Jakob Böhme who developed a complex theosophical system from 1612 to 1624, founded on original vision.

Starting with *Aurora* in 1612, Böhme strove to explain that the creative Will of the Divine Trinity (beyond all human knowledge) revealed itself in creation *through four successive stages*, all of which may be experienced as feminine forms. The first reception of the Divine Will is perceived as a mirroring where the purely transcendent subjective becomes objectified to God Himself. This first 'mirror' is Böhme's *Mysterium Magnum*. From here the Will proceeds to the dynamic process of the 'Divine Nature', a sevenfold 'wheel' or circulation: a Divine 'sport' or playground where the seven fountain-spirits rejoice in free play, a loving tussle (*Ringen*)[238] which celebrates the polarity of unbounded Divine energy and its expression in evanescent mobile formations. Such free 'sport' results in the spiritual pleroma of the Divine Nature, the seeds of creation, the archetypes of Plato, Philo, and the Neo-Platonists, which Böhme understands as the *Jungfrau Sophia*. Finally, as a result of Lucifer's rebellion, the Divine Will as present in the pleroma is moved to a further externalization: the Creation of the Universe even as we see it today.

Clearly Böhme knew something of the older Kabbalistic traditions but we are very uncertain as to how he encountered them after

1612. Still, the fact remains that Böhme continued to assert a fourfold 'descent' or 'objectification' of the Divine Will. With enlightenment, the human spirit can retrace the 'pathways' of creation in ascending order. This takes the meditating mind from empirical Nature to its archetypes in the Sophia / Wisdom pleroma (also examined by Bulgakov), to the great 'wheel' of fountain-spirits (where movement and metamorphosis is 'faster' than any one form), and finally to the 'first Mother', *Mysterium Magnum*. Obviously, there is a considerable overlap here with the four Kabbalistic levels of Atziloth, Briah, Yetsirah and Asiah.[239]

In a sense following the pioneering work of Bulgakov on Sophia and Mary, few have achieved more today in Old and New Testament studies than Margaret Barker. She has argued convincingly that the O.T. Law was originally *vision*, and that Ezekiel saw into the Divine Feminine (fourfold) that was expressed as *chayyah*, the 'living one' of Ez. 10:17: her evidence and argument, at the highest level of Hebrew studies, are simply incontrovertible.[240] But what does all this really mean? *'Pamina lebet noch'*?

As Beckh painstakingly investigated the Divine Feminine between 1924 and 1930, he set out a vast range of metaphors and traditional images. From anthroposophical natural science he discussed Wachsmuth's four ethers and related this to the Tree of Life; he understood that the Tree and the Goddess were expressions of the same source; he investigated the hieroglyph and the traditions of Isis; he understood the Bride of the Lamb and The New Jerusalem; he presented the story of Snow White.[241] He explained that the Tree of Life was still with us, but becomes obscured in waking consciousness.[242] No one else during these years did more to convey a glimpse of the radiant Divine Feminine.

There was still a final threshold to cross. In his last years, 1930-1937, aged 55-62, Beckh continued to compose music for The Christian Community, and returned to the earlier 1923 text, *The Essence of Tonality*, to expand it into *The Language of Tonality in the Music from Bach to Bruckner* (pub. 1937). He published two small musical compositions, *Psalm 23* (the text his own translation) and *The Roses of Damascus*, and was writing a new work on music during his final months of earthly life, *The Mystery of Musical Creativity: Man and Music*.[243] However, before these tasks he had realized that his extensive studies on the Gospels of Mark and John required a certain clarification, which we can initially simplify as: What is the *substance* of The New Jerusalem?

Threshold 4 1930-1931: The Christ-Consciousness enters the pre-natal / post-mortem condition

As the distinguished Professor of Indology, Beckh applied the clearest logical thinking to what should be understood by *nirvana* in the Pali Canon of Buddhist thought. The analysis in Part 2 of *Buddha's Life and Teaching* (1916) is a model of exposition. It is just here, however, that Beckh points out, with abundant evidence, that the Buddhist 'step-ladder of meditation leads in its latter stages to an inner experience of a "this-side" *nirvāṇa* (*diṭṭhadhammanibbāna)'.*[244] This is to say that in advanced meditation the subject will encounter within him / herself a true 'realization' of the post-mortem and pre-natal condition of consciousness *while still in incarnation.* It will be remembered that Beckh had three such experiences during his life, albeit involuntary. In fully awake consciousness, assisted by immense scholarly learning, the publication explained Gautama Buddha's teaching on 'this-side' *nirvāṇa* to the satisfaction of the logical intellect.

When Hermann Beckh was living in the Stuttgart seminary, we are reminded by Gundhild Kačer-Bock, her sister Rosemaria and by others who knew Beckh well, that he would make a particular point of showing them Venus or Sirius in the night sky, usually above Stuttgart, and that he maintained a collection of beautiful crystals. It is not difficult to imagine the Professor pondering and meditating on them: how has supernal light come to find itself in cold, hard physical matter? The question stood before him whenever he observed snowflakes, ice-covered mountains or simply frost on the windowpanes of his attic room in Urachstrasse 41.

During the 1920s Beckh published a range of periodical articles approaching the question from a number of different angles. Among the most attractive are his contemplative verses on The New Jerusalem, his discussions of Isis, most of all his meditative findings in the story of Snow White. More thorough analyses are then to be found in the two books on the gospels. In 1930 Beckh was completing *John's Gospel: The Cosmic Rhythm—Stars and Stones,* but then found that something more still needed to be said. Between 1930 and 1931 Beckh continued to write extensively on the stars and a new astrology for the Priests' *Rundbrief* while composing what was intended to be a fairly short Appendix for John's Gospel and also publishing the intense study *The Parsifal=Christ=Experience in Wagner's Music Drama.* Very quickly the planned Appendix became a fully-fledged work in its own right with the title *Vom Geheimnis der Stoffeswelt (Alchymie)* in 1931. Among

Beckh's works, this is the text that has been most often reissued, but the two volumes complement each other.

The 1931 *Parsifal* expresses the *realization* that the music drama progresses through four distinct stages, that it develops through deepening levels of Mystery. All of Act 1 presents the young, unknowing Parsifal 'in the region of the Grail' where he listens to Gurnemanz but has to admit that he does not know what the Grail is. Act 2, Sc. 2 presents Parsifal many years later in Klingsor's magic garden overcoming Kundry and coming to understand Amfortas' wound. Act 3, Sc. 1, is Good Friday where the death of Titurel is reported, and the music drama reaches its climax with the renewal of the Earth, the *Karfreitagzauber*, and then, Sc. 2, the unveiling of the Grail. Regarding the spring-like renewal of the Earth, Beckh adds the observation, 'The Earth is transformed into a shining monstrance.'[245]

In the penultimate paragraph of the study, Beckh presents his final overview:

In the four steps of the Parsifal-path, Wagner presents in artistic images that same Mystery which is enacted at the altar in The Act of Consecration of Man of The Christian Community.

These four 'steps' or stages are then summarized:

> The Liturgy of the Word or 'Proclamation of the Gospel'.
> The Offertory: 'the soul has to step through the gate of purification'.
> Transubstantiation: 'bread and wine radiate in the light of renewed purity'.
> Communion: 'the human being as *bearer of the Cup*'. [My emphases.]

As both scholar and artistic visionary, Beckh had striven through the 1920s, with publications culminating in the two gospel studies, to convey what he had experienced as the Divine Feminine as the provider of spiritual nourishment in the most defined sense, whether as Sanskrit *soma*, Avestan *huoma* or Hebrew *manna*. As we have seen above, the Divine Feminine was perceived as the one source of light and renewed life, the Tree of Life which radiates the uncreated light which is normally invisible. For Beckh this was also what is presented in the Grail vessel. But this left the question, what of the vessel itself? Beckh had to extend the gospel studies into what he had found beyond the final threshold: *Vom Geheimnis der Stoffeswelt: Alchymie* had to be written.

Between 1904 and 1922 Hermann Beckh had cultivated first a professorial knowledge of Buddhism and then a mature understanding of what Rudolf Steiner was presenting. It is now known that when he was called up in autumn 1916 to serve as a foot-soldier on the Eastern Front the one book that he took with him, along with the trench-digging tools, was *Occult Science—An Outline* at the very same time that *Buddha's Life and Teaching* saw publication in Berlin. The one thing that was abundantly clear to him as he took shelter in an empty house in Romania on Christmas Eve 1916[246] was that perception depends on levels of consciousness; with both Buddhism and anthroposophy, the supersensible beings that are encountered on different levels on the Path are themselves states or expressions of the changing consciousness.

When he composed *Buddha's Life and Teaching* in 1915-1916 Beckh did not oversimplify Buddhist teachings. Part 2 of the book set out, with full scholarly apparatus, an impressive analysis of the complex series of stages of meditation to be encountered by the Buddhist disciple on four levels. In due sequence we find *saddhā* (belief), *samādhi* (meditation), *paññā* (realization), and *vimutti* (liberation). Within *vimutti*, a fourth stage of exalted contemplation (*dhyāna*) is described closely following texts in the Pali canon. Beckh carefully explains that this fourth stage is the highest attainable as 'this-side' *nirvāṇa*. 'If', thus it is said in the passage on meditation of the Dīghanikāya (SPhS 83):

> If the spiritual or mental element (*cittaṃ*) has been thus concentrated, purified and filled with light, free from all impurities and earthly passion, compliant and pliable, steadfast and unmoving, then he directs this spiritual element towards the realizing vision (or 'seeing realization', *ñāṇadassanaṃ*).
>
> That which presents itself first to his vision is his own body, his own being, which he then sees as if split into a duality: a physical being, constituted by the four elements which is the result of physical heredity (*mātāpettikasambhava*) and which carries the conditions of decay and dissolution in itself, and another one, a principle of spiritual consciousness (*viññāṇa*) which permeates that physical being in the same way as a coloured thread drawn through a pure, stainless, polished eight-sided precious stone, and it is said that he sees this his physical body which is subject to decay and traversed by the thread of the consciousness-soul as if *from the outside* like someone who takes a precious stone into his hand and says: this is a precious stone with these particular characteristics, and here a coloured thread has been drawn through it.[247]

In this powerful image, the archetype of the physical body displays its crystalline nature, a precious stone through which the 'coloured thread' of *viññāna* is drawn. The 'eight-sided precious stone' of the Pali Sāmaññaphala Sutta 84 is *veḷuriya* from which classical Greek *beryllos* comes by way of metathesis, i.e. beryl. Although in later publications Beckh preferred to represent this as a diamond, Part 1 of *Buddha's Life and Teaching*, given over to a painstaking examination of Gautama Buddha's life in history and legend, had drawn the reader's attention to a pertinent detail in the Lalitavistara account of the Buddha's birth.

Beckh tells the Sanskrit Lalitavistara story of the birth, as follows:

> The gods offer Queen Māyā their abodes for her to reside in until the birth of the Bodhisattva. By way of his magically effective concentration, the Bodhisattva causes Māyā to be seen in all those divine abodes at the same time. He himself rests in the womb in the position of yoga meditation (*paryaṇka*). So that no earthly impurity may tarnish him, a shell of radiating beryl shine surrounds him (*ratnavyūhabodhisattvaparibhoga*) which is transported into Brahmā's heaven by the gods after his birth and kept as a sacred relic there. In that night, when the Bodhisattva enters his mother's womb, a lotus grows from the earth reaching up to Brahmā's heaven. Only Brahmā himself is able to see this lotus. Whatever is available as powerful essence in the wide compass of the worlds is present as a drop of honey in this lotus. Brahmā himself offers this drop of honey in *a bowl of beryl* to the child in the womb, and the Bodhisattva accepts the refreshment in order to show himself gracious to the god. Nobody would be able to tolerate this drop of power except the Bodhisattva in his last earthly existence.[248]

The 'bowl of beryl' here is made of Skr. *vaiduryā*, beryl, the Sanskrit form of Pali *veluriya*.

Neither here in the 1916 *Buddha* nor at any other time does Beckh point out this extraordinary coincidence, which is more than simple philology, although he must have been fully aware of it. Certainly, the restrictive format of the publisher Sammlung Göschen limited the amount of discussion; the text studiously avoids any mention of Rudolf Steiner and anthroposophy, apart from a footnote reference to *Riddles of Philosophy*. Nevertheless, in 1916 Beckh *realized* that in Buddhist tradition at the deepest level of meditation the physical body appears as a pure crystal formed out of beryl, and that *the same substance*—we could say 'hypostasis'—forms the vessel which contains the sacred nourishment to sustain life.

From time to time between 1922 and 1924 Beckh considered the Grail, especially in the 1923 *Das Geistige Wesen der Tonarten*, *The Essence*

of Tonality (regarding Wagner) and at Christmas within The Christian
Community. While central Europe had to contend with Drews' 'Christ
Myth', Beckh continued to explore the realm of the twenty-four musical keys and the zodiac, as we have seen, but he was also under some
pressure to make it clear that he was a Christian priest and not a Buddhist professor. The result was the publication of *From Buddha to Christ*
in 1925.[249] Here was the principal opportunity to bring together the university scholarship on Buddhism and what he had heard in Wagner's
Parsifal. Beckh reintroduces the eight-sided stone and retells the Lalitavistara story at some length immediately after explaining that a great
deal of Christian esotericism is to be found in the Grail legend and then
stating, 'The Holy Grail is also beheld many times as a bowl of beryl.'
The persistent image recurs in the traditional story of 'the bowl of beryl
or emerald' presented by the Queen of Sheba to Solomon, and the nineteenth-century story from August Schultz wherein the precious jewel
that fell from Lucifer's crown becomes the Grail vessel.[250]

By 1931 Beckh had approached the Grail from many sides, most
purposefully in the two substantial studies of Mark and John. The new
publication, for Rudolf Geering Verlag, now set out to bring light into
the subject of the Mystery of matter itself, but for a broad readership.
In consequence, the account largely moves within familiar territory.
The alchemical 'Stone of the Wise' naturally finds many synonyms
and closely related images: *terra lucida*, the philosopher's stone, Oetinger's thesis on the salt crystal[251] all testify to the substance or hypostasis of Paradise and the Resurrection Body, and all within Beckh's
comprehensive grasp are indicative of the Eucharist and The New
Jerusalem. It can easily appear that the author is spreading out ad-lib
over subjects that are dear to his heart, but this is to mistake the text.

Once again Beckh presents the octahedral *veḷuriya* from the
Sāmaññaphala Sutta with reference to *Buddha's Life and Teaching*, but
now adds the observation:

> These occasional echoes in Buddha of what is still retained from later
> ages of Indian wisdom appear to us all the more remarkable, considering
> the otherwise diminishing awareness of alchemy as well as the astrology
> connected to it. Reading between the lines of Buddhist traditional texts,
> mysteries of the zodiac as well as planetary wisdom may still be discov-
> ered in which genuine primal wisdom is contained ...[252]

'Beyond' or 'farther in from' sleep, Beckh had three experiences of
a pre-natal consciousness during his life. He felt that this was his

homeland from which he been estranged at birth, and that some intimation of this could always be rediscovered in crystal formations. This was confirmed by the exalted vision of the octahedral stone, *veḷuriya*, as the realization of the physical-material body and the coloured thread of a raised consciousness that runs through its midst.

After a brief mention of the legendary jewel that fell from Lucifer's crown to become the substance of the Grail vessel, *Alchymie* presents two short observations on beryl. First, with reference to the colour-circle, the 'yellow-green' crystal conveys 'the mediating colour', which represents 'the spirit of Christ'. The second realization follows an analysis of the sequence of signs in the zodiac wherein beryl is found to correspond with the Lion. Implicit here is the notion that the primordial origin of the physical-material body is to be found in the sacrificial outpouring of Divine warmth.[253] For Hermann Beckh, two associations are implicit. On one hand, his considerable knowledge and attraction to crystals could not avoid basic mineralogy: beryl is found to form some of the Earth's largest crystals (several *metres* along the axes) and is thus able to be shaped into substantial artefacts such as bowls or chalices. Then, as a consecrating priest, Beckh realized that the Christian Sacrament at Communion is precisely the 'mediating' element of divine substance.

Yet for all this, the evidence in texts and Beckh's personal fourfold path only present something of a greyscale route-map or a spider's web cast over the vibrant personality. One can imagine explaining to him the series of thresholds, the Buddhist and Biblical passages, *vaiduryā*, and *veluriya*, while walking along Urachstrasse in 1931 only to be met with a beaming smile and his booming voice. 'Of course! Of course!' he would say. 'Don't you see it all?' And he would point to the reddening glow of sunset, Venus as the Evening Star, and the fresh peach blossoms.

The creation of man and the archetype of the physical body called to resurrection? Lacking a diamond, Beckh would always show the two Bock sisters a piece or two of beryl which he kept in his crystal cabinet.

If ever there was a token of genius it is the natural, and then cultivated gift to *realize* the marriage of immense scholarly learning and personal spiritual insight with the simplest perceptions of everyday life.

GUNDHILD KAČER-BOCK: A TRIBUTE

Author of:

1993 *Emil Bock Leben und Werk* ('Emil Bock: Life and work')

1995 *Die Mysteriendramen im Lebensgang Rudolf Steiner* ('The Mystery Dramas in the Rudolf Steiner's Life')

1996 with Michael Debus, *Das Handeln im Umkreis des Todes* ('Dealing with death')

1997 *Hermann Beckh Leben und Werk* (*Hermann Beckh: Life and Work*, TL 2021)

2007 *Die Christengemeinschaft in Stuttgart* ('The Christian Community in Stuttgart')

2008 *Wie hat Rudolf Steiner gesprochen?* ('How did Rudolf Steiner speak?')—from the literary estate.

Editor of Emil Bock's works:

(1) Collected and edited the material:

1961 *Rudolf Steiner: Studien zum Lebensgang* (*The Life and Times of Rudolf Steiner*, tr. Lynda Heburn, 2 Vols. Edinburgh: Floris Books 2008)

1961 *Briefe* ('Letters')

1997 *Das dreifache Mariengeheimnis* (*Threefold Mary*, tr. Christiane Marks. London: Rudolf Steiner Press 2004)

(2) *Prepared new editions of:*

All seven volumes of the Biblical studies, from *Urgeschichte* to *Apokalypse* (*Genesis* to *The Apocalypse of St John*. Edinburgh: Floris Books)

Reisetagebücher ('Travel Diaries')

Romanische Baukunst und Plastik in Würtemberg ('Romanesque buildings and sculptures in Würtenberg')

Das michaelische Zeitalter ('The Age of Michael')

Der Kreis der Jahresfeste ('*The Rhythm of the Christian Year*', Edinburgh: Floris Books 2000)

Boten des Geistes ('Messengers of the Spirit')

Das Neue Testament ('The New Testament', Stuttgart: Urachhaus 2014)

A Special Personality: The H.B. Biography—a book review

Johannes Lenz

 This appreciation of the life and work of Hermann Beckh appeared at the end of 1997. Gundhild Kačer-Bock, to whom we already have to thank for the basic work *Emil Bock: Leben und Werk* (1993) has written another biography of a co-founder of The Christian Community. As an eyewitness and one who experienced the destiny of this important epoch, she feels called as hardly anybody else to report on the personalities who formed the beginning of the Movement for Religious Renewal.

Hermann Beckh lived from 1875 to 1937. He came from a well-to-do industrialist family in Nuremberg; he took an increasingly individual path. Already as a five-year-old he was granted experiences that led him on to 'the other side' of existence. These made him aware of his origin out of the spiritual world; they expanded his day-consciousness to cosmic perspectives. He suffered at school but qualified in 1893 with one of the best school finals in Bayern. [With a scholarship] he entered the Maximilianeum by the River Isar in his beloved Munich. There he devoted himself to National Economics, then he read Law, and finally in 1899 wrote his dissertation—which won a prize—that was published as his first publication. A sentence that the young Judge had to pass on a poor couple caused him to quit his post right at the beginning of a promising career.

A first basic change in his life led to a new beginning. In Kiel, Bonn and Berlin he qualified after a second round of full study. He learnt Tibetan and Sanskrit; the 33-year-old earned a second doctorate. Later he was awarded a position as tutor for Tibetan philology at the University of Berlin and finally a seat as a Professor without a chair. At the same time through a requested leave, he entered the next big change of his biography.

On 14 December 1911 Hermann Beckh heard a lecture by Rudolf Steiner on the prophet Elijah held at the Architects' House. Already by 1913 the teacher became a pupil and underwent a decisive turning to spiritual schooling. Out of a personal spiritual relationship to Buddhism and to Gautama Buddha he published in 1916 a two-volume work on Buddhism, which even today retains its high academic standing. Through meeting Friedrich Rittelmeyer, he suddenly came upon the group destined to found The Christian Community. As an experienced pastor and founder of communities, Rittelmeyer regarded Beckh as hardly suitable for this profession. The Professor, however, made it clear that for his 'whole development and striving for the founding of a new spiritually created Christian cult would be *the* fulfilment of his life'—'Now I am here and belong with you; and even if you did not want me, you will not be able to send me away!'

Urachstrasse 41

The profoundly spiritual, highly original, lonely judge, researcher of language and scholar went through the final and decisive turning point. He became a priest. With his calibre he belonged with Friedrich Rittelmeyer and Emil Bock after the ordination 1922 not only to take part in the birth of The Christian Community in Stuttgart, but also to engage his unusual abilities in teaching at the new Priests' Seminary. An extensive lecturing activity began. His experience in spiritual subjects he delivered with such fiery enthusiasm that many people during these years experienced through him the reality of the spirit, even if he went right over the heads of his listeners. He helped train many priests of the first generation, bringing to their awareness the world-encompassing spiritual greatness of Christianity.

When Hermann Beckh died on March 1, 1937, he had sacrificed 15 years of his strength to build up the young Church. In himself he formed a unique and energetic element amongst the variety of personalities of the group of founders. His written work, exactly catalogued at the end of the biography [yet with several omissions—*Ed.*], embraces the code of civil law, Tibetan studies, Buddhist studies, the Old and New Testaments including studies on the Gospels of Mark and John, and leads to the language of tonality and the spiritual essence of the musical keys.

Gundhild Kačer-Bock is to be thanked that she has considerably expanded the sparse (existing) sources through her own research, for the first time evaluating the 34 letters to Rudolf Steiner and a series of letters to Marie Steiner, and furthermore included personal reports. Finally she adds personal memories in a tender and loving manner, describing the life and work. The grateful reader wishes more such appreciations of personalities in the group of founders of The Christian Community.

The Great Friend

Gundhild Kačer

(*Die Christengemeinschaft*. March 1967. 145-49)

On 4 May 1967 the birthday of Professor Beckh, the anniversary of whose death was commemorated in the March issue, comes round for the 92nd time. For many people Hermann Beckh today is known as the significant expert in early Eastern wisdom, as the many-sided researcher and scholar and as the author of numerous basic works: *The Source of Speech; Buddha's Life and Work; Mark's Gospel: The Cosmic Rhythm; The Departure of the Perfected One*; and *The Language of Tonality*, to name only a few. Some individuals will also recall the memoirs of his childhood and youth which were printed in this journal after his death. But how did a child experience this human being?

The question can be raised, whether it is justified, to publish quite personal memories from one's own childhood. The attempt may nevertheless be hazarded, because in Beckh's friendship with a child—to be recounted below; it was the writer of these lines—something objective of his person speaks beyond the initially subjective, personal experience: his great love of children, which was an expression of his love and devotion to the forces of childhood in people and the world. And whoever has experienced his intimate connection to the beauty and wonders in nature can perceive at the same time the heavenly forces and childlike forces that were alive in him.

The child has just learned to walk, can hardly speak. It clearly espies the door of the flat in the old Urachhaus is open; in a trice it has disappeared and clambers on all fours a storey higher, where Professor Beckh in his study sits working at his writing desk. It is true he is always in a hurry to work and has no time, but the child's visit is never denied. On the contrary. And now this visit is played out like a ceremony, repeated for years in the same manner so that the details through its oft-experienced rhythmical repetition impressed itself on the child for all time.

From the beginning he accepted the childish form of his academic title as his own kind of special name. He was never called other than ''Fesser Beckh'; the concept 'uncle' in this case would have been completely unimaginable. On the arm of the great friend first the pictures on the wall were greeted one by one. Next to the door Dürer's hare, then a woodcut of Snow White in the glass coffin, next to which a sad dwarf sits. Further on a picture of the Himalayas and a large photograph of the mountain near Einödsbach near Oberstdorf, associated with a significant experience as a child. In the little adjoining room, a colour photo of the snow-covered Matterhorn and a coloured picture of the Egyptian Sphinx. Over the piano was the *'Isle of the Dead'* by Arnold Böcklin [Swiss painter, 1827-1901], but this picture was expressly not included in the greeting because it is only 'for the grown-ups'. On the writing-desk next to a photo of Beckh's deceased sister there is a picture of Rudolf Steiner, and with an often-repeated, 'and that is the dear, good Dr Steiner', the round of pictures is completed.

But on the writing-desk are to be found, next to the books and papers, many precious things. Here is a large mountain crystal with its black twin, a splendid morion [i.e. a smokey quartz]; a giant mother-of-pearl mussel, in which one can hear the sea murmuring; and a prism, in which one sees the rainbow and when you look through it creates magically around the objects wonderful coloured rims.

On special occasions—almost every time—a glance may be cast into the many drawers of a cupboard nearby in the room on the left, that contained many mysterious treasures: stones in all colours and forms, crystals, seashells, corals, fossil ammonites and, as a very special attractive riddle—a piece of amber enclosing a little midge caught since primeval times. How long has it lain there? When 'Fesser Beckh in a letter to the eight-year-old included a whole list of minerals that he had seen in a museum, he spoke to the child of a world long known to her. The names have a well-known sound.

The 'precious-stone game', as one could call it, was not omitted on any occasion during the early years. The great friend sat himself on the sofa that stood behind the writing table, the child astride on his lap so that it directly saw the tiepin with the shining red ruby. He took the pin in both hands, which with each question he raised in the air and lowered again. Is this a tourmaline? No.—Is this an amethyst? No.—Is this a sapphire? No.—Is it a beryl? No.—With each question the voice became more dramatic, the child's arms more energetically raised and brought down. Is this a topaz? No.— Is this a chrysoprase? He shook his head.—The tension grew with the drama. Now the voice became like threatening, growling thunder! But suddenly it became soft and tender and enticing: Is this perhaps a ruby? And a game ended with chuckling laugher from both players.

The end of the visit was formed by the musical part. 'Fesser Beckh played on the piano and the child sat by the player next to the deep notes on the chair of the writing-desk—from *Anna Magdalena Bach's Notebook*, and especially from Schumann's *Album for the Young*: 'The Wild Rider', 'The Merry Peasant', '*Träumerei*' ('Dreaming') and 'Knecht Ruprecht' ('Black Peter'). Quite soon the child learns to recognize the individual pieces in advance according to the notation, and the many black notes of 'Knecht Ruprecht' frightened the child a little each time. Sometimes more demanding pieces, like Beethoven's 'Moonlight' Sonata appeared in the programme, but always the iron rule was: if a mistake occurred during the playing, then everything was bungled: '*alles verpatzt*'—he said '*verbatzt*'—and one had to start once more from the beginning, even when the mistake occurred in the last bars. This rule also applied when Professor Beckh in later year on special request recited his composition of 'The Rose of Damascus' or 'Psalm 23' indicating the singing voice with an ensouled humming.

But the friendship not only took place in his study under the roof. Often the whole house resounded right down to the ground floor where the seminarists took their lessons, when the child with the help of the friend with great noise was allowed to jump down the steps—first two, then three, four, five steps—until this game, too, ended in raucous laughter. Or the friend visited with a posy of violets when the child was ill, told fairytales—especially Snow White—or read Morgenstern's '*Kätzchen ihr der Weide*', whereby already through the tender sound of the voice one could feel the soft, velvety sheen of the catkins. Especially festive moments, which were announced mostly for weeks before and expected with festive excitement, were the annual visits to the first blossoms on the peach-trees of Urachstrasse and the walk to the hill of the Kanonenweg in order to see the Evening Star or Jupiter. These impressions are unforgettable, where the sight of the blossoming tree or the shining of the star in the light evening sky relate to the indescribable joy and capacity for enthusiasm of the old friend at whose hand the child was permitted to experience it.

*

Letters to a Child

from Hermann Beckh

A postcard with two white cats to the 5-year-old:
Dear little Gundhild!
The two little cats in the picture are a little stupid. They think they are little Gundhild and Rosemaria and so they love each other and always want to play with each other. When I come back, we will play again that little piece in A-major, the old one and the new one. And Rosemaria is also allowed to be there. Warm greetings,
Your Fesser Beckh

Letter to the 5-year-old from the Tegernsee:[254]

Dear little Gundhild!
Here I send you, before we see each other again, some arnica; because you are the big sister and already knew yourself that these are arnica and heal when you cut yourself or burn yourself or get stung or receive knocks or fall down, or when the other children annoy you. Some other yellow flowers which nearly look like arnica, are not real arnica and are not able to heal, but the ones I send you are the real, *quite genuine* ones. I found them at the foot of the mountains, there are only very few, but between Holzkirchen and Oberwangau where I recently passed by there are *lots and lots*. There the meadows are completely full. All this lies in Upper Bavaria where the people cannot say *Eichhörnchen* ('squirrel'), but where they always say *Oachkatzl*. Now quite soon I return to Stuttgart. I am already back early on Tuesday with you and little Rosemaria. Then I bring you what the bears have given me for you, and Rosemaria will get something small that is pink. Always be nice to her and show her the little butterfly. I wonder whether your little brother still recognizes me. Please greet him from me.

From your Fesser Beckh

Letter from Oberstdorf to the 6-year-old

Dear little Gundhild!
Unfortunately, I could not write for your birthday as I was travelling and had lots to do. But I did know it was your birthday and thought

Gundhild with 7-month-old Rosemaria

about you. It rained on your birthday and all the flowers were wet and hid themselves. I could find no gentian. But today the sun shines again and they all came out again and where I went today there were gentians, lot of them, big and small ones. From Switzerland I sent little gentians to your little sister, but because you are the big sister, I send you the big gentian. Look after them and show them to your little sister and brother; greet them well from me, also your father and your mother. On Saturday I return again to Stuttgart but will be there only for three days, and then comes the big journey to north Germany. There everything is *Nord Deutsch*—North German.

Warm greetings, from Fesser Beckh

Letter from Dresden to the 7-year-old:

Dear little Gundhild!

Here I live in a big castle, you know, where your father lived with your mother in the spring. I tell you, it is *magnificent*. My rooms are *gigantic*, and the candelabra up on the ceiling with many, *very many* electric candles is *gigantic*, and the city Dresden is *gigantic*, much bigger than Stuttgart, and soon you will also be *gigantic* when you've been a few years in the Waldorf School and Frl. Heydebrand will no longer

be able to look up to you. And *so* clever … Many people come to Frau Exc[ellency] von Schlützer, and then I speak to the *many* people. And before that I was in Chemnitz. There were also many people. And then I come to Leipzig and then Thüringen, where also Eisenach lies, you know, where the story happened with the devil and the inkwell. But this time I will not get to the Wartburg. And just think, I am with Uncle Koschützki in Berlin. Yesterday I was with Exc[ellency] von Schlützer in the great gallery of paintings, you know, where there is the great picture of Mother Mary and the child Jesus, where the Pope is on it and Saint Barbara and many little angels and the two angels below, who look like *this*, and the clouds and much light …
Warm greetings, from your faithful Fesser Beckh

Letter from Dresden to the 8-year-old
… I often think when you were little Dédele and poured the water from the little flowers into your bed, instead of flowers you always said 'Dédale'. You have nearly forgotten this, but the flowers, especially the roses, remember everything. Dr Steiner told us this once. And, you know, when you sometimes feel lonely or unwell, just think about the little rose and the gentian and the good Doctor Steiner and on the little Venus-star and of the little child Jesus, Mother Mary and the ox and the ass.
Greetings to you, your dear mother and your dear siblings,
With warmth, yours Fesser Beckh

Letter from Dresden to the 8-year-old:
Dear Gundhild!
Now, it has taken so long to get around to writing to you since it's so busy here. First, I was in Berlin, where your father goes so often and gives so many lectures there, every evening. Berlin is *enormous*, much larger than Dresden, and Stuttgart is absolutely small in comparison. And the houses too are gigantic, and the streets really wide. There are not only trolley-busses, but real trams, and an underground train that runs under the earth in a long tunnel, and the trams are all electric, but not so boring as in Stuttgart. And there is also a train, where you travel for a long time under the earth, and when you come up you are already in the middle of the woods. And in the woods are beautiful lakes, and all the people are happy to get there. From Berlin you go on to Dresden … And once I travelled to Freiberg. It lies in the *Erzgebirge*. There is a gigantic museum of minerals. They have large crystals,

lots, mountain crystals and amethysts and turmalines. A really big tourmaline is especially beautiful. And a big *Iceland Spar*, in which you see the rainbow. And many other stones. One is called fluorite, another malachite, and yet another is called alexandrite, and another *zinnwaldite*, and one is called *coper uranite [chalcolite]*, and another *pyrolusite*, and another zinc blende, and one is called *Labradorstein*, and in general they have so many names that you can't remember them all, and they shine and glitter in all colours, and have the most varied crystal forms.

Tomorrow, I journey to Eisenach, to Wartburg, where the story with Luther with the devil and the ink-pot took place.
Warm greetings from your Fesser Beckh

Letter from Walsertal to the 9-year-old:
Dear little Gundhilde!
Yesterday I was once more in the high mountains, when it became so steep as I had never gone up in my whole life, just as in the picture that you once painted for me, when you were still a little *Dédele*, you know, that picture where Fesser Beckh is picking gentians in the high mountains. And as I was up there yesterday, I came to a high mountain meadow, and there all around me were indeed a lot of gentians, lots and lots, deeply blue. In spring this year, I could not find them, but now in summer I found them right up high. Down below they grow in spring, so that are called spring gentians, they are also called 'flowers of heaven', that's why I want to send you some from here. And just think, there were also some prunellas with little black-brown negro-heads that smell like vanilla. And many forget-me-nots, but they are mountain forget-me-nots.

See you soon in Stuttgart,
Warm greetings to you, your dear mother and Rosemaria and Fried-wart.

Warmly yours, Fesser Beckh

A letter from Upper Bavaria to the 10-year-old:

Dear little Gundhilde!
Here I send you before I come home some blue gentians from the Bavarian highland, which I found today in Maithenbeth, near Haag.

It was a wonderfully beautiful day today … There were so *many* gentians, you can't imagine, and in the background the high mountains, the snow-covered Alpine chain.

When this letter arrives, I might already be back in Stuttgart. Soon I have to move on to Dresden, and your father will be back from Palestine.

The first of May today with so much light and sunshine was beautiful, like the light of Paradise which you once painted. I had to think a lot of your picture of Paradise.

Warm greeting,

Yours, Fesser Beckh

Memories and Appreciations of Gundhild Kačer-Bock

Friedwart Bock[255]

Gundhild Johanna Bock was born 21 May 1924 in Stuttgart; she died on 9 January 2008.

The day of her birth and the day of her death was a Wednesday.

A good week after her birth Emil Bock, her father, asked Rudolf Steiner for a name for his child. The next day he received the answer, 'The child should be called Gundwart Johannes'. A moment's thought—after Rudolf Steiner was told the child was a girl—he said, 'Then, let's say, Gundhild Johanna.' He added the memorable explanation, which he probably only gave with this child. The first name would connect with the nationality, the ancestral stream. The second name expresses the future orientation, the Christian element. Gundhild felt her names really did belong to her. *Hild* means 'struggle'; *Hild* also means 'struggle'.

It is a Mystery, a riddle from God concerning every child. We frequently try to read from the days of childhood what life is likely to bring for this child—and what this child would bring to the world. So, it appears to me a key is given to approach the being Gundhild Johanna by looking into her childhood.

She was the eldest of four siblings; her parents were young, 28 and 29 years old. Her first memory was of picking berries at about two years old. Michael Bauer bent the branches for her. He said how important it was that children pick the berries themselves.

A main characteristic as a child was observing other children involved in activities and at play. She writes in her memoirs that the pictures she received as a child grew further, had retained their validity. Her school reports present the child as an observer standing at the side of the teacher.

Her biography clearly shows the seven-year periods.

Shortly after her 14th birthday the Waldorf School was closed. The address of Count Bothmer places impulses for her further biography. A year later her mother dies at the birth of her youngest sister. This 14th/15th year of her life shows in many ways the end of her childhood.

In the middle of the next seven-year period her father is taken to a concentration camp and Gundhild tries to keep contact and does all she can for his release by travelling to Berlin.

At 21 years old she takes part in The Act of Consecration of Man, which was once again permitted, a day before her 21st birthday. From now on she plays for the service, looks after the vestments, and begins anthroposophical work under the guidance of Gottfried Husemann.

Again in May, at the end of her 4th seven-year period, she concludes her study of Archaeology, History of Art and Russian History with the exams and is awarded a Doctorate with 'The House of Württemberg in Russia'.

In 1959 she held her first lecture in Rudolf Steiner House in Stuttgart. Her motto was and remained all her life: one must offer one's services.

In a conversation with her father she said, 'You do know that I did this to please you?' Her father answered, 'I hope you do this for its own sake.' An austere-loving relationship is expressed here. A letter from her youth is preserved in which the 18-year-old writes, 'My only great love is my father.'

Gundhild Johanna Kačer-Bock took part from 1952—she is 27 years old—in the work of the Stuttgart Initiative group. The first meeting takes place on the second day after her marriage.

Her theme is carried to her by life: she spoke at numerous memorial meetings—at over 100 funerals. Her relation to those who had died and to the world after death was exceptionally strengthened during her life. Thus, she practised what increasingly became her own concise manner of speaking.

This quality with the spoken word she used in an admirable fashion also in her written style and with the editing of her father's life's work. Her final project, 'The Christian Community in Stuttgart: Chronicles 1922-2005' (2007) reflects for us this deep conscientious and incorruptible manner of speaking and writing.

Was there a really private area in the life of Gundhild Johanna Bock? In the school holidays of her [teacher] husband she went on journeys.

On account of the Nordic part of her name, the couple journeyed independently like the Norse people—not with a tent, yet with an invincible campervan on the trail of the Nordic Mystery-stream to Carnac in Brittany, to Scotland and Ireland, and repeatedly to Greece and Crete.

Gundhild Johanna Kačer-Bock was born on Earth and into Heaven on the day of Mercury. The struggle is hidden in these names. She did not live with nimble feet. She emphasized the yellow brightness of Mercury through the blue surrounding him. Blue appears to me to be the colour of her being. Blue, which gives a boundary to yellow. Her father had spoken about this when for her 10th birthday he wrote in her album the following verse:

> Behold the heaven's pure Blue —
> it is God's dress.
> Behold the Stars unending Twinkling —
> they are God's love.
> Behold the Sun's warming Light —
> it is the Will of God.
> The Sun's warming Light,
> it shines in your heart,
> The Stars unending Twinkling,
> it shines in your soul.
> May the pure Blue of heaven,
> shine through your whole life.

Memories and Appreciations of Gundhild Kačer-Bock

Johannes Lenz

Gundhild Johanna Kačer (21 May 1924—† 9 January 2008)[256]

On 9 January 2008 during the season of Epiphany Gundhild Johanna Kačer died. Whoever was active in the anthroposophical work in Stuttgart in the Society Meetings and in the office, whoever was active in the Anthroposophical Society in Germany has met her and knew her. Besides her spoken and significant written work, she created a body of work which called the souls of those who had died to a conscious focus. Following the funeral rites she held more than 100 addresses by the coffin. During memorial meetings she brought the picture of these souls as recollections. Thus, an essential part of her work was directed towards the threshold of the spiritual world. She represented substantially in ever new impressive ways the ancient saying *'memento mori'*—'remember the dead'—which in the renewal of the ritual reminds the human being in the face of death that s/he is accountable to the spirit.

She was born in Stuttgart, in the Urachhaus. This was the first house of the growing Christian Community, which was founded in 1922. Here lived under one roof Friedrich Rittelmeyer and Emil Bock, the leading priests of the new Church.

Emil Bock was the spokesman of the priests' group. He liaised with Rudolf Steiner, and prepared the discussions, collecting all the questions which received suggestive answers. Her mother Marguerete, née Seumer, was not only supposed to run the household under extreme restrictions, but also had to bring up her children: in 1927 Rosemaria was born, in 1928 Friedwart and in 1939 Marguerete. She died six days after the birth of the fourth child. All the children up to the present day are active in several realms of anthroposophical work [Friedwart † 23 May 2010, Pentecost; † Marguerete 1 April 2014].

Thus, Gundhild Johanna grew up in a family such as Rudolf Steiner describes in his book *Knowledge of the Higher Worlds: How is it Attained?* that real 'family-souls' are active in the individual members of a single spirit. Through her work one can see how she remained faithful to this all her life. Her baptism name was given by Rudolf Steiner. He described that the first name should express the folk-element of the language and cultural realm; the other name the future Christian element, 'the Christian name'. Friedrich Rittelmeyer carried out the Christening. The godparents were Gertrude Spörri and Eberhard Kurras. Professor Hermann Beckh, living in the house, took the child to his heart. Later she wrote his biography *Hermann Beckh: Leben und Werk* as the fruit of this intimate relationship. In 1931 she began in Class 1 of the Waldorf School with the venerated teacher Caroline von Heyderbrand. After seven years of beloved school time in 1938 the Stuttgart Waldorf School had to close—on her 14th birthday. She felt this blow deeply. Until her *Abitur* (school finals) in 1944 she had to attend a state school.

After the end of the War, she helped to build up The Christian Community that had been forbidden in 1941 and laid the basis for an intensive anthroposophical youth work. From 1946-52 she read History, History of Art and Archaeology at the University of Marburg. She obtained her doctorate with a dissertation on 'The House of Württemberg in Russia'. The closing of The Christian Community in June 1941 brought imprisonment for her father. He was held until February 1942 in a concentration camp. Before this she repeatedly had to speak with the Secret Police in order to take necessary provision to him. The tension of this time pursued her through her whole life. In October 1952 she married Jan Kačer who became a teacher at the Krähewald Waldorf School, Stuttgart. They were united her whole life. Both travelled, as all young people do, to Carnac in Brittany (23 times!), to Ireland, Scotland and Greece. She broadened her scientific studies through these travels. Beyond this she grew into the extended anthroposophical work. Her clear and trained conceptual capacities and the ability to write led her to edit her father's life's work. This flowed into the [official] authentic biography *Emil Bock Leben und Werk* (1993). In 1995 she published *Die Mysteriendramen im Lebensgang Rudolf Steiners*; in 1996 out of her work for those who have died *Das Handeln im Umkreis des Todes* jointly with Michael Debus; in 1997 there appeared *Hermann Beckh Leben und Werk* and, thanks to her karmic calling, finally in 2007 *Die Chronik der Stuttgarter Gemeinde*, which was the mother community of The Christian Community from the early days onwards.

Gundhild Johanna Kačer was cremated in Prague on 14 January 2008, The Act of Consecration of Man for the eternal soul was celebrated on 19 January—all within the regal season of Epiphany this year. The thoughts about her were filled with deep respect for the achievements of her life. Her upright character, the never swerving stand for anthroposophy, her ethical nature and her adequate and authentic spoken and written words, all this created an obvious authority, which accompanied her with extreme humility. One can adequately meet her thoughts and deeds when the living presence of this soul is felt out of feelings of gratitude.

Up the Stairs
Hermann Beckh and the Divine Feminine 1921-1929

Neil Franklin, Ph.D.

One may easily imagine little Gundhild Bock aged four or five (1929/30) running up the stairs of the Seminary house in 41 Urachstrasse to visit the Professor in his attic study and to gaze again at his crystals, seashells, pictures of the Alps and the Himalayas, and his favourite woodcut of Snow White in her crystal coffin, set in a romantic landscape of forest and rocky fells. He played the piano for her, and he told her stories; this memory is included above.[257]

On Saturday 16 February 1929, then, Gundhild may have kept her promise to 'Fesser Beckh, as she called him, and made her way up the stairs towards the end of the afternoon to listen to a favourite story, one indeed that Beckh most loved. It was a bitterly cold day in Stuttgart, scarcely getting above freezing point, and snow lay thick over the town and its busy streets. February 1929 was a very cold month for all of Europe, the coldest in fact since 1895, which Hermann Beckh must have recalled from his student days in Munich. He shovelled more coal into the iron stove. Were the windows coated in frost? The Atlantic low pressure had finally collided with the high centred over northwest Russia (Stuttgart had earlier shown 1030mb) with consequent record amounts of snowfall—that very day 182 cm, recorded as six feet of snowfall.[258]

Hermann Beckh must have been kept fairly busy during the day. The coming week was the start of Lent: there were vestments to get ready and the altar cloth needed changing in the ground-floor chapel. Perhaps he had prepared an address for the congregation; he had been invited to present at least one lecture to another centre of The Christian Community,[259] teaching in the Seminary needed to be prepared, and the continuing work on *John's Gospel: The Cosmic Rhythm—Stars and Stones*, then an article on Indian yoga for *Gäa Sophia* was needed.[260] Above all, however, his only sister Marie, living just around the corner with their mother, was in the final stages of a terminal illness.

I can see Professor Beckh, now aged 53, composing himself, looking out through his western window. The sun was very low in the sky and the rooftops over Spittlerstrasse gleamed with the white snow tinged by the red of the declining day. When Gundhild came in they talked about her family and her new sister Rosemaria, how she herself was nearly ready for school; biscuits were produced, and Gundhild settled into the sofa.

> *There was once a poor widow who lived in a lonely cottage. In front of the cottage was a garden wherein stood two rose-trees, one of which bore white and the other red roses. She had two children who were like the two rose-trees, and one was called Snow White, and the other Rose Red ...*

I would want to ask *how* Hermann Beckh told the story. Certainly, with his tremendous abilities of recall, with which he was born, it is most likely that he rarely had to *read* a story. And most importantly, with the Hermann Beckh who was profoundly grounded in the origins of speech we can be pretty sure that every word carried its due weight and each sentence its own rhythm. In other words, when he told the story of Snow White and Rose Red to her, little Gundhild would have heard the truth of the matter, something that the grown-up 'Fesser Beckh cherished with all the strength of his warm heart and willing devotion. Is it just possible, with some slight study aided by a freedom of imagination, to approach the loving *holiness* of what Gundhild heard?

The Law

Some thirty years previously the young Hermann Beckh had acted as a judge in criminal cases and had originally gained his first doctorate (Dr Jur.) with his analysis of the 'burden of proof' required by a new Code of Bavarian Civil Law. While performing his duties as a judge there must have been the inner experience of implementing the law as it had been established. In other words, when the judge spoke it was not, in the first instance, a matter of personal opinion or a flourish of personality, though these were not absolutely excluded. The experience could only be 'the Law speaks through me'. Put in other words, Hermann Beckh as a judge must have had a sense that he as an individual was obliged to speak forth what was at the time accepted Law and the foundation of good civil order.

Yet Beckh quickly came to realize that such Law, particularly as written in the Bavarian Code, was to some extent an artificial authority; he found it primarily existed to defend the rights of the wealthy and their ownership of property—then it punished. After he had resigned his judicial position, Beckh wanted to argue the case that this Bavarian

Code was an extension of old Roman laws: it was not adapted to either true Christian values or German life and traditions. As William Blake had also understood with the figure of Urizen, the authority of such laws readily became a new tyrant whose principal function was oppression.

The very idea of a Code of Laws goes back to Roman times. The Code is a codex, a book as we know it today, and the law (*lex, legis*) is what is written down and can be read (*lego*). *Ius* is what has been commanded, *iubere, iussi*. Whether it is the Code of Napoleon or the Bavarian Code of Civil Law we have the expression of the arbitrary power of the state.

As a first contrast to a Code of Law, understood as 'positive laws' belonging to one state, the rationalizing *philosophes* of the middle and late eighteenth century developed the theory of 'natural law'. *Above and prior to* positive laws we find universal human rights. This was a revolutionary idea in the 1750s and 60s and was ably expounded by the sharp pens of Diderot, de Jaucourt and Desmahis, especially in the grand *Encyclopédie* of 1751-1772. Their immediate target was oppression, particularly that of slaves and of women, and one of its chief exponents, apart from the ancient regime in general, was the system of clerical law. De Jaucourt's article '*Égalité naturelle*' in Vol. 5 of the *Encyclopédie* (1755) rings out:

> *Natural* or *moral equality* is therefore based on the constitution of human nature common to all people, who are born, grow, live and die in the same way.
>
> Since human nature is the same in all people, it is clear according to natural law that each person must value and treat other people as so many individuals who are naturally equal to himself, that is to say, as people like himself.
>
> Several consequences ensue from this principle of the *natural equality of people* ...
>
> 1. It follows from this principle that all people are naturally free, and that the faculty of reason could only make them dependent for their own welfare.
>
> [original italics, my translation]

Clearly the American Declaration of Independence and the Declaration of Human Rights were not far off, nor was the French Revolution, the end of slavery and ecclesiastical courts, though the liberation of women still had a long way to travel. What matters here, however, is that our judge Hermann Beckh, profoundly steeped in the history of law, would have found the basic theory *in Europe* entrenched in a rational argument appealing to *natural law* that is both absolutely universal and *above positive law*.

Of course, the same period of the European Enlightenment also witnessed the rapid growth of the understanding and formulation of scientific laws along with the development of experimentation and mathematics, often driven by commercial concerns. Whether it was Newton on gravity, Priestley on nitrous oxide, or Benjamin Franklin on electricity, the discoveries had enormous popular appeal as well as the often-unpredictable impact on national economies. At the same time, however, there was growing certainty that *the natural world was regular*, it displayed incontrovertible and universal laws. For Hermann Beckh, such scientific laws must have included the notion of hypotheses open to challenge, but also the insight that the seashells and crystals that he lovingly showed to Gundhild clearly displayed a geometrical *order* which has an exalted origin. Like *lex* and *ius*, *ordo* has its roots in the Roman desire for ordering life in neat patterns, especially legions and the rules of inheritance. Understandably, then, the monastic life later wished to develop its own *ordo* and we find members of the Benedictine *Order* pledging obedience to imposed rules, but such *regularity* is clearly different from the regularity of the crystal forms familiar to Beckh, equally Mendeleev's Periodic Table, or Einstein's equations for General Relativity. Here we need to distinguish, if possible, the idea of law as imposition from what may first be called *natural lawfulness*, something that is truly innate *within* both the world and mankind. The term here is only a temporary scaffolding.

In the early 1920s, shortly before little Gundhild was born and perhaps while Professor Beckh was still adjusting his rooms in Urachstrasse 41 and working out a *modus vivendi* with Friedrich Rittelmeyer, Emil Bock, Gertrude Spörri, also with his mother and sister just around the corner,[261] he had the notion of setting out a range of key points concerning *rights* in a short article. The result was published as '*Zur Wandlung des Rechtsbegriffs in Menschheitsbewusstsein*' ('The Changing concept of Rights in Human Consciousness') in *Anthroposophie*, 04. Jg. 1922/23, on 17 May 1923. After a brief discussion of Roman law or *ius* (that which has been commanded), Hermann Beckh did not feel that it was necessary to turn to classical Greek *nomos* or to law (Torah) in the Hebrew world, though we will need to mention the latter in due time. Instead, he was able to draw our attention to the Indian concept of *dharma*:

> ... *dharma* is the higher natural lawfulness, through which all cosmic development is carried and ordered. Today's lexicography only finds it tiresome to find the connecting bridges between the different meanings of the word *dharma*: right, law, religion, duty, moral, sacrifice, nature, quality, etc. We only find them and with them the characteristic nuances of the Indian concept of *dharma* when we recognize how within it the concept of the natural and of the moral flow together in a manner which for the Western consciousness is initially somewhat strange.

After some eighteen years, 1902-1920, of studying Sanskrit, Tibetan and Pali to the very highest level in Europe, and being offered the newly created Chair for Tibetan in the University of Berlin with the status of Professor Emeritus; after eleven years of working with anthroposophy and corresponding with Rudolf Steiner, 1911-1923, Hermann Beckh faced the question that, in contrast to Roman law and the Bavarian Code, there would be a 'higher natural lawfulness' working both in human nature and in the universe. If *dharma* is not the bedrock of the question, it would be necessary to consider the early Vedic literature:

> This concept of *dharma* lies closer to the earlier Vedic concept *ṛta*, *r(i)ta*, which word not only signifies the cultic ordering of the sacrificial ritual, but also the cosmic ordering, the course of the year, the course of nature, and the lawfulness of the starry cosmos. The original basic meaning of *r(i)ta*, from the root √*r*, 'to move oneself', is 'rhythmical movement', which can indeed be recognized in the word from its root and its sounds, also its relationship to the Gk. *rhythmos*. *R(i)ta* originally delineated the rhythm of nature, the cosmic rhythm. The early Indian felt in his cosmic-cultic thinking how, as it were, through the cult, the sacrificial ritual stems from the cosmic rhythm, into which, fallen out of this rhythm, the earthly events are returned.

In other words, the *regularity* of the world-whole was also earlier experienced as *rhythmical*, and one cannot avoid the observation that this is a far cry from the ordering of Roman legions. In 1929-1930, while telling Gundhild the story, Professor Beckh must have experienced that he had moved on from being the representative of Bavarian positive law to being a priest of The Christian Community. Here there is the assurance that ritual, daily, weekly, seasonal, is the direct expression of 'cosmic ordering', the greater Law that is *ṛtá*.

Indeed, the concept and the experience of ṛta are so far-reaching for the European mind that it required S.T. Coleridge to find an appropriate poetic expression, and one that is rooted in music. It was in Clevedon in Somerset, 20 August, 1795, that he heard the notes produced from 'The Aeolian Harp' in his open window:

The Aeolian Harp

…And now, its strings
Boldlier swept, the long sequacious notes
Over delicious surges sink and rise,
Such a soft floating witchery of sound
As twilight Elfins make, when they at eve
Voyage on gentle gales from Fairy-Land,
Where Melodies round honey-dropping flowers,
Footless and wild, like birds of Paradise,
Nor pause, nor perch, hovering on untamed wing!
O! the one Life within us and abroad,
Which meets all motion and becomes its soul,
A light in sound, a sound-like power in light,
Rhythm in all thought, and joyance everywhere—
Methinks, it should have been impossible
Not to love all things in a world so filled;
Where the breeze warbles, and the mute still air
Is Music slumbering on her instrument….

And what if all of animated nature
Be but organic Harps diversely framed,
That tremble into thought, as o'er them sweeps
Plastic and vast, one intellectual breeze,
At once the Soul of each, and God of all?

Here, then, is a European experience of ṛta: the wisdom and spirit of the universe is also *the one life within us and abroad, a light in sound, a sound-like power in light, rhythm in all thought.* I imagine that some of this must have radiated out from 'Fesser Beckh to Gundhild as she sat in his study in 1929, and it also has a reasonable inference. We can now remove the temporary scaffold 'natural lawfulness' and introduce 'the signs and spiritual realities of the Imaginative world' (R. Steiner, *Occult Signs and Seals.* GA 156). For Hermann Beckh—as also Wordsworth, Coleridge, Goethe, Novalis and Rudolf Steiner—Imaginative understanding is *as totally lawful* as analytical reason. What was daringly grasped by our French *philosophes* as natural law has now been extended beyond universal reason to a new consciousness of *ṛta*. If so, we may find that the pictures of Snow White and Rose Red are embedded in the most profound *lawful* realities of the Imagination. Furthermore, in the history of law and rights, if the elucidation of *natural law* grounded on *reason* in the second half of the eighteenth century brought in a new era, resulting in both the American and French revolutions, then there is every reason to expect that the continuing unfolding of the signs and spiritual realities of the Imaginative world, *the Laws of the Imagination*, should prove to be equally fruitful. Beckh's destiny to become involved, as a young man, with judicial matters was not some kind of accident or wrong turning.

On the mountains and beside the lake

'And when they looked round they found that they had been sleeping quite close to a precipice, and would certainly have fallen into it if they had gone only a few paces further ...'

It would be a mistake to conceive of Hermann Beckh largely as a housebound scholar thumbing his way through hundreds of dictionaries, learned articles and sacred texts. While not attempting to diminish the scholarly achievements, especially in the University of Berlin, the countless hours of preparing Tibetan and Sanskrit manuscripts for printing and publication,[262] it is right to come to a true appreciation of the fact that the Professor preferred to spend his time walking alone in the high mountains in all weathers. Like Wordsworth, Beckh was a hardy man given to great exertions in remote places, striding up mountains and sleeping in the open when necessary.

We know now from his biography that he spent very considerable periods wandering, for example, around Garmisch, Sonthofen and Oberstdorf, scaling the Widderstein and the Zugspitze a long time before the current amenities were installed. These were dangerous places and the story of Hermann Beckh caught in a snowstorm high up a mountain is there for all to read—trying to wrap up, burying his feet in his rucksack and lasting out the night. It was in the high lands, too, that as a child he had his first experience of a spiritual nature, one that fostered him all his life.[263]

It is therefore easy to understand his response in 1925 when asked by members of The Christian Community to contribute an article on The New Jerusalem.[264] This was a most exalted theme which Beckh did not want to approach head-on but then neither did an outright refusal seem appropriate. The consequence was the publication of 'The New Jerusalem', a poetic work in iambic metre rather in an ambulatory style, an interweaving of observation and meditation while standing on high land. This is the sole poetic composition which he published during his life, and worth careful consideration.

Here the living heart of Beckh's imagination is characteristically brought to bear on the contrast between the personal experience of standing among high mountains and the sight of the fog-wrapped city in the far distance. With The New Jerusalem of the book of Revelation in mind, the poem turns to consider the pure nature of snow and ice crystals, the crystalline harbingers of what will become the resurrection body in the future. It is precisely here that Hermann Beckh observes:

> Today everything earthly is covered
> with a radiant dress of heavenly light,
> from myriads of snow-crystals
> a shining countenance of the Sun
> glitters towards me reflecting the heavens,
> in that which, falling out of the heights of heaven,
> has then become the tender earthly covering.

With both a number of lectures by Rudolf Steiner and Günther Wachsmuth's *The Etheric Formative Forces* (1924) in mind, Beckh is at pains to impress upon the reader that the *snow-crystals* shining in the clear light of the mountains are a concrete expression of the light of Paradise. Naturally this is linked to the language of Revelation, quoted in the poem:

> And I, John, saw the holy city
> like a virgin who, in a white dress
> adorned like a bride, prepares herself for the wedding.

Beckh does not hesitate to bring in a number of imaginative analogues for the shining ice encountered in the mountains: we find the Grail descending from heaven to earth and Novalis' Arcturus, 'the town of the ice-flowers and crystal-plants',[265] and knowing the author, it is perfectly understandable that the figure of Snow White in her crystal coffin should also appear in her full splendour:

> And in this world of snow and ice crystals
> a familiar fairytale picture was created for me,

the picture of a child which as white as snow
as red as blood, as black as ebony wood,
on a high mountain in a crystal coffin
lay in a sleep of death,
wept over by friendly animals showing pity,
owl and raven, nocturnal birds,
fluttered around; the dove of light hovered above.

And it is just at this moment that the poem introduces, in the briefest and most delicate manner, the resonant image that we find in the original story. The Grimms' tale says, '*Then they were going to bury her, but she still looked as if she were living, and still had pretty red cheeks.*' With the greatest sense for Imaginative truth (or lawfulness) Hermann Beckh created the verses:

Thus in death it appeared sleeping —
the radiant colour of life,
life's blossoming colour remains,
the fresh red of its cheeks, because the decay
could not reach its bright being.
[Emphases added]

This is no slavish following of the original source. Such stories do not contain arbitrary embellishments or some kind of accidental detail. Beckh understands that the purest *white* of snow, ice crystals, or frost *can be touched by rose.*

If the winter of 1928/29 was especially cold and laden with snowfalls, then it is worth bearing in mind that the eighteenth century offered still greater extremes of temperature. At 11 a.m. on 16 September 1798, Wordsworth and Coleridge departed from Yarmouth en route to Cuxhaven. After a period of staying together in Hamburg (there were some unhappy experiences in the city—when Wordsworth complained about the price of bread the baker knocked the loaf out of his hands and refused to refund the money) the two later agreed to separate. Coleridge travelled on by himself to Ratzeburg, a short distance south of Lübeck, on 30 September and most fortunately we still have his letters and notebook entries from this time.[266]

By now Coleridge had accumulated a great number of notes for 'The Ancient Mariner' with a special interest in the old seafarers' first-hand observations of icefloes, icebergs and frozen seas. He had made a start on the poem on 14 November 1797, and we can trace numerous sources for ice standing high above the masthead, the terrible cracking or groaning sounds made by icebergs, and 'snowy clifts' which he had noted from the accounts of earlier voyages in high latitudes. Nothing, however, had prepared him for what he saw on a bitterly cold day in the middle of January 1799.

The event is recorded in a letter to his wife Sarah, dated 14 January: the entire Ratzeburg See was that morning 'one mass of thick transparent ice'. A month previously he had noted 'the thunders and howlings' of the breaking ice, but now 'the moment the Sun peeped over the Hill, the mist broke in the middle, and in a few seconds stood divided, leaving a broad road all across the Lake; and between these two Walls of mist the sunlight *burnt* [sic] upon the ice, forming a road of golden fire intolerably bright ...' Coleridge was once again by the lakeside on the following evening as the sun was setting, making keen observations to include in the same letter, and it is just here that the essential point is made:

> On the evening of the next day, at sun-set, the shattered ice ... appeared of a deep blue, and in shape like an agitated sea; beyond this, the water, that ran up between the great Islands of ice ... shone of a yellow green; but all these scattered Ice-islands, themselves, were of an intensely bright blood colour—*they seemed blood and light in union* [my emphasis].

It is precisely this natural interweaving of pure, cold white and warm red that invites reverence and makes us pause. Whether we approach the subject as the Lily and the Rose of the Song of Solomon or through Hermann Beckh's article on Snow White, we should have no doubt that the image, seen as the Bride in Revelation and in the Heavenly Jerusalem of 1925, is that of a divine feminine. In one of his earliest lectures, subsequently shaped into an article, Beckh had also drawn on his extensive linguistic knowledge to share the perception that the dawn can be experienced as the goddess Aurora, the Eos of classical Greek. In turn, he explained, the word Eos (dawn) is directly related through historical Indo-European philology to the Sanskrit Ushas, also meaning the Goddess of Dawn,[267] to whom twenty hymns are dedicated in the sacred verses of the Rig Veda.

From Eve to Isis

'... There they found a big tree which lay felled on the ground, and close by the trunk something was jumping backwards and forwards in the grass, but they could not make out what it was.'

Between 1922 and 1929 Hermann Beckh proceeded indefatigably to extend his meditative insights and meticulous scholarship in many areas, united in one spirit and founded both in Christ and in The Christian Community. The large number of published articles and the major books of this seven-year period,[268] between the ages of 47 and 54, reveal the most valuable insights in the approach to music, Indian, Avestan and Classical Hebrew sacred traditions, to the world of the stars, and ultimately to Mark's Gospel. The scope is enormous, but among the publications (a good number of which have scarcely seen the light of day since that period) one can perceive a consistent loving care to find a true and right approach to a specific feminine form within the lawful Imagination or the 'Signs and Spiritual Realities of the Imaginative World'.

It may also be said in passing that such signs of *ṛta* tend to leave external marks on the movement of history; they write their own signatures. Earlier in the day of 16 February 1929, Hermann Beckh may have been up at his usual hour, stoking up the fire and scratching away some of the frost from his window on the eastern side of the house. Peering out over the rooftops and perhaps pondering how the structure of the John's Gospel differed from what he had deciphered in *Mark's Gospel: The Cosmic Rhythm* lying on his desk, he would have observed Venus as the Morning Star in Sagittarius. Perhaps, too, the early dawn was becoming slowly tinged with red. He may well have appreciated at that moment that the life of The Christian Community could acknowledge certain forerunners in comparatively recent European history, without going further back in time, as he preferred, to the Rig Veda or the Zend Avesta. He would recall that the principal work which set out a new Rosicrucian theosophy for the West was Jakob Böhme's *Aurora or Morgenröte in Aufgang*— the Morning Redness, announcing a new way for Christianity in 1612 when the darkness of the impending Thirty Years War was growing ever more ominous. In the mid-eighteenth century it was Diderot who had commissioned the triumphant titlepage for the complete *Encyclopédie*: a radiant Lucifer (Morning Star) or 'Light-bearer' proclaiming universal rational Enlightenment. After the French Revolution the very same figure appeared on top of the column in the Place de la Bastille: an end to oppression. The newer transformation of thinking at the end of the nineteenth century was signalled by the theosophical periodical *Lucifer*, followed by Rudolf Steiner's *Luzifer* which became *Luzifer Gnosis*.[269] Here then was, Beckh mused as he continued to observe the start of a new day, three hundred years of striving. It was time to get back to work.

Over the seven years Beckh had continued to elaborate on the feminine, and it would be quite wrong to see the relevant publications as ad hoc occasional pieces. From the small book on Genesis, *Der Urspung im Lichte*, 1924, through 'Snow White' (*Die CG* 1924), 'Maya' (*Die CG* Christmas 1924), 'The Heavenly Jerusalem' (1925), 'Egyptian Hieroglyphs' (*Gäa-Sophia* 1926), 'The Mysteries' (*Die Drei* 1926), 'Mount Meru' (*Gäa-Sophia* 1927), and 'The Rainbow's Revelation' (*Die CG* 1928)[270] he had continued to work out a unique understanding of the Feminine within the Divine Nature consistent with anthroposophy and The Act of Consecration of Man. In fact, the issues continued to concern him throughout his later life, with major milestones being marked with the extensive exposition of John's Gospel, *Der kosmische Rhythmus, das Sternengeheimnis und Erdengeheimnis im Johannes-Evangelium*, 1930, and *Vom Geheimnis der Stoffeswelt (Alchymie)*, 1931. Here it is possible to outline very briefly the stages of the discovery.

Starting with the earliest lectures and articles on language, 1921-1922, we find Hermann Beckh applying the most varied philological resources to demonstrate that the aspirate h in its many Indo-European forms represents a feminine out-breathing, a movement from inner force to outer manifestation. The Hebrew *Yahveh* itself is an expression of the divine masculine, *yod*, the feminine *he*, and creative-actualizing power of *vau*. The creative Godhead as Elohim is equally masculine-feminine, and consequently the formation of primordial Adam (Adam Kadmon), as the image and likeness of God, reproduces the aboriginal union of masculine and feminine.[271] In 1924 Beckh wrote:[272]

> 'And the deity created man in their image, in the image of the divine they created him. And they created him male-female.' With this, perhaps the most powerful sentence of the Bible, we are presented with a Mystery, which in the truest meaning of the word is still a Mystery of the future.

The same period sees Beckh lecturing in Zürich ('*Yehi ôr*, Let there be Light') and tracing three stages in the progressive manifestation of the feminine within the Divine Nature. As a mirror to the Godhead (Böhme's *Mysterium Magnum*, the First Mother) there is, in classical Hebrew, H-Y-H, He—Yod—He; from here emerges ħ—y—h, where ħ represents the rougher aspirate, heth. The subsequent externalization is presented as H—V—H, or Eve, the 'mother of all living' before the Fall.[273] The evolution of consciousness has externalized the perception of the world-all, and Adam is now able to speak, to give names.

By 1924 Beckh was in a position to make a substantial contribution to the newly founded series of publications, *Christus aller Erde* with *Our Origin in the Light: Pictures from Genesis*. Yet this had been immediately preceded by a short article, 'The Names for the Divine' for the first Christian Community periodical, *Tatchristentum*. It is just at this moment that the author introduces an essential new insight, with a pertinent glance at Michelangelo's *Creation of Adam*. While the feminine Divine Nature does indeed enter the course of evolution accompanying humanity, as it were, through Noah's Flood and the disintegration of language at the Tower of Babel, *at the same time.*

> ... a mysterious female figure is indicated by Michelangelo: the human female half, as the primordial feminine of the world, Eve, is still dwelling in the spiritual heights with the divine Creator.[274]

The same language immediately entered *Our Origin in the Light*:

> A mysterious female figure in Michelangelo's painting also hints at the fact that the human being's female half, as the primordial Female of the world, Eve, still remains in spirit.[275]

In the same year Hermann Beckh turned his attention away from Genesis to consider his favourite image: Snow White asleep in the crystal coffin. After several poetic touches regarding the 'heights of the Sun', the 'mysterious star-formations of the snowflakes, ice crystals' and the 'maternal covering of snow', he concludes:

> And the awakened soul, the Eternal feminine in us, Snow White, finds the union with the highest 'I', which from regions of cosmic light, the highest cosmic love, stoops to her.[276]

That Christmas, December 1924, the new periodical *Die Christengemeinschaft*, taking over from *Tatchristentum*, published a startling article by Professor Beckh with the challenging title 'Queen Maya: the Christmas Mystery in the Indian Flower Garden'. While the central argument in these pages is that the 'pure virginal element of the cosmos' is also 'the radiant Earth still in the light of Paradise' having close connections with the Indian perception of Maya, the author is now able to add that the Eve who went forward with the evolution of consciousness, congealing, as it were, into the Samsara of apparent hard matter, should be conceived as 'the Mystery of the Virgin *veiled since eternity*'. Characteristically, the article makes an immediate link with Novalis 'poetically the *cloudy veil of the divine Virgin* weaves in the songs of Mary in Novalis' before taking the significant step:[277]

> As the expression of deep cosmic Mysteries (the image of Mary) lived in early Egypt, in those pictorial depictions of the goddess Isis, who carries the child Horus in her arms.

Beckh had found the image that he was searching for. The feminine aspect of Divine Nature was *both* the 'Isis' retained with the uncreated light of Paradise *and also* the dusky veil which shrouds her—*both at the same time*. In the quest for adequate concepts and formulations in these years, however, Beckh was fortunate to see the publication of Günther Wachsmuth's *Etheric Formative Forces* in 1924 where he could find an anthroposophical terminology ideally suited to his vision and experience—the language of the four ethers.[278]

In 1925 this was immediately applied to the story of Buddha's Passing (*Mahaparinibbanasutta*) in Beckh's third article for *Die Drei*.[279] The blossoms which shower down upon the Perfected One from the two Sala trees are from the Tree of Life, now understood as 'All the realms of the higher life-element that remained back in Paradise, of *the life-ether and sound-ether*, open up' (my emphasis). Further observations followed in 1926 with articles contributed to *Die CG* regarding the nature of Mary,[280] culminating in the fairly short but penetrating piece 'Sun and Star' that was issued in the July edition.[281] Here we find an analysis of the veil that covers the Divine feminine:

> Already the early Indian, the Vedic poet, knew that the impulse of his thinking actually is condensed sunlight, sunlight which awakens light and love. Our consciousness today is completely carried by the weaving being of light. Even this thinking of today, which caught in the world of matter does not see the spirit-ether being of light in its truth, lives in the ether-element of this light. But the element of light has become a veil for thinking, hiding from it the higher element of life. The harmonies of light are silent for it; the life of light has died.

It remained to encapsulate what was meant by 'the life of light', and in contrast to the language of the four ethers Beckh opted for the 'human Mysteries of the cosmic harmonies and of the cosmic life'. However, at the same time as these shorter publications were in production Beckh had been in discussion with Günther Wachsmuth who, among numerous responsibilities, was also the editor of *Gäa-Sophia*, the *Jahrbuch* of the Natural Scientific Section of the School for Spiritual Science. The decision was taken that *Gäa* would issue an extensive article from Beckh which would explore his extraordinary discovery that ancient Egyptian hieroglyphs for Isis confirmed Wachsmuth's analysis of the four ethers and their formative manifestations in the natural world. The resulting publication 'Etheric Formative Forces and Hieroglyphs'[282] presents the fullest analysis of a threefold feminine that Beckh ever set out for the public, and it requires a careful reading.

In essence, the article analyses both the various original names and hieroglyphs of Isis. The names are simply given from Brugsch[283] as 'the one from the primal beginning', 'the primal picture of all pictures', 'the queen of goddesses and women', 'the mistress of the year's beginning' (relationship to the star Sirius), 'the brightest amongst the shining ones', 'queen of the Earth', 'mistress of warmth', 'mother of god', 'lady of the birth-chamber', 'giver of life', 'leading mistress of magic', 'mistress of love'. Beckh's own detailed analysis of the hieroglyphs proceeds to demonstrate that Isis herself should be seen as the 'Eternal Feminine', or Cosmic Love, represented by the Tree of Life. Since the Fall of man and the consequent evolution of consciousness this is now *withheld* from everyday experience and comprehension.[284]

A second aspect of the Feminine is found by Hermann Beckh in the perception that the 'frozen cosmic harmonies'[285] of sound-ether can enter our experience when contemplating ice crystals, snowflakes and frost. The discussion willingly accepts and refers to Wachsmuth's term 'cold light'. This one aspect of the veil of Isis was precisely what Beckh had noticed in 'The Heavenly Jerusalem', on his journeys in high frozen mountains, and very probably when spending the night immersed in the deep snow. Further, Hermann Beckh as Professor of Indology (Sanskrit, Pali and Tibetan) is now able to put the case that the Sanskrit word *sisira*, pronounced *shishira*, could mean cold, snow, ice, frost and the cold time of the year. Modern dictionaries agree, adding also 'mountain'.[286] Having closely studied the work of Rudolf Falb on Quechuan and the ancient Inca inscriptions,[287] Beckh can now observe that what appears to be the very same word, *sisira*, is found in both Sanskrit and Quechuan. In the latter it is said to mean 'woven' or woven material.

In the folk imagination Snow White and numerous 'ice-queens' represent this experience of 'frozen light'. In the following year, 1927, Beckh extended this aspect of the Eternal Feminine in his next article for *Gäa* on Indian Cosmogony and Mount Meru: the 'ice-maiden' is also discovered with the stories of Isolde (the name itself witnesses to the connection with ice (*Ishild* = *Eishilde, Eisholde*), and also with Brunhilde.[288]

The third aspect, or the second quality of the veil of Isis, for Beckh is the simple fact, which he himself had experienced in the mountains, that a covering of snow acts as a warming mantle. He had written in Snow White:

> ... from the maternal covering of snow, which so softly and lovingly covers the rigid Earth protecting the shoots slumbering in the depths. The maternal element of the world speaks to us out of this warming love.[289]

Now in 1926, Beckh can relate the warmth-ether woven in the veil of Isis to bring together once more the natural-scientific work of Günther Wachsmuth and the forum of *Gäa-Sophia* with the linguistic findings of Rudolf Falb.[290]

> With Falb we also frequently find the meaning of this word *(sisira)* as 'veil of mist', the watery veil of the light, the 'tear pearls of the Sun'. And on the other hand, the rosy sunrise and red sunset is also associated with the veil of mist, or veil of duskiness, especially in the mountains when this appearance that today is called *Alpenglühen,* 'alpine glow', appears, which for the early people was something thoroughly sacred, revealed in the red of the mountains (Falb 433). From this Peruvian meaning of the word *sisira* 'red of the mountain', there easily arises for Falb the meaning 'red colour' that is the same word in Hebrew (only with other vowels): *shasher.* [Jer. 22;14, usually translated as 'vermilion'.] We recall that red is also the colour-tendency of the warmth-ether, as well as the sphere is its form-tendency, in the same way as in the mountains the Sun-veil is revealed as red in colour ...

Later in the decade, Beckh continued to present the Divine Feminine Nature especially in two articles for *Die Drei* entitled 'Isis',[291] and 'The Name Isis',[292] going on in 1928 and 1929 to compose 'The Rainbow's Revelation'[293] and then 'John and the Word'[294] for *Die Christengemein-schaft* before finding that the hour had struck in 1929 for the gigantic undertaking of his study on Mark's Gospel.[295] All the same, for Wachsmuth's *Gäa-Sophia* the 1926 article on Isis and her representation in hieroglyphs constitutes the most mature, precise analysis that he made, even if later work continued the broader application of findings.

It is one thing to say with the intellect that the Divine Feminine Nature is threefold: the withdrawn source of love and creation, of cosmic harmonies, lies with the Tree of Life normally inaccessible except in sleep. Her higher life-ether travels with us in the veil of warm reds, or warmth-ether; her tone-ether is found in the veil of cold ice and snow, the frozen light-ether. It is something quite different, however, to experience this as Hermann Beckh did in the mountains, and to expand in such a way, the original insight regarding the three forms of Eve suggested by the study of Classical Hebrew, H-Y-H, ħ—y—h and H—V—H into an exegesis of the Egyptian throne hieroglyph ⌐⌐, combined with the hieroglyphs for 'loaf of bread' and for 'queen' to confirm the overall meaning, Isis:[296]

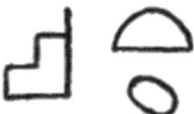

In all probability only Beckh could have constructed the confirmation, which needed to encompass, inter alia, Sanskrit, 'The Departure of the Perfected One' in Pali, and a passing notice of Quechuan inscriptions in Peru, a confirmation which rests on the unshakeable experience and knowledge of the universality of Imaginative Laws. The Eternal Feminine (*das Ewig-Weiblichen*) was revealed to Beckh in the form of the black Queen of the Night, studded with stars, and the Dawn. Such an Imaginative form, however, is not just a matter of simple observation and a knowledge of traditional lore and legend.

1928-1929 Virgo

'The old mother lived peacefully and happily with her children for many years. She took the two rose-trees with her, and they stood before her window, and every year they bore the most beautiful roses, white and red.'

'Is that the end of the story?'

'Yes, Gundhild, it is. It's time for supper. Good night and sleep well.'

'But,'Fesser Beckh, where did they live? Are they still there today?'

Later that night, in the early hours of Sunday morning, when Gundhild and most of the household were fast asleep, Professor Beckh found himself pausing from the intense study of John's Gospel. He had just rewritten a note for Section 3 of Part 1: 'For the early Egyptians the star Spica ['the sheaf'] was in the constellation of the Virgin, as similarly the fixed star Sirius, and the planet Venus is an Isis-star, a revelation of Isis.[297] It might need emending'.

Just after 2 a.m. Hermann Beckh turned off the light. He stared out of the eastern window, where indeed Virgo was rising, and he could make out both

Spica and Vindemiatrix gleaming in the dark sky now that the waxing moon had set.[298] *A hard frost was setting in. It was true that his colleagues and many friends had congratulated him on what had become known as 'the Mark book'. There was considerable satisfaction that his scholarship and meditations on Virgo had been warmly received both as regards the cycle of musical keys, which he had addressed earlier, and now as an inspiration for an understanding of the Parable of the Sower, the Feeding of the 4,000, and finally the Last Supper itself. It was fitting and right that he had explained several times in learned articles that the Divine Feminine Nature could be experienced as a source of heavenly nourishment, and he had been able to trace her footsteps through the ages: Sanskrit* soma, *Avestan* huoma, *Egyptian* Isis, *the manna in the wilderness. It was clear for all to see. Yet what had happened to the Divine Bread? Arthur Peake had convinced most of the world in 1919 that manna was either coriander resin or the 'crystallized honeydew of certain insects'.*[299]

'Everywhere people are hungry,' thought Hermann Beckh, 'and they are given stones.' Later that day he was to put on the vestments for the last Sunday of Trinity before Lent, that is the last Sunday in Epiphany in the Lutheran tradition and consecrate the bread and the wine once again. 'How many times,' he mused, 'have people found their way to the Supper understanding little but with a willing heart and loving devotion?' He then recalled Gundhild's questions: Snow White and Rose Red, 'Where did they live? Are they alive now?'

Yes, Gundhild, I can tell you where they lived, and yes, they are alive now but have fallen into a deep sleep with their mother …

They lived together for a long time in the Middle Ages in great retirement and then appeared in Amsterdam in 1651. The book Bahir—*the word means* Brightness—*saw them:*

> The Holy One, blessed be he, kept the divine light for the future to come. It is the measure of all the valuables that are in the world. It is the power of the precious stone that is called socharet that is red marble and dar that is pearl. [Esther 1:6].[300]

They were often found in the cloisters, especially in Bohemia, where they were known as the Lily and the Rose, and very many beautiful hymns were composed in their memory.[301]

The two girls visited Lombardy in 1558-60.[302] *when the great Zohar saw the light of day in Mantua. Its very opening words are:*

> 'Like a rose among thorns, so is my beloved among the maidens' … For there is a rose, and then there is a rose! Just as a rose among thorns is coloured red and white ….[303]

Before that they dwelt in Jerusalem where tradition holds that they were seen by Solomon who probably had the clearest view of them:

> *I am the Rose of Sharon, the Lily of the Valleys* [Song of Solomon, 2:1].

But even before that time they lived together in ancient Babylon. When the astronomers looked into the night sky at the stars we now call Virgo, they saw not one divine lady, but two. To the East, closest to the Scales, they revered she who was called Mul Ab Sin, or sometimes Mul Ki Hal. She represented fallow land especially good for sowing cereals, and her name is generally expressed as 'The Furrow' (like Sitā, heroine of the Rāmāyan). Her greatest jewel, held in her left hand below, was the star we call Spica, or the ear of wheat. For thousands of years this star was seen as the source of divine bread. To the ancient Greeks it was Στάχυς (Stachys), to the Syrians Shebbelta, Chüshe to the Persians, Çparegha in the Avesta, all meaning the same ear of wheat. For the Sanskrit world the star of the White Lady was Citrā, the Lamp or the Pearl.

To the West, closer to the Lion, the Babylonians saw, experienced and reverenced the great goddess Sarpanitu, known to the astronomers as Mul E Ru, the date-palm or 'The Frond', a symbol (Greek 'phoenix') of rebirth, which she bore in her uplifted right hand. Her great star was known to the Greeks as Προτρυγετής (Protrygetes), the grape-gatherer or grape-harvest, rendered as Vindemiatrix by the Romans ... [304]

By mid-February we can be confident that the text of *John's Gospel: The Cosmic Rhythm—Stars and Stones* was nearing completion. In *Mark*, Beckh had painstakingly traced the structure of the entire gospel, focusing on the seasonal relationships of the zodiac signs to the Earth and the three years of Christ's ministry. He had deciphered what he termed the 'Pisces-Virgo' axis of the 'etheric cross' as divine nourishment and found its highest manifestation in the Last Supper.[305] His earlier observations on Soma, Huoma, Isis and manna are pertinent here. Now, with John's Gospel, he had found that the structure was very different, and the focus had to be on Lazarus, he who is sick, that is, the becoming of John himself. In all probability this subject is the most difficult that Beckh had to address.

Presumably between 1928 and 1929 he addressed two qualities which could be attributed to Virgo, both relating to Mary Magdalene in the context of John 12 and the narration of the raising of Lazarus. In the final version of the publication, we find the discussion in Part 3 of Section 3. In the gospel we see:

> the disciple of Christ raised out of the grave, and at the same time we glimpse the sister-soul Mary Magdalene, linked with the Fishes, with

the sign of resurrection and serving love, at the same time the sign of the Virgin. And we recall how we always recognized the constellation as the *constellation of the Last Supper.'*[306] [Beckh's emphases.]

However, the discussion then goes on to refer back to the earlier exposition of Mark's Gospel (p. 302ff. in the English translation, TL p. 250ff.), Departure of the Perfected One, and Rudolf Steiner's *Man in the Light of Philosophy, Theosophy and Occultism* (GA137). 'Characteristic of this sign (Virgo)', Hermann Beckh now claims, is the Christ's 'farewell to the outer world' and:

> Of all signs the Virgin is the sign of the Mysteries of the Earth (cf. John 12:24) that in the gospel is always significantly united with the Mystery of the Last Supper.[307]

By 1930 Hermann Beckh had spent many years considering the Divine Feminine Nature and the quest had passed through many cultures and languages, through indications presented by Rudolf Steiner, the signs of the heavens and the two gospels. At an exalted level he was to find that the search still required a penetrating examination of the traditions of philosophical alchemy, that is, the mysteries of Earth-substance, which led to the little book *Vom Geheimnis der Stoffeswelt,* Stuttgart, 1931. He had repeatedly enlarged on the knowledge, in fact, that such substance is the Bride of Revelation, though he had avoided drawing our attention to the fact that 'I AM the bread of life' and 'I AM the true vine' in the seven I AM-sayings of John's Gospel represent the beginning and the end of a new engagement. He had also avoided pointing out that such 'substance' (Latin *substantia*) translates *hypostasis* (Greek) and that through Christ we are to be enhypostasized in the Divine Nature. He preferred other terms.

In reading Hermann Beckh's collected works we find ourselves hovering precariously between the need for colder, icier intellectual scholarship and a warmer full-bloodied imagination. As in so many things it is difficult to tell precisely where 'facts' end and imagination or interpretation begins or where ideas become ideals. With the texts we approach the person, and it is impossible to exaggerate the huge gratitude to all who knew him and left their memories for us today, perhaps above all to Gundhild for her biography of Beckh, and to her sister Rosemaria who has given us wonderful photographs and recollections. I do not find that a colder scholarship is always the best means to approach the workings of the spirit in a great man.

On Sunday 17th February I would expect to have seen Hermann Beckh in the chapel of the Seminary participating in The Act of Consecration of Man. I expect that he was wearing the vestments for Trinity, and I expect that the Gospel Reading which he may have read himself was Matthew 17:1-13, the Transfiguration. It is probable that he received the bread and wine and the blessing of peace.

I know that the woman who was most dear to him, his sister Marie, passed over the threshold eight days later on the 25 February, and that Hermann Beckh dedicated his new work on John's Gospel to her. As for the 'sister-soul', Beckh would read in Proverbs 7:4 'Say to wisdom (Heb. *hokmah*, LXX *sophia*)) you are my sister.'

The first section of *The Zohar, Haqdamat Sefer ha-Zohar*, employs the fiction of introducing Rabbi El'azar in the act of teaching on three names of God.[308] On the lowest rung there is Elleh, אלה, 'these'. 'These' are the things we think we know, and we can point to them and give them names, all that we 'know' of the revealed Divine Nature. A naïve beginning. Above Elleh we find that we are full of questions: *Mah*, מה, 'what?' We know we don't know but are still seeking concepts, percepts, things. Never satisfying. But above this we may find a higher name of God, *Mi*, מי, ['Who?']. When we consider the 'what' of Beckh's publications we can only go so far. Above and beyond the 'what' there lies the awesome presence of the man himself, the 'who'. We have reached the top of the stairs. In a different context, in 1921 Hermann Beckh quoted a sentence[309] dealing majestically with this:

> And so, we stand here, perhaps indeed at the boundaries where we have to venerate in all humility what cannot be researched.

Fig. From left to right: Rosemaria; the beloved au pair, Rosa; the children's mother Marguerete Bock, née Seumer; and Friedwart (c. 1932/33).

Book Reviews

John's Gospel: The Cosmic Rhythm—
Stars and Stones[310]

Hermann Beckh. Translated by Alan Stott

Herman Beckh reveals the living stream of Johannine Christianity in this recently published book translated by Alan Stott. His insights have been sourced by correlating the events depicted in the gospel with the star signs which accompanied Christ as He walked the roads of Galilee with His disciples.

Beckh was a scholar of Sanskrit, philosophy and other disciplines such as mythology, music and poetry. However, when he met Rudolf Steiner and learnt about anthroposophy and The Christian Community, this worldview became the nexus of all that he had mastered before. He recognized that sum of all truth is the outpouring of love that is manifest in the person of Jesus Christ. This review is written in the centenary year of the founding of The Christian Community. Beckh was one of the founding-priests of The Christian Community and was present at the celebration of the first Act of Consecration of Man. His writings show him to be a person of deep devotion, which along with his poetic imagination helps to illustrate what he has to say. However, a word of caution is needed here, as the reader requires some stellar knowledge to be able to follow the indications that Beckh gives in the reading of the constellations. Beckh describes the individual events of the gospel and shows how these influence each other in the broader canvas of development, for example the wedding at Cana, the transfiguration, the raising of Lazarus and the witness of the beloved disciple at the crucifixion. We are familiar with these events, and what is new is in the cross pollination that Beckh brings in his vision of how one event affects another. It is as though we are seeing these relationships for the first time as he opens the doors to the heavenly pastures.

Beckh places the raising of Lazarus at the pivotal point of the gospel. 'One can say that the raising of Lazarus was the outer deed that incorporated in this one individual, through his initiation, the Knowledge of Truth, in the light-filled consciousness that Christ wanted to lead humanity to.' In this respect, Lazarus is born again as the first free man. This moment already anticipates the deed of Golgotha, when from the cross Christ surrenders His divine 'I' to the 'I' of humanity. The Act of Consecration of Man today celebrates this fact where the faithful express their longing in their aspiration to commune with the body and the blood of the Resurrected One, in the hope of one day becoming free.

Hermann Beckh gives us the opportunity to discover new aspects of the gospel which can broaden our basis for understanding these mysterious truths. As an example, he says of the Last Supper, 'Christ gives a sop to Judas and in doing so Christ took the dark deed of betrayal on to himself. He had to will this dark deed itself because without it the great Mystery for the advance of the earth and humanity would not be brought into effect.' This insight puts in a starkly different light whatever we may have thought about Judas as the betrayer, and indeed the position of Christ who effectively releases him from the dreadful weight of guilt by taking this onto Himself. In contrast to this sombre mood, we have another example of Beckh's poetic description of the Last Supper, made as though he had been there as a witness of the great tenderness that flowed in the Upper Room at that time. 'In the image of the one on Jesus' breast as the inspirer of the outpouring of what goes beyond the gospel—one is brought into the intimacy of the love of Christ for His disciples and how He lovingly prepared them for the future.' The love of Christ for His flock permeates every word of the Farewell Discourses and the High Priestly Prayer (Jn. 17) which has become the cornerstone of our sacramental life.

The reader who perseveres with this book will be rewarded by being excited at moments, inspired at others. They will also have to labour hard to read the signs to navigate round the rocks that are in the way. However, for the more experienced traveller, these same rocks may be experienced as beacons of light.

Review by Douglas Thackray

Hermann Beckh: Life and Work

Gundhild Kačer-Bock, translated by Maren and Alan Stott

At the founding of The Christian Community in 1922 it was agreed that the new Seminary in Stuttgart was to have three incumbent teachers who were to live in the splendid new house. Friedrich Rittelmeyer and Emil Bock were given the ground floor and first floor respectively, with added responsibility for executive and administrative decisions. The top attic floor was provided for Hermann Beckh who had responsibility for teaching the relationship of Christianity to earlier religions, and who, as the only Professor among the 48 founding priests, could most inspire the spiritual growth of the new community.

Beckh's extraordinary biography was meticulously researched and lovingly written by Gundhild Kačer-Bock and published by Urachhaus in 1997, marking a great milestone in the records of The Christian Community. Having known the Professor since she was a child in the Stuttgart Seminary, Gundhild was able to combine early memories with factual discoveries resulting in a rounded picture of a truly great man who was both a pioneer in the spirit and a warm colleague. It is impossible to avoid the insight that Beckh had the most profound knowledge of ancient languages and texts—Tibetan, Sanskrit, Pali, Avestan, Hebrew (as well as Latin and Greek)—and could relate this knowledge to his own personal path of spiritual development as a priest at the altar.

It is precisely because this biography is a secure testimony of Beckh's spiritual greatness during the first fifteen years of The Christian Community that Maren and Alan Stott have undertaken the much-needed task of supplying an English translation of the biography with considerable extra material. The publication is a significant step forward within the overall project of providing an English edition of *The Collected Works of Hermann Beckh* (including generally unknown articles, typescripts and a complete manuscript of his unfinished final work) before the centenary of the founding arrives in 2022. Hermann Beckh was not a peripheral voice among the numerous speakers for the establishment of The Christian Community. He emerged as the brightest star among the constellations and blazed a path which today we are only beginning to understand and appreciate.

The biography shows that Hermann Beckh (1875-1937) was one of Rudolf Steiner's most distinguished pupils who remained loyal to his teacher since he first met him close to Christmas 1911. Steiner was actively seeking a circle of highly competent and gifted individualities around him, both for his own lifetime, and who would continue to carry his great legacy out into the world after his death. In these pages we find that Beckh was one of those souls intimately connected with significant and most poignant moments in Steiner's life.

In 1913 he was admitted to the Esoteric School as a chosen pupil. The biography indicates that Steiner gave lectures particularly with Beckh in mind and that there is an extensive correspondence between them awaiting investigation in the Dornach archives. On New Year's

Eve 1913 he attended an unforgettable evening dedicated to the poetry of Christian Morgenstern. Marie Steiner recited several of the poems with the seriously ill poet himself in the audience. Rudolf Steiner added a deeply moving tribute at the end of which he took several red roses from a vase, stepped off the podium and walked to where Morgenstern was sitting, handing the roses to him with further words of heartfelt appreciation. For a short while in 1914 Beckh joined the carvers working on building the all-wooden Goetheanum, with Steiner regularly present to give instructions. In 1913 Beckh is present at the very first public eurythmy performance, an art which he deeply treasured. His relatively short military service during World War I with the German army in the Balkans, especially Romania, must have prepared him for a dramatic event in 1922 when Steiner was giving a public lecture in Munich. Rumours had spread that trouble was brewing. All was going well during Steiner's talk when suddenly the lights went out, stink bombs were thrown, and an attempt was made to attack Steiner on the podium. Beckh had been chosen together with other leading anthroposophists (Kolisko, Noll, Bückenbacher) to form a bodyguard to defend Steiner from such attacks. Noll and Beckh threw back the attackers so that Steiner could reach the safety of the Green Room.

September 1922 brings another pivotal event in Beckh's complex life, the founding of the Movement for Religious Renewal, otherwise known as The Christian Community, with Steiner himself in the White Hall of the Goetheanum only about three months before the devastating arson attack, which took place in the same room on New Year's Eve 1922. Beckh had felt prompted to join this group of mainly young people seeking new ways for the religious life. There is a reverberating anecdote of his loud statement on the stairwell of Rittelmeyer's vicarage, 'Now I am here and belong with you; even if you don't want me, you will never get rid of me.'

Many of the insights and stories relating to his life are woven into this remarkable biographical document by Gundhild Kačer-Bock. This now appears in English for the very first time and gains in poignancy when one reads how at a young age (she was the eldest daughter of Emil Bock) she would visit Beckh in his attic flat of Urachstrasse 41, Stuttgart, which housed them both. No matter how busy he was, he always found time to speak with her. Despite his immense erudition, Professor Beckh retained a childlike sense of wonder about the world in all its aspects, and so the visit of this young child was something he deeply valued. They built up a particular ritual during the visits. They would greet the pictures, the shells and fossils, and the wonderful array of precious stones. Her favourite game was 'naming the stones' which always produced a lot of noisy merriment. He would play to her on his piano and tell fairy stories. To her and her siblings he was always "Fesser Beckh' (no one apart from his sister and mother seems to have addressed him as Hermann). On his visits he would write home delightful notes on postcards; a number are included in the book. 'The first of May today was beautiful, like the light of Paradise which you once painted. I thought a lot about your picture of Paradise. Warm greetings, yours, 'Fesser B.'

Over the 318 pages of this handsomely produced book a rich, highly nuanced series of pictures of a remarkable personality emerge. The all-too-short autobiographical fragment of about 50 pages is included, leaving off with his student days in Munich. In its very moving style, it offers many keys to unlock the deeper layers of Beckh's being. We read of the deep love of the high mountains, especially the Bavarian Alps, beginning in early childhood. Here among the peaks and the precious mountain flowers (gentians and arnica) he feels much closer to the worlds of spirit than in the lowlands and certainly the cities (although Munich is the only city where he truly felt at home). At the age of five, in a powerful supersensible experience, he felt in a body-free consciousness a realm beyond our narrow earth-existence, 'on the other shore of existence', from where the true human 'I' originates and where the 'wafting cosmic breath is perceptible'. At the same time, he felt an almost unbearable compassion for humanity. The experience was repeated later in life, as if to remind him of his deeper destiny that he eventually discovered.

We can be most grateful to the team of translators and editors who have worked tirelessly for several years and who now continue to bring out the *Collected Works of the Rev. Prof. Hermann Beckh* in time, hopefully, for the centenary of The Christian Community in 2022. The translations read well, and the editing is of a fine quality, the layout with its subtitles an improvement on the German edition. Maren and Alan Stott, Neil Franklin (the General Editor) and Katrin Binder deserve much praise, thanks and encouragement for their loving commitment to Hermann Beckh, as do the publishers Anastasi Ltd of Leominster [and, after they closed down, the project was taken on by Temple Lodge, Forest Row], who unconditionally back these publications which signal a new perspective in our understanding of the first generation of teachers in The Christian Community, their great stature, knowledge and intentions. Hermann Beckh now stands before us as a most distinctive leading personality to be revered and loved.

Review by Christopher Cooper

The Language of the Stars

Hermann Beckh, Rudolf Frieling

During the brief window between the two World Wars, the Rev. Prof. Hermann Beckh (1875-1937) led research at The Christian Community Seminary in Stuttgart. In those precious years he published on music, Buddhism, the cosmic rhythm in the gospels, alchemy, the origin of speech and the ancient Mysteries. By 1930, in his contributions to the priests' *Newsletter*, he had produced the most far-reaching account of the cosmic order ever written. The typescript of this great work was destined to gather dust in the Berlin *Zentralarchiv*—until it was rediscovered in recent years. Published here for the first time, it is the crowning masterpiece to Beckh's *Collected Works*.

The translated and annotated text of *The Language of the Stars* is accompanied by Rudolf Frieling's (1901-1986) in-depth application of Beckh's principles of the cosmic starry order to the Creed of The Christian Community. Frieling later led The Christian Community until his death. Historically, Frieling's response to Beckh's magisterial studies on the cosmic rhythm in Mark's Gospel and John's Gospel was what caused Beckh to 'pick up [his] pen this very day' and produce his unique account. It is in fact the first attempt towards a new knowledge of the stars, according to Rudolf Steiner's initial stimulus in Leipzig 1913 (GA 149), who hoped the astrologer present would respond. This gentleman failed to do so; it remained for Beckh, who was also present at the lecture-course, to take up the challenge himself. At the time Beckh asked Steiner what he should study of astrology. The answer? 'Nothing, only anthroposophy.' This the author did, thus substantiating his claim: 'Astrology is a concern of the Christ and the work of Michael.' Frieling himself concludes: 'To emphasize once more that without Beckh's books all this would have been impossible or would have hung in the air. My *Contributions* are only the consequences that are drawn out of Beckh's insights for the theological and liturgical realm.'

Through ever-deepening meditation guided by Rudolf Steiner, and his vast knowledge of Tibetan, Sanskrit, Pali and Avestan sacred texts—scarcely to be equalled in Europe at the time—and not to forget a considerable quantity of music, Beckh came to the first-hand realization that human and cosmic life was ordered. He perceived directly that this cosmic order was *good*, as originating from the World-Will; *true*, as from World-Thinking; and *beautiful*, as from World-Feeling. All three could be personally experienced in disciplined consciousness that could enter dream, sleep and pre-natal life. This, then, was Beckh's method and inspiration, as shown in this extraordinary work.

Drawing for the most part on Steiner's *Occult Science: An Outline*, Beckh begins with a detailed account of the Uranus aspect. This, he rightly points out, is largely neglected. The subject invokes a huge perspective of cosmic history. For Beckh, astrology is not primarily about birth horoscopes; he quotes Steiner remarking that even an initiate at the end of his life would be cautious to undertake such an investigation. Beckh's concern is to awaken perception, for which, he claims more than once, a study of musical tonality was his pathway. Simply put, after Imagination comes Inspiration and Intuition. Beckh, genuinely humble one suspects, shares his investigations into the spiritual archetypes.

Rudolf Frieling

Hermann Beckh and Rudolf Frieling (photo: left) worked spiritually side by side, 1930-1932, after Beckh had published his studies of the Gospels of Mark and John and Frieling had written some works of orientation on *Sacred Playing* (1925), *The Seven Sacraments* (1926), *Sacrament and Ritual* (1928), and *The Holy Mount* (1930). While contributing their articles for the priests' *Newsletter* as well as the monthly journal *Die Christengemeinschaft*, Beckh was composing *Alchymy* (1931) and Frieling was working towards the highly significant *Sacred Number in John's Gospel* (1933).

Both writers had come to realize that life in general, the gospels and the sacramental work of The Christian Community in particular, were expressions of spiritual beings working through the ordered path of the starry heavens. Rudolf Steiner's indications were taken up with great earnestness to address a central topic. The heart of the new Christ-centred astrology was not to underestimate the formative forces of the starry signs and planets but to emphasize that for each person they provide the house into which the individual enters at birth. The householder, the 'I', however, is free in Christ to respond originally and creatively throughout the individual's life.

When Beckh attended a conference of astrologers—all fine people, he says—he found that the principal lack was an approach to rebirth and *karma*. What is written in the stars at birth is an expression of 'The Book of Destiny' which we have brought with us as a result of previous lives. He explains that he has seen this directly when looking at his own birth horoscope and life-challenges.

The Appendices also contain articles referred to in the text, several appreciations and relevant book reviews. With this publication, we are given the opportunity to appreciate not only a deeper approach to anthroposophy, but also to re-assess the universal scholar Hermann Beckh, of whose legacy Emil Bock in his final publication (1959) wrote: 'An abundance of books came into existence whose significance perhaps will only be properly appreciated in the future.'

This could be a call to our present, the twenty-first century. Here dedicated search for the creative archetypes, fundamental anthroposophy, can receive a fresh impulse from authors who have inspired generations of priests worldwide, including Dr Alfred Heidenreich and Adam Bittleston in Britain. Consequently, we are also looking forward with immense gratitude and interest to the sixteenth title of the project, the forthcoming *Collected Articles* of Prof. Hermann Beckh [2023].

Review by Dr Kenneth Gibson

The Language of Tonality in the Music of Bach to Bruckner

Hermann Beckh, translated by Alan Stott

At long last, several important books that explore the holistic nature of music and its cosmic origins have been made available in English—for the first time. We have Heiner Ruland's *Expanding Tonal Awareness* and Christoph Peter's *The Language of Music in Mozart's 'The Magic Flute'* (Anastasi 2015)—which at the same time is the definitive study of the opera. To these must now be added the substantial achievements of arguably the greatest figure of them all, Prof. Dr Hermann Beckh (1875-1937). His works have only been available in German (excepting his standard book on Buddhism, translated into Japanese and Dutch), and there is much treasure still to come. Anastasi, based in Leominster, Herefordshire, have now issued Beckh's *The Language of Tonality* in a handsome paperback edition, with helpful layout (a welcome advance on all the German editions). Alan Stott's concise and very readable translation is a true labour of love in which Beckh's clear, but rather complicated German style has been successfully surmounted. The translator has even risen to the challenge to complete a *Collected Edition* of this legendary writer, one of Rudolf Steiner's closest pupils. In 2004 (rev. 2008) Anastasi issued Beckh's *The Essence of Tonality* (written in 1922; new edition, TL 2022). Now in *The Language of Tonality* Beckh takes his ideas considerably further, embracing the Western musical language from Bach to Bruckner. He concentrates, however, on Richard Wagner (1813-83) and the evolution of this composer's use of the musical keys in all the major music dramas, from 'The Flying Dutchman' to 'Parsifal'. In his Introduction, Alan Stott puts Beckh's ideas into a clear modern context. The book includes an article by Beckh on 'The Mystery of the Night in Wagner and Novalis', an inspiring contribution on Beckh and music by Lothar Reubke, interesting memories by August Pauli and a survey of the author's career by Gundhild Kačer-Bock (Beckh's biographer).

The universal scholar Hermann Beckh, Dr jur. et Phil.—*ein Original*, as the Germans would say—who gained his first doctorate with a work on Civil Law, worked as a judge before changing career to pursue independent studies in Eastern languages; in the process he mastered six ancient languages to add to his complete fluency in six modern languages! He lectured at the University of Berlin, where, hearing a lecture by Rudolf Steiner in 1911 on Elijah changed his life. Resigning from academic life in 1921, he aimed to work as an independent scholar for anthroposophy. But in 1922 he heard of plans to found the Movement for Religious Renewal, The Christian Community. Beckh joined immediately as a founder priest, taking on the task of founding the Seminary in Stuttgart. Two monumental studies, *Mark's Gospel: The Cosmic Rhythm* and *John's Gospel: The Cosmic Rhythm—Stars and Stones* (1928 & 1930) are both available from Anastasi [now TL 2021] by the same translator. These gospel studies contain several references to the musical keys —to a polymath like Beckh the subjects mutually correspond. This born educator, a very accomplished pianist able to illustrate his lectures at the piano with ease from memory, enjoyed playing piano duets of the Masters with his friends and colleagues Lic. Emil Bock, Dr Rudolf Frieling and Dr Alfred Heidenreich.

Beckh's 1922-essay *The Essence of Tonality* pictures the twelve musical keys and their interrelationships in the form of a 'tone-zodiac', linking them to the course of the day, the seasons of the year and the human form, as a vast cosmic rhythm. Beckh understood the circle of fifths of the musical keys not merely as abstract theory, but as the deepest organizing principle, to be lived and experienced, that is, inwardly *heard*. These ideas, expounded in lectures over many years, appeared in later works, such as *Wagner and Christianity* (1933) and *The Parsifal Christ-Experience* (1930, available in one volume TL, 2022), before finally coming to fruition in a crowning magnum opus, *The Language of Tonality*. Beckh completed his book in 1936, though in considerable pain from a progressing cancer of the kidneys. The book was posthumously published in 1937; the terrible turmoil of World War II and the aftermath effectively buried it, certainly it did his other impressive works. Since those years Beckh has been known, if at all, in German editions—until now.

Although the title runs 'from Bach to Bruckner', the central core of the book is devoted to how Wagner, apparently totally intuitively, explored the cycle of key-relationships in his music dramas. Beckh's first chapter, 'The Circle of the Musical Keys' explains the deeper connections between, for example, C-major and its polar opposite in the circle, F#-G♭-majors, also G-major and D♭-major, E-major and B♭-major, all of which also form triangles with other keys. The circle of keys moves, like the day and the year, progressively lighter and higher, then after the transition in F#-G♭, to the keys with flats, D♭, A♭, B♭ and F-majors. The minor keys normally depict the shadow side of the key-centre. The remaining chapters explore each of these key-centres in detail, constantly referring to examples from the Masters; much of the music is quite familiar. Beckh moves on to specific passages in Wagner's 'The Flying Dutchman', 'Tannhäuser', 'Lohengrin', 'The Ring', 'Tristan and Isolde', 'The Mastersingers' and finally 'Parsifal'. No written musical examples are given—strictly not necessary, as Beckh describes relevant passages from each work using Wagner's text, here printed with the original German and in English translation side by side. Wagner-lovers will have the advantage in recognizing passages and are encouraged to place them in the context of the whole work performed in one's mind. But this book is not only for musicians; the musical terminology is widely used but kept to a minimum. Music-lovers will find Beckh's insights a revelation, a stimulus to revisit this controversial, yet considerable artist.

At the time Beckh was writing (during the difficult 1920s and 30s), the language of music, like the visual arts, was passing through various stages: tonality, atonality, bitonality, polytonality, neo-classicism, dodecaphony, et al. After the War, some music sank even deeper into the subterranean realms of 'organized noise', electronic 'music' and the rise of the 'avant- (but really *derrière!*) garde'. But music is not to be mocked; it has taken quite a time for the truer understanding of music and its mission to re-surface again. The twenty-first century will expect from us a much more holistic remembering of the source of music, often called the 'universal language'. In this respect, is could be that Hermann Beckh really was writing for the future, as Emil Bock, for one, maintained; his vision (or 'audition') is for a time when music's true destiny and purpose should re-awaken. That time is now; this is *the* book to assist in that process.

Review by Michael Jones

Collected Articles (1922–1938)

Hermann Beckh

It is nearly ten years since the first publications undertaken by Alan and Maren Stott, Neil Franklin and Katrin Binder devoted to the writings of Hermann Beckh, initially with Anastasi Ltd, and now (in revised editions) by Temple Lodge. This initiative received a boost in 2006 with the publication in '*Der Europäer*' of three of Beckh's articles exploring musical creativity—a discovery which motivated Alan Stott to research extensively all surviving material (some of which only existed in MSS in Australia). This collection of articles amounts to a unique and considerable literary achievement, involving ancient Indian languages, religion, artistic criticism, anthroposophy, and Beckh's close participation in co-founding The Christian Community in 1922.

  Hermann Beckh (1875-1937), lawyer, philosopher of language, musician, Christian priest, all-round universal scholar—*ein Original,* as the Germans would say—originally trained in Law, but as a circuit-judge was soon disillusioned. He gave it up to focus on ancient Indian languages, particularly Sanskrit; soon he was appointed Professor of Oriental Studies at the prestigious Humboldt University in Berlin. In 1911 he attended a lecture on Elijah given by Rudolf Steiner which changed his life—in article No. 21 (1925), he expressed this encounter: '*To meet Rudolf Steiner is to become acquainted with the living word ... To awaken through this word means to find the forces that hitherto slumbered in depths of the soul, and then through one's own will to use these forces consciously.*'

In 1920, disappointed with the narrow academicism at the university, Beckh resigned his position resolving to work as a freelance lecturer in anthroposophy. Later he joined the founding of The Christian Community, which he experienced as the goal of his life. The group photograph of ordinands on page 3 is revealing— Beckh is sitting right at the back, slightly detached from the main group '... as if leading from behind?' says the caption. Another way of saying it is that his writings are also for posterity, which could be our present. The fact is, he was never allotted a congregation, although he assisted in Dresden and elsewhere, but was assigned by Friedrich Rittelmeyer to lecture at the new Seminary in Stuttgart. There he inspired a generation of priests and lived in his own attic apartment, affectionately known by everyone as 'The Professor'.

This substantial volume of 642 pages contains a staggering 70 + individual articles grouped under various subjects, of which 14 are posthumous publications appearing after Beckh's death in 1937. Grouped chronologically, each year is preceded by a brief but informative editorial of the *Sitz im Leben* of The CC in Germany, together with events in the Anthroposophical Society, and later references to the developing difficulties under the rise of National Socialism. *Collected Articles* can be grouped into: (a) 'Word and Language in the Light of Anthroposophy'—16 articles starting with the principle of the Primordial Word and forming links with the Indian languages, Hebrew, German, English and others. Beckh's mastery of word-association is particularly revelatory; (b) 25 articles cover his very thorough insights into Buddhism, the Rig Veda and other texts, and in particular the relationship of the Buddha and his last pupil Ananda, who failed to ask the vital question. In retrospect, as Beckh clearly relates in several articles, it was inevitable that the Buddha was not to unite with the Earth but to attain *nirvana*; he died some 500 years before Christ—who *was* destined to remain united with the Earth, making the Buddha the great forerunner of this future 'Turning Point of Time'. (c) Christology and The Christian Community are described in more than a dozen articles, including the groundbreaking first draft of 'the cosmic rhythm' in Mark's Gospel. (d) Goethe, Novalis, Wagner, Nietzsche (in relation to his *Zarathustra*) and other literary figures are discussed, some in book reviews written for the monthly journal '*Die Christengemeinschaft*'. Finally, Beckh gives us astonishing insights into the esoteric background to the fairy-tale 'Snow White'; his own delightful children's story 'The Little Squirrel, the Moonlight Princess and the Little Rose' ends this impressive collection.

As one would expect from such a thoroughly prepared volume, the helpful notes are extensive; a list of Beckh's other works and publications is also given. Consequently, *Collected Articles* must rank as one of the most important collections of writings by any largely unpublished author in recent times. A higher price, perhaps, than some anthroposophical publications, but indisputably worth the outlay; the abundant material surveyed from so many facets will enormously reward all efforts to absorb it. And not to forget mentioning Beckh's own pick of articles published in *From the Mysteries—Genesis—Zarathustra* (TL 2020), as well as items from the literary estate, *Hermann Beckh: Celebration* (forthcoming).

Review by Michael Jones

The Song of the Earth (1935)

Hermann Beckh

Source: http://idb.ub.uni-tuebingen.de/opendigi/thlb_056_1935#p=57 (here in English translation)

Concerning his translation of the Hymn to the Earth (Atharva Veda XII, 1), the author himself says that he wrested it from an extraordinarily difficult original text in long, arduous toil and, despite all his efforts to grasp the exact meaning of the words, tried at the same time to give the whole thing the poetic and artistic form that the poetic momentum of the original text demands. One must concede that it is a poetic achievement. I question whether his interpretation of the Hymn is correct in every respect. He interprets it in the sense of The Christian Community's conception of Christ, following the example of Rudolf Steiner. The anthroposophical interpretation already emerges in the explanations, but especially in the Appendix, 'The Name of Christ and His Being in the Atharvaveda Hymn'. I know that the author considers the way of his interpretation to be a deeper science, and he may apologetically smile at my lack of spirituality, when I tell him that it's not really a science, just a more or less ingenious gimmick. But I cannot judge otherwise.

Review by Schomerus, Halle a. S., Journal of Theological Literature

Kalidasa's Meghaduta

Hermann Beckh

With these two papers. Dr H. Beckh introduces himself into the academic world. The last-named publication he has recently presented as his thesis to the University of Berlin; he has subjected the Tibetan translation of Kalidasa's Meghaduta to a most careful and minute study.

In the first treatise he gives a critical edition of the text in Tibetan characters based on a comparison of the three Tanjur copies of St Petersburg, Berlin, and London, and accompanied by an elaborate array of critical notes. Then follows a literal translation after the Tibetan text, which is very instructive, as the author has added in parentheses many Tibetan-Sanskrit equivalents and imparts full explanations of many poetical phrases and compositions, from which Tibetan lexicography will obtain a rich harvest. These results, the author promises to work up in a third paper.

In the second contribution he is engaged in the question as to what can be learned from the Tibetan version regarding the Sanskrit text. Of primary importance here, of course, is an inquiry into the time when this translation was made. The epoch of the translators named in the colophon is thus far unknown, but from internal evidence the conclusion is warranted that the Tibetan Meghaduta refers to the 13c CE. One of the most interesting results of Dr Hermann Beckh's investigation is that the Tibetans were not acquainted with the commentary of Mallinatha. In many respects this Meghaduta translation is greatly distinguished from the usual method of Buddhist texts, being extraordinarily free and skilful. The author lays stress on the understanding with which the translator has grasped, upon the whole the thoughts of Kalidasa, and reproduced in his language the intricate style of the Mahakavaya. Among the various Sanskrit editions, the Tibetan version stands nearest to that of Wilson (Calcutta, 1813), and is farthest removed from that of Mallinatha, but it cannot be looked upon as the genuine and original text of Kalidasa, as doubtless unauthentic stanzas have been received into it. The independence of the translation renders it difficult to establish confidently the Sanskrit reading which may have crossed the mind of the Tibetan. Dr Beckh scrutinizes all cases with an almost microscopic analysis, and dwells on the passages where the Tibetan version harmonizes with Wilson and the Singhalese edition against Mallinatha.

Altogether the merits of the author's most thorough and painstaking work, on which he deserves hearty congratulations, can hardly be overestimated, and it is not too much to say that it presents the best that has been done for years in the line of Tibetan philology. No one who takes an interest in Kalidasa can pass by his investigation, and no student of Tibetan language and literature should neglect to work through this text with his translation and notes, which will reveal to him an entirely new and unsuspected form of this interesting idiom. We also wish to express our undisguised satisfaction at welcoming in Dr Beckh a new worker in this woefully neglected field and one who bids fair to advance its cause by the intelligence and quality of his work. We take the opportunity of calling his attention to the Tibetan version of Açvaghosha's Buddhacarita in the Tanjur, which would well repay a complete edition and translation. Several have begun to cope with it; the late Dr Wenzel was the first to lay hands on it, and the late Dr Huth kept the same plan in mind. I myself then studied a great portion of the work, when other duties called me away from it, with bare chance of the hope of resuming it, but I am convinced I do not err in cherishing the belief that Dr Beckh is the right man for this task.

Review by B. Laufer, The Monist. Vol. 17, No. 4 (October, 1907).

[Berthold Laufer (1874-1934), an anthropologist and historical geographer with an expertise in East Asian languages.]

Notes

1 H.B., *The Language of Tonality* (Anastasi 1915 ed.), p, 59.
2 See, *Die Christengemeinschaft*, 14. Jg. April 1937, Eng. trs. by A.S. in: *Hermann Beckh and the Spirit-Word*. Anastasi 2015 (out of print).
3 Gottfried Husemann, Die Begründung der Christengemeinschaft. In 'Mitteilungen ...' Heft 22, 1952. Reprinted in: *Erinnerungen an Rudolf Steiner*, Gesammelte Beiträge aus den 'Mitteilungen aus der anthroposophischen Arbeit in Deutschland' 1947-1978. Ed. Erika Beltle u. Kurt Vierl. Stuttgart: Verlag Freies Geistesleben. 1979. 306. Eng. tr. in *H.B. and The Spirit-Word*, Anastasi, 2015, 157-59.
4 Vorwort to *Neue Wege zur Ursprache*, Stuttgart 1954, p. 5.
5 *The Language of the Stars* began as a series of 'Contributions' to the *Priests' Newsletter*, 1930-1933. Beckh intended to revise it for publication, but circumstances and his death prevented this from happening until the English translation was published by TL 2020.
6 Edwyn Clement Hoskyns, ed. Francis Noel Davey, *The Fourth Gospel*, London, Faber & Faber [2]1947.
7 E.C. Hoskyns, *Cambridge Sermons*, SPCK 1938, 70.
8 Aleksandr Solzhenitsyn's Nobel Prize lecture (1970) is available online: https://www.nobelprize.org/prizes/literature/1970/solzhenitsyn/lecture/#:~:text=ONE%20WORD%20OF%20TRUTH%20SHALL,writers%20of%20the%20whole%20world.
9 Illust. from *Wikipedia: https://www.rigpawiki.org/index.php?title=Twelve_deeds*
10 Original held in the Rudolf Steiner Nachlass, Dornach, Switzerland. Eng. tr. M. & A. Stott.
11 O.S. = Rudolf Steiner, *An Outline of Occult Science/ Esoteric Science*, GA13.
12 *Priester-Rundbrief* No. 68, 04 Nov. 1926, 14-17. Eng. trans. A.S.
   In his descriptions of the 'cosmic rhythm' in the gospel, Beckh goes to some length to explain the zodiac through relationships of squares, or crosses (in steps of three on the circle) and triangles (steps of four). His description of the 12-pointed star (steps of five) is much briefer (*Mark's Gospel*, TL 2021, 33f); this relationship is presented once more in *The Language of the Stars* (TL 2020, 276f). The present contribution clarifies the 12-pointed star, with some welcome details—*Ed.*
13 An unpublished article in typescript, held in the Zentralarchiv der Christengemeinschaft, Berlin, Eng. trans. by A.S.
14 More details on this concept in a further article. [A possible reference to a projected series. The present article (no date) reads like an introductory fragment—*Ed.*]

15   http://resources.ipsissima-verba.org/documents/extraordinary-form-order-of-mass-all-draft-9.pdf

16   What we are discussing here is more the form of worship, the form of the Apocalypse, rather than its actual content. Consequently, we forego entering into details. Yet to give at least *one* example: at the first trumpet, when it is said how 'all green grass was burned up' [8:7], we can think of these images of the breath of materialism that passes over the earth in such a way that all the germs of sprouting spiritual life are suffocated. Wherever this breath blows, we feel that 'grass no longer grows'. [H.B.]

17   One would need, as Novalis did in his linguistic *Fragments*, different degrees of translation [...]—*H.B.*   Novalis, *Fragment* No. 68:
'A translation is either grammatical, or modifying, or mythical.
Mythical translations are translations of the highest kind. They represent the pure, perfected character of the individual work of art. They do not give us the real work of art but the ideal of it. There still does not exist, I believe, a complete example of such a translation. But in the spirit of many a critique and description of works of art clear signs are to be found. A mind is needed where the spirit of poetry and the spirit of philosophy have saturated each other in all their fullness. Greek mythology is in part such a translation of a national religion. The modern Madonna too is such a myth.
Grammatical translations are translations in the usual sense. They require a great deal of learning—but only discursive abilities.
Modifying translations, if they are to be genuine, demand the highest poetic spirit. They easily slip into travesty-like Bürger's Homer in iambics—Pope's Homer [in rhyming couplets]—all French translations. The true translator of this kind must indeed be an artist himself and be able to produce the idea of the whole at will in one way or another. He must be the poet of the poet and thus be able to let him speak according to his own and the poet's idea at the same time. [FN: For Novalis, a truly poetic translation demonstrates the kind of critical reflection needed for Romantic creativity, hence his belief that the translator must be 'the poet of the poet'. He approved neither of the poet Bürger's attempt at translating Homer into German iambics (1771), nor of Pope's translations into heroic couplets made fifty years earlier.]
The genius of humanity stands in a similar relation to each single person. Not only books but everything can be translated in these three ways.'
(Novalis, *Philosophical Writings*, Translated and edited by Margaret Mahny Stoljar. State University of New York Press, 1997, 33f. Download: https://ia601404.us.archive.org/23/items/novalis-philosophical-writings/novalis-philosophical-writings.pdf)

18   This sentence is from H.B. 'The Apocalypse & the ACM', also kept in the *Zentralarchiv* (see previous article)—*Tr.*

19   Rudolf Frieling's study of the Creed, completely approved by Beckh, appeared in the priests' *Rundbrief*. Eng. trans. in H.B. and F.R., *The Language of the Stars*, TL 2020, 345-443.

20   We recall the story of Manoah (Judges 13), where the angel of annunciation says, 'Why do you ask my name, seeing it is wonderful?' 'Wonderful' is simply *phel'ī*: 'secret'. Cf. Isa. 9:6—*Ed.*

21   Lawrence A Waddell, *The Buddhism of Tibet, or Lamaism*, London 1895. Online: https://archive.org/details/buddhismoftibeto00wadd/ page/114/mode/2up/ See also Wikipedia article: Laurence Waddell.

22   Unrevised lecture notes dated 31 May 1927, from a typescript held by the Zentralarchiv der Christengemeinschaft, Berlin. Eng. trans. from the German by M. & A.S. 2023.

23   Lecture notes, dated 7 June, 1927, unrevised by the lecturer; typescript kept in the files of Zentralarchiv der Christengemeinschaft, Berlin. Eng. trans. M. & A. Stott, 2023.

24   https://www.friedrich-schiller-archiv.de/gedichte-schillers/highlights/die-kuenstler/

25   Rudolf Steiner similarly describes the musical motifs Schiller experienced prior to poetic composition:
'First of all an undefined melodic motif was living in his soul, something musical, upon which the words were arranged like a string of pearls. In this way he attached the prose words to the musical motifs.'
 Lecture, Penmaenmawr, 26 August 1923, in *Eurythmy as Visible Speech*, RSP 2019, 178—*Tr. note.*

26   *Privatdozent*; no direct equivalent term in English. Beckh was a professor without a chair—*Ed.*

27   Rudolf Steiner, *Knowledge of the Higher Worlds* [GA 10]. Chapter 6, 'Some Results / Effects of Initiation'.

28   *Privatdozent* refers to Beckh's position as 'extra-ordinary Professor without a chair'—*Ed.*

29   The final lines of Fr. Schiller's, *Wallenstein's Camp (Wallensteins Lager)*. Sc. 11, Chorus. Tr. James Churchill.

30   Beckh's article 'Schneewittchen' appeared in *Die CG*, Aug. 1924, 138-46. Eng. tr. in *Collected Articles 1912-1938*, TL 2023, No. 15, 118-30, also *Alchymy*, TL 2019, 114-26.

31   'Our Lady's Little Glass'. Legends for Children, No. 7. The Brothers Grimm:
Once upon a time a wagoner's cart which was heavily laden with wine had stuck so fast that in spite of all that he could do, he could not get it

to move again. Then it chanced that Our Lady just happened to come by that way, and when she perceived the poor man's distress, she said to him, 'I am tired and thirsty, give me a glass of wine, and I will set your cart free for you.'—'Gladly,' answered the wagoner, 'but I have no glass in which I can give you the wine.' Then Our Lady plucked a little white flower with red stripes, called field bindweed, which looks very like a glass, and handed it to the driver. He filled it with wine, and then Our Lady drank it, and in the self-same instant the cart was set free, and the wagoner could drive onwards. The little flower is still always called Our Lady's Little Glass.

32   Alfred Meebold [1863-1952], *Der Weg zum Geist. Versuch einer Seelenbiographie*. München: Piper & Co. 1917.

33   In this letter the sign for Mercury always contains this dot in the circle—*Ed.*

34   A window consisting of four panes of glass is pictured—*Ed.*

35   Usually taken as dark blue—*Ed.*

36   Beckh appears to use the 'new' German edition (1913)—*Ed.*

37   Johann Wolfgang Goethe. 'Über den Granit'. Münchner Ausgabe. Bd. 2.2. München: Hanser 1987. Granit II, pp. 503-507.

38   Ref. untraced—*Ed.*

39   2 Cor. 5:2-4; cf. Rom. 13:14; 1 Cor. 15:54; Gal. 3:27—*Ed.*

40   John 19:38.

41   John 19:30.

42   Hermann Heisler (1876-1962), a counterpart to Rittelmeyer, who—in Steiner's words—was the 'martyr' of the foundation of The Christian Community—*Ed.*

43   *Die Christengemeinschaft*, März 1967. 79-82.

44   Rudolf Meyer, *The Wisdom of Fairy Tales*, Edinburgh: Floris Books 1988/95. Rudolf Meyer, *Die Weisheit der Schweitzer Märchen*. Schaffhausen: Columban-Verlag 1944. Time and again the reader comes across acknowledgements that yet fail to reappear in the books and studies by those people Beckh inspired. No doubt he would be pleased that others—for example, like Meyer, one of his followers in the Seminary—find their destiny in standing for what they do (Lk. 17:10). The price seems to be that Hermann Beckh himself has tended to become forgotten by later generations precisely in his spiritual stature (cf. Lk. 10:20)—*Tr. note.*

45   From: Newsletter, Prague, in *Rundbrief* 'In Memoriam Hermann Beckh'. May 1937. 34f.

46   Cf. Rudolf Steiner, *True and False Paths* … (GA 243). Lecture Torquay, 22 August 1924. All published translations of the passage on music at the end of this lecture-course are faulty. For an accurate tr. of the passage see the Appendix in Lea van der Pals, *The Human Being as Music*, Anastasi 2014. 120-23.

47 From: *Rundbrief, In Memoriam Hermann Beckh*. Mai 1937. 31f.

48 From *The Christian Community Journal*, March 1938, vol. 7, 65-75 (slightly edited A.S.). Dr Heidenreich was a founder priest of The Christian Community. With Marta Heimeran (1895-1965), he brought this 'Movement for Religious Renewal' to the British Isles. The story is told in Alfred Heidenreich, *Growing Point*, Edinburgh: Floris Books 1979—*Tr.*

49 No other mention of a visit to England seems to exist, rendering this statement questionable.

50 *Die Christengemeinschaft*, April 1937, p. 20.

51 Beckh's biographer claims it took place during a summer school in Zürich—*Tr. note.*

52 From *Mitteilungen aus der anthroposophischen Arbeit in Deutschland*, Johanni 1975, pp. 139-41.

53 Kurt von Wistinghausen (1901-1986), a founder priest of The Christian Community who also lived in Urachhaus during those early years. He edited *Die Sprache der Tonart (1937)* for the press—*Ed.*

54 From the motto of *Alchymy: The Mystery of Substance* (Germ. ed. Basel 1931). Eng. tr. TL 2019. 'Our Origin in the Light: Pictures from Genesis', in *From the Mysteries*, TL 2020.

55 Hermann Beckh, *Der Mensch und die Musik*. Chapters I, II, and parts of Chapter XI were first made available to the public in *Der Europäer* in 2005 (Vol. 9, Nos. 9/10), 2006 (Vol. 10, Nos. 9/10) and 2007 (Vol. 12, Nos. 2/3). English tr. of the complete text, *The Mystery of Musical Creativity: The Human Being and Music*, tr. & ed. by A.S. TL 2016, with extra material. Both quotations from Chapter I.

56 This was achieved in another way by Hermann Pfrogner in *Lebendige Tonwelt* (Munich 1976) and by Christoph Peter in *The Language of Tonality: Mozart's 'The Magic Flute'* (Germ. ed. Stuttgart 1983/97); Eng. tr. A.S. Anastasi 2014. (TL forthcoming.)

57 Hermann Beckh, 'From my Life', memoirs reprinted in: Gundhild Kačer-Bock, *Hermann Beckh: Life and Work* (Germ. ed. Stuttgart 1997, 87), TL 2016, 59.

58 Hermann Beckh, *Von Buddha zu Christus*, Stuttgart 1925. 96f. Eng. tr. *From Buddha to Christ*, TL 2019. 'Schneewittchen', in *Die Christengemeinschaft*, Vol. 1, 1924, No. 5. Eng. tr. 'Snow White' in *Collected Articles 1922-1938*, No. 15, TL 2023, 118-30. Also, in *Alchymy*, TL 2019, 114-26.

59 Eng. tr. in *John's Gospel: The Cosmic Rhythm—Stars and Stones*. Anastasi 2015, 459–77. TL 2021, 358-72, also *Alchymy: The Mystery of the Material World*, TL 2019, 100-13.

60 New German edition 2011 by Thomas Meyer, Perseus-Verlag, Basel. We would like to draw readers' attention especially to the postscript.

61   The letters from Hermann Beckh to Gertrud von Hohnhorst written in Sütterlin handwriting are kept in the Zentralarchiv der Christengemeinschaft, Berlin.

62   Germ. Original in *Die CG*, 1938/39, 242ff; 78, 55ff.

63   In his *Die Taten der Apostel: Zur Apostelgeschichte des Lukas*, Stuttgart: Urachhaus 1992, Johannes Lenz notes how the silent John supports Peter. In his cartoon of the healing of the lame man (V & A Museum, London), the painter Raphael depicts how 'John with his right hand points in blessing towards the lame man sitting on the ground, whereas Peter is active with both hands' (34). In his studies on the gospel, Beckh particularly emphasizes the profound supportive role John plays in the early Church—A. S.

64   H. Beckh (1931). *Vom Geheimnis der Stoffeswelt (Alchymie)*. Basel: Rudolf Geering, p. 79. English translation in H. Beckh (2019). *Alchymy: The Mystery of the Material World*. TL, p. 64.

65   H. Beckh (1922). *Anthroposophie und Universitätswissenschaft*. Breslau: Verlag Preuss und Jünger. English translation, 'Anthroposophy and University Knowledge', in H. Beckh (2019) *The Source of Speech*. TL, 181-207. This lecture, challenging the contemporaneous academic world by suggesting what anthroposophy could contribute, was presented to the University of Berlin on 30 November 1921.

66   A personal memory of the occasion in 1918 by Rudolf Meyer: In memoriam Hermann Beckh, in 'Rundbrief in memoriam Hermann Beckh', typescript A186, Nr. 186, May 1937. We are indebted to Rudolf Gaedeke for supplying this text from the *Zentralarchiv der Christengemeinschaft*, Berlin. Eng. tr. above pp. 127-31.

67   Novalis (1997). Miscellaneous Observations, 17, in M.M. Stoljar (ed. and trans.) *Novalis. Philosophical Writings*. Albany: State University of New York Press, p. 25.

68   W. Blake (1972) *Blake: Complete Writings*. Edited by Geoffrey Keynes. Revised edition. Oxford: Oxford University Press, pp. 793-94.

69   H. Beckh. *Alchymie*, op. cit., p. 86; Eng. tr. 69.

70   See e.g. W. Pagel (1982) *Paracelsus. An Introduction to Philosophical Medicine in the Era of the Renaissance*. 2nd, revised ed. Basel: Karger, pp. 65-9.

71   Fr. G. von Hohnhorst (1937) in *Rundbrief*, op. cit., p. 12, Eng. tr. above pp. 163-67. Hermann Beckh's own recollections appear in G. Kačer-Bock (1997). *Hermann Beckh Leben und Werk*. Stuttgart: Urachhaus, pp. 65-6; Eng. tr. pp. 43-4.

72   Hermann Beckh's life and work within The Christian Community, 1922-37, coincides with the period which witnessed both the rise of form-criticism following the publication of Rudolf Bultmann's *History of the Synoptic Tradition*, 1921, and the Christian applications of I-Thou principles developed by Ferdinand Ebner in *The Word and the Spiritual Realities*, 1921.

73   H. Beckh (written 1931?) On Steiner und Buddha: Neubuddhistische Geistesströmungen und Anthroposophie. This article originally written for the *Zeitschrift für Buddhismus* but not published, exists as a typescript made from Beckh's own Sütterlin handwriting by G. Kačer-Bock. English translation in H. Beckh (2016) *Collected Articles 1922-1938*, No. 51, TL 2023, 434-50.

74   These include a lecture for the Schopenhauer Society presented on 8 July 1927. Reduced version H. Beckh (1927) in *Fünfzehntes Jahrbuch der Schopenhauer-Gesellschaft für das Jahr 1928*. Intro. Hans Zint. Heidelberg: Carl Winter's *Universitätsbuchhandlung*, 1928; and, H. Beckh (1933) Anthroposophie, epistemologische Grundlage für die Astrologie, in *Astrologie 1933. Vorträge und Bericht des XII. Astrologen-Kongresses* Stuttgart 1933. Herausgegeben im Auftrage der Astrologischen Zentralstelle E.V. von Dr Hubert Korsch, Düsseldorf 1933. pp. 67-9, 69-71. English translation of both articles in *Collected Articles*, op. cit., Nos. 38 & 52. Our gratitude to Alan Stott tracing these articles.

75   Diether Lauenstein, 'Nachwort des Herausgebers', in Hermann Beckh, *Der Hingang des Vollendeten*. Stuttgart: Verlag Urachhaus. 1960. 177.

76   Alfred Heidenreich, *The Christian Community Journal*, March 1938, 66f. Reprinted in *Hermann Beckh & the Spirit-Word*. Anastasi, 170. See also pp. 138-49 above.

77   Friedrich Rittelmeyer, *Die Christengemeinschaft*. April 1937. 20. Eng. trans. in *Hermann Beckh & the Spirit-Word*. Anastasi. 129.

78   A colleague from Tibetology at Göttingen University recently appreciated Beckh as one of the great pioneers of the discipline whose contributions are still highly regarded.

79   Winternitz 1929, 3.

80   Winternitz 1929, 6. Hermann Beckh, *Der Hingang des Vollendeten*. Verlag der Christengemeinschaft. Stuttgart 1925.

81   Winternitz 1929, 29.

82   The book was taken from the market and copies were destroyed during the Nazi years. As a member of The Christian Community, Beckh was not a tolerated author; public interest in Buddhism during this time was not allowed. For more details, see Gundhild Kačer-Bock. *Hermann Beckh: Life and Work*. TL 2021.

83   This is not the place to explore the interface between publications such as Beckh's *Buddhismus* and the context of WWI or the subsequent inter-war years; however interesting such an exploration would be, it should be undertaken by someone with the necessary expertise.

84   Tilmann Vetter, *The Ideas and Meditative Practices of early Buddhism*. Leiden: Brill 1988: xv.

85   The reference is to *Hingang* (Eng. tr. *Departure* … TL 2023). Winternitz, 19.

86   This contribution by Katrin Binder originally appeared in *Festschrift* (2016) marking the centenary of the first edition of Beckh's *Buddhismus* (1916) and celebrating the publications of the English translation, alongside *The Mystery of Musical Creativity* and the translation of Gundhild Kačer-Bock's biography, *Hermann Beckh: Life and Work*. Further significant publications followed: *From Buddha to Christ* (2019), *The Departure of the Perfected One* (2023), several important essays in *Collected Articles 1922-1938* (2023) and *The Song of the Earth* (2024), for all which Dr Binder was in the lead as transcriber, translator and editor—*Ed.*

87   Rudolf Steiner, *The Gospel of St Luke* (GA 114), lecture 2. Basel, 16 September 1909.

88   Hermann Beckh, *Buddha und seine Lehre*, Stuttgart: Verlag Freies Geistesleben 1958/98/2012. 43. Eng. trans. *Buddha's Life and Teaching*, TL 2019, pp. 42-43. The account is from the Lalitavistara.

89   'In eurythmy the word becomes *movement*—and this movement *is speech.*' Zimmermann (2013), 12 (emphases in the original).

90   The encouraging words of Frank Teichmann (1937–2006) concerning my plans should not remain unmentioned. We were grateful for deep insights into the cultures of early Egypt and Greece. His efforts exceeded this to the training of thinking; he was able to stimulate others to think for themselves.
      The works of and with Frank Teichmann: http://www.geistesleben.de/urheber/frank-teichmann

91   The three lectures were reprinted together (Stuttgart 1954); Eng. trans. in: Hermann Beckh, *The Source of Speech*, TL 2019.

92   Kačer-Bock (1997), 30. Eng. tr. (2021), 18.

93   Ibid., 246: Letter to Rudolf Steiner of 24 Jan. 1916: '[...] I recognize precisely that what I have assimilated through your writings and lecture-cycles, also to deepen my Indian studies, is invaluable, and connections have become clear to me that earlier I could not have imagined.'

94   Ibid., 244.

95   The Christian Community was founded in 1922 as 'a Movement for Religious Renewal'. http://www.christengemeinschaft.org

96   Beckh (1954), 13.

97   Oliver Heinl refers to this *Fragment* of Novalis in his book *Einblicke in das Wesen der Sprache* (2013), stimulated by Hermann Beckh, as he himself reports (cf. *Nachwort*), 154.

98   Schulz (1981), 743.

99   Mauthner, Fritz (1912): Zur Sprachwissenschaft. http://www.textlog.de/31001.html/

100 Beckh (1954), 21.

101 *Rig-Veda. Das heilige Wissen Indiens* (2008), ed. & Intro by Peter Michel. Marix Verlag. Wiesbaden. VII.

102 All Sanskrit words are written in IAST: 'International Alphabet of Sanskrit Transliteration.'

103 The tradition of Vedic was recorded in 2003 by UNESCO in the collection of masterworks of the aural and immaterial heritage and in 2008 added to the list of the immaterial cultural heritage of humanity. http://www.unesco.org/culture/ich/en/RL/00062

104 'The above evidence suggests that the meaning of the word "Veda" underwent a development. […] "Veda" appears to have been used […] as an approximate synonym of mantra and brahman "sacred utterance".' Bronkhorst (1989), 132.

105 'Veda is the breathing of Brahmān' *Mukhopadhyaya* (1999), 126.

106 *anādinidhanaṃ brahmā śabdatattvam yad akṣaram |*
     vivartate ´rthabhāvena prakriyā jagto yataḥ | | 1 | | W. Rau (2002). *Bhartrharis Vākapadīya*, Stuttgart. 3.

107 Ibid., X.

108 Ibid., Verse 48, 12.

109 *'nityāḥ śabdārthasaṃbadhās tatrāmnātā maharṣibhiḥ'* Ibid., Verse 23, 7.

110 Padoux (1992), 7.

111 Geldner, K. F. (2008) [1](1951): *Rig-Veda Das helige wissen Indiens*. Wiesbaden, 248.

112 Bṛhaspati, the priest of the gods. In: Monier Monier-Williams: *Sanskrit-English Dictionary*. Clarendon Press, Oxford 1899, 737, coll. 1.

113 Geldner (2008), 249.

114 As can be recognized in the word itself: (Sanskrit, ऋषि, *ṛṣi*, from dṛṣ : to see).

115 M. Witzel (2007), 428.

116 Beckh (1954), 20.

117 Stenzler (1876-78) 17, Chap. 1: 'On the tenth day, the father of the woman lets her rise, feeds the Brāhmaṇas and gives the child the name.'

118 Steiner (1994), 146.

119 Reference on p. 3.

120 Beckh (1954), 18.

121 Cf. 18.

122 Peter Lutzker has described this theme in great detail in his book *Der Sprachsinn* (1996), in which he investigates the perception of speech as a sensory process.

123 On the meaning of Sphota, see: http://www.iep.utm.edu/bhartrihari/#H5

124 Beckh (1954), 22.

125 Beckh (1954), 35. Emphases added.

126   Dvija signifies 'twice born'. The following event is worth noting in connection with the above-described theme of name-giving. The teacher asks the name of his pupils, in order to follow this by giving him a new one. This name is whispered and immediately forgotten, like a fleeting baptism, for the new life waiting for him.
'This is followed by the giving of a new name, when the preceptor takes the right hand of the boy into his own and asks him his old name. The guru gives him a new name, which is only uttered at the time of this particular ceremony, and then promptly forgotten, the old one alone being used.' M.S. Stevenson (1920), 34.

127   Ibid., 59-60.

128   Geldner (2008), 235-36.

129   Rau (2002), Verse 164, 36-7.

130   Beckh (1954), 55-57.

131   Ibid., 56-7.

132   *anupāsitavṛddhānāṃ vidyā nātiprasīdati* Staal, Fritz (2008), *Discovering the Vedas.* 300. Frits Staal, philosopher, linguist and Indologist, began in 1975 to research and document the *Agnicayana* or Fire Sacrifice, a more than 3000-years-old Vedic ritual, the oldest ritual still practised today.

133   Hermann Beckh. *Buddha's Life and Teaching.* TL 2019.

134   Hermann Beckh, 'Etymology and the meaning of speech-sounds in the light of spiritual science', in *The Source of Speech.* TL 2019.

135   Hermann Beckh, *Die Beweislast nach dem Bürgerlichen Gesetzbuch.* Beck: München 1899. Download: http://dlib-pr.mpier.mpg.de/m/kleioc/0010/exec/books/%22103926%22

136   Hermann Beckh, 'The Physical and the Spiritual Origin of Speech' in *The Source of Speech.* TL 2019.

137   'The Hebrew letter *vau* … is the image of the most profound, the most inconceivable mystery; the knot which unites, or the point which separates nothingness and being … is the universal convertible sign, which makes a thing pass from one nature to another; communicating on one side with the sign of intellectual sense [*vau* as vowel], which is itself more elevated, and on the other, with that of material sense [*ayin*], which is only itself more abased.' *The Hebrew Tongue Restored*, tr. N.L. Redfield, Putnams 1921, 334.

138   Hermann Beckh, 'The Physical and the Spiritual Origin of Speech.' Lecture held June 1921 in Zurich.

139   Information on the Sumerian language is taken from the following sources: Delitzsch, Dr phil. Friedrich, *Smerisches Glossar*, Leipzig 1914; Black, J.A. Cunningham, G., Ebeling, J., Flückiger-Hawker, E., Robson, E., Taylor, J., and Zólyomi, G., *The Electronic Text Corpus of Sumerian Literature* (http://etcsl.orinst.ox.ac.uk/), Oxford 1998–2006; Friedrich,

Johannes, *Kurzgefaßtes Hethitisches Wörterbuch*. Heidelberg 1991; Halloran, John A, *Sumerian Lexicon*—Version 3.0. 1996–2009.

140 *Plays by August Strindberg*. Tr. Edwin Björkman. London: Duckworth & Co. 1912. https://archive.org/details/playsstrindbjork00striuoft/. Hermann Beckh also considers the episode in the 1921 essay 'Let there be Light'. English translation in *The Source of Speech*, TL 2019—*Tr. note*.

141 The 'four living creatures' [AV/KJV: beasts] τέσσαρα ζῷα also appear in Rev. 4:6. 'In the midst of the throne, and round about the throne, were four living creatures full of eyes before and behind'—*Ed*.

142 For Northrop Frye's early observations on the MS, see *Fearful Symmetry*, Princeton, 1947. The Liddell family later donated the MS to The British Museum. Yeats' transcripted text was published in *The Works of William Blake*, Quaritch 1893. A full photographic facsimile of the MS was published in *Vala or The Four Zoas*, ed. G.E. Bentley Jnr., Oxford University Press 1963. The line quoted here occurs at the top of the page marked '23' by Bentley.

143 A more expanded account is provided in J.J. Stoudt, *Jacob Boehme*, Wipf and Stock, Eugene 2004, 212-13; first edition Seabury Press 1957.

144 N.V.P. Franklin, 'His Most Hideous Pilgrimage, unpublished thesis', University of Wales 1979.

145 Fr. S. Bulgakov, *The Holy Grail and the Eucharist*, N.Y., Lindisfarne Books 1997.

146 Ibid., 33.

147 Ibid., 56.

148 Ibid., 33, 43.

149 Ibid., 45.

150 The English translation by Ruth and Hans Pusch of Rudolf Steiner's *Twelve Moods* (Spring Valley: Mercury Press) with 'A Satire' is also included in GA 277a, RSP 2019, pp. 73-5.

151 W.B. Yeats, *A Vision*, Werner Laurie, 1925, revised and expanded 1937, 1956.

152 Quoted by Yeats in the essay 'Swedenborg, Mediums, and the Desolate Places', 1914, to accompany Lady Augusta Gregory, *Visions and Beliefs in the West of Ireland*, which reached publication in 1920.

153 H.B., *John's Gospel: The Cosmic Rhythm—Stars and Stones*, tr. A.S., Anastasi 2015, 291; TL p. 222. Beckh here alludes to Albert Steffen's *Lebensgeschichte eines Jungen Mannes*, 126, which had appeared in 1928.

154 H.B. *The Language of Tonality in the Music of Bach to Bruckner*, Eng. trans. A.S., Anastasi 2015, 186-87; TL forthcoming.

155 Ibid.,185.

156 *The Mystery of Musical Creativity*, Chapter 8. Cf. Chapter 8, p. 70f.

157 Ibid., Chapter 12, from Schopenhauer's *Neue Paralipomena*.

158   The 'etheric cross' is discussed in Beckh's *Markus-Evangelium*, Rudolf
       Geering 1928, 32, Eng. trans. *Mark's Gospel*, TL 34, and in *Die Sprache der
       Tonart*, Stuttgart 1937, in the section on 'The Keys of the F-major Cross'.

159   *The Mystery of Musical Creativity*, Chapter 13.

160   Chr. Peter, *The Language of Music in Mozart's 'The Magic Flute'*, Eng. trans.
       A.S., Anastasi 2014, 356; TL forthcoming.

161   Ibid., 212.

162   Ibid., 219.

163   Typescript A186 'Rundbrief in memoriam Hermann Beckh'. Our thanks
       to Dr Gaedeke for supplying the information.

164   *The Holy Grail and the Eucharist*, op. cit., 34.

165   Engl. tr. by A.S., *Rests and Repetition in Music*, Anastasi 2014, 16.

166   The three lines of the Latin Trinitarian, Rosicrucian verse, using the
       simple Latin number-alphabet, yield three numbers that Bach uses as a
       structural device, particularly the numbers of bars of certain pieces (see
       Helga Thoene).

167   Helga Thoene (Düsseldorf) said in a telephone conversation concern-
       ing Hertha Kluge-Kahn's work, 'Ich habe es *gründlich* studiert'—'I have
       studied it *thoroughly*.'

168   Written in full, David 'the beloved' in Hebrew = 24 (R.M. Benson. *War-
       Songs of the Prince of Peace*. London: Murray 1901—a commentary on the
       Psalms in a class by itself).

169   28 is a *'numerus perfectus'*, a 'perfect number': the sum of all the numbers
       from 1 to 7; the sum of its factors: $1 + 2 + 4 + 7 + 14 = 28$. Wikipedia '28
       (Number)' points out further special mathematical features.

170   Percy Scholes, *The Listener's History of Music*, OUP. 1947/54/74, makes
       rudimentary observations. We note in addition that Prelude No. 1 com-
       pares with Bach's Prelude No. 1, *WTC* Bk. 1: e.g. Bach writes 35 bars; uses
       all 12 notes with 23 discords. Chopin writes 34 bars, uses all 12 notes (bb.
       12-21) and 24 discords.

171   *Chopin Complete Works*. I Preludes. Editors I.J. Paderewski, L. Bronar-
       ski and J. Turczyński. Instytut Fryderyka Chopina. Warsaw. 1949. On
       p. 65, the Commentary on b. 23 (an important esoteric number) may
       correctly justify the change to 'the altered root of the subdominant
       seventh chord of E-minor (A-C-E)', but of course it misses the point
       made in my text.

172   For practical purposes, I re-wrote No. 17, although I recognize Beckh
       aligns A♭-major to the Archer, the star-sign governing the Crucifixion in
       both Mark's and John's Gospel. Jukes, Bach (Nissen, Kluge-Khan) and
       Beckh find Last Supper events here. Washing the feet of the bride is part
       of Jewish marriage rituals. The inner story of Chopin's *Prelude* No. 17
       can indeed share the conception of Christ's marriage to humanity. Why

11 concluding bass primes *forte*? Perhaps because the positive symbolism of 11 = 6 + 5, the hierogamic (sacred) marriage?

173 The notes B-A-C-H, being adjacent, will obviously make the appearance of the motif questionable in a richly chromatic work. This observation, as abstract criticism, ignores the evidence of musical context, which is a tangible indication of the composer's intentions. Likewise, to argue that 'Chopin doesn't think like Bach' is to beg the question. Furthermore, the categories 'romantic', 'classical', etc, are too broad and relative to be of much critical use (for example, in Mozart's day, some of his slow movements were described as 'romantic'; Bach's rich and 'romantic' harmony is a commonplace …). Actual compositions in any case are not confined to systems of classification. Labels suggesting categories, however, are certainly useful in libraries and for those who make catalogues or arrange the shelves for commercial wares. However, the subject here, of celebrating the circle of fifths, has little to do with styles and genres and everything to do with the inherent musicality in all tonal music. Esoteric intention works with *the law of inverse proportion, the less obvious the creative principles, the more powerful the effects.* Of course, no clues are to be found in Chopin's letters, nor in Debussy's for that matter—lack of evidence here depreciates nothing of these meticulous craftsmen, who are the very opposite of their popular images. The issue is this: Chopin's *Preludes* sound spontaneous but are scrupulously fashioned. Indeed, many great composers were also renowned improvisers at the organ or piano, but their *written* compositions are the product of much toil. That craftsmanship goes further than conventional wisdom admits is the subject of intense research today (cf. the Introduction by A.S. to the English-language edition of Prof. Beckh's *The Language of Tonality*).

174 The keys of Chopin's *Nocturnes*, op. 27, 1 and 2 are C#-minor & Db-major respectively; listen to what happens in the silence *between* the C#-major ending of the first, to the Db-major opening of the second. The keys and opus number relate to Beethoven's C#-minor *Sonata*, op. 27, 2, the 'Moonlight' (the 3 movements are written in C#-minor, Db-major, C#-minor). In Chopin's 'Raindrop' *Prélude* this key-scheme is reversed: Db-major-C#-minor-Db-major.

175 L.H. finger 2 in No. 2 (Alla-breve = 2/2 = 2 minim beats to the bar) plays twice on every beat in every bar of the L.H. part. Prelude No. 2 in A-minor is usually hailed as the 'most original' creation of all Chopin's Preludes. Chopin takes over directly from the end of No. 1 and writes 14 bars of transition with modulations before arriving at A-minor. The insistent interval-pattern is supplied by the 'theme' of Bach's name (sounding in the minor like a 'Dies Irae' chant). Here Chopin is plainly 'improvising'

as he accesses the metamorphosis between the pieces and puts what he hears directly onto paper.

176   If so, then Chopin might be 'adding his own name' six times in No. 4 that has so much B-A-C-H in it: C-H appears in the treble 6 times, the number of letters in his name—though this ignores one, or even two instances appearing in the transition bar 12. Notice, however, the bass bb. 21-22. What would Schumann have made of these observations? His 'ABEGG Variations', op. 1, was written in 1830; 'Carnaval', op. 9, 'Little Scenes on four notes' of his name (the musical letters are S-C-H-A = E♭-C-B-A) was composed 1834-35; Chopin began work on his *Preludes* in 1831.

177   Rudolf Steiner, *Knowledge of the Higher Worlds* … (GA 10). Tr. G. Metaxa, rev. H.B. & L.D. Monges. New York: Anthroposophic Press 1947. 36. Tr. C. Bamford. Hudson N. Y.: Anthroposophic Press 1994, 39.

178   This triune conclusion arrived after reading Alfred Cortot, *In Search of Chopin*. London & New York: Peter Nevill 1951.

179   The pianist Walter Rummel, who premiered Debussy's *Preludes* Bk. 2 and the *Etudes*, reports:
      'I spent the afternoon today with Claude Debussy in his quiet study overlooking the Bois de Boulogne, which was steeped in a sunset haze. I asked him whether he was inspired to create in these terrible days of war and slaughter. He glared at me and abruptly replied: "I am never inspired; I am either well-disposed or badly disposed, but I am never inspired—composition to me is like this" (and he took his penknife and began to scratch on his blotter); a constant effort at working on a surface, trying to take off the outer matter and working through from the outer impression to the kernel.' Charles Timbrell, *Prince of Virtuosos: A Life of Walter Rummel American Pianist*. Lanham, Maryland/ Toronto/ Oxford: The Scarecrow Press 2005, 49.

180   Hermann Beckh, 'Rhythmical Events in the Gospel', in *Collected Articles*, No. 47, 411-17; also, in H.B., *Mark's Gospel*, TL 2021, 369-75; H.B., *John's Gospel*, TL 2021, 341-47. See also: 'Cosmic Ritual Experience in Humanity's Past and Future', in H.B., *CA*, No. 4, 59-64.

181   Hermann Beckh, *The Essence of Tonality*, TL 2022. The expanded account, *The Language of Tonality*, Anastasi 2015, is planned to be reissued TL 2025.

182   R. Steiner, *Art as Seen in the Light of Mystery Wisdom* (GA 275), Lect. 3, 30 Dec. 1914, RSP 1984, 37.

183   All English versions available online omit the title page. The translation of Michael Wilson includes the Preface to the first edition on pp. xxvii-xxx. In the later German editions (1918), Steiner incorporated the first Preface in the 'Second Appendix'. The above quotation appears there as the book's concluding words.

184   R. Steiner, *The Gospel of St John* (GA 103), lect. XII, Hamburg 31 May 1908. AP Spring Valley, 1962, 174f, emphases added.

185 R. Steiner, *Speech and Drama* (GA 304), lect. 3, Dornach 7 Sept. 1924, 68.

186 See the English edition of R. Steiner, *Eurythmy as Visible Singing* (GA 278), tr. and commentary by A.S. Appendix 9: 'A Right Balance between Heaven and Earth—Art as a WAY: the Way as ART', RSP 2019, 469-87. Germ. tr. in Stefan Hasler (Hg.), *Der Toneurythmiekurs von Rudolf Steiner*, Dornach 2014, 40-55.

187 R. Steiner, GA 278, lect. 3, 4, etc.

188 R. Steiner, *The Course of My Life* (GA 28). Chap XXXIII, concluding paragraph.

189 R. Steiner, *The Boundaries of Natural Science* (GA 322), lect. 8. AP/Steiner-Books 1987.

190 H. Beckh, *Collected Articles 1922-1938*, TL 2023. No. 53, 469-95.

191 Gundhild Kačer-Bock, *Hermann Beckh: Life and Work.* TL 2021, 115. Emphases added.

192 Hermann Beckh, *Collected Articles*, TL 2023. No. 47 (1930), 411-17.

193 R. Steiner, *The Book of Revelation and the Work of the Priest* (GA 346), RSP, 1998. 84, 104 & 237.

194 Regarding thunder, cf. the conversation with Sylvester in Novalis, *Henry von Ofterdingen*, Part 2, Dover Pub. 2015, pp. 123-25. Milo Mahan, 'Mystic Numbers', *Collected Works*, II, New York 1875, 218, advises:
'Numbers, in fact, symbolize principles rather than dogmas; they are suggestive rather than definitive; colourless in themselves, they readily assume the color of surrounding objects; having as it were, a negative and positive pole, their meaning takes a negative or positive hue according to the pole which happens to be presented.'

195 Friedrich Hiebel, *Entscheidungszeit mit Rudolf Steiner*, Dornach 1986, 392-402, three endnotes p. 436. (This exemplary essay is missing from the English translation, *Time of Decision*, SteinerBooks 1989.) Eng. tr. by A.S. in *Farther In*, No. 2, Dec. 2021, 33-9.

196 A. Stott, 'Rudolf Steiner's Written Style' in 3 instalments: *Farther In*, No. 2, 40-8; No. 3, 7-13; No 6, 18-26.

197 GA 278, lect. 3.

198 The theologian and trained musician Chr. Rau, *Struktur und Rhythmus im Johannes-Evangelium*, Stuttgart 1972, traces the remarkable artistic form of John's Gospel. Eng. tr. by A.S. currently seeking a publisher. Summarized in Chr. Rau, *The Four Gospels*, Lindisfarne Books 2024.

199 R. Steiner, 15 Sept. 1907. GA 101.

200 Cf. Sylvia Eckersley, *Number and Geometry in Shakespeare's Macbeth*, Edinburgh: Floris Books 2007.

201 Cf. E.W. Bullinger, *The Companion Bible*, Oxford 1909-1921, currently Kregel Grand Rapids. On the literary form of the gospels, see especially

Christoph Rau, op. cit. where each centre is identified and the stages leading to it and from it.

202   'In the seven days of the week the soul experiences its own rhythm.' Wilhelm Hoerner, *Zeit und Rhythmus*, Urachhaus, Stuttgart 1991; after R. Steiner, Berlin, 2 Jan. 1909, in GA 107; the 'I' is related to the number one, the astral body to the number 7, the etheric body to 4 x 7 days, or the months; the physical body to the year.

203   See C.G. Jung, 'The Philosophical Tree', *Alchemical Studies*, Collected Works, Vol. 13, Princeton Univ. Press 1967/ Routledge & Kegan Paul, London 1968, 251-349.

204   *PoF*, tr. Wilson, 49; tr. Poppelbaum rev. (1939), 49; tr. Stebbing (1992), 47; tr. Lindeman, 57; tr. Lipson, 60.

205   She goes by a multitude of names. See Margaret Barker, *The Mother of the Lord*, Vol. 1, Bloomsbury, T&T Clark 2021; and Part 2, *The Great Lady: Restoring her Story*, Sheffield Phoenix Press 2023.

206   The lecture-title of 2 Dec. 1922, 'Human expression through music and speech' is missing in the English translation, in *The Inner Nature of Music and the Experience of Tone*, AP 1983. Beckh's repeat lecture in Stuttgart would seem to have been given in October, possibly November, of that year.

207   Further research would address such issues of terminology and traditions. To assist serious work, new editions of 'the basic books' are called for with revised layout (German originals), and for revised English translations (to retain the sentence order). Files are already prepared in both languages, the sentences simply arranged to show both chiastic rhythms of 7 and of 12.

208   Regarding Bach, see: Hertha Kluge-Kahn. *Johann Sebastian Bach: Die verschlüsselten theologischen Aussagen in seinem Spätwerk*. Wolfenbüttel u. Zürich: Möseler Verlag. 1985.
Hans Nissen. Der Sinn des 'Wohltemperierten Klaviers II. Teil'. *Bach-Jahrbuch* 1951-52. 54-80. Online:
https://doi.org/10.13141/bjb.v19521567/ (Some typos are apparent, e.g. numbers of bars.)
Helga Thoene. To date, Frau Thoene has published detailed analytical studies on the G-minor Sonata (*Cöthener Bach-Hefte 6*, Veröffentlichungen des Historischen Museums Köthen/Anhalt 19. Köthen, 1994), *D-minor Chaconne* (Dr ziethen verlag, Oschersleben 2003), the A-minor, (2005) & C-major Sonatas (2008).

209   From 'In the Power of Sound'; 1828, pub. 1835.

210   Cf. 'It is when the word is added to the element that the sacrament results as if itself also a kind of visible word.' Augustine (354-430), *On the Gospel of John* (Trac. 80.3).

211 More is meant than the usual term 'absolute music'. 'Pure music' here refers to what is inwardly heard, that is, the inherently expressive relationships of notes and rests before all questions of sensory manifestation—*A.S.*

212 Milo Mahan, *Collected Works*, Vol. 2, Pott, Young & Co, New York 1875, 223.

213 John Michell, *How the World is made … Sacred Geometry*, Thames & Hudson, London 2009, 79.

214 This article first appeared in H.B., *The Language of the Stars*, TL 2020, 503-20. A translation into German exists in MS awaiting a publisher.

215 For translated observations from friends and colleagues, see *Hermann Beckh and The Spirit-Word*, Anastasi, Leominster, 2015, p. 121ff.

216 In GA 61. See also: 'Meeting Rudolf Steiner', in H. Beckh, *Collected Articles 1922-1938*, No. 21,TL 2023, pp. 180-88.

217 The early illuminated print *'All Religions are One'*.

218 Or 'in the shadow / protection of God'.

219 Thus understood by Margaret Barker D.D. in several publications, including *Temple Mysticism: An Introduction*, SPCK, London, 2011, p. 33.

220 A reliable account is provided by Arthur Green's Introduction to *The Zohar*, Vol. 1, Stanford University Press, 2004, pp. xlvi-liii.

221 The title, appearing numerous times in the Books of Enoch to represent Messiah (the anointed one) is taken up by Isaiah 42:1-4 and applied to Jesus, Matthew 12:18.

222 Sammlung Göschen, Berlin, reprinted several times. See also the one-volume edition with Intro. by Heimo Rau, Freies Geistesleben, Stuttgart 2012. Eng. trans. by Dr Katrin Binder, *Buddha's Life and Teaching*, TL 2019.

223 Hermann Beckh, *Buddha's Life and Teaching,* Temple Lodge 2019, p. 10f.

224 *Anthroposophie*. Nr. 46. 17 May 1923. Eng. trans. in H.B., *Collected Articles 1922-1938*, No. 5, Temple Lodge 2023, pp. 65-8.

225 Preuss & Jünger, Breslau, 1923. Eng. trans. *The Essence of Tonality*, Temple Lodge 2022.

226 Edited with a Foreword by Rudolf Meyer, Urachhaus, Stuttgart; Eng. trans. 'Indology and Spiritual Science', in *The Source of Speech*, TL 2019.

227 The word encompasses a range of meanings, including 'mood', 'atmosphere', 'state of mind' as well as a musical key, pitch or tuning.

228 See also Neil Franklin, 'Up the Stairs', in *Festschrift: Essays in Honour of Hermann Beckh*, Anastasi, 2016, 181-212, reprinted here pp. 304-24.

229 Contribution X (RB 122, 17 May 1931); Eng. trans. included in H.B. *The Language of the Stars*, TL 2020, p. 141. See also pp. 149, 174f., 180, 192, 208, 226, 234.

230 See Gershon Weiler, *Mauthner's Critique of Language*, Cambridge University Press, 2009.

231 Jena, 1921, 2nd. ed. 1928.

232 Ellic Howe, *Uranias Kinder*, Weinheim 1995, p. 195.

233   Available in English as *The Etheric Formative Forces in Cosmos, Earth and Man: A Path of Investigation into the World of the Living*. Vol 1, translated by Olin Dantzler Wannamaker, 1932, Anthroposophic Press, New York.

234   Albert Steffen, *Mani*, Verlag für Schöne Wissenschaften, Dornach und Stuttgart, 1930.

235   Ibid., p. 51.

236   Margaret Barker, *Temple Mysticism*, op. cit., p. 57. For a thorough investigation into the subject of the Divine Feminine in the O.T., see the same author's *The Mother of the Lord: The Lady in the Temple*, Vol. 1, Bloomsbury T. & T. Clark, Lindon and N.Y., 2012, especially pp. 80 ff. and *The Great Lady: Restoring her Story*, Sheffield Phoenix Press Ltd, 2023.

237   In the French translation, *La Sagesse de Dieu*, trans. C. Andronikof, 'L'Age d'Homme', Lausanne, 1983, pp. 42-3.

238   In the Introduction to the Pritzker edition of *The Zohar*, Stanford University Press, Stanford, 2004, p. xlvi, Arthur Green emphasizes that the sequence of Sephiroth constitutes a circulating process. However, this need not be limited to a simple circle.

239   Briefly summarized by Gershom Scholem, *Major Trends in Jewish Mysticism*, Schocken, N.Y. 1995, p. 272.

240   *Temple Mysticism*, op. cit., p. 65.

241   See especially H. Beckh, *Ätherische Bildekräfte und Hieroglyphen*, Gäa Sophia, Bd.1, Beitrag 33, Oct. 1926 (Eng. tr. in *Collected Articles*, TL 2023, No. 31, 258-68); 'Das Neue Jerusalem' in *Gegenwartsrätsel im Offenbarungslicht*, Christus aller Erde, Band 16, Verlag der Christengemeinschaft, Stuttgart, 1925 (Eng. tr. in *John's Gospel*, TL 2021, 359-72; also, in *Alchymy*, TL 2019, 100-13); Schneewittchen, *Die Christengemeinschaft* Jg. 1, Nr. 5, Aug. 1924 (Eng. trans. 'Snow White', in *Collected Articles*, No. 15, 118-30; also, in *Alchymy*, 114-26).

242   H. Beckh, *Aus der Welt der Mysterien*, Rudolf Geering, Basel, 1927, 120. Eng. trans. *From the Mysteries*, TL 2020, 208f.

243   The complete text of the MS, newly transliterated from Beckh's Sütterlin handwriting by Dr Katrin Binder, trans. by Alan & Maren Stott, TL, 2019. Five chapters (in German) were published in three articles in *Der Europäer*, Basel 2005/06/07-08. http://www.perseus.ch/archive/category/europaer/europaer-archiv/.

244   *Buddha und seine Lehre*, op. cit., p. 219; Eng. trans., 205.

245   H. Beckh, *The Parsifal=Christ=Experience*, Anastasi, 2015, 109, out of print; also, in the double volume *The Essence of Tonality* with *The Parsifal-Christ-Experience*, TL 2022, 129.

246   G. Kačer-Bock, *Hermann Beckh: Life and Work*, Anastasi, 2016, 142f; rev. ed. TL 2021, 105f.

247   *Buddha und seine Lehre*, 185. Eng. trans. *Buddha's Life and Teaching*, 174.

248   Ibid., p. 39; Eng. trans., 38f.

249 H. Beckh, *Von Buddha zu Christus*, Verlag der Christengemeinschaft, Stuttgart, 1925. Eng. trans. of the complete text, with extra material, *From Buddha to Christ*, TL 2019.

250 The legends of the Queen of Sheba's bowl of beryl presented to Solomon and the jewel from Lucifer's crown had previously been brought together in H. Beckh, 'Maya. Das Weihnachtsmysterium im Indischen Blüten-garten', *Die CG*, Dez., 1924, 254-58 (Eng. tr. In *Collected Articles*, TL 2023, No. 18, 144-50). The presentation of the bowl is said to be depicted in an early stained-glass window in the Church of St Urban, Strasburg. See San Marte (pseudonym for A. Schultz), *Parcival, Rittergedicht von Wolfram von Eschenbach, Im Auszuge mitgetheilt von San Marte*, Magdeburg, 1832.

251 F.C. Oetinger, *Das Geheimnis von dem Salz*, Frankfurt and Leipzig, 1762 (reprint edition currently available). The unorthodox Lutheran theologian was much influenced by Böhme and Swedenborg. In all probability Beckh would have read Emil Bock's discussion of Oetinger in *Boten des Geistes*, Stuttgart 1929, when Beckh was writing his principal study of John's Gospel. Oetinger is frequently mentioned by R. Steiner as a significant pioneer for the reformation and renewal of Christianity.

252 H. Beckh, *Vom Geheimnis der Stoffeswelt*, Rudolf Geering Verlag, Basel, 1931, 19. Eng. tr. *Alchymy: The Mystery of the Material World*, TL 2019, 21.

253 Ibid., 125 and R. Steiner, *The Inner Realities of Evolution* (GA 132), Berlin, 31 Oct. 1911, lecture 1; see also R. Steiner, *Occult Science—An Outline*, Chap. 4, section on 'Ancient Saturn'.

254 Two letters contain references to Beckh's story for very little children 'The Little Squirrel, the Moonlight Princess and the Little Rose', first translated, with coloured illustrations by Tatjana Schellhase, published in *Festschrift: Essays in Honour of Hermann Beckh*, Anastasi 2016, 246-53; also *Hermann Beckh, Life and Work*, TL 2021, pp. 231-37; also without illustrations, *Collected Articles*, TL 2023, No. 72, 604-607—*Tr. note*.

255 The Editor especially thanks Rosemaria Bock for much of the following information—A.S.

256 From *Nachrichten für Mitglieder* Nr. 26/08, pp. 3-4.

257 Memories of Hermann Beckh's study and her visits to him at this period are found in Kačer-Bock, G. (1997). *Hermann Beckh: Leben und Werk*. Stuttgart: Urachhaus. Henceforth as LW. English translation, *Hermann Beckh: Life and Work*, TL 2021.

258 Weather details for West and Central Europe from www.Wettercentrale, de. For Britain and general overview of the very cold winter in 1929: booty.org.uk/booty.weather/climate/1900-1949.
   For the iron stove, *Kanonenofen*, see LW, 195.

259 Announcements of such conferences and lectures for this period were usually included in a loose page inserted in the periodical *Die Christengemein-*

schaft where they can sometimes be found today. Tracing Beckh's participation in the conferences is an area of research which has only begun.

260   Beckh, H. (1929). Das Indische Yoga. *Gäa-Sophia Jahrbuch der naturwissenschaftlichen Sektion der Freien Hochschule für Geisteswissenschaft am
Goetheanum*, Dornach. Band III, pp. 183-212. English tr. 'Indian Yoga',
in Hermann Beckh, *Collected Articles 1922-1938*, TL 2023, No. 46, 382-93.

261   Lichtensteinstrasse 10. LW, 192, Eng. tr. 136. Gundhild tells us also that
Hermann Beckh would have his meals there, and that 'later' he also slept
there. The latter may have been due to the need to accompany his mother
after the passing of his sister Marie. The house would have been some
five minutes' walk from the seminary.

262   See the publications, still valuable today: *Beiträge zur tibetischen Grammatik, Lexikographie, Stilistik und Metrik, in Abhandlungen der Königlich Preus-
sischen Akademie der Wissenschaften* (1908). Berlin: R. Pischel. Verzeichnis
der tibetischen Handschriften—1 Abt. Kanjur, in *Die Handschrftenverze-
ichnisse der Königlichen Bibliothek in Berlin, Bd. 24.* (1914) Berlin: Verlag
Behrend und Co. Reprints of both are readily available.

263   Most details presented in this paragraph are from LW, 21, Eng. tr. 11; LW,
55-87, Eng. tr. 36-59 reproduces Beckh's own account of his early years,
stressing his love of mountains and high land. The incident of supersensible experience is found on pp. 68-9, Eng. tr. 45-7.

264   This poetic offering of Hermann Beckh's surprised his six colleagues
who collaborated for the little volume on the Apocalypse, *Gegenwartsrätsel im Offenbarungslicht* ('Present-day riddles in the light of revelation'),
Verlag der Christengemeinschaft, Stuttgart, 1925, 105-21. Based on passages from the vision of John on Patmos we know as the Apocalypse
(Book of Revelation) concluding the New Testament, Beckh's poetic lines
(in iambic metre) may possibly owe something to passages from Victor Hugo's (1802-85) gigantic dream-vision *La Légende des Siècles*. Beckh
himself acknowledges the holistic visions and thoughts of the spiritual-scientific fragments of Novalis. My thanks to Alan Stott for this note,
taken from 'The New Jerusalem' in Hermann Beckh (2015) *John's Gospel*,
Anastasi, p. 459. TL 2021, 358 (also in *Alchymy*, TL 2019, 100-113).

265   Novalis, *Heinrich von Ofterdingen*, Chapter 9.

266   The relevant details here regarding Coleridge's interest in ice and the
frozen lake are taken from John Livingston Lowes (revised edition
1930), *The Road to Xanadu*. Quotations here are from the 1978 Picador
edition, 124-26. On Wordsworth and Coleridge travelling to Germany
and their stay in Hamburg see K.R. Johnston (1998). *The Hidden Wordsworth*. New York: Norton, Chapter 25. The full text of the letter to Sarah
is published in E.L. Griggs (editor) 1956. *Collected Letters of Samuel Taylor Coleridge*, Oxford: Clarendon Press, 459-70. Such was the impact of

the experience with the white and red ice at Ratzeburg that Coleridge adapted some details from the letter for publication in two issues of *The Friend* (Nos. 16 & 18, December 1809) and in *Biographia Literaria*, 1817, ii, 213-14 and 234-36.

267 H. Beckh (1921). *Der physische und der geistige Ursprung der Sprache*, Stuttgart. Reissued (1954) in *Neue Wege zur Ursprache*. Stuttgart, Urachhaus. For full bibliographic details and events surrounding the original lecture in Stuttgart on 7 September 1921, see H. Beckh (2021), *Hermann Beckh: Life and Work*, TL.

268 Four major books and 57 articles within this period have so far been located and edited for *The Complete Works of Hermann Beckh* (note written January 2016).

269 First issue of *Lucifer*, by H.P. Blavatsky, September 1887, London. *Luzifer* (R. Steiner) Berlin, June 1903. *Luzifer-Gnosis* (R. Steiner) first issue January 1904, Berlin.

270 The periodicals are *Die Christengemeinschaft* (*Die CG*), a monthly then edited by Friedrich Rittelmeyer. *Gäa-Sophia: Jahrbuch der Naturwissenschaftlichen Sektion der Freien Hochschule für Geisteswissenschaft am Goetheanum Dornach*, edited by Günther Wachsmuth 1926-1932. *Die Drei, Monatsschrift für Anthroposophie, Dreigliederung und Goetheanismus*, editorial board 1922-1935: Ernst Uehli, Jürgen von Grone, Kurt Piper, Emil Leinhas, Hans Erhard Lauer, Hans Büchenbacher, Carlo Septimus Picht.

271 See H. Beckh (1921). *Etymologie und Lautbedeutung im Lichte der Geisteswissenschaft*, reprinted in *Neue Wege zur Ursprache*. Stuttgart: Urachhaus 1954, 25, Eng. tr. in H. Beckh (2019) *The Source of Speech*, 112, and H. Beckh (1922) '*Wort und Sprache im Lichte der Anthroposophie*' in *Das Goetheanum* 1922-23, 252, Eng. trans. in *The Source of Speech*, 72.

272 H. Beckh (1924). *Der Ursprung im Lichte (Bilder der Genesis)*, Band 7 of *Christus alle Erde*. Stuttgart: Verlag der Christengemeinschaft, 23f. Eng. tr., 'Our Origin in the Light: Pictures from Genesis', in *From the Mysteries*, TL 2020, 5-53.

273 H. Beckh (1921). '*Es werde Licht*' *(Jehi ôr) Schöpfungsurworte der Bibel*. Stuttgart: Verlag Der Kommende Tag. Reissued in *Neue Wege* (1954), 104. Eng. tr. in *The Source of Speech*, TL 2019, 154. The article is based on a lecture Beckh gave in Zürich to 'university people' on 21 June, 1921, shortly after Rudolf Steiner had spoken there.

274 See *Tatchristentum* 1. Jg. 11. February 1924, 122-24. English translation in *Collected Articles 1922-1938*, TL 2023, No. 13, 106-10. *Tatchristentum* was the first monthly periodical for The Christian Community, running from 1923-24, edited by Fr. Rittelmeyer.

275 H. Beckh (1924). *Der Ursprung im Lichte*, op. cit., 31. Eng. tr. H. Beckh (2020), *From the Mysteries*, 25.

276   H. Beckh (1924). *Schneewittchen* in *Die CG* 1924, 145. English translation *Collected Articles 1922-1938*, TL 2023, No. 15, quotation p. 129. For the importance of Snow White in Beckh's life in the period generally in review, see LW 197-98, Eng. tr. 140f. The woodcut which he had in his study of Snow White is by Karl Thylmann 1888-1916: 1913 woodcut (30 x 32 cm) described as: *Über einer Baumlandschaft erhebt sich in der linken Bildhälfte ein Felsen. Obenauf befindet sich Schneewittchen im gläsernen Sarg, getragen von zwei Zwergen. Die Sargträger bilden den Abschluss des Zuges aus Zwergen, die die Felskuppe überqueren. Auf dem Sarg sitzen Vögel.* 'In the left part of the picture, rising above a wooded landscape, a hillside, on the top of which Snow White is seen in a glass coffin, borne by two dwarves. The coffin bearers form the end of a procession of dwarves who cross the top of the hillside. Birds are sitting on the coffin.'

277   H. Beckh (1924). *Maya. Das Weihnachtsmysterium Im Indischen Blütengarten, Die CG* (December) 1924, p. 254. Beckh regularly submitted seasonal articles for *Die Christengemeinschaft*. English translation as 'Queen Maya: the Christmas-Mystery in the Indian Flower-Garden' in *Collected Articles*, No. 18, 144-50.

278   G. Wachsmuth (1924). *Die ätherischen Bilderkräfte in Kosmos, Erde und Mensch. Ein Weg zur Erforschung des Lebendigen.* Stuttgart: Verlag Der Kommende Tag. Eng. trans., *The Etheric Formative Forces in Cosmos, Earth and Man*, London & New York 1932. Beckh was clearly impressed by Wachsmuth's discoveries that the four ethers left distinctive forms in substance which he (Beckh) could trace both in Egyptian hieroglyphs and in Sanskrit.

279   H. Beckh (1925). '*Buddhas Hingang*'. *Die Drei*, V. Jahrgang, März 1926, 917-34. Eng. tr., 'Buddha's Passing', in *From the Mysteries*, TL 2020, 185-201.

280   See especially H. Beckh (1926). 'Maria im Fernen Osten: Das Problem der Kuan Yin'. *Die CG* Jg. 2, Nr. 10, Jan. 1926. Eng. tr. in *Collected Articles*, No. 24, 199-201. This was a review of Richard Karuz (1925) *Maria im Fernen Osten*, Leipzig-Munich-Vienna: Otto Wilhelm Barth Verlag. Richard Karuz (1867-1945) was a professional ethnologist who originally studied medicine. He met Rudolf Steiner in 1920 and became a regular lecturer at the Goetheanum.

281   H. Beckh (1926). 'Sonne und Stern', *Die CG* Jg. 3, Nr 4, 1926, 97-9. Eng. tr. in *Collected Articles*, No. 27, TL 2023, 212-14.

282   H. Beckh (1926). '*Ätherische Bilderkräfte und Hieroglyphen*' in *Gäa-Sophia*, Bd. 1, Dornach, 383-93. English translation from *Collected Articles*, No. 31, TL 2023, 258-68.

283   H.K. Brugsch (1885). *Religion und Mythologie der Aegypter*. Leipzig: J. C.Hinrichs. 2nd edition 1891. Online text https://archive.org/details/religionundmyth02bruggoog

Heinrich Karl Brugsch (1827-94) held the prestigious position of Director of the School of Egyptology at Cairo, producing a substantial number of scholarly works concerned with ancient Egypt. Judging by the number of references included in his own publications, Hermann Beckh found Brugsch to be a reliable and inspiring source.

284 *Ätherische Bildekräfte,* op. cit., 388. English translation from *Collected Articles*, No. 31, TL 2023, 258-68.

285 Ibid., 392, Eng. trans., 267.

286 In common use today is M. Monier-Williams (2008). *Sanskrit-English Dictionary* (revised) Brown University, online. www.sanskrit-lexicon.uni-koeln.de/monier/

For *'sisira'* this provides: 'cool, chilly, cold, frigid, freezing; m.n. cold, coolness, hoarfrost, dew; the cool or dewy season (comprising two months, *Magha* and *Phalguna* or from about the middle of January to that of March); m.n. of the seventh month of the year; of a mountain.' My thanks to Dr Katrin Binder for this observation.

287 R. Falb (1883). *Das Land der Inka in seiner Bedeutung für die Urgeschichte der Sprache und Schrift.* Leipzig: J.J. Weber. Online at: https://archive.org/details/daslandderincai00falbg.

The inscription is said to be 'on an ancient Peruvian temple-monument, the prehistoric Sun-gate monument of Tiahuanaco on Lake Titicaca'. English translation from *Collected Articles.* The 'Gateway of the Sun' and the inscription can still be visited today. In the article under consideration, Beckh observes with scholarly rectitude that he is personally unable to confirm Falb's reading of the inscription (*Ätherische Bildekräfte,* op. cit., 392, Eng. trans., 266f.).

288 H. Beckh (1927) 'Berg Meru', in *Gäa-Sophia*, Vol. 2, Dornach 1927, 284-300.

As images of the 'ice-maiden' Beckh comments on Isolde and Brünhilde:

If we want to see in solid earthly form that which according to its inner nature is life-ether, sound-ether and cold light, we find in the *ice-crystal* the most expressive symbol for all this. Even in the word 'crystal' precisely the sounds of the Egyptian name of Isis (similar to those of the name 'Christ') are significantly contained. It may be added that we indeed also find the ice in Brünhilde original homeland Iceland, and furthermore in the name *Isolde*, that is related to Ishild (= Eishilde, Eisholde). Isolde is the bearer of the higher life-element in the Celtic Mysteries, which again is connected with the Egyptian Isis-Mysteries, as Brünhilde is the bearer of this element in the Teutonic Siegfried-Mystery.

English translation from *Collected Articles*, No. 37, 310-25.

289 H. Beckh, *Schneewittchen*, op. cit., 138. Eng. tr., *Collected Articles*, No. 15, 118-30, quotation p. 119.

290   H. Beckh, *Ätherische Bilderkraft*, op. cit., p. 392. English translation in *Collected Articles*, No. 31, TL 2023, 258-68.

291   H. Beckh (1925) 'Isis. Die Sternen Weisheit der Altägyptian Mysterien und ihre Zusammenhang mit Zarathustra' in *Die Drei*. 1925. Reissued in *Aus der Welt der Mysterien*, 1927, Basel: Verlag Rudolf Geering. Eng. trans. in H. Beckh (2020), *From the Mysteries*, TL, 150-69.

292   H. Beckh (1926). 'Zum Namen der Isis', *Die Drei*, 1926. Reissued in *Aus der Welt der Mysterien*, op. cit. English translation in H. Beckh (2020) *From the Mysteries*. TL, 170-75.

293   *Die CG* 1928, pp. 260-64. English translation in *Collected Articles*, No. 42, 351-55.

294   H. Beckh (1928). 'Johannes und das Wort', *Die CG*, 1928. Eng. tr, in *Collected Articles*, No. 40, 339-43.

295   H. Beckh (1928). *Der Kosmische Rhythmus im Markus-Evangelium*. Basel: Rudolf Geering Verlag. English translation: *Mark's Gospel: The Cosmic Rhythm*, Anastasi 2015. Rev. ed. TL 2021.

296   H. Beckh, *Ätherische Bilderkraft*, op. cit., p. 388. Eng. tr. in *Collected Articles*, No. 31, TL 2023, 258-68.

297   H. Beckh (1930). *Der kosmische Rhythmus, das Sternengeheimnis und Erdengeheimis im Johannes-Evangelium*. Basel: Rudolf Geering Verlag. Reference here to the Eng. tr. *John's Gospel: The Cosmic Rhythm—Stars and Stones*, Anastasi 2015, 80; TL 2021, 54.

298   For phases of the Moon in 1929, see http://www.timeanddate.com/calendar/?year=1929/

299   A. Peake (1919). *A Commentary on the Bible*. London: T.C. and E.C. Jack.

300   Ed. E. Collé and H. Collé (2014). *The Bahir: The Brightness*. No details of publisher. P. 122 English text, p. 123 Hebrew text.

301   A fine example is the Latin hymn '*Ad honorem et decorum Matris Domini*' in G.M. Dreves (Ed.) (1886). Analecta Hymnica Medii Aevi I. Leipzig: Fues Verlag (R. Reisland).
        Reprint available through Primary Source Edition. The second verse of the hymn includes the words: *Ergo ora omni hora / Rosa, Lilium.*

302   First printed, but the work is supposed to be about 200 years older—*Ed.*

303   D.C. Matt (Translation and Commentary) (2003). *The Zohar*. Pritzker Edition. Stanford: Stanford University Press, 1.1a.

304   On Babylonian astronomy: R. Hinckley Allen (1899). *Star-Names and their Meaning*. G.E. Stechert, reprinted New York: Dover Publications, 1963; G. White (2008). *Babylonian Star-lore*. Revised ed. London: Solaria Publications.

305 H. Beckh (1928). *Der kosmische Rhythmus in Markus-Evangelium*. Basel: Rudolf Geering, 104-10; 3rd ed. (1997) Stuttgart: Urachhaus, 113-19. English translation as *Mark's Gospel: The Cosmic Rhythm*. TL (2021) 102-107.

306 H. Beckh (2021). *John's Gospel: The Cosmic Rhythm—Stars and Stones*, Anastasi 358; TL 276.

307 Op. cit. Anastasi 359, TL 276.

308 *The Zohar*. Pritzker edition, op. cit., 1.1b.

309 H. Beckh (1921) *Etymologie und Lautbedeutung im Lichte der Geisteswissenschaft*. Stuttgart: Verlag Der Kommende Tag, reissued in *Neue Wege* (op. cit.) 17. Eng. tr. in *The Source of Speech* (2019), 112. Beckh is quoting from Wilhelm Mayer-Rinteln (1905). *Die Schöpfung der Sprache*. Leipzig: Grunov.

310 Book Review in *Perspectives*, March-May 2022, 29f.

The Works of Prof. Hermann Beckh Dr jur. et phil.

'An abundance of books came into existence whose significance perhaps will only be properly appreciated in the future.' (Lic. Emil Bock, 'Hermann Beckh' in *Zeitgenossen Weggenossen Wegbereiter*, Stuttgart: Urachhaus 1959, p. 132)

Die Beweislast nach dem Bürgerlichen Gesetzbuch
'The burden of proof according to the Code of Civil Law' Prize essay, awarded distinction from the Law Faculty the University of Munich München und Berlin 1899. Download: http://dlib-pr.mpier.mpg. de/m/kleioc/0010/exec/books/%22103926%22/

Ein Beitrag zur Textkritik an Kālidāsas Meghadūta
'A contribution for the text criticism of Kālidāsa's Meghadūta' Doctorate dissertation approved by the Department of Philosophy of the University of Berlin 1907.

Die tibetische Übersetzung von Kālidāsas Meghadūta
'The Tibetan translation of Kālidāsa's Meghadūta' Edited and with a German translation, Berlin 1907/2011.

Beiträge zur tibetischen Grammatik, Lexikogaphie, Stilistik und Metrik Habilitationsschrift. Berlin 1908.
'Contributions to Tibetan grammar, lexicography, style and prosody' Inaugural dissertation.

Udānavarga
A collection of Buddhist sayings in the Tibetan language Berlin 1911 (also reprinted by Walter de Gruyter, 2013).

Verzeichnis der tibetischen Handschriften
'Catalogue of Tibetan MSS in the Royal Library in Berlin' (Vol. 24 of the Manuscript Catalogue)
First division: Kanjur (Bhak-Khgur)
Berlin 1914/2011/14.

Buddha und seine Lehre
Vol. 1: *Der Buddha*. Vol. 2: *Die Lehre*.
Sammlung Göschen. Berlin & Leipzig 1916. Third edition 1928.
Later one-volume editions, Stuttgart: Urachhaus 1958/98/2012.
Tr. into Dutch (1961) and Japanese (1977).
Eng. tr. *Buddha's Life and Teaching*, Tr. Katrin Binder, Temple Lodge 2019.

'Rudolf Steiner und das Morgenland' in *Vom Lebenswerk Rudolf Steiners*
Ed. Friedrich Rittelmeyer, München: Chr. Kaiser 1921
Reprint by HP, Univ. of Michigan (www.lib.umich.edu) (download: www.archive.org).
Eng. tr. in *Hermann Beckh and the Spirit-Word*, Anastasi 2015. 33-65; also in *The Source of Speech*, TL 2019, 16-71.

   • *Der physische und der geistige Ursprung der Sprache*
'The physical and the spiritual origin of language'
Stuttgart 1921.
   • 'Es werde Licht!' (JEHI OR)
'Let there be light!' (JEHI OR) The primal biblical words of creation and the primal significance of the sounds in the light of spiritual science.'
Stuttgart 1921.
   • 'Etymologie und Lautbedeutung'
'Etymology and the significance of speech sounds in the light of spiritual science'
Stuttgart 1921/2013.
All three essays on language (above) reprinted in
Neue Wege zur Ursprache, Stuttgart 1954
Eng. tr. *The Source of Speech*, with all relevant essays and articles. Temple Lodge, 2019.

Anthroposophie und Universitätswissenschaft
'Anthroposophy and University Knowledge'. Breslau 1922.
Eng. tr. in *Hermann Beckh and the Spirit-Word*, Anastasi 2015. 71-101; also in *The Source of Speech*, Temple Lodge 2019, 181-207.

Vom geistigen Wesen der Tonarten
The Essence of Tonality: An Attempt to view musical Problems in the Light of Spiritual Science. With diagrams. Breslau 1922. Third edition 1932.
Eng. tr. Anastasi 2008; corrected ed. double volume *The Essence of Tonality* with *The Parsifal=Christ=Experience in Wagner's Music Drama*, Temple Lodge 2022.

Der Ursprung im Lichte. Bilder der Genesis
'Our Origin in the Light: Pictures from Genesis.' Stuttgart 1924.
Eng. tr. in *From the Mysteries*, triple volume with 'Zarathustra'. Temple Lodge 2020.

Von Buddha zu Christus
From Buddha to Christ
Stuttgart 1925 (tr. in Norwegian, Oslo 1926);
Eng. tr. of a short digest Floris Books 1978.
New Eng. tr. of full text with additional material, Temple Lodge 2019.

'Das neue Jerusalem'
'The Heavenly Jerusalem'
A poetic work, in the collaborative work *Gegenwartsrätsel im Offenbarungslicht*
('Present-day problems in the light of revelation'), Stuttgart 1925.
Eng. tr. incl. in *John's Gospel: The Cosmic Rhythm—Stars and Stones*. Anastasi 2015, 459-77; rev. ed. Temple Lodge 2021, 358-72; also in *Alchymy*. TL 2019, 100-13.

Der Hingang des Vollendeten
The Departure of the Perfected One: The Story of the Buddha's Transition from Earth to Nirvāṇa (Mahāparinibbāna Sutta of the Pali canon).
Translated and with an Introduction. Stuttgart 1925/1960. Eng. tr. *Buddha's Departure*, TL 2023.

Zarathustra
Stuttgart 1927
Eng. tr. with additional articles, in *From the Mysteries*, triple volume with 'Genesis', Temple Lodge, 2020.

Aus der Welt der Mysterien
From the Mysteries
Seven articles (reprinted). Basel 1927. Eng. tr. as triple book with 'Genesis' and 'Zarathustra', Temple Lodge, 2020.

Der kosmische Rhythmus im Markus-Evangelium
Mark's Gospel: The Cosmic Rhythm

Basel 1928/1960/1997.

Eng. tr. Leominster: Anastasi 2015; rev. ed. Temple Lodge 2021.

Der kosmische Rhythmus, das Sternengeheimnis und Erdengeheimnis im Johannes-Evangelium John's Gospel: The Cosmic Rhythm—Stars and Stones
Basel 1930.

Eng. tr. Anastasi 2015; re. ed. Temple Lodge 2021.

Das Christus-Erlebnis in Dramatisch-Musikalischen von Richard Wagners 'Parsifal'
The Parsifal=Christ=Experience in Wagner's Music Drama
Stuttgart 1930.

Eng. tr. with 'Richard Wagner and Christianity' (1933) and essays by Emil Bock (1928) and Rudolf Frieling (1956), Anastasi 2015; double volume with *The Essence of Tonality*, TL 2022.

Vom Geheimnis der Stoffeswelt (Alchymie)
Alchymy: The Mystery of the Material World
Basel 1931/1937/1942/2007/2013.

Eng. tr. with Introduction and Appendices, Temple Lodge 2019.

Der Hymnus an die Erde
The Hymn to the Earth: From the Old Indian Atharvaveda: A memorial to the oldest poem and to the early Aryans. Stuttgart 1934/1960.

Eng. tr., TL 2024.

Psalm 23 aus der Heilige Schrift
Psalm 23: Newly translated from the original text and set to music, op. 7. Stuttgart 1935.

Die Rosen von Damaskus
The Roses of Damascus. 'Thibaut von Champagne'. The ballad by Conrad Ferdinand Meyer. For solo high voice with piano accompaniment set to music, op. 8. Stuttgart 1937.

Die Sprache der Tonart
The Language of Tonality in the Music from Bach to Bruckner with special reference to Wagner's Music Dramas
Stuttgart 1937/1987/1999. Eng. tr. Anastasi 2015; rev. ed. TL forthcoming (2025).

Richard Wagner und das Christentum

'Richard Wagner and Christianity'
Stuttgart 1933.
Eng. tr. in *The Parsifal=Christ=Experience in Wagner's Music Drama.*
Anastasi 2015. Reprinted in double volume with *The Language of Tonality*, Temple Lodge 2022.

Indische Weisheit und Christendom
'Indian Wisdom and Christianity'
10 articles reprinted and 9 articles from the literary estate
Stuttgart 1938. Eng. trans. in *Collected Articles (1922-1938)*, Temple Lodge 2023.

The Mystery of Musical Creativity: The Human Being and Music
A recently discovered history of music in MS, Sütterlin script, 'Der Mensch und die Musik' (1936):
Five chapters pub. in three articles in *Der Europäer*, Basel 09.2005/09.2006/02.2007-08.   http://www.perseus.ch/archive/category/europaer/europaer-archiv
Fully restored text translated into English, with Appendices, Temple Lodge 2019.

The Language of the Stars: Zodiac and Planets in Relation to the Human Being with a chapter on the Anthroposophical Soul-Calendar (1911-12) (1930-33)
by Prof. Dr Hermann Beckh, and
'The Cosmic Rhythm in the Creed: for readers of Beckh's books (1930-31)' by Dr Rudolf Frieling.
with an Introduction and Book Reviews by Rudolf Frieling and others, translated from the German by Maren & Alan Stott edited by Neil Franklin.
Temple Lodge Publishing 2020.

Collected Articles 1922-1938, including posthumous publications, 72 items translated into English by Maren and Alan Stott: ed. & with Introductions by Neil Franklin, Temple Lodge 2023.

Three Further Publications:

Hermann Beckh: Leben und Werk
by Gundhild Kačer-Bock, Stuttgart 1997.
Hermann Beckh: Life and Work

Eng. tr. by M. & A. Stott, Anastasi 2016; rev. edition, eds. Neil Franklin and Katrin Binder, TL 2021.

Hermann Beckh and the Spirit-Word: Orientalist, Christian Priest and Independent Scholar, Anastasi 2015 (out of print). Introducing the Collected Works of Hermann Beckh.
Contents includes:
- H. B., 'Rudolf Steiner and the East'
- H. B., 'Anthroposophy and University Knowledge'
- H. B., 'Meeting Rudolf Steiner'
- Alan Stott, 'Hermann Beckh and the Twenty-First Century'
- Numerous appreciations by Beckh's colleagues and his biographer.

Festschrift in Honour of Hermann Beckh, Anastasi 2016 (out of print).
— on the centenary of *Buddha und seine Lehre*,
— the first publication of *The Mystery of Human Creativity: The Human Being and Music*, and
— the Eng. tr. of the biography by Gundhild Kačer-Bock, *Hermann Beckh: Life and Work*.

*

A full errata and addenda list is available upon request from: alanstotty@gmail.com

Useful addresses for researchers:
www.rudolf-steiner-bibliothek.de/ or also
bibliothek@rudolfsteinerhaus.org
Jörg Ewertowski (Stuttgart)

Das Zentralarchiv der Christengemeinschaft
Gubener Str. 47a
10243 Berlin
Tel. Archivburo: +49-30-609 785 12
archiv@christengemeinschaft.org
Archivleiter: Thomas Prange
Tel: +49-176-81281909

https://goetheanum.ch/en/documentation/library

https://en.anthro.wiki/

A note from the publisher

For more than a quarter of a century, **Temple Lodge Publishing** has made available new thought, ideas and research in the field of spiritual science.

Anthroposophy, as founded by Rudolf Steiner (1861-1925), is commonly known today through its practical applications, principally in education (Steiner-Waldorf schools) and agriculture (biodynamic food and wine). But behind this outer activity stands the core discipline of spiritual science, which continues to be developed and updated. True science can never be static and anthroposophy is living knowledge.

Our list features some of the best contemporary spiritual-scientific work available today, as well as introductory titles. So, visit us online at **www.templelodge.com** and join our emailing list for news on new titles.

If you feel like supporting our work, you can do so by buying our books or making a direct donation (we are a non-profit/ charitable organisation).

office@templelodge.com

TEMPLE LODGE

For the finest books of Science and Spirit